Quoting God

Quoting God

How Media Shape Ideas about Religion and Culture

edited by

Claire Hoertz Badaracco

Baylor University Press
Waco, Texas USA

Book Design by Gryphon Graphics
Cover Art: modified version of *American Gothic*, 1930 by Grant Wood; courtesy of
    Friends of the American Art Collection. All rights reserved by The Art Institute of
    Chicago and VAGA, New York, NY
Cover Design: design concept by Claire Badaracco; composition by Pollei Design

Chapter 1 is adapted from "Journalism and the Religious Imagination," in *People of
    Faith: Religious Conviction in American Journalism and Higher Education* by John
    Schmalzbauer. Copyright (©) 2003 by Cornell University. Used by permission of
    the publisher, Cornell University Press. Another version of this essay appeared as
    "Telling Catholic and Evangelical Stories: The Impact of the Religious
    Imagination," in *U.S. Catholic Historian* 20, no. 2 (2002): 25–44.
Chapter 3 expands "Misprints? Falun Gong and the First Amendment," in
    Commonweal, June 6, 2003: 10–11.
Chapter 9 is from "'Our Lady of Guadalupe as a Cultural Symbol: 'The Power of the
    Powerless,'" in *Liturgy and Cultural Religious Traditions,* ed. Herman Schmidt and
    David Power, 25–33. New York: Seabury, 1977.
"The View" by Richard Rodriguez is from the Lehrer News Hour Essay, July 8,
    2002.

Library of Congress Cataloging-in-Publication Data

Quoting God : how media shape ideas about religion and culture / edited by Claire
Hoertz Badaracco.
    p. cm.
  Includes bibliographical references and index.
  ISBN 1-932792-06-6 (pbk. : alk. paper)
  1. Mass media--Religious aspects--Christianity. 2. Mass media and culture. 3.
Christianity and culture. I. Badaracco, Claire.

BV652.95.Q86 2005
201'.7--dc22
                                            2004019144

To My Students

Contents

Acknowledgments

I wish to thank Dr. Jon Pray, vice-provost for educational technology at Marquette University, whose unwavering good humor and steely nerves met each challenge calmly along the way as we developed the "linked classroom," where many of the authors in this volume conversed via teleconference with my students in media and religion. Thanks also are due to Dean William Elliott, whose leadership of the College of Communication provided the equipment and technical support, and whose intellectual interest in the global electronic classroom helped make this work possible. Without the initial seed grant from the JNET broadband network directed by Dr. Richard Vigilante, and similar small grants from the Marquette University Simmons Fund over a four-year period, as well as small grants from Santa Clara University and Loyola University–New Orleans, the multisite course "Cultural Identity, Media, and World Religions" would not have been realized.

Among those to whom I owe a special word of thanks are those in Merton Studies—especially the late Dr. Robert Daggy, former director of the Merton Center at Bellarmine College. Thanks also to the Center for Communication and Culture, to Robert White, S.J., of the Department of Communication at Gregorian University; to Brother William Biernatski, S.J.; and to Stewart Hoover of the University of Colorado at Boulder, one of the intellectual leaders in the field of media and religion. Thanks to all those who joined in linked, national conversations with us, especially to Dr. Charles Haynes of the First Amdendment Center; and to Dr. Yvonne Haddad of the Center for Christian-Muslim Understanding at Georgetown University. Thanks also are due to my colleagues and fellow collaborators in the "linked" electronic classroom: Dr. Paul Soukup, S.J.,, of the faculty at Santa Clara University, Dr. Catherine Wessinger of the faculty of Loyola University-New Orleans, and Dr. Richard Malloy, S.J., of the faculty of St. Joseph's-Philadelphia.

Particular thanks go to all the contributing authors, and especially to my editor, the director of Baylor University Press, Dr. Carey C. Newman, whose excitement about this project made it happen, and to Diane Smith, Production Manager at Baylor University Press. This book was a joy to produce. My hope is that those who read it will discover in it as much satisfaction as did the contributing authors and this editor.

Foreword

John Dart

Time was when weaving essays together from scholars and journalists into one book, as this volume has done, might have seemed contrived if not ill-advised. In the early 1990s, a common faculty view was that popularizing research for the public amounted to "dumbing down" complex ideas. And, some said, why talk readily to journalists and be victimized by error-prone, superficial reporting? Academics like Harvey Cox, Martin Marty, and Elaine Pagels were the exceptions who kept avenues open to popular media without damaging their academic standing.

When, at the start of 2004, a well-credentialed sociologist of religion, Christian Smith, railed against what he called "religiously ignorant journalists" in the evangelical-oriented *Books & Culture* (January–February, pp. 6–7), it seemed as if scholarly disdain for media professionals was alive as ever, at least on religious subjects.

But the experience of the American Academy of Religion indicated otherwise. The AAR launched, in August 2002, a computer database of more than 5,000 scholars of religion, catalogued by fields of expertise and complete with their telephone numbers and e-mail addresses. Designed for journalists, Religionsource saw only a handful of scholars asking that their names be removed in its sixteen months. "Overwhelmingly, the scholars in the database with whom we've talked are enthusiastic about being included and talking to journalists," said Kyle Cole, AAR religion news adviser. Many volunteered their home or cell phone numbers. "Scholars [see] it as an opportunity to educate the public about their field," he said.

Religionsource reflects AAR's relatively recent philosophy of encouraging scholarly and journalistic interaction and enhancing "public understanding of religion." Likewise, late in 2003 the Society of Biblical Literature started a Web site that each month features articles on a different theme written for lay persons and scholars alike. The approaches complement the goals of book publishers, who, under sales pressures, increasingly urge scholars to write for nonspecialists.

This new cross-breeding is very timely, no less, for this book. Contributors have illustrated how religious practice is suppressed by some nations, or mischaracterized by outsiders, or is so subtly influential as to be imperceptible but for the diligence of serious scholars and earnest journalists. Clarity about the future use and abuse of religion will be crucial as the United States and other nations seek to justify national security measures and aggressive military moves in the face of terrorist atrocities. Simplistic religious rhetoric from political figures calls for scholars and scribes to wield a swift communications scalpel with an integrity befitting both professions. Consumers of mass media (all of us) need insightful analysis from both journalism and academia.

This is not to ignore religious leaders, who most people hope will add a moral voice for charity and justice. Indeed, religious, intellectual, and press constituencies are guaranteed free expression in the U.S. Constitution's First Amendment. Yet these three do not usually see themselves as blessed bedfellows.

Ongoing tensions between organized religion and the secular, ever-pervasive news media, for instance, in 1992 prompted the Freedom Forum's First Amendment Center at Vanderbilt University to ask me (with the *Los Angeles Times* providing leave time) and Jimmy R. Allen, the last "moderate" president of the Southern Baptists, to research causes and offer solutions. Our 88-page *Bridging the Gap* study was published in 1993 and widely distributed. Fortunately, it coincided with a broadly felt consensus in journalism that improved news coverage of religion, ethics, and spirituality was a worthy priority just as an economic upturn enabled news budgets to grow. Our recommendation that journalistic outlets and religious organizations learn more about each other was aided greatly by a steady stream of conferences, intensive seminars, and other educational vehicles. Foundations such as Lilly Endowment and Pew Charitable Trusts continue to support initiatives too numerous to cite here.

Much has changed since 1993, and even since 2000 when an updated version of *Bridging the Gap* was published. Many people keep up with events partly through the Internet, which is both bad news and good news. The "urban legends" and false reports parading as "what the establishment won't tell you" mislead the gullible. But religious leaders, scholars, and journalists can now acquire solid information with unprecedented speed. Admittedly, we may favor resources that echo our preconceived views.

Thus, a special burden falls on scholarship and journalism to be true to facts and findings, and fair toward conflicting theories and plausible alternatives. Professionals in both endeavors have a "calling" to be not only fact-finding but also sensitive and frank, ultimately letting the chips fall where they may.

A final note on bias as it pertains to news reporting: some electronic and print news outlets blur the line between opinion and straight reporting, but the most reputable media normally label the gradations from even-handed reporting and news analysis to commentary and outright opinions. In judging news output, organizations, consumers, and scholars alike should make distinctions between these two poles. Even at the straight-news end, most journalists no longer speak of "objective" news reports, preferring instead to say they strive toward fair, accurate, and balanced reporting.

Equally as important as the news content are the story choices made. To be sure, the competitive business nature of news ensures that most developments of interest will surface—whether the pack-journalism pursuit of celebrity foibles, or the more significant wrongdoing in powerful political, legal, and corporate circles. News agencies do choose how much to use and whether those stories will be on page one or lead off the 6 p.m. news. In other words, most readers should be aware that choices are made daily by news gatekeepers—a necessity usually welcomed by people leading fast-paced lives.

Upon taking early retirement from the *Times* and joining the *Christian Century* as news editor, I barely altered my journalistic style except in choices of stories to edit and write. Both publications have a national and international perspective, but the bimonthly magazine serves as a news and commentary journal with special attention to mainline Protestant denominations. Though the magazine has a big helping of stories on Methodists, Presbyterians, Episcopalians, and trends in church life, major Catholic, evangelical, Muslim, and religious-sociopolitical issues are not neglected. The reason *Century* has been an enduring magazine, I believe, is its blend of clerical, scholarly, and journalistic contributors.

Secular (religiously neutral) news organizations have long relied on clergy leaders as sources on religious developments. But journalism's increased use of religion scholars, who take a nonpartisan approach akin to that of journalists, enables the news media to put faith matters into a richer context.

Introduction

Quotation and the Life of Public Texts

Claire Hoertz Badaracco

Today's news media—electronic and digital news in papers, magazines, radio, and television—disseminate ephemeral glimpses of ordinary language used in common by global publics. On the basis of snapshot or serial reports, mass media audiences learn daily about the deeper realities of life and death that define individual, state, and national identity. With reporters as global storytellers, people determine the identity of others as friends or enemies; judge the legitimacy of past reports; and imagine their futures with hope. Analogous textual expressions of spiritual yearning that seek to name or to identify the enduring materialize in all types of public spaces. Seemingly incongruous, ephemeral commercial culture functionally shelters the unchurched from confrontations with traditional religious culture by mimicking or "quoting" the deeper cultural values that often are resisted by the disbeliever as untranslatable or lacking currency in the present day. By this I mean that the superficial, material, or ephemeral culture is a substitute for what many people seek and name as the deeper realities traditionally housed in religion.

As the essays in this book suggest, both the fast-paced culture of media and the unchanging verities of traditional religions based on sacred texts are

1

enacted daily, lived out, reimagined, and reframed as contemporary truths; and this occurs in multimedia environments that are multilogual—that is, many voices speaking simultaneously in multiple modes of electronic dissemination. Rather than thinking about these two levels of culture as distinct, either in confrontation or parallel, it is more accurate to think about how they constantly inform one another and are, to an increasing extent, blurred, indivisible, and inherently connected. As the velocity of information increases, the degree to which the two levels of culture shape and speak to one another becomes more complex and increasingly difficult to discern as separate voices. Though this blurring is most obvious in current debates about separation of church and state, secularism and national identity, fundamentalism, and public expression of private belief, the debate also plays out in popular entertainment and uses of media to house collective memories defining culture. Though multimedia avenues of public expression continuously reframe eternal questions about the meaning of being itself, more mundane matters are simultaneously addressed: in any textual or visual narrative network, roles are assigned—storyteller, audience, interpreter.

Issues of authenticity and authority pertain in the search for factual or objective truth. All types of media—including expressions of the material culture in film, commodities, Internet, and music—thrive on improved and increasingly diverse modes of delivery and novelty in the manner of reporting stories. While diversity in an information age connotes positive and progressive change, it also means modification of habitual practices based on accepted definitions and norms, and that can pose a threat to social groups whose identity is rooted in sameness rather than difference. In this sense, mediated cultures and religious cultures are incongruent: the one saturated in difference and innovation, the other immersed in values based on tradition, authority, and authenticity.

Over the past quarter-century, religious cultures have adapted media technology in order to deliver their messages both to adherents and to the unchurched. The adaptation of multimedia or generationally friendly modes by traditional religions evangelizing prodigal youth is a postmodern homily expressed in religious rock music, videos, novels, film, Internet, and cybercafes. All forms of media, including public relations campaigns designed for persuasion, talk shows, and mass rallies, have been adapted from secular to religious culture by sectarian groups. This applies equally to the ancient desert religions as well as to newly created ones. Technology has changed the role of media from agenda setter and gatekeeper to an as-yet-unnamed role that has to do with the perception of self-identity and the scale and scope of the self in relation to the local, regional, and universal community.

Once it was the role of the preacher from the pulpit to tell churchgoers about biblical history and explain the stories of biblical texts in order to enliven the faith of those in the pews. Today the role of storyteller as exclusively the role of the religionist has been overtaken by others. When mass media transmit stories, they are more horizontal and lateral than vertical, and the commercial direction of the dissemination has had a profound influence on the styles of religious communication and on messages about hope, transcendence, endurance, triumph, and what it means to be human. Mass media modes of transmission affect how people think about the identity of their social groups, the quality of the culture in terms of its aesthetic and spiritual vitality, and the significance of faith as a formative and deliberative motivational force for social good. Much of the mass media and material culture in the late twentieth century would seem to trivialize religious faith, but world events and political life have served to elevate the previously unrecognized importance of faith as an inescapable influence on the quality of social institutions and civic life.

Marshall McLuhan's definitive explanation in *Media Studies* of the relationship between technology and meaning contends that in all types of media the content contains another medium. His analysis of cultural processes explains that print is made up of written words, and the written word is made up of a silently spoken conversation, the nonverbal thought processes of the authorial self reporting outward to other selves. The nonverbal is made print. News stories can turn the verbal, the spoken word, into print, which is turned into digital or electronic pulse by broadcasters relying on news stories for telecast. More recently and with more subtlety, the film industry has introduced the practice of putting products with recognizable logos as advertisements in narratives, in which characters are casually shown using identifiable products that the audience also has used. Each product advertised in a film or magazine contains an emblem; as a commercial design, the logos contain iconic meanings relevant to the company that produces the product. As received by the consumer, logos provoke reactions both positive and negative, acceptance or resistance, not only in response to the product but also to the reputation or image of the nation where the company produces the product. For McLuhan, the message of media is the change that it introduces into human life.

One must, as Benedict Anderson observed, "have" a nationality.[1] National identity circumscribes choices and opportunities as well as patterns of media consumption. Anderson asserted that nationalism never has had any great philosophical "ism" thinkers; consequently, all nations must "imagine" themselves, based on an idealization of horizontal comradeship. The connections that patriotic citizens feel with their communities are realized through actions. Audiences are like citizens. They belong to imagined communities linked not through action but through passive reception. The news, as a cultural product, is similarly invented and reinvented each day, printed on sheets with no definitive story genre except objective reiteration of the spoken word into a print medium. Anderson saw evidence that readers imagined the connection between and among stories, interpreting the layout of editors. The top of the morning news may be relegated to a small mention by evening, and sleeper stories, conversely, may blow up during the course of a day and achieve greater gravity or significance as facts are revealed. The imaginative connection Anderson defined, though, in addition to the similarity in layout, texture, and feel between the newspaper and the ordinary book, is that imaginative connection between the producer of print and the writer's marketplace. The mass consumer audience, the attention of the reader or consumer, becomes indispensable for the success of fiction as well as the news. As social institutions, both religion and media rely on the construction of an imaginary loyalty to the larger group: neither are democratic. Although the media may uphold a pretense of interactivity with advances in technology, the economic infrastructure that fuels converged, global media corporations controls the agenda.

Important changes in contemporary political life connect the ways in which mediated and religious cultures influence imagined collective identities in "the most religiously diverse nation" in history.[2] Charles Haynes has argued that elementary and secondary public schooling ought to include education about world religions and that adverse reaction to the political issue of allowing prayer in public schools has caused K-12 educators to refrain from teaching children about understanding, not just tolerating, religious differences. Such a curriculum would assert the case for the importance of beliefs as a universal and global phenomenon, linking students with a greater understanding of their own ethnic heritage, the country's foundational history, and recently "re-imagined" civic obligation as moral duty, that of the citizen in a civil society to help construct the Common Good.[3] This would require that an educated person have a deep understanding of the struggle and legitimacy of all religious groups to claim a place in the national identity that is indivisible from their religious and philosophical beliefs.

The children of the information age are so accustomed to the pace of change introduced by media that they need to be educated to understand how slowly traditional religious cultures change—sometimes at a glacial pace, members resisting change even to the death. They also need to understand that the civil role of believers or adherents is to conserve memories and stories of their shared collective past, uniting those in the present day with ancestral publics, spiritual ghosts still empowered by their recollection in the minds of the bereaved, those who have braved displacement, disappointment, and profound social and cultural change. One owes something to those who went before: this is a fundamental human yearning, even among those who have little regard for formalized religion and actively dispute theology as having ideological bias.

Donald Shriver's historical analysis of modern nations in warfare concluded that nations need, as part of their historical imagining, an ethic for enemies that incorporates reconciliation and forgiveness.[4] Rosemary and Herman Ruether in *The Wrath of Jonah* discuss how the national psyche of religiously identified Middle Eastern nations, which for generations could not speak about their wounds, brooded over history but could not mediate it or make public their epistemology of loss.[5] Resentment is as much a source of political corruption as is revenge, and both can change in profound and politically devastating ways the spiritual vitality of a national culture. The Israeli-Palestinian conflict is a parable not only for the Middle East but for the interaction between fundamentalism and modernism. As Martin Marty and Scott Appleby have argued in *Religion, Ethnicity, and Self-Identity*, tribal religionists have adapted well to the introduction of new technologies, and their faith communities have become more entrenched as they become more adept at the use of media.[6]

As long as religious practices were discrete, a little bit of an embarrassment among the intellectual and political elite, and religion reporters wrote for the back pages of the Saturday paper, the threat of religion in public life was the farthest thing from the public mind. Martin Marty argues that it has been the traditionally accepted practice of separating public affairs and religious faith that effectively created in the Middle East the type of political climate and historical conditions that foster the simmering resentment discussed by the Reuthers. It would follow from this argument that the current public voice of religion is a positive development and that, rather than dilute the religious practices of adherents, it revitalizes their faith. However, the impact of the religious lobbyist on the public square and the effect mediated evangelism has on those who would prefer to take the word *God* out of the Pledge of Allegiance, bar prayer from public occasions, and rule out the expression of public religion in monuments remains a matter for legal debate.

The American Religious Freedom Restoration Act precludes the type of reactive political restriction employed by the French; whether by veil, *hijab*, turban, or felt hat, Americans have the right to wear their religion on their sleeve. However, some would argue that the threat of religion to progressive thinking is greater that the threat to religion of political or ideological progress. The "ism" that could be said to have been the driving creative force for how moderns imagined themselves had to do with machinery, not social organizations, as Walter Benjamin's analysis of the age of reproduction explained—there was no turning back the clock. Technology, a type of new secular religion, promised to improve the lives of all it touched by offering new and improved means of managing daily life, and to explain, if not eliminate, the suffering so often equated historically with religions.

Marty asserts that there was an "informal pact" epitomizing the modernist imagination that separated religious expression from public life. Media use by religionists for political and evangelical aims blurs the popular understanding in the United States about the meaning of the First Amendment. Faith-based initiatives raise questions about the role of public religion in a media democracy, the changing role of religion in civic life in constructing social capital, how we imagine ourselves as a nation, and how we identify enemies.[7]

Until recently, most academics treated religion only as a secondary factor in the construction of ethnic and national identity, but the indisputable sociopolitical force of global fundamentalism and violence has changed that, as Marty and Appleby, among a number of others, have established. This volume strives to bring together two segments in contemporary mediated religious culture: academics working within what Stephen Carter termed in the title of his book "the culture of disbelief," who treat religion as an interesting intellectual problem; and reporters, who are workers in an information economy that constitutes the media culture, often blamed by religionists for undermining spiritual values. This book proposes that the relationship between media culture and spiritual culture is foundational; that the relationship between news values and religious values in political life is influential; and that the relationship among science, modernity, and disbelief is pivotal in social fragmentation or consolidation.[8]

The idea for this volume began in my media and religion classroom, an innovative collaboration using JNET broadband to link several Jesuit campuses in three regions of the United States. The once-experimental course entitled "Cultural Identity, Media and World Religion," is now a part of the Marquette University Core Curriculum. As JNET expanded into AUSJAL to include Central and South America, we are able now to link students of media and religion in Milwaukee with those in Santiago, Chile, among other places, making possible a student community that crosses borders, cultures, and language differences. This book is envisioned as a reader for those engaged in conversations and similar discussions in other communities about cultural diversity in world religions, cultural identity, mediated religion, and national identity; about how media influence public opinion, popular beliefs, and political ideas about both the cultural identity of God and the spiritual basis upon which a national identity is imagined.

This is an edited volume, a "multivocal" blend of voices representing many viewpoints rather than a monologue or monograph. It is the appropriate medium through which to disseminate the ideas emerging from the past eight years of study, pedagogical development, and discussions with thought leaders of national influence, including Charles Haynes, Yvonne Haddad, Stewart Hoover, and Stephen Carter in Aspen Institute Leadership Seminars, among many others whose work and ideas have been important to me as a scholar and to the growth and development of the work we do collectively as teachers and writers interested in religion, media, and spiritual values in public culture.

Among media scholars interested in religion, and among religion scholars beginning to study the languages of media, this avenue of inquiry is relatively new. Many scholars have published important works, but this volume is unprecedented in its collaborative tenor. It represents the conversation of an engaged, multidisciplinary, and multireligious group. This is not a closed or limited consortium of like minds but an association of interested colleagues, on the news beat and in academe, who do not necessarily agree. This is the medium into which we invite our readers.

A variety of methods and approaches are used by interdisciplinary scholars to address the subject of mediated religious culture in this book; scholars use rubrics from sociology, history, mass media, theology, and religious studies. Though the cultural model of American journalism and the religious imagination serves as the bedrock paradigm, the book explores cross-cultural and subcultural mediated practices within media in Tibet, Japan, Mongolia, the Vatican, the Middle East, and among Muslims and Mexican Americans in the United States, Chinese immigrants in New York City, and old regular Baptists in Appalachia. These topics are taken up in order to study how media shape public perception, popular beliefs about religious practices, media habits, and collective identities.

All of the national journalists whose commentaries appear here are reporters for the mainstream press. The foreword is contributed by John Dart, a veteran religion writer for the *Los Angeles Times* and now news editor of *Christian Century*. His benchmark attitudinal study about spiritual climates in American newsrooms for the Freedom Forum preceded a decade of scholarship by academics.[9] Dart's commentary is balanced by the conclusion, contributed by Gustav Niebuhr, a veteran *New York Times* religion reporter and now communication and religion professor. As John Dart points out, our medium is also our message: religion scholars and journalists who report on religion should work harmoniously together. Our work collaborates in constructing reality, and day-to-day life is realized contextually. Altogether, informing one another, we are part of the macronarrative linking contemporary with ancient cultures by virtue of the spiritual imagination and religious practices that characterize what human values mean across time and culture.

This book is a collection of reflective essays grounded in field experience and academic research designed to serve interested readers and faculty as a resource for discussions about realizing spiritual life in a secular world. Our editorial aim is to reach a global audience—any reader interested in the processes of cultural formation and the spiritual architecture of public life. For it is the publicly declared word and image that determine self-perception, community definition, and national identity; and it is the stories through which people identify the religious meaning of their lives that determine not only how audiences use media, but which medium they prefer. Though audience ethics is beyond the scope of topics covered in this volume, the role of the audience as "cocreator" of the spiritual culture is propositional.[10]

By including, along with academic essays, journalists' commentaries written "from the news desk," we assert that mediated religious culture is not just a two-way street—two oppositional forces of theoretical and applied views in creative tension or dialogue—but a confluence of multimedia, social attitudes, political climates, and public opinion. The formation of media and religious practices and their cumulative influence on cultural identity is complex; and the longitudinal changes, as well as the multimodal and multivocal characteristics of the conversation, make neat answers seem shallow, suspect. Both mediated culture and religious culture require the active engagement of audiences to sustain both imagination and belief. Indeed, academics and scholars of religious studies, mass media, and mediated religion need to find ways to develop connections with the religion journalists whose written words help shape popular ideas about culture.

No longer relegated to the Saturday religion page, reporters covering religion often see their bylines on the front page. Much of the American population imagines itself to be both religious and patriotic, yet partisan differences can be constructed through public opinion polls between those who attend church and those who do not; and political platforms include stances for or against abortion, school vouchers, or the display of religious symbols such as the Ten Commandments, the crèche, the Star of David, or other worn religious symbols in public places, including schools. As the Center for the Study of Religion in Public Life has established, substantive correlation between religious identity and partisan political affiliation shapes the American democracy.[11]

The medium through which the audience receives information in turn influences the styles of expression in news as well as commercial styles in mainstream programming and also in related multimedia—in advertising, sitcoms, music, video, Internet, and film. Imperceptibly, these mediated forces shape public opinion about the many "threats" to the free exercise of religion in a mediated democracy, including the ethics or legitimacy of media consolidation and its existing or potential power to homogenize culture in the global communication economy. How media workers in world centers of production gauge audience reception determines the frequency and duration of the new ideas being introduced and the choice of stories told, which stories make the "cover" of newsmagazines, or which are repeated on air. Cumulatively, the repetition of violence, the dissemination of stereotypical images about ethnicity, the media's obsession with the body as a commodity, the estrangement of sexuality from love and family, and the constant dumbing down of relationships into contests—all these reiterate embedded clichés in middlebrow culture about the superficiality of material existence. This contributes to the popular opinion that surface culture rather than deep culture is the more enduring. Yet marketing theory shows that the entire information economy thrives on cycles of built-in obsolescence, ephemeral messages, fickle tastes. The technology that disseminates media products in the consumer economy functions in even shorter boom-and-bust cycles, but what is long-term is the ability of media technology to reinvent new modes of dissemination. In fact, media technology has outraced the ability and talents of multimedia programming to fill the hundreds of channels, stations, and outlets with information of value. As social critics denounce the surfeit of entertainment and the resultant coarsening of celebrity and fan culture, surface culture obfuscates the ability of the public to digest complexity of any kind, whether that information is about science or political life.

When the audience embraces surface culture, it does so without a sense of its collective power, its ability to imagine itself as a community with economic and political clout to shape media products. There is a sense in which the inability of media workers to imagine well and often enough to fill all forms of multimedia channels has left the audience with a self-perception of its helplessness as a victim of cultural domination by a global media machine impervious to its resistance. This circumstance has led some to conclude that public rituals of democratic electoral politics or material evidence in romantic or mystery fiction, football, global sports contests, jazz, and the movies help fill the void in American spiritual culture, feeding the human thirst for improvisation, imagination, and recognition of otherness.[12]

Just as the guiding editorial concept for the creation of this volume is that the production of mediated religious culture is not just a two-way street, it is also the governing editorial principle informing this work that "faith matters." By this I mean that belief in a higher power connects the believer to the imagination of an ordered universe in which each human life has value because it is lived in connection with others and for the good of the whole. In this volume, diverse faith and philosophical viewpoints are represented among both academics and journalists, including the skeptic and agnostic. Many faiths make for a good story. But the assertion that faith matters in a book for a university press, especially in the culture of disbelief that pervades secular universities even among religion scholars, begs the larger question regarding how popular audiences come to know with conviction what they believe, especially with regard to how they respect, perceive, and resist religious differences, and how they choose to identify themselves with mediated as opposed to real communities.

CONCEPTUAL AND THEORETICAL FRAME

The title for this volume of collected essays—*Quoting God*—refers on one level to how the media report religion news, to their use of the quoted word as fact in stories about religious conflict, lived faith, and religious language used in the public square. *Quoting God* also refers to how traditional and emerging religions, including those described by media as "cults," "terrorists," "fundamentalists," "prophets," or "evangelists," mix the language of spiritual authenticity with authority. That mix proposes a connection between the common reader and the Author of the Book, meaning all the ancient texts (Bible, Qur'an, Torah), as the source of original Wisdom written by male prophets, inspired by a universal, timeless, yet privileged religious source of being, identified in religious cultures by names such as God, Yahweh, Allah, Wisdom, Buddha, the Divine. Debates about whether all religions worship the same God, while well beyond the scope of this pluralistic volume, are alive and well in the media and in American political culture.

The title of this book also refers to the mediated processes of quotation or reiteration through which contemporary religions, both ancient and new, allege their authenticity. Each identifies as "on their side" a God who is, to borrow Anderson's phrase, a "horizontal comrade," a neighbor on speaking terms only with a clique of followers, involved in their win-loss scenarios, be they petty and muscular, such as a sports game, or more devastating , such as a "just" war.

The mediated or popularly quoted God exists in the collective unconscious as a locus of reception. Not unlike the audience, one is powerful, the other powerless—but both are viewers. The imagined relationship between authenticity and the authority of the "ultimately concerned" Viewer demands that the journalist as participant-observer be outside the religious culture in order to achieve objectivity, as the scribe and transmitter of events and the teller of tales, recording conversations overheard or tales retold. Among the many questions this book strives to raise in the minds of our readers is whether that place for a religion writer has a theological or philosophical rationale and a cultural consequence that contributes to the formation of deep culture.

This editorial perspective builds on the meaning-making activity that Clifford Geertz and other important academics thought responsible for constructing religion, though it is nearer to the literary view of texts his followers applied in field stories told to anthropologists.[13] The ideas in this volume focus on the problems of cross-cultural formation of religious information and its impact on both the practices that make up surface media culture and the deeper culture as well. We do not extend the argument to include the generational issues of the life-course research field, how religious practices vary according to demography and maturation, or theoretical issues in ritual studies that address differences in the consumption and practice of mediated culture.[14] These analytical frames are of course important, because historical epochs as well as human aging are determinants in establishing cultural identity. The focus of this volume is the media and the languages of cultural formation where the variables of interpretation of public texts shape the idea of collective, national, and individual identity.

The emphasis in this volume is on the production of social "texts" in all facets of media, with an emphasis on news, but including material culture. News stories and the quotations on which they are built are witness narratives of real events. The principle of narrative objectivity strives to construct a reality, imbued in the words themselves, that exists apart from the meanings ascribed to the words by readers, created out of psychological need or ideological necessity. A journalist and ethnographer differ in how they use imagination and fact in their storytelling; yet they are both cultural interpreters, narrators about "otherness," building their "webs" of meaning from language about events and facts. This use of language is distinct from the symbolic or iconographic language used in advertising, in film, and in visual communication for the purposes of commercial design.

This book is interested in the cultural identity of God as ascribed to the Unknown by secular forces, chief among which is the global news and mass media industry. While national identity is often described as a construct based on the history of a people moving from the periphery to the center of mainstream culture, or as a result of assimilation among ethnic or immigrant groups, the stories told about a culture by outside observers, about the people struggling to name the culture, are a critical and most compelling part of that formation process. We think story is at the heart of how prejudice is reframed. The identity of the storyteller is paramount within the discussion of the cultural identity formation of communities and nations, and the role that media play in asserting national identity on a global stage.

What identifies the reader of mediated stories is not interpretation of a static Word, but a nationalized image of God. In American media, God is often portrayed as the Pretty American: in a commodity culture, God is a word on money, on legal cornerstones. That idealized American divinity blurs the values framed by the Constitution, including separation of church and state, and the freedom of speech that gives rise to a platform for public debate as a right and also as a grace.

Discernment, a reflective religious practice among contemplative traditions, referring to the seeker's willingness to empty the self in order to receive God's will, also means that knowing the Author's intention is the spiritual source of one's personal religious identity and the perception of the other's religious authenticity. Saints have claimed discernment as the avenue through which they conversed with God in order to know Divine Will. As the daily global press reports, similar claims about privileged access to truth have been made by wayward clergy, terrorists, religious extremists, and suicide bombers. Knowing the self and knowing the faces of God are part of a social dialogue for believers: a conversation between ancient public texts inscribed by evangelists and prophets, and intuited understanding by meditating on the Word (*lectio divina*), the work of the religious imagination. The work of this volume suggests that religious imagination pervades contemporary media cultures, though it takes different forms of public expression, in visual art and in verbal and written stories, and in distorted ways, in material culture and in violence.

"Quoting God" in the secular sense is a source of suspicion, embarrassment, ridicule, and friction between and among factions in the public square, as it is between tribes, countries, and within nations. In its extreme partisan and patriotic form, the imbued values of the patriotic God who takes sides are the bedrock source of religion's potential for violence.[15] As it is used here, *quotation* is intended as a theoretical term referring to the processes of imitation or mimesis in an aesthetic context to frame reality, episodes in history, and those subversive events resulting from disordered identity that dispute the authenticity and authority of the past as it is introduced to new audiences in the present.

Quotation traces the focus of the "gaze" of readers: it is a fulcrum between an imagined future, centered in the present, but always harkening back in history and in time. In religious mediated culture, the word *origin* is the locus of dispute. This applies both to text and to image. Whether an artist "quotes" Caravaggio or Michelangelo, every act of interpretation by the next generation of artists changes the original.[16] Every act of seeing visual images or reading literary quotations involves transformational, interpretative values that thrive in the heart of mystery for believers. In a parallel culture, the world of the secular unbeliever, a comparable level of engagement occurs through multimedia products imbued with "magical" powers to lift the receiver from humdrum life.

In art history, literary history and textual studies, and in theology, anthropology, and cultural history, interpretation involves an array of actions, including deconstructing, resisting, inventing, and accepting. All of this intellectual and psychological work leads to stages of belief, or degrees of disengagement from former beliefs, part of the process of growth or transformation. All of this depends on intuitive, imaginative, and graced powers of the mind and heart to create lessons about living that endure. History and cultural memory are necessary for such power to resonate in media and in popular culture.

In journalism, reporters act as cultural storytellers, embedding the language of others as textual "objects" within the narrative frames they construct. In media, the text aspires to be objective while at the same time it enjoys being subjective, the focus of disputed truth and the center of the action. Reporting as storytelling is both borrowing and constructing; it is a consolidating sociolinguistic force rather than a force for social fragmentation. Each quotation is recorded, cropped, framed, attributed, placed as important within the narrative structure, publicly displayed where it can be argued against or disputed. Through this process, and by virtue of its publicity, it accrues authenticity over time.

Not just the journalist but all media engaged in the production of material and secular cultures include an audience as a player on a public platform that involves interpretation of authenticity, authority, intention, originality, imitation, and power. The applied ethical concern at the center of this book is how power relationships (among churched and unchurched in mediated and material subcultures) affect mass audience beliefs. Personal and subjective beliefs about value and truth shape "objective" storytelling—

construed as subjective when aesthetic in visual communication, but as objective when occurring in news reporting and ethnography. The uses of media by an audience lead us back to basic issues of content, programming, production, and the values informing texts and publicly reported talk by secular leaders about faith.

The concept that there is an "independent life" of a text (a concept derived from literary criticism, implying that meaning is in the eye of the beholder rather than the writer, that language can be manipulated beyond the author's intention) is anchored by the concerns outlined above about authenticity and authority as mediated social processes and by the obligations of audience as receivers. A quoted text that can be read as an object, acquiring public meaning as symbol, beyond its author's intention, is an ongoing, interdisciplinary theoretical concern debated extensively in the relevant academic literature of several disciplines outside of communication and mass media, including art and literary history, and cultural studies. Only rarely do such discussions involve faith practices or beliefs in the religious sense.

While the work of this book builds on prior academic discussion from fields where religion is not the focus of concern, it is engaged with the intellectual problem of how the audience or public reader sees a mystical connection between words and common language over time and how that influences their appetite for the similarities between the ancient and new that reside in the historical and collective memory. More than any other medium, it is the common language used in public texts interpreted by storytellers that shapes notions of identity. Moreover, how the audience sees mystical authenticity or spiritual authority as "real" influences their attitudes toward the validity of the "Unknown,"[17] the future history of a people. The mass public audience engaged spiritually with interpretation of mystery in ancient religious literature differs from the response of an audience that yearns for mystery, thirsts for the miraculous, and enjoys the freedom of a vacationer in a constructed public space (liminality) through the consumption of cultural productions of media work in film, books, sitcoms, advertising, and material products in the consumer culture. Yet the consequences depend, not on an author's intention, but on the audience's reception of the text.

To the extent that sacred texts are unfamiliar, their meaning as a quotation is lost on the receiver or audience, as both literary and art historians have described. Not knowing the stories shared by others is a source of alienation and violence, and it is ultimately a powerful, subversive force against the values of the national or imagined identity. Recovery of a sense of connection to a remembered past, to the macrostory of creation and wisdom extant in all world religions, works as a consolidating force in spiritual cultures by increasing participation in shared knowledge about the language of human life—its brevity and loves.

This theoretical description is central to the theological and historical concerns of this book and serves as a bridge to the conceptual frameworks of mass media studies by McLuhan, Anderson, and many others. If the life of a mass media audience and the life of a common reader work to fragment spiritual cultures, what means shall we seek as transcendent in the material, mediated culture to answer the question who is God? This is a rather different question than who is your God? Undoubtedly it is through knowledge of the Other's images of God that we understand our own more clearly, and the investigative reporter's quotations of daily imaginers may serve as a transcendent bridge.

OVERVIEW OF THE VOLUME

The conceptual and theoretical frames described above thread together seemingly disparate chapters grouped broadly into three sections. Chapters 1–4 of the first section focus on the legal and constitutional frames informing national identity and the ideological climates of newsrooms within which journalists construct the mediated religious public square. Chapters 5–8 in the second section develop the theme of reporting across cultures, the delicate role of the reporter who negotiates two cultures as participant-observer within subcultures, and the movement of religions from personal prayer to activist public voice through, and mirrored in, media. Writers address the relationship between news value and the political subcultures that work to close down rather than open up religious communication. Chapters 9–12 in the third section explore the role of the lack of scientific and theological information, the gap between faith and reason, the failure of faith to communicate with the larger mass public through media because of the complexity of religious issues, and current issues in religious ideology as seen in conflicts between science and religious dogma. Contributing authors in this volume imply that there is a culture of absence in national identity that contributes to the rise of material manifestations through commodities and through media products in order to achieve a sense of belonging.

Working in a Publicity Economy

As religious people move from the posture of a private conversation with God through prayer to a more visible, public position to raise their voices in testimony about their faith, conversion experiences, and life before and after encountering religion, they encounter resistance from the secular culture. Within that resistance, they find new avenues of communication that assimilate their once private voices in the marketplace and in the public square.

JOHN SCHMALZBAUER presents research based on interviews with leading syndicated and mainstream news reporters; he describes components of the Catholic and evangelical Protestant imagination and how that sectarian identity process shapes styles and types of newswriting. He constructs as contrasting outlooks two streams of religious imagination: Catholic sacramentalism and evangelical biblicism, analogical Catholics and dialectical evangelicals, Catholic communitarianism and evangelical Individualism. Within the context of the quotation theory described above, two publics emerge based on their response to the Bible as a public text. His inquiry addresses the consequences of these differences. Creating a typology of storylines based on longitudinal content analysis, he finds three predominant themes in religion newswriting: culture wars, cultural consensus, and communitarianism. Schmalzbauer associates high-profile journalists with specific types of stories.

JOHN BUESCHER discusses the difficulty of reporting about an Asian culture from the United States and talks about the receptivity of Buddhist monks for radio news. His essay presents a nuance concerning the uses subcultural practices make of so-called intrusive media, demonstrating the Buddhist's meditation on what is present rather than what is absent. In the context of the theoretical frame of the book, one might suggest that meditation is an integrative and subtle force of reading that constructs resistance by accepting all forms of intrusion, even radio, as natural.

C. WELTON GADDY cautions that at this time in American history, as the fabric of the nation's religious diversity makes it more important for mutual respect among religious peoples, God talk in the public square is divisive because it is specifically associated with partisan and sectarian attitudes. Gaddy argues that religious rhetoric should play a role in the political life of a nation, without proponents and partisan advocates building an altar in the mediated public square for their special interests or causes. Whether issue-based politics are waged by the elected or the self-described Elect, freedom and inclusion should be the tenor of religious language used to interpret public texts, especially prayer.

MOHAMMED EL-NAWAWY enumerates cultural and legal reasons for Middle East news climates and regulations. Because of the historic, dominant relationship between government and media in Arab countries, freedom of expression is a cultural concept limited by politics and by law, while censorship is tolerated and even expected as a form of civic responsibility.

PAUL MOSES examines the constitutional issues relevant to the immigrant Chinese press in New York and the Falun Gong. He explores the role of the immigrant press informing political and public attitudes about the authenticity of a "foreign" religion, native to China.

PETER SMITH provides three case-level stories about faith-based initiatives in recent news in which the First Amendment and freedom of religious expression are in conflict. Public monuments are emblematic of the church-state tensions in public policy debates lived out in the service sector.

REBECCA MOORE undercuts the popular usage of fundamentalism as a synonym for antimodernity. She frames the argument from the perspective of religious studies: the idea of backwardness associated with biblical literalism and intense readings of patriarchal religious texts is inaccurate. Rather, the adept use of media by fundamentalists of the Middle East puts contesting religionists squarely in the center, in the mediated culture that defines both modernity and postmodernity.

COREY FLINTOFF observes how ideas of social authority mix with journalistic objectivity in Mongolia, while he was on assignment, teaching and working with broadcast journalists. Among Mongolian journalists and media workers, he found attitudes that were more fundamentally religious about secular politics than they were political about religious fundamentals.

PAUL BOYER discusses how the best-selling *Left Behind* series by Timothy LeHaye, a minister and Old Testament scholar, commodifies millennialism through narrative, and in tapes, comic books, and T-shirts. Boyer provides a clear and concise historical description of the nature of this belief and draws important connections with the ideology governing U.S. foreign policy in the Middle East and war in the biblical holy lands.

ASLAM ABDALLAH analyzes press stories about Islam since 9/11. He argues that Americans' ignorance about geography and other cultures leaves them mentally vulnerable to accepting distortions reported in the U.S. and global press about the nature of the conflicts in the Middle East and affects their perception of "objective" journalism.

JOHN P. FERRÉ argues that the celluloid imagination of mystery has distanced Americans from death and that the audience's epistemology of loss creates a need for new mediated forms of obituaries in multimedia on highways and on the Internet.

MARK PINSKY argues that the American way of death is shaped by historical memory, less from what the audiences know personally about loss than from how their real experiences of loss imitate their knowledge of death through media.

RICHARD GARDNER studies the role of collective memory in the self-naming of a culture. He argues that recollections of loss define the epistemology of a people, who read themselves as they are being read by outsiders—as both victims and victimizers. When a religious cult emerges, the historical background defines the public response to the pathology of religion.

TERESA WATANABE explores the religious contradictions in Japanese life today, where the reflective moral life of a nation is more secular than religious, where consensus restrains people from discussions about religious sectarian preferences, and where affiliations are nominal. Yet the national identity is formed in the absence of sectarianism: the spiritual is pervasive; loyalty to nation, ancestors, and family are stronger identifiers than external expression of belonging to religious organizations.

HOWARD DORGAN explores the subtleties of cross-cultural observation, based on his thirty years of research in Appalachia exploring early morning *Gospel Hour* radio broadcasting. The culture he explores is in America, yet far from its popular values. Dorgan studies the insider-outsider relationship as one that hinges on a balanced focus on the present, when he, as the participant-observer-visitor, is embraced by the warmth of a religion that is not his own. An accomplished ethnographer, Dorgan supplies both reflections on his three decades of applied methodology and insight into a pristine American subculture loyal to its deep roots in religious traditions that have much to do with identity of family, community, and the mountain culture. At the same time, this region epitomizes the problem of translating deeply held private convictions from one culture to broader ones. Surrounded by affluent secular and material culture, the people Dorgan researched are deeply enmeshed in their beliefs, using simple, stark, and biblically fundamental ways to test their own faith.

ADAM PHILLIPS explores the role of the reporter as storyteller. The writer who is a media worker is not an ethnographer, strictly speaking, but a participant-observer who must strike a balance between journalistic objectivity and empathy with the subject, not unlike Dorgan's experience of being embraced by those whose faith he did not share. Welcoming strangers is to a degree taken as seriously by good storytellers as by faithful believers in remote regions practicing a pure form of faith based more on inherited patterns of expression than on clergy. Writers must to some degree cherish the story of the day, hold the actors in high regard, tread lightly where deep faith practices or grief of an extraordinary nature occurs, whether in New York City or in the Middle East.

VIRGILIO ELIZONDO contributes his classic essay, a definitive, historical baseline against which to measure the plethora of literature about the importance of the Marian apparition at Guadalupe as a political and spiritual icon in Hispanic culture.

RICHARD RODRIGUEZ observes the ironic position of being a participant-observer of one's self in a religion of one's own: he is both insider and outsider, belonger and the excluded. That contradiction is the source of his poetry, centered in the present, yet full of historical memory, a style reminiscent of biblical Lamentations.

JAME SCHAEFER takes up the complicated problem of journalists translating issues in science for a skeptical audience. She argues that journalists need to educate themselves about the theological mind, a method consistent with scientific investigation. The lack of knowledge about science on the part of journalists makes it possible for partisan religionists to politicize science in controversies over stem cell research and creationism taught in schools. Schaefer cites examples of quotations about science and religion in media and explores the assumptions behind them. As a means to think more clearly about the field, she provides a succinct typology of ways to think about conflicts between religion and science.

JOE WILLIAMS provides a light-handed but candid case study about the notion of "fairness" in reporting on politicized scientific issues. He explains the pressures science reporters are up against in facing activist publics for whom life-and-death issues are rooted in deeply held religious principles on which they define their political as well as national identity.

PAUL SOUKUP provides a map to the Vatican's speech designed for global public audiences—a mixed media of evangelism, dogma, and media relations that complicates reception. Among the important resources about values in modern media culture, he explicates little-known and less-often-read documents about the role of media, advertising, and news in the modern world. These important public texts are produced over the course of several papacies, particularly the papacy of John Paul II, who coined the phrase "the culture of death," in reference to the culture of the American media. These documents are interesting examples of how ancient wisdom confronts mediated culture, raising questions about the need for a media champion to serve as interpreter in order for ideas to thrive.

DAVID CRUMM responds to media inquiries about what threatens the practice of religion in America culture. His observations suggest that it is not estrangement from Roman styles of formal high-church communication that keep public texts such as papal documents hidden from the collective mind—it is the postmodern saturation of ephemeral cultural diversions that dates Vatican styles of communication used to address the deep moral issues about media use and its impact on modern life. The shopping mall contains quasi-religious practices that compete with older traditional religions.

GUSTAV NIEBUHR provides an emblem and model of the reciprocal relationship between both religion newspeople and the scholars who research religions. These two groups work together in a synchronous conversation that includes the audience and that leaves readers better informed and less vulnerable to misunderstandings about religion.

The field of media and religion has grown and become established in the decade since John Dart and James Allen first surveyed American newsrooms about reporters' religious attitudes. Events such as 9/11 and wars in the Middle East have marked the early twenty-first century as an historical age in which religion and politics, and the politics of religion, have been confused with battles over land, power, and the lack of forgiveness, what Donald Shriver termed *An Ethic for Enemies*. At the beginning of the twenty-first century, it appears that global media homogenizes cultures, while religion, which ought to dissolve differences, serves to divide people according to their unknown, inexplicable beliefs and their frail mysteries. The media machinery that dominates global exchange of information carries within it the mechanics of reproduction and the power to repackage old messages as new: these have to do with the importance of storytellers and the nature of universals, the human life stories and impact of news events on the actual realities of audiences globally. Across linked networks and webs of media communities, ideas about religion move so quickly that the tech-savvy audience becomes blasé, insensitive to the subtle changes in language that affect collective attitudes and shape prejudice and popular beliefs. To borrow McLuhan's concept cited at the beginning of this essay, consider how unexamined change contains habit, and each habit contains attitudes of mind, and naming of meanings contain prejudice and biases, and within these is the mirror that reflects the readers' resistance to the Other.

Chapter 1

Journalism and the Religious Imagination

John Schmalzbauer

At the height of the Clinton-Lewinsky scandal, William Powers wrote in the *National Journal* of the rise of a "Roman Legion" of Irish Catholics in the Washington press corps, arguing that such journalists were especially critical of Bill Clinton's behavior. Noting the scorn expressed for President Clinton by Cokie Roberts, Mary McGrory, Tim Russert, and Chris Matthews, Powers asked if it was a mere coincidence that so many of them had come out of the same church. Later in the article, he argued that "the moral history of the church" was "reflected in their views," adding that "the desire for complete honesty is of course very Catholic." Was Powers right? Did the "moral history" of Catholicism shape the journalism of Roberts, Russert, and Matthews in a way that led them to be harder on Bill Clinton? To what extent are the stories of American journalists influenced by their religious backgrounds? This essay examines the impact of the religious imagination on the journalism of people of faith.

One of the most striking things about the journalistic profession is its claim to tell stories without morals. In the textbook version of reporting, journalists come to a story *tabula rasa*. Political, moral, and religious convictions are checked at the newsroom door. In light of American journalism's public disavowal of moral questions, what place does religious faith play in the crafting of stories? Given the historic commitment of American journalists to the ideology of objectivity, there would seem to be little room for a religious or moral imagination. Journalists simply report on the world; they are not supposed to judge it.[1] Yet few scholars take the textbook version of the profession at face value anymore.[2]

In *The Content of the Form*, Hayden White writes that "narrative is not merely a neutral discursive form," but instead reflects choices about the representation of reality that have "distinct ideological and even specifically political" consequences.[3] Along the same lines, media sociologist Michael Schudson argues that journalism's conventional story forms "reinforce certain assumptions about the political world" while narrowing "the range of what kinds of truths can be told."[4] By including some newsmakers, plotlines, and explanatory frameworks while excluding others, journalistic narratives dramatize an implicit vision of what aspects of reality are politically and morally significant. Investigative journalists defend "traditional virtue by telling stories of terrible vice."[5] Foreign correspondents condemn torture by calling attention to the suffering of victims. "Insofar as journalists are defenders of a set of values," writes sociologist Herbert Gans, "they are more than technicians who transmit information from sources to audiences."[6]

THE CATHOLIC AND EVANGELICAL IMAGINATIONS

Given the value-laden character of journalistic narratives, what role do religious values play in the stories of Catholic and evangelical journalists? This essay focuses on the news stories and columns produced by twenty journalists interviewed as part of a much larger study of the place of faith in professional life.[7]

Just as media analysts have rediscovered the importance of narrative, scholars from across the disciplines have increasingly stressed the role of stories in transmitting religious identities. From Bible stories, to the lives of the saints, to civil religious stories of "Christian America," such narratives furnish believers with a set of cultural resources to make sense of the world and to "talk about the good society."[8] This study argues that Catholic and evangelical journalists work at the intersection of two public storytelling communities: the profession of American journalism, and their own religious traditions. Along with the cultural conventions of the journalistic profession, the Catholic and evangelical traditions help fill the "cultural toolkits" of my respondents, providing the "building blocks" (stories, symbols, and metaphors) from which their news stories and columns are constructed.[9]

In *The Catholic Myth*, Andrew Greeley writes that Catholics and Protestants tell "different stories of God," arguing that the differences between the two heritages are "but manifestations . . . of more fundamentally differing sets of symbols."[10] Concurring with Greeley, Robert Bellah argues that there are deep differences between the "Protestant cultural code" and its Catholic counterpart.[11] Along the same lines, scholars have called attention to the presence of a Catholic sensibility in the works of figures such as John Ford, Andy Warhol, Flannery O'Connor, and Martin Scorsese.[12]

What are the components of the Catholic and evangelical Protestant imaginations? Given the internal pluralism of American Catholicism and American evangelicalism, it is dangerous to make any firm generalizations. Nevertheless, I would like to call attention to three sets of opposing qualities that capture some of the differences between the two traditions that scholars have identified.

Catholic Sacramentalism and Evangelical Biblicism

In the opening paragraphs of *The Catholic Imagination*, Andrew Greeley provides an evocative description of the sacramental orientation of American Catholics:

> Catholics live in an enchanted world, a world of statues and holy water, stained glass and votive candles, saints and religious medals, rosary beads and holy pictures. But these Catholic paraphernalia are mere hints of a deeper and more pervasive religious sensibility which inclines Catholics to see the Holy lurking in creation. As Catholics we find our houses and our world haunted by a sense that the objects, events, and persons of daily life are revelations of grace. . . . The workings of this imagination are most obvious in the Church's seven sacraments, but the seven are both a result and a reinforcement of a much broader Catholic view of reality.[13]

This Catholic focus on the physicality of religious symbols and rituals is in sharp contrast to evangelicalism's reverence for what Peter Thuesen calls "the leather-bound shrine in every home."[14] By stressing the inerrancy, infallibility, inspiration, and truth claims of Scripture, evangelicals have pointed to the Bible as a central point of contact between human beings and God.[15] While these differences are by no means absolute, evangelicals have tended to see *words* (and the Word of God) as more sacred than *things*.[16]

Analogical Catholics and Dialectical Evangelicals

The Catholic confidence in the capacity of rituals and symbols to mediate the sacred is related to an even more profound difference between the two religious traditions. In *The Analogical Imagination*, theologian David Tracy argues that the Protestant and Catholic traditions incorporate different models of the relationship of God to the world and of Christianity to human culture.[17] While the Protestant tradition tends to view the world as full of sin, the Catholic tradition sees the world as "charged with the grandeur of God."[18]

Because of their more culture-affirming orientation, Catholics are more likely to view human society, the body, and the material world *analogically* (as analogies for the divine), looking for "similarities-in-difference" between "God, self, other selves and world."[19] By contrast, the Protestant tradition emphasizes the *differences* between creation and creator, nature and grace, and sacred and profane.[20] The qualities of this "dialectical imagination" are especially apparent in evangelicalism. More than any other branch of American Protestantism, evangelicals emphasize the boundaries between Christ and culture, sacred and secular, and church and world.[21]

Catholic Communitarianism and Evangelical Individualism

Andrew Greeley observes that "Italian American films, from *Mean Streets* through *Moonstruck*, *Sleepers*, and *Johnny Brasco*" are "about an intense family life, intricate extended family relations, and a close-knit neighborhood community."[22] From Weber and Durkheim to Greeley and Bellah, social scientists have long contrasted the communitarian orientation of the Catholic tradition with Protestant individualism. While the "Protestant cultural code" places enormous stress on personal faith, Catholicism sees the individual as embedded in a network of relationships and groups.[23] In sharp contrast to Catholic communitarianism, evangelicals have been "largely incapable of seeing how supraindividual social structures, collective processes, and institutional systems" shape human beings.[24] Along the same lines, recent surveys indicate that the vast majority of American Catholics consider "social justice" a central part of being Catholic.[25] By contrast, evangelicalism has emphasized personal morality and individual responsibility, embracing a "moral reform agenda" of family values and opposition to abortion.[26]

This sketch of the Catholic and evangelical imaginations should not obscure the internal pluralism of both religious communities. Sociologist Christian Smith warns against "treating conservative Protestants as a monolithic social group," noting that evangelicals "can be found spread across the political and ideological map . . . taking positions as diverse as pro-American conservatism, traditional liberalism, peace-and-justice activism, and theonomic reconstructionism."[27] Similarly, historian David O'Brien argues that "after two centuries of organized existence in the United States, the American church has not evolved a coherent understanding of its public role and responsibilities."[28] From the pacifism of the Berrigans to the conservatism of William F. Buckley, American Catholics have integrated their religious views with a host of conflicting ideologies.

THE RELIGIOUS IMAGINATION
IN AMERICAN JOURNALISM

What difference do the Catholic and evangelical imaginations make in American journalism? This study analyzes the stories of twenty Catholic and evangelical journalists.[29] Assessing the influence of religion on these journalists was a difficult task. Besides the limitations of working with a small sample (ten Catholics and ten evangelicals), I had to contend with the fact that most journalists had written hundreds (and in some cases thousands) of news stories and columns over the course of their careers. Instead of analyzing every story written by every journalist, I chose to begin with a sample of approximately fifty stories per journalist.[30] These stories were culled evenly from across the careers of journalists in the sample using LexisNexis. As broad themes emerged, I would then search for additional stories using key words such as "culture wars," "community," or "justice."

Eventually, I began to recognize recurring patterns in the stories of my respondents. For example, it became evident that the evangelical journalists Cal Thomas, Fred Barnes, and Russ Pulliam had an affinity for the "culture wars" account of American politics, emphasizing the boundaries between conservative Christians and secular liberals. In a similar way, Catholics E. J. Dionne and Peter Steinfels returned to the themes of consensus and moderation in story after story. As I worked through a sampling of stories from individual journalists, I found it helpful to keep in mind an insight now commonplace among media scholars: Journalists tell the *same stories* over and over again, plugging new facts into "preexisting plotlines."[31] Mark Silk writes about this tendency in *Unsecular Media*, identifying seven recurring storylines that he calls the "topoi" of religion news.[32]

Borrowing a page from Silk's approach, I have identified five recurring storylines that seem to reflect the influence of the Catholic and evangelical Protestant imaginations in the stories of my respondents.[33] I will discuss two of these storylines in this essay. Although these storylines do not begin to exhaust the multitude of religious themes found in their writings, they do illustrate the influence of Catholicism and evangelicalism on their work:

1. Culture Wars: This storyline of polarized conflict between religious conservatives and secular liberals embodies the dialectical, individualistic, and morality-oriented outlook of the Protestant imagination.
2. Cultural Consensus: Reflecting an analogical emphasis on "similarities-in-difference,"[34] this storyline stresses dialogue and points of agreement between liberals and conservatives, Catholics and non-Catholics, religious and secular.

To a large extent, these two storylines embody the Catholic and Protestant imaginations as described by Tracy, Greeley, and others. While Catholics have told stories that are analogical and communal (the "cultural consensus" storyline), evangelicals have emphasized individual morality and the truth claims of the Bible (the "culture wars" storyline). At the same time, not all Catholic and evangelical journalists have told stories that conform to the textbook version of the Catholic and Protestant imaginations. Along the same lines, some Catholic journalists (though none in the sample) have made use of the culture wars storyline. These deviations from the standard accounts of the Catholic and Protestant imaginations are a reminder of the internal pluralism of both traditions.

Besides reflecting the religious backgrounds of their creators, the stories of my respondents have been shaped by the values and organizational divisions of professional journalism. In *Deciding What's News* (42–69), Herbert Gans describes eight "enduring values" that characterize the American news media: "ethnocentrism, altruistic democracy, responsible capitalism, small-town pastoralism, individualism, moderatism, social order, and national leadership." Many of these values are also shared by Catholic and evangelical journalists and have been integrated into the two storylines listed above. For example, there are deep affinities between political "moderatism" and the story of cultural consensus. Nevertheless, *some* of the enduring values (moderatism) are in tension with *some* of the storylines (culture wars).

Along with the enduring values outlined by Gans, the stories of Catholic and evangelical journalists have been influenced by the organization of news reporting into bureaus, beats, and topical specializations—what sociologist Gaye Tuchman calls the "news net." Because the reporting of journalists is limited to a relatively narrow range of organizations, sources, and topics, news is allowed "to occur at some locations but not at others," and even opinion columnists are constrained by the need to write about national politics.[35] The challenge for Catholic and evangelical reporters has been to find ways of telling the stories they want to tell (culture wars, cultural consensus) in their particular spot in the news net (the White House, the United Nations, national politics).

Catholic and evangelical journalists have told stories at the intersection of professional and religious worlds. The stories they have written are both like and unlike those of their professional colleagues. Like other journalists who juggle multiple identities (African American journalists, gay journalists, women journalists), they have engaged in a process of cultural bricolage, grafting the stories of their religious communities onto those of American journalism.[36] The remainder of this essay will examine how Catholics and evangelicals have brought their religious commitments into American journalism through the storylines of culture wars and cultural consensus. Along the way, it will look at how they have articulated a fit between these storylines and the values and topical specializations of American journalism, creating hybrid story forms that reflect the influence of both social worlds.

The Culture-Wars Storyline: Cal Thomas

Sociologist Christian Smith argues that "evangelicals operate with a very strong sense of boundaries that distinguish themselves from non-Christians and from nonevangelical Christians."[37] Nowhere is this more the case than in the rhetoric of Christian conservatives in American politics. In his 1992 book *Culture Wars: The Struggle to Define America*, James Hunter described the affinity of conservative Protestants (and other religious conservatives) for the dualistic picture of the world contained in culture-wars rhetoric. On issues such as abortion, the family, school prayer, and the media, the leaders of the new Christian right have drawn sharp boundaries between themselves and their political opponents. In contrast to the analogical imagination's focus on "similarities-in-difference," such rhetoric pictures a clear distinction between Christianity and the world. By opting for a language of difference rather than similarity, negation rather than affirmation, and conflict rather than consensus, the culture-wars storyline comes close to being a pure expression of the dialectical imagination.[38]

Although several studies have shown that most American evangelicals do not view the world through a culture-wars lens, the culture-wars storyline has been used by a number of the evangelical journalists interviewed for this project (including Fred Barnes of the *Weekly Standard* and Russ Pulliam of the now-defunct *Indianapolis News*). By far the most interesting use of this storyline can be found in the writings of the syndicated columnist Cal Thomas, who works for the *Los Angeles Times* syndicate. Although Thomas has moderated his rhetoric in recent years, he continues to be an outspoken advocate for religious conservatism. According to David Astor in *Editor and Publisher*, Thomas's column appears in more than five hundred newspapers, making it the most widely syndicated political column in America—surpassing the columns of George Will, Robert Novak, and Ellen Goodman in the number of newspapers reached.[39]

Consistent with the military metaphor of "culture wars," Thomas's 1987 collection of columns is entitled *Occupied Territory*. According to Dean Riddings's review published in the *Fundamentalist Journal*, "Thomas's raging red necktie [on the cover] tells the story," adding that Riddings "is angry that the conservative worldview" is "virtually absent" from "the public arena."[40] While Thomas uses the term "culture wars" only occasionally, a culture-wars map of the world is implicit in much of his writing. In column after column, Thomas describes a struggle between two polarized camps battling for the soul of the nation. On one side are "conservatives," "social and religious conservatives," "Christians," the "Christian Right," and the "champions of traditional morality." On the other side are the "liberal secularists," the "pagan left," the "'heroes' and 'heroines' of the '60s," the "'60s flower children," "feminists," "television journalists," the "big media," the "entertainment industry," the "tenured radicals," the "bigots" (against Christian conservatives), and the "protected classes."[41] The binary oppositions that run through Thomas's columns map out a clearly defined battle between two sides:

Conservatives	Liberals
Christians	Secularists
The Greatest Generation	Baby Boomers
Pre-1960s/1980s	1960s
Ordinary Women	Feminists
Ordinary Americans	Media Elites/Academics

James Hunter argues that "defining the enemy" is a key feature of culture-wars rhetoric.[42] As this list makes clear, Thomas's journalism divides the world into two warring factions.

Thomas regularly marshals public opinion surveys to show that a majority of Americans agree with the positions of religious conservatives.[43] While religious conservatives are portrayed as the guardians of middle-American values and the "Judeo-Christian tradition," liberals and the mass media are depicted as the agents of America's moral destruction ("Clinton's" B7). In one column, Thomas blames the "imposed immorality" of the "pagan left" for divorce, teen pregnancy, abortion, single-parent families, and murder ("Religious Right" B7). In another he accuses "liberal secularists" of having "spiritually strip-mined" America ("Making Sense" B7). In yet another, he uses Hollywood celebrities and the media to symbolize the general moral decay of American society, holding up actor Hugh Grant's encounter with a prostitute as a sign of a general "sexual impurity in entertainment and real life." For Thomas, both Grant's sex scandal and a *Newsweek* article on bisexuality are "evidence of social decay," a "new strain of depravity," and a sign that "jumbo jets full of societal viruses are stacked up over our nation" ("Hugh Grant" B7). The metaphors of impurity, sickness, and decay are repeatedly used to draw boundaries against liberals, secular humanists, and the entertainment industry.

Time as well as political ideology is given moral significance. For Thomas the 1960s in general, and the 1962 Supreme Court ruling against school prayer in particular, are the symbolic starting points of America's spiritual and moral decline. "The liberals said no" to school prayer "and no it has been for 32 years," writes Thomas in a 1994 column. Linking this anniversary to a larger process of societal decay, he argues that "our prayerlessness has promoted our growing secularism, and, many argue, the decay of our society into violence, lawlessness, and moral poverty" ("Making Sense" B7). As the children of the 1960s, baby boomers are singled out as especially culpable for the demoralizing of American culture. Comparing them to the virtuous men and women of the World War II generation, Thomas characterizes the "'heroes' and 'heroines' of the '60s" as "intellectual and moral dwarfs who can't see beyond their own comfort and for whom sacrifice was sitting still long enough to listen to a lecture from their parents about why they should love their country" ("Final Insult" B7). Contrasting the piety of the Pilgrims with the secularism of "those who proclaimed God dead in the '60s," Thomas notes that it is "fitting that at Thanksgiving time, a national holiday that celebrates prayerful thanks, there would be a controversy about prayer in public schools" ("Making Sense" B7). Along the same lines, he holds up the faith of the "Founding Fathers" as an antidote to the contemporary reign of secular humanism ("Spiritual Wall" B7).

Why does Thomas draw such sharp boundaries between religious conservatives and secular liberals? In *Redeeming America: Piety and Politics in the New Christian Right*, political scientist Michael Lienesch provides a clue, noting that religious conservatives have tended to describe "the polity in dualistic terms, as a place of good and evil, right and wrong, allies and enemies."[44] While such dualistic rhetoric has deep roots in American evangelicalism, it also serves a strategic purpose by mobilizing supporters against a common enemy through fund-raising letters, speeches, and political campaign slogans. Before assuming his current position as a columnist for the *Los Angeles Times* syndicate, Cal Thomas worked for Jerry Falwell's Moral Majority.

Besides echoing the rhetoric of the new Christian right, many of Thomas's columns have been influenced by the storytelling conventions of American journalism. In an insightful piece in the *Columbia Journalism Review*, James Hunter describes the journalistic "predisposition to dichotomize," arguing that "the narrative structure of most journalism depends in large part upon the interplay of antagonists and protagonists, heroes and villains, victims and victimizers, and so on." By contrasting the views of Christian conservatives and liberal secularists, Thomas fits his stories into journalism's "grid of rhetorical extremes."[45]

Thomas's stories also echo a number of the "enduring values" that Herbert Gans argues are implicit in American journalism, including social order, individualism, and nationalism. By focusing on the moral degradation of American society, the decline of the family, and the "breakdown of culture," Thomas traffics in what Gans calls "social disorder news." Social disorder stories often engage in the "romanticization of the past" while expressing a "fear of contemporary disintegration."[46]

The enduring journalistic value of individualism is also on display as Thomas returns again and again to the themes of "morality" ("Moral Issues" B5), "individual character" ("Crime" B7), and "virtue" ("Lost Virtue" B7). His columns locate the problems of American society in the nuclear family or in individual lives, ignoring the larger social context of neighborhoods, churches, and civil society. Government is viewed as part of the problem in columns that call for "smaller government, less dependence on the state and a reformation in moral and social values" ("Newt" B7). This single-minded focus on personal character to the exclusion of larger social institutions reflects evangelicalism's individualistic "moral reform agenda."[47]

Consistent with evangelicalism's emphasis on the authority of the Bible, Thomas occasionally appeals to the biblical text. In a column on abortion, he quotes extensively from Psalm 139 ("You created my inmost being; you knit me together in my mother's womb. . . . I am fearfully and wonderfully made") ("Mr. Theologian" B7). Yet the civil-religious myths of American society (the story of Thanksgiving, the heroism of the "Greatest Generation") figure much more prominently in his columns than the stories of the Bible. Thomas is a *nationally* syndicated political columnist. Because of his position in the news net, Thomas locates his stories of moral decline within a narrative of the American *nation* rather than the story of the Christian church, reflecting journalism's emphasis on the "nation as a unit" and "national leadership."[48] Instead of relying on Christian terminology to make his arguments (which he does only occasionally), Thomas appeals to "absolutes" ("RU-486" B7), "virtue" ("Lost Virtue" B7), "objective standards," and "morality" ("Moral Issues" B5). In the words of Dean Ridings in the *Fundamentalist Journal*, Thomas is "careful to let reason, statistics, and authorities—on both ends of the pole—present his case."[49]

While the culture-wars storyline can be found throughout Thomas's corpus, it does not entirely dominate his work. Indeed, Thomas uses a small number of pieces to tell stories of agreement between conservatives and liberals, extolling the virtues of what Gans calls political "moderatism."[50] Along the same lines, Thomas's 1999 book (cowritten with former Moral Majority staffer Ed Dobson) articulates a Christian critique of the new Christian right. *Blinded by Might: Can the Religious Right Save America?* argues that "we must not . . . demonize those with whom we disagree."[51]

While attempting to be conciliatory, Thomas and Dobson use words like "secularists," "secular establishment," and "secular left" to describe their political opponents.[52] Consistent with the dialectical outlook of the Protestant imagination, they stress the tensions between Christ and culture, church and world, and evangelicalism and America. While softening the rhetoric of the religious right, they do not eliminate the boundaries between Christian conservatives and the outside world. Far from minimizing evangelical distinctives, they highlight the contrast between "true Christianity" and the immorality of contemporary society. Despite its criticism of the religious right, *Blinded by Might* reflects the ongoing influence of the culture-wars framework on evangelical political thought.

The Cultural-Consensus Storyline:
Peter Steinfels and E. J. Dionne

Reflecting a very different religious sensibility, Catholics Peter Steinfels and E. J. Dionne have rejected the culture-wars narrative in favor of what might be called the cultural--consensus storyline. Instead of focusing attention on the right and the left, Steinfels and Dionne have written about the center. Instead of pitting one era of American history against another (the 1960s versus the 1950s, the Pilgrims versus the baby boomers), they have focused on the ambiguities in each generation's experience. In place of Cal Thomas's martial metaphors, "occupied territory" and "culture wars," they have used words like "consensus," "agreement," "dialogue," and "complicated."[53]

Demonstrating a keen awareness of the story forms of American journalism, Steinfels and Dionne have criticized the "preexisting plotlines" and "frameworks" of culture-wars reporting, arguing for narratives that do justice to the complexities of American life. In Harvard's *Nieman Reports*, Steinfels wrote that he has tried to "give voice and visibility to those people and positions that get squeezed out when conflicts involving religion are reported only in terms of two sides—conservatives and liberals; orthodox and dissenters—rather than the spectrum of perspectives that normally exists."[54] In the same way, E. J. Dionne lamented the fact that the 1960s have been the subject of rival conservative and liberal "parodies," arguing that "each misses the other's truth and each fails to grasp how painfully complicated the 1960s were."[55]

Steinfels writes a religion column ("Beliefs") for the *New York Times* (at the time of the interview, he also served as the *Times's* senior religion correspondent). Dionne writes a political opinion column for the *Washington Post*. Despite differences in beats and genres, both have exemplified the analogical imagination as described by David Tracy and Andrew Greeley. According to Tracy, "analogy is a language of ordered relationships articulating similarity-in-difference."[56] It focuses on the ways in which phenomena are *like* rather than *unlike* each other.[57] By encouraging the building of bridges rather than the building of walls, analogical thinking makes it possible for people of faith to engage in dialogue with those from outside their traditions.

In describing the political and religious landscape of American society, Steinfels and Dionne have told stories of similarities-in-difference, highlighting points of agreement between conservatives and liberals, left and right, and secular and religious. Conversation, dialogue, and a meeting of the minds figure prominently in each man's work. Reflecting his location in the news net—the religion beat—many of Steinfels' news articles and columns use academic, religious, or political meetings and conferences as the scenic backdrop for stories of dialogue and agreement. One such column told of a United Nations meeting in Copenhagen where the "Vatican converged with feminist lobbies" and "the forces of faith agreed, with each other and their secular counterparts." Criticizing the journalistic motif of conflict, Steinfels asked, "Was this a classic example of 'no conflict, no news?'" ("Beliefs" 18 March 1995). Likewise, in a news story on the United Methodist's General Conference meetings, he reported on the "conference's determination to steer a cautious middle course on homosexuality." The article cited a Methodist bishop who had said that "he came to the General Conference last week fearing" he "would witness 'a dramatic exhibition' of polarization," adding that "up to now . . . I haven't seen it" ("Methodists" A22). Finally, Steinfels wrote that the election of an Eastern Orthodox priest to the presidency of the National Council of Churches "represented 'a growing pluralism' and recognition of an Eastern Orthodox tradition that could mend the breach between liberal and conservative Christians" ("Orthodox" A30).

Occupying a very different position in the news net—national politics—E. J. Dionne has incorporated similar motifs in his analysis of American politics, using public opinion data to ground a consensus interpretation of American culture. In a column focusing on the extremism of the Anita Hill/Clarence Thomas hearings, Dionne argued that "the country as a whole is not as neatly polarized as are the Washington-based interest groups," noting that "the polls showed pluralities or majorities of women supporting Thomas and a significant majority of men backing Hill," showing "us that the world out there is far more complicated than men versus women, left versus right" ("After the Brawl" C1). Rather than portraying sharp partisan divisions *between* liberals and conservatives, Dionne has focused on the ambivalence many Americans feel "within themselves about many of the social changes of the last two decades." Citing a *Times-Mirror* survey on gender roles, Dionne pointed out that while "68 percent of those surveyed said that 'too many children are being raised in day care centers,'" a similar percentage "rejected the idea that 'women should return to their traditional role in society.'" From these findings, Dionne concluded that "conventional political labels like conservative and liberal, even Democratic and Republican, are of little use describing the American electorate" ("Survey" D27).

Dionne articulated the same themes in his 1991 book *Why Americans Hate Politics*, arguing that the "cause of this false polarization" between liberals and conservatives is "the cultural civil war that broke out in the 1960s" (11). In sharp contrast to the polarized discourse of elites, Dionne noted that "in truth, America's cultural values are a rich and not necessarily contradictory mix of liberal instincts and conservative values" (14). On abortion, he argued that "evidence from polls is that even on this question Americans resist yes/no answers," and that on other social questions, the "public's ambivalence suggests how deep is its thirst for compromise on the issues raised by the cultural civil war that began in the 1960s" (19). Rejecting "an 'either/or' politics based on ideological preconceptions," Dionne called for a "'both/and' politics based on ideas that broadly unite us" (14). In doing so, he exemplified the analogical imagination's emphasis on similarity-in-difference (both/and), emphasizing common ground over ideological polarities (either/or).

Both Steinfels and Dionne have condemned the use of inflammatory language in the public square, calling for a return to civility and reasoned public discourse. In his column on the Clarence Thomas/Anita Hill debate, Dionne sharply criticized both liberal and conservative willingness to "flout all the rules in order to win," arguing that "it is precisely when the issues at stake involve such explosive matters as race and sexuality that the country has a right to expect politicians, and especially the White House, to do more than just play around with social dynamite for cheap political points" ("After the Brawl" C1). Rejecting the "polarizing denunciations" of religious debates over homosexuality, Steinfels' praised the unusual civility of *New Republic* editor Andrew Sullivan's speech on "The Gay Catholic Paradox." "What was noteworthy about his speech at Notre Dame," wrote Steinfels, "was the manner in which he presented the case," avoiding "cheap shots" like using AIDS "as an emotional club for winning agreement." The Notre Dame students were "impressed . . . with Mr. Sullivan's seriousness, with the way in which he argued his case within the framework of church teaching, and with the tone of the argument" ("Beliefs" 17 February 1995).

Finally, both Dionne and Steinfels have highlighted the similarities-in-difference between Catholicism and American culture. In his final months as a Vatican correspondent for the *New York Times*, Dionne wrote an article on "America and the Catholic Church," beginning with a vignette from the 1780s. "Long before it was popular to do so," he noted, "a Roman Catholic clergyman from the United States favored celebrating mass in English instead of Latin, the election of the leadership of the American church by its own priests instead of its appointment by Rome, and a strong role for the laity. The man in question was not a latter-day Catholic dissident, but John Carroll, the first Catholic bishop of the United States, elected by his fellow clergymen in 1789" ("America" A1). By drawing on what Philip Gleason calls the "new Americanism" in Catholic historiography,[58] Dionne and Steinfels have emphasized the democratic strain within American Catholicism. Along the same lines, many of their news stories have challenged the binary storyline of the church versus the modern world. Instead of characterizing John Paul II as a staunch traditionalist at war with modernity, Dionne wrote that "to assert that he is 'anti-modern' is too simple, since the 66-year-old Pope is himself a man of paradoxes and contradictions, the latter being one of his favorite words" ("Pope" A1). Likewise, in his *Nieman Reports* article on the religion beat, Steinfels criticized those stories which descend from "the tension between religious faith and the 18th-century Enlightenment," calling for a more nuanced account of religion and modernity.[59]

To what extent can the analogical style of Dionne and Steinfels be attributed to their liberal Catholic religious backgrounds? In an autobiographical essay published in 1965, Steinfels described the influence of two styles of Catholicism on his intellectual development:

> The Politician is my father's child: he read *Theology and Sanity* in high school (I think Cogley and *The Commonweal* were his, too) and admires the realistic things Eugene McCarthy has said about the nature of compromise; he understands strategy, waiting, the double effect, and sees five sides to every question. The Prophet is the son of my mother: his was Dorothy Day and the *Catholic Worker* and *The Woman Who Was Poor* and he wonders if the world is not beyond strategy and at what point calculation is the death of the soul. Every Christian, I think, carries these two figures within his soul and senses the tension between them.[60]

Sometime between the 1960s and the 1980s, this tension was resolved in favor of the Politician. One of Steinfels's early intellectual heroes was *Commonweal* editor John Cogley. In the 1940s Cogley separated himself from the Catholic Worker movement, criticizing the Worker for its total pacifism.[61] Echoing the trajectory and views of his hero, Steinfels has emphasized the motif of compromise while identifying "five sides to every question." His stories bear a much greater resemblance to the analogical rhetoric of Cogley and *Commonweal* than they do to the pages of the *Catholic Worker*.

On several occasions Dionne too has called attention to the Catholic roots of his politics. In a passionate *Washington Post* column following Pope John Paul II's visit to Denver in 1993, Dionne urged the press to focus on liberal Catholicism's contribution to American public life. "My heroes in American Catholicism," he wrote, "are the progressives, people like Archbishop Rembert Weakland, Father Bryan Hehir and Peggy Steinfels, the editor of *Commonweal*, the lay Catholic magazine" ("Church" A21).

The careers of Dionne and Steinfels must be seen in the context of the ongoing interaction between American liberal culture and Catholic intellectual life.[62] As Catholics, they are the intellectual heirs of John Cogley and Eugene McCarthy. As liberal intellectuals, they reflect the influence of non-Catholics such as Reinhold Niebuhr, Arthur Schlesinger Jr., and Daniel Bell.[63] Scholars of rhetoric have long pointed out the affinities between certain metaphors and ideological traditions such as liberalism, conservatism, and Marxism. By praising consensus, paradox, and complexity, Steinfels and Dionne have appropriated the vocabulary of postwar American liberalism. As historian Godfrey Hodgson points out, "irony, paradox, complexity, and other safely non-political abstractions" became the metaphors of choice for liberal consensus thinkers such as Daniel Bell, Richard Hofstadter, Reinhold Niebuhr, and Arthur Schlesinger Jr.[64] They are also congruent with American journalism's emphasis on moderatism.[65]

American Catholicism has not always enjoyed such a harmonious relationship with the liberal tradition. As recently as the 1940s and 1950s, prominent American liberals depicted Catholicism as a dangerous threat to

American democratic values.[66] Perceived as hierarchical, authoritarian, and intolerant by liberal elites, American Catholics were criticized for violating what Jeffrey Alexander calls the "discourse of civil society."

Postwar *Commonweal* Catholicism of the sort exemplified by John Cogley was a response to the liberal denunciation of Catholic culture found in books such as Paul Blanshard's *American Freedom and Catholic Power*.[67] By focusing on "neutral grays" rather than black and white, liberal Catholicism helped integrate Catholics into the world of liberal public intellectual discourse.[68] In recent years, Peter Steinfels and E. J. Dionne have brought a similar approach to religion and politics into American journalism. This combination of religious and democratic values was apparent in Dionne's comments at a forum on the religious right. Noting that civil society "is the place where most of these arguments should take place," Dionne argued that the "purpose of democratic politics is not to provide chances to pronounce anathemas or to cast fellow citizens into darkness."[69] By drawing firm boundaries against incivility, intolerance, and "pronouncing anathemas," while emphasizing the importance of vigorous public debate, Dionne and Steinfels have demonstrated the capacity of American Catholics to play by the rules of democratic civil society. They have also exemplified the analogical imagination.

CONCLUSION:
THE CATHOLIC AND PROTESTANT IMAGINATIONS
IN AMERICAN JOURNALISM

In *The Outrageous Idea of Christian Scholarship*, George Marsden asks what difference Christian commitments could "possibly make" in academia. Answering his own question, Marsden argues that the underlying commitments of Christian scholars have a "real impact" on their work.[70] This article has posed a similar question, asking what difference religious commitments make in the world of journalism. Drawing on recent scholarship on the Catholic and Protestant imaginations, we have argued that Catholic and evangelical journalists tell stories that embody the theological assumptions of their religious traditions.

These theological assumptions are clearly evident in the two storylines profiled above. While the columns of Cal Thomas dialectically highlight the conflicts dividing Christian conservatives from secular liberals, the stories of Peter Steinfels and E. J. Dionne point to analogical "similarities-in-difference" connecting right and left. Consistent with what Robert Bellah terms the individualism of the "Protestant cultural code,"[71] Thomas's columns revolve around issues of personal morality.

To be sure, not all of the Catholic and evangelical reporters I interviewed have reflected the theological perspectives usually attributed to their own traditions. The handful of stories Cal Thomas tells about liberal-conservative common ground are a departure from evangelicalism's dialectical outlook. In *The Catholic Myth*, Andrew Greeley notes that "the analogical and dialectical imaginations exist side by side" in the minds of many individuals (p. 45). Such deviations from ideal typical accounts of the Catholic and Protestant imaginations call attention to the internal pluralism of the Catholic and evangelical traditions.

At the same time, it is striking how closely the stories of Catholic and evangelical journalists have reflected the outlook of their respective traditions. Consistent with the theories of Tracy and Greeley, the storyline favored by Catholics (cultural consensus) has been more analogical. By contrast, the evangelical Protestant storyline discussed above (culture wars) has been biblicist, dialectical, individualistic, and focused on personal morality.

In mainstreaming the Catholic and Protestant imaginations, my respondents have brought the story forms of their religious communities into secular journalism. Cal Thomas's columns for the *Los Angeles Times Syndicate* do not look all that different from the ones he wrote for Jerry Falwell's *Fundamentalist Journal*. Though they are a departure from his editorials for *Commonweal*, the religion stories of Peter Steinfels betray his long association with the magazine. Indeed, the columns of several respondents have appeared in both the Catholic and evangelical press. *Commonweal* now features the *Washington Post* column of E. J. Dionne.

In bringing their religious commitments into the news, my respondents have had to translate their beliefs into a form that makes sense to those outside their religious traditions. While Cal Thomas has couched his critique of secular humanism in the language of American civil religion, Peter Steinfels and E. J. Dionne have appropriated the vocabulary of postwar American liberalism. In these and other ways, they have made connections between their religious commitments and the storytelling conventions of American journalism.

Admittedly, many of the stories Catholic and evangelical journalists write look just like the stories of their secular colleagues. Yet just because the "theological footprints" of the religious imagination are subtle, this does not mean that they are not there.[72] Until recently, many film critics ignored the influence of Catholicism on the films of John Ford, Frank Capra, and Alfred Hitchcock. Thanks to the scholarship of people like Paul Giles, Lee Lourdeaux, and Richard Blake, it has become increasingly difficult to overlook the impact of religion on the works of these filmmakers.[73] My research has uncovered a similar Catholic sensibility in the world of American journalism. Though many observers are unaware of the presence of religious themes in the pages of the *New York Times* and the *Washington Post*, it may be that they have not looked closely enough.

1: View from the News Desk

Radio in Tibet: A Portable Window on the Sacred

John B. Buescher

A couple of years ago, an old nomad who had settled in Lhasa wrote us a letter at the Voice of America's Tibetan Broadcast Service and had a tourist he met smuggle it out of Tibet. He wrote that each morning he circumambulated the sacred path around the central Jokhang Temple. But while others might have carried in their sheepskin tunics portable silver reliquaries, he carried in his a shortwave radio with an earplug so he could listen to our news shows undisturbed. Despite intense Chinese efforts to jam our signal, he often plucked our program out of the rarefied air. He was, and is, not alone in this. Across Tibet, pilgrims en route to holy sites and monks sitting in morning services are plugged in. Our letter writer wanted us to know he was a devoted listener, no matter that people were forbidden to tune in to what the authorities called "enemy radio." I drew one more conclusion from his letter, however: that he found listening to our show to be in harmony with praying and walking his ritual rounds, which seemed extraordinary to me—after all, it is just a news show.[1]

More than one of our listeners have distilled the main reason they tune in to our programs to the fact that occasionally they can hear the voice of the Dalai Lama coming out of the radio set. Like the nomad's letter, their testimony invites us to see the radio receiver as a portable window on the sacred. Not long after our broadcasts began in 1991, a Communist Party official from a rural district of Tibet complained in a letter to his superiors that villagers had the annoying habit of gathering together to listen to our programs. While they clustered in silence around a radio, they clasped their hands together as if praying, or fingered their prayer beads. If a sound clip of the voice of the Dalai Lama happened to come on during a news report, they prostrated themselves as if in his presence.

Whose activities are most covered by the *Washington Post*? Over the long run, it is naturally the president's. So in our Tibetan broadcasts, reporting on the Dalai Lama's activities has a prominent place, and we use longer clips of his recorded voice than we would if our audience could hear him elsewhere. Our practice coincides with the preferences of those listeners who regard all of his speech as precious and would object to more of a soundbite approach. To some extent, then, we act as a channel for his voice to the people of Tibet, a voice that, in itself, they regard as a grace, whatever he is speaking about.

Through our programming, the Dalai Lama, physically absent from Tibet for more than forty years of exile, is present there, although only implicitly. Our broadcasts have ended his exile from Tibet, but only by way of a similitude, a foreshadowing of a possible future return of the sacred human center of Tibet. Broadcasting our programs, then, is like creating an image inside Tibet of an unrealized but possible Tibet, a restored sacred land, a mandala constructed not out of sand but out of sound. It is a Tibet that has not been overwhelmed by China, but one where Tibetan language and culture stand next to others—where all the news of the world, for example, can be conveyed in Tibetan, just as it can be in English, or Chinese, or Hindi.

At the ancient Tashilhunpo Monastery, the traditional residence of the Panchen Lama, south of Lhasa in Shigatse, the mummified body of the previous Panchen Lama, who died in 1989 under mysterious circumstances, is displayed in a glass case. Enrobed in layers of ceremonial brocades, he is seated in the lotus posture with his eyes closed as if in meditation. There is an object in the case with him—his Bakelite art deco table radio, seeming to float on cloth waves of embroidered gold. I like to imagine him there, tuned in to us.

We beam news over the high plain of Tibet, where people tease it out of the ether and catch it in little metal boxes and release it as a fragile stream of sound. The radio signal seems an embodied Buddhist lesson in the transitory nature of things in this world. So is the news itself, of course, which, like a river, is never constant. Our news announcers run to the studio microphones, clutching their scrawled scripts with the ink still wet as if the paper is an anchor, but each news item written on it dissolves through their fingers into the stream of events even as they finish reading it. So also does each program dissolve. Even as they walk away from the microphone, what's left of it? And so will our Tibetan broadcasting service dissolve, having arisen from impermanent causes and conditions, including many that are technological and political, and liable to disappear again at any time. And so too dissolve all the forces and systems and states and people that animate the stories we broadcast—"They all go into the dark . . . the vacant into the vacant." And so do our listeners. And so do we. Dissolve and disappear like bubbles skittering along the surface of water, like specters of voices floating away on a stream of static.

Everything we do amounts only to the quotidian things that radio reporters and news broadcasters always do—prodding reluctant sources, looking for news leads in meandering interviews, checking facts over the phone, staring at computer screens, rummaging for extra batteries for recorders, trying to get cabs across the city during a snowstorm. None of these activities seem religious. So how does our work have an effect on the religious life of our listeners?

The content of our programming is not explicitly religious, nor is it often about religion. Even when the Dalai Lama appears in a news item or a feature, we almost always cast the lead as news—*Dalai Lama Draws Hundreds of Thousands to Central Park, Urges Religious Tolerance*. On the rare occasions, perhaps two or three times a year, when we interview him at length, most of the discussion is about political matters. Our show is international and regional news, and like any other news program, it consists largely of tales of war, disaster, hunger, greed, hatred, anger, desire, pride, accomplishment, failure, and celebrity—the old round of suffering and redemption that is always new—and is always news.

Nevertheless, we do report stories about religious issues. Some of these have made the newscasts here as well—*Pedophilia Scandal Spreads among Catholic Clergy. U.S. Episcopal General Convention Okays Actively Gay Bishop. Federal Court Orders Removal of Ten Commandments Monument from Alabama Courthouse. Protestant Clergy Divides over Iraq War. Pope Paul Tells Polish Crowds to Reject Consumerism. Anti-Western Sentiment Dominates Islamic Academies.* And on and on. Afterward, how well does our audience really understand the controversy over the Ten Commandments monument? It's hard to say, but you might also ask the same question about the viewers of *FOX News Tonight*.

Before we began our broadcasts, I was naïve. If asked, I would have said that our hardest challenge would be the countless unprecedented translations, large and small, that we would have to make each day for our Tibetan audience to convey to them the news of the rest of the world. These would be fascinating puzzles in coining phrases about spent nuclear fuel rods and computer viruses, or ways to translate "Pontiff" and "apocalyptic." This is how I thought about cross-cultural reporting.

More than ten years later, I now believe that our hardest challenge is not how to convey to our Tibetan listeners information about the rest of the world but how to convey to them information about themselves. Consider, as one category of this, stories about Tibetan religion as it appears abroad— *Fifth Avenue Boutiques Sell Tibetan Wrist Rosaries as Fashion Accessories, Tibetan Sacred Painting Exhibition Opens in Major New York Gallery, Neuroscientists Discuss Nature of Thought with Buddhist Meditation Masters, Tibetan Teacher Recognizes Los Angeles Child as Reincarnate Lama, Beastie Boys Lead Off Tibetan Freedom Concert with "Bodhisattva."* You've probably seen variations on some of these stories. But the difference between you and a Tibetan sitting in Tibet is that you can understand each of these events as extraordinary—in short, as *news.* But does a Tibetan listener think that most Americans are Buddhists, or that most Western scientists revere Buddhist teachings on the nature of the mind, or that most Western doctors believe that Tibetan medicine has something substantial to offer medical science? How does she think a rosary came to be a chic, expensive accessory? How does he imagine that the aggressive punctuated sounds of hip-hop came to be linked with the compassion of the Bodhisattva? Does he understand how exceedingly odd but also perfectly fit most Americans would regard the naming of a child from Los Angeles as a reincarnated lama? If he doesn't, will he get the wrong idea about Tibetan Buddhism's ultimately small but fantastical place in America?

We also have stories about local news in Tibet that concern religion. The difficulty with these stories is a different and unsurprising one for us—finding the news when authorities allow no reporters into Tibet without official escorts and when they regard ordinary Tibetans who pass on information to foreign broadcasters as guilty of trading in state secrets. Such an environment is like a news desert, with only the bravest of stories venturing out to compete for recognition with the insubstantial mirages of rumors. Under these conditions, most of the stories we do get recount the stark outline of fairly severe suffering and lack the background details that allow a nuanced comprehension of the situation—*Authorities Bulldoze Buddhist Center in Serthar and Send Thousands of Residents Away, Lhasa Police Install Surveillance Cameras around Downtown Temple, Party Officials Set New Restrictions on Display of Dalai Lama's Picture on Home Altars, Monk Activists' Prison Sentences Extended.* As tough as it is to get hold of such news from inside Tibet, broadcasting it back into the region is one of our most important jobs. There is no question that spreading such news amplifies the efforts of Tibetans inside and outside Tibet who hope to protect and strengthen their religion, although we do not have that goal in mind when we broadcast. They have the same effect as news stories about the Dalai Lama conducting the Kalachakra Initiation in India for hundreds of thousands of devotees or about the Karmapa fleeing Tibet and arriving in India.

We also have stories that put Buddhism in an unfavorable light—*Thai Monks Patronize Prostitutes, L.A. Temple Accused of Improper Donations to Gore Campaign, Dalai Lama Warns Monks against Laziness.* And some still harsher ones—*Tibetan Nuns Protest Traditional Bar against Their Full Ordination, Struggle Surfaces over Choice of Karmapa Successor, Shugden Worshippers Claim*

Oppression by Dalai Lama, Dalai Lama Followers Blame Stabbing of Cleric on Shugden Followers.

What's our goal here and our obligation to our audience? The head of the United Front for Tibet—that is, the party's regional propaganda chief—once visited VOA and testily complained to me that we didn't broadcast news that was sympathetic to Chinese rule. He said we should broadcast good news instead. I thought of an image of smiling girls sewing uniform patches for People's Liberation Army soldiers and an image of liberated peasants pushing hygienic buttons at a hydropower installation. I'd seen some posters like this from the cultural revolution.

Another time an agitated official from the Dalai Lama's organization visited and loudly lectured us. He made the point that the American government had given us the money for our show in order to inspire Tibetans and give them hope, and so, he asked, why were we broadcasting stories about contentious religious issues and upsetting people?

What I'd like to have said to them both is that news is whatever *feels*—or even *smells*—like news, no matter whether it seems good or bad to anyone in particular. It's hard enough for us to dig out the news and get it on the air. If we also had to calculate whether each news item or feature was good or bad for any of our listeners, we'd be far too busy to ever report anything. That's what I'd like to have told them.

Instead, I told them the old Taoist story about the farmer whose lone horse runs away. His neighbors say, "What a terrible misfortune was losing your horse!" He, however, is unsure. Next day, his horse returns, accompanied by another, a wild one. His neighbors say, "What great good fortune you have!" He, however, is unsure. Next day his oldest son, riding the wild horse, falls off it and breaks his leg, making it impossible to help the family in the harvest. "A terrible misfortune," say his neighbors. He, however, is unsure. Next day, a warlord's army sweeps through the area, taking away all the young men to fight in a bloody war but leaving the farmer's son because of his broken leg. "What great good fortune for you," say his neighbors. And so it goes. A news reporter, I told them, should be like the farmer—carefully following the news, day by day, and reporting it, without concluding whether it will be good or bad news for anyone in particular. That's a working description of what we're obliged to give our audience—a free press.

But now we've arrived at the nub of reporting across cultures. And here, I confess, I *have* puzzled over, in a general way, whether our broadcasts benefit our audience. How deeply are we implicated in their lives? Inexact audience research done a few years ago indicated that almost half of the people of Tibet were regular listeners to our programs, but we're not interfering with a pristine culture, as if we were violating the Star Trek Prime Directive. Tibetans' culture and religion have been repeatedly and massively interfered with and affected by Indian Buddhist saints, Mongolian warlords, Nepali Gurkha soldiers, Victorian British adventurers, czarist Russian spies, Han

Chinese communist revolutionaries, and latter-day capitalist entrepreneurs. And like everywhere else in the world, Tibet has a long history of internal struggles as well. We do not think of our goal as either to lock or unlock the museum doors of Tibetan culture and religion, but to help our listeners negotiate the currents of social and political change to their benefit. Nevertheless, part of that requires remembering the Tibetan past—including its religious beliefs and traditions—keeping its spark flamed and carrying it into a future where it encounters the rest of the world. It is in that spirit that we have offered our listeners such fare as feature programs on the celebrations during religious holidays in old Tibet and documentary history programs on the destruction of Tibetan temples by young Chinese and Tibetan Red Guards.

Tibetans have learned what Westerners think of Tibetans—that they are saintly, extraordinarily compassionate conveyors of a culture of peace, from a place where sectarian differences in religious views are relatively unimportant and where reign universal toleration that is consonant, although until recently unfamiliar, with modern democracy and science. In our broadcasts, they've heard Western Buddhists and Taiwanese politicians and Hollywood movie stars tell them this about themselves. They've even heard their own spiritual leader say something like this from exile. And I guess that to some extent they've accepted it as true. Before, many of them may have been compassionate, but now their possession of an extraordinary degree of compassion is part of their articulated self-identity, part of what it means to be Tibetan and Buddhist. The articulation of that identity has occurred partly through our broadcasts, although I am uncertain whether it expresses the hard past or the ambiguous present or the hopeful future. Is the articulation of that identity good or bad? I don't know, I answer, like the farmer who lost his horse.

While Tibet never really was sealed away from the rest of the world, its borders with the rest of the world have never been easy to cross. Restrictions on the flow of communications to and from Tibet continue. But the restrictions also impoverish internal communication among Tibetans within Tibet. It would otherwise occur, in part, through a news media. Tibetans could represent themselves to themselves, refining and expressing their identity as a people, and testing and adjusting their religion to new times, as well as to the reflection in the mirror of what others think. Without that, our programming offers them a poor substitute that nevertheless looms large in importance—giving them, in a fragmented community, an image of who they are, who their leader is, what Tibet is, and what Buddhism is all about.[2]

Chapter 2

God Talk in the Public Square

C. Welton Gaddy

When President George W. Bush announced, shortly after the September 11, 2001, terrorist attacks against the United States, that he wanted to lead a crusade against terrorism, his choice of the historically weighted word "crusade" spawned alarm, anger, and resentment throughout the Muslim world. Negative reactions to the president's choice of the word "crusade" also poured in from other persons sensitive to the tragic nature of that term, given the atrocities perpetrated when evangelical Christians murderously invaded Muslim countries in medieval times. To his credit, the president paid attention to the negative outbursts against his choice of terminology and did not use the word "crusade" again in speaking of his war on terrorism. However, in the fall of 2003, a worse-case-scenario elaboration of the ideology behind the word "crusade" showed up in the rhetoric of a military general chosen by the Pentagon to hunt down Osama bin Laden, Saddam Hussein, and other major figures in terrorist activities aimed at the United States.

Lieutenant General William G. Boykin used God talk to explain the mission, motivation, and confidence of success with which he approached his military charge. Boykin spoke of his mission in terms of a clash between the Judeo-Christian values of a Christian nation and the work of Satan. Dressed in full military uniform and explicitly identifying himself as an evangelical

Christian, the general declared, "We in the army of God, in the house of God, kingdom of God have been raised for such a time as this."[1] Exuding confidence regarding the ultimate success of his work, Boykin reflected on an earlier victory over a warlord in Somalia, explaining, "I knew my God was bigger than his, I knew that my God was a real God and his was an idol."[2]

NBC's *Nightly News with Tom Brokaw* obtained and aired several videotapes of Boykin speaking to different religious groups over a period of two years. The substance of the general's remarks represents the sine qua non of God talk. In June of 2002, during a speech at the First Baptist Church of Broken Arrow, Tulsa, Oklahoma, Boykin described the United States' escalating battle with terrorism as an engagement between Osama bin Laden, "the enemy,"and President Bush—"a man that acknowledged that he prays in the Oval Office. A man that's in the White House today because of a miracle. You think about how he got in the White House. You think about why he's there today." The general went on to explain, however, that the real enemy is not bin Laden but "a spiritual enemy." "His name is Satan," Boykin declared, "And if you do not believe that Satan is real, you are ignoring the same Bible that tells you about God. Now I'm a warrior. . . . And what I'm here to do today is to recruit you to be warriors of God's kingdom."

On another occasion, at the First Baptist Church in Daytona Beach, Florida, in June of 2003, Boykin detailed a specific engagement in his battle with evil when, in Mogadishu, he went after an ally of Aideed named Osman Atto. Boykin recalled Atto's boasts that he would never be captured because, in his words, "Allah will protect me." Boykin said that with confidence that his God was bigger than Atto's god, he prayed, "Lord let us get that man." Three days later, according to the general, Atto was taken captive. Boykin recalled his encounter with Atto once he was searched and confined. "With no one in there but the guard . . . I looked at him and said, 'Are you Osman Atto?' And he said, 'Yes.' And I said, 'Mr. Atto, you underestimated our God.'"

The high-ranking military leader's comments reek with an easy equation between "we are right" and "those whom we oppose are wrong." Phrases like "our God" indicate the assumption of a divine blessing on the U.S. mission that justifies all action. Of course, non-Christians and residents of other nations, as well as many outraged Christians in this nation, saw the matter from a totally different perspective.

Perhaps the most frightening aspect of General Boykin's religion-laced, militaristic-focused rhetoric is its close similarity to the spiritual arrogance, harsh religious judgment, and promises of violence present in the vitriolic rhetoric of Osama bin Laden and other terrorists who also justify their actions with divine motivations. In February of 1998, like Boykin in June of 2002, bin Laden neatly divided the world into believers and unbelievers. Citing antipathy toward secularism and a lack of morality in government, bin Laden called on every Muslim who believes in God "to comply with God's order to kill the Americans and plunder their money wherever and whenever they find it." Echoing Boykin's recruitment of "warriors of God's kingdom," bin Laden defined hostility toward America as a "religious duty."[3]

This comparison of the rhetoric of Boykin and bin Laden is in no way intended to suggest that the motivations of the two men were identical. It simply suggests that when God talk is used to justify violence, one commentator's (or commander's) rationale sounds just like another's. General Boykin left the general public envisioning, not a national imperative to defend the United States against terrorists, but a spiritual mission—a kind of battle of the gods—to prove the superiority of one faith over another.

Early in the presidential campaign of 2000, numerous warning signs pointed to a proliferation of religious rhetoric generally, and to God talk particularly, from the next resident of the White House. Then vice president of the United States Al Gore indicated that answering the question "What would Jesus do?" would be an integral component in his process of political decision-making. George Bush, at that time governor of Texas, cited Christ as the most important and influential philosopher in his life. More than once the campaign rhetoric of these two candidates suggested a competition to win the title "Holy Man of the Year" rather than an electoral race for the presidency of the United States.

The president of the United States is a political leader, not a spiritual leader. Every person who occupies the Oval Office carries a constitutional mandate to serve as a leader for all of the people in the nation, not as a leader exclusively for citizens who share his particular faith or find meaning in the language of his personal religious tradition.

As election officials in Florida recounted the votes that finally made George W. Bush the president-elect of the United States, little did anyone know how much the lines between the role of faith in the president's personal life and the role of faith in his leadership of the nation would be blurred. Few anticipated the extent to which God talk would dominate the presidential rhetoric of George W. Bush.

George W. Bush arrived in the Oval Office convinced of the power of religion to change life. Religion had changed his life, and he wanted other people in trouble to experience the benefits of faith that he had learned firsthand. Reportedly, Bush took the oath of the presidency holding the conviction that God had "called" him to run for president—"God wants me to do this, and I must do it," he had told a minister named James Robison.[4] Indeed, Bush later seemed to confirm his understanding of such a missional motivation in his presidency by offering no word of caution, protest, qualification, or disassociation when, prior to his speech to the Association of National Religious Broadcasters in Nashville, Tennessee, in the February of 2003, he was presented as "God's man for this time."[5] Predictably, then, from his earliest days in the Oval Office, the president fashioned policies such as the faith-based initiative—which, for the first time in the nation's history, channeled public tax dollars into pervasively religious institutions, even houses of worship—and punctuated his public rhetoric with the language of faith and references to God.

Fundamentalist Christians in particular have applauded the president's use of the language of faith in speeches from his bully pulpit. Late in 2003, however, even the religious fundamentalist sector of the American public occasionally began to criticize the president's God talk. Speaking at a news conference with Tony Blair in November of 2003, the president stirred a firestorm of public protest when he told a reporter that Muslims and Christians worship the same God. Richard Land, a leader in the Southern Baptist Convention, an advisor to the president, and a representative of many people in conservative religious traditions, declared that the president was "simply mistaken." Similarly, Rev. Ted Haggard, president of the National Association of Evangelicals challenged Bush's observation declaring, "Muhammad's central message was submission; Jesus' central message was love. They seem to be very different personalities." Continuing his critique of President Bush's assertion that Christians and Muslims worship the same deity, Richard Land said, "We should always remember that he is commander in chief, not theologian in chief."[6] The remarkable unanimity of agreement between fundamentalist and progressive religionists evoked by Land's remark pointed to the seriousness of the problems related to the president's ventures into theological elaboration and articulation of God talk.

The president's remarks in the United Kingdom were neither his first nor final attempt at doing theology for the nation. In the aftermath of the tragic explosion of the space shuttle *Columbia* and the deaths of the seven astronauts on board, President Bush addressed the nation, offering consolation, the substance of which had been drawn from the heart of the tradition of Christianity, specifically from the text of the fourth Gospel in the New Testament. The president concluded his brief remarks by saying, "The crew of the shuttle Columbia did not return safely to Earth; yet we can pray that all are safely home."[7]

Was the president implicitly questioning whether or not all of the astronauts whom he had mentioned had fared well in the afterlife? Actually, the president's prayerful plea that each of the crewmembers had arrived "safely home"—a petition inspired by Christian scriptures—conveyed the Christian hope that all of the deceased astronauts had reached heaven. But not all of the astronauts on the shuttle were Christian. The grieving family members and friends of at least one of the members of the crew could have been offended, rather than comforted, by the president's message.

Once again, a problem could have been avoided had the president spoken as the political leader that he was and not attempted to speak as the religious leader of the nation. Presidential rhetoric that suggests that God is intervening in events, God is on America's side, and God chose George Bush to be the president of the United States is problematic at best.[8] Any time that the president embraces doctrinal declarations when speaking as the nation's leader, he implicitly suggests that people who hold a different theological point of view do not matter to him as much as those who share his particular religious point of view. At stake also is a suggestion that the nation does, in fact, contrary to a constitutional prohibition, have an "established religion." All of the people in this land deserve a chief executive who can address a moment of national grief in inclusive language.

Using God talk to advance public policy has also been a hallmark of the Bush administration, especially the president's use of God talk in his appeals for passage of legislation supportive of his faith-based initiative. Typical of this policy-oriented religious rhetoric were the president's remarks to a Bush-Cheney '04 lunch late in December of 2003—"Our government should never fear the influence of faith in the lives of our average citizens. We ought to encourage faith-based programs to help solve problems." Which faith? we well might ask the president, before inquiring as to what business the government has using federal tax dollars to fund any faith.

Perhaps the boldest and most objectionable of all of President Bush's faith-based requests for an endorsement of his faith-based initiative came during his 2003 State of the Union address. President Bush spoke of the "wonder-working power in the goodness and idealism and faith of the American people." Critics of the president who suspect that his use of religious language is a coded means of reassuring the religious right of his identification with their theology and appreciation for their cause did not miss the linkage between the president's "wonder-working power" statement in support of his legislative agenda and the words "wonder-working power in the blood of the Lamb" from the chorus of the old gospel song "Power in the Blood." However, the president's chief speechwriter, Michael Gerson, explained that such religious language is "not code, it's our culture."[9]

President Bush has used the language of God talk to address foreign policy concerns as well as domestic initiatives. Though the president has not employed the divine name in the blatant manner of General Boykin, he has voiced a level of judgment that many religious people feel is most properly left only for a divine perspective. Prior to his approval of preemptive strikes against Iraq by U.S. military forces, President Bush frequently spoke about this international challenge in moral absolutes, for example, categorizing Iraq and other nations like North Korea as components of an "axis of evil" and "the forces of darkness" in his 2003 State of the Union Address. His sweeping demonization of entire nations left no room for any benevolent or helpful distinction between the wrong—indeed, the evil—done by a corrupt government or its highest leader and the moral character of other people living under that government.

Elaine Pagels, an expert in the theological development of concepts of good and evil and a student of the historical uses of those terms, considers such morally absolutistic talk by the president as "the language of religious zealots."[10] For President Bush to suggest that disagreement with him or his foreign policy springs from a deficiency in morality represents an assumption of the kind of all-knowing wisdom traditionally attributed only to God. Yet the president relentlessly persisted in the use of such absolutistic rhetoric, several times declaring that all who were not with us in our foreign policy initiative were against us. On at least one occasion, the president labeled a preemptive invasion of Iraq as an act "in the highest moral traditions of our country."[11]

In reality, a tremendous difference exists between arguing that a foreign policy initiative is in the best interest of this nation and using the terminology of religion and morality to justify that initiative. Intended or not, the president's merger of political and religious language clearly suggested that the speaker's way was the right way—indeed, God's way—and that all who disagreed with him had chosen another path. That meaning was most readily apparent in the president's references to the United States as a "blessed nation"—defined in language from the Christian scriptures related to the advent of Christ, "light [that] shines in the darkness. And the darkness will not overcome it"—and in his address to Congress on the September 11 horrors, assuring victory in the nation's cause: "The course of this conflict is not known, yet its outcome is certain. Freedom and fear, justice and cruelty have always been at war, and we know that God is not neutral between them."[12] Simply put, through a variety of expressions, more than once President George W. Bush has declared, "God is on our side."

True to historical precedent, the president of the United States has significantly shaped the manner in which other people use the language of faith. God talk is a pervasive phenomenon in American culture in the first years of the new millennium.

Americans have long used the phrase "God bless America," from Irving Berlin's song popularized by Kate Smith, to express positive sentiments about the nation. More recently, the public has elevated these words to the status of a mantra spiritually, a slogan nationally, and an advertisement commercially. Currently, "God bless America" can be found printed on pizza boxes, placarded on portable signboards surrounded by flashing lights, and spoken as the solemn (though intended as uplifting) conclusion to many a politician's public speech. "God bless America" are the lyrics of patriotism blared across a crowded stadium during the seventh-inning stretch of a World Series baseball game and part of a congregational liturgy quietly spoken during a gathering for corporate meditation or public worship. A sometimes intensely personal prayer for the nation, "God bless America" takes on at other times the nature of a national pep rally cheer or a war cry.

The public's present infatuation with "God bless America"—whether as genuine prayer for a righteous nation, as patriotic boast of divine blessing, or as strategic rhetoric employed to build support for politician's candidacy for public office or for a national policy—epitomizes the reality, confusion, and danger of God talk in the public square. So pervasive is the God-talk phenomenon that it has contributed significantly to the politicization of religion and "religiofication" of politics in the national public square.

THE POLITICIZATION OF RELIGION
AND THE RELIGIOFICATION OF POLITICS

A proliferation of God talk generally and among politicians especially is altering views of democracy, jeopardizing appreciation for religious pluralism, weakening the cords of national unity, and even threatening the stability of the historic constitutional guarantee of religious liberty. How did this happen?

G. K. Chesterton once described the United States as a nation with the soul of a church. That description of the United States, though dated by its lack of recognition of the vast religious pluralism that now characterizes the nation, points to the historical reality of a political state with a passionate and an abiding appreciation for religion. Indeed, many students of this government argue that the nation cannot be understood correctly apart from awareness of the substance of the nation's religious center.

In recent years, well-organized, relentless activists have attempted to move beyond the historic mutual appreciation between religions and government in America to a full-scale integration of religions and government—politicizing religion by using how people vote on a litmus-test agenda of social-political issues to define authentic faith, and "religiofying" politics through studied efforts to use the machinery of government to advance the missions, values, and doctrinal stances of sectarian traditions.

Early in the 1970s a relatively small number of power-oriented persons, possessing both political expertise and intimate knowledge of the language of faith and of people of faith, launched a carefully constructed campaign to make the American public fearful of an epidemic of immorality in a nation fed by a steadily escalating preeminence of secularism over "the one true religion." When popular, media-savvy religious leaders heralded the involvement of evangelical Christians in politics as the solution to these disturbing problems, scores of evangelicals responded positively to this call, quickly setting aside a previous disdain for politics to foster a marriage of politics and religion. Groups like the Moral Majority, the Christian Roundtable, and the Christian Coalition began to define faith in terms of support for a specific political agenda and to interpret morality on the basis of a person's advocacy for certain candidates for public office and for particular legislative initiatives.

Streetwise politicians, in turn, responded positively to the strong-arm tactics of this significant new, vocal, and hyperactive constituency often known as the religious right, a movement that many scholars now consider the most significant religious movement in the twentieth century. Clergy pledged to deliver votes for candidates "ordained by God," and candidates seeking such a lofty endorsement spoke the language of faith in their appeals for the support of people of faith.

With traditional boundaries between religion and government blurred if not successfully erased in the psyche of a large segment of the American public, it is little wonder that God talk is now so much a part of government as well as religion. Reciprocally, the politicization of religion and the religiofication of politics encourage more God talk.

USES AND ABUSES OF GOD TALK: WHAT IS NEW?

Nothing is inherently wrong with the presence of religious rhetoric in the public life of the nation. To be sure, the absence of religious language in a nation that places such a high value on religion would be far more difficult to explain than the presence of that language. But not all God talk is the same; nor is it even religious in substance or motivation. Even as some God talk has about it the ring of authenticity—an honest reference to personal faith locked in a struggle to understand and comment on social-political issues—other God talk has about it the clang of deception or manipulation, the language of faith used to promote a particular politically partisan or narrowly sectarian agenda.

Responsible decisions about the appropriateness or value of religious rhetoric in the public square must take into consideration the motivation of the speaker and the consistency (or lack thereof) between the substance of the speech and the nature of religion. Examining a specific instance of God talk should involve inquiry about the impact of that particular language of religion on the integrity of religion and the consequences of this rhetoric for the democratic process. Though God talk cannot be easily categorized, such rhetoric typically emerges for a political reason and serves an ideological function.

God talk sometimes appears as *a natural expression of personal faith*. Given that religion is a vital component in self-identification and that religious language is a natural articulation of religious devotion, it is to be expected that religious people, including public figures, will refer to their faith from time to time as they do their work. Since many individuals enter the realm of public service motivated by religious convictions related to strengthening the nation and helping people in need, God talk comes as naturally in their speech as does talk about case studies, proposed legislation, and concerns about an impending election.

Confessional talk—religious rhetoric that springs from personal faith— especially on the part of national leaders, must, however, be recognized for what it is: the language of self-identification. A personal confession of faith is not to be confused with evidence of special political authority, superior wisdom, or unique electoral advantage. Public officials have a responsibility to speak of their chosen religion not in a manner that even hints at judgment of or discrimination against other religions, but in a manner that strengthens a democratic society—recognizing that the rights of minorities are as important as the rights of the majority and using a vocabulary that does not exclude whole segments of their constituencies.

President Dwight D. Eisenhower exemplified responsible confessional-religious language, identifying himself as "the most intensely religious man I know," then hastening to explain, "That doesn't mean I adhere to any sect." Eisenhower made clear his citation of the importance of religion related to the health of democracy and thus the strength of the nation—"A democracy cannot exist without a religious base. I believe in democracy." Speaking of America as a religious nation toward the end of his presidency, President Eisenhower observed, "Recognition of the Supreme Being is the first, the most basic expression of Americanism" and declared, "Without God, there could be no American form of government, nor an American way of life."[13] Yet he seemed open to an affirmation of any deity called "God" being used for that purpose.

To be sure, a person need not hold such a generalist, nontradition-specific view of religion in order to use religious language responsibly in the public square. The God talk of a particular religious tradition like Islam or Christianity can be as respectful of others and their religions as the language of a thoroughly civil religion.

At times God talk is employed as *a studied strategy for advancing public policy.* Nothing is more emotional than religion—unless it is politics. To unite religion and politics in support of a common cause is a powerful—and, often, winning—strategy in numerous endeavors. Few politicians focused on passing a particular piece of legislation, gaining support for a controversial initiative in public policy, or winning support for a nominee to a governmental post can resist a temptation to coopt the powerful emotion of religion in an effort to secure success for their respective causes.

During a senatorial debate on President Bush's proposal for massive tax cuts as a way of addressing a faltering economy, Democratic Senator Mary Landrieu addressed a proposed tax bi;; amendment appealing for guaranteed financial support for adoption agencies. Concluding an impassioned plea for acceptance of her amendment, the senator declared, "God wants you to vote for this amendment!" This obviously legislatively driven comment about the will of God stands in sharp contrast to the observation of a minister who lost his seat in Congress to a religious right candidate wielding religious rhetoric to establish himself as the God-ordained person for that legislative post. "No one speaks for God in American politics," said John Buchanan.[14]

Amid contentious debates on the confirmation of controversial nominations for judicial appointments during the 108th Congress, religion itself and the language of religion became major subjects of discussion in the Senate Judiciary Committee. While considering President Bush's nomination of

William Pryor to the 11th Circuit Court of Appeals in Atlanta, the rhetoric of religion meshed with strident, partisan political arguments in a manner that cheapened religion and diminished the recognized authority of the Senate Judiciary Committee to speak on matters of constitutionality. Interestingly, the inappropriate use of religion in this debate was prompted by the God talk of the candidate whose nomination for a seat on a federal bench was under consideration. Early in his judicial career, William Pryor had observed that "our political system seems to have lost God" and declared that the "political system must remain rooted in a Judeo-Christian perspective on the nature of government and the nature of man."[15]

Given the necessity that a federal judge appreciate the nation's religious pluralism that defends the "no-establishment of religion" clause of the Constitution, senators had a responsibility to examine this candidate carefully regarding his commitment to religious liberty. However, the examination became a partisan rhetorical battle in which Republican members of the Judiciary Committee charged the Democratic members of that committee with a bias against Catholics and advanced a public relations campaign against Democratic senators called "No Catholics Need Apply." Once it became clear that most of the Democratic senators on the Judiciary Committee were themselves members of the Roman Catholic Church, a much-needed discussion on a judicial nominee deteriorated into a battle of words aimed at distinguishing "good Catholics"—those who supported confirmation of the nominee—from "bad Catholics," those who opposed confirmation for Mr. Pryor.

Similar to the use of God talk as a strategy for advancing public policy is the employment of God talk as *a tool of electoral politics*. For example, though his own personal faith was more a form of Americanism than a reflection of any specific denomination, in 1912 Teddy Roosevelt launched his campaign to win the national presidency, declaring, "We stand at Armageddon and battle for the Lord."[16] Such transference of authority—religious to political—has proven to be a powerful means of attracting loyalty for candidates running for a political office. Not infrequently, today's politicians use religious language to position themselves as recipients of a blessing both from servants of God and from God. Unlike the rhetoric of the earlier Roosevelt, however, the religious authority claimed by contemporary candidates for public office has a much more particularistic religious ring to it.

During the presidential primary elections in 2000, the director of the Christian Coalition in Iowa, Bobbie Gobel, spoke to the press about her efforts to winnow the field of Republican presidential hopefuls "godly" enough to be president. Ms. Gobel indicated that she saw only "a manageable handful" of candidates that would increase the likelihood of a "godly" person being elected. While engaged in a rather uncivil conversation with Dan Quayle, former vice president of the United States, Ms. Gobel questioned whether or not Mr. Quayle should remain in the race for the Oval Office. Mr. Quayle responded to Ms. Gobel's question with the assertion, "If God is in this, I will be the next President of the United States."

No wonder candidates scramble to speak in a manner that establishes the credibility and attractiveness of their religious identity. A public intrigued with God talk responds positively to this strategy.

Sadly, many religious leaders are more than willing to accommodate candidates in search of religious credentials. Since the rise to power of the religious right and a solidification of its role as a major player in political campaigns, more and more candidates for public office seek endorsements and engage in rhetoric that establish them as "chosen by God," "divinely ordained," "God's man for this hour in history" or a "blessed candidate."

The Interfaith Alliance, the national faith-based, grassroots organization in which I serve, recommends that voters question candidates who employ God talk as a campaign tactic, as well as ask all candidates to speak candidly about their appreciation for religious pluralism and their commitment to continuing the constitutional mandate for an institutional separation between religion and government. During the 2004 election, the 150,000 members of the Interfaith Alliance who come from over seventy different religious traditions are being asked to confront candidates with the following questions: What role should and do your religious faith and values play in creating public policy? What are your views on the constitutional guarantee of the separation of church and state? What active steps have you taken and will you continue to take to show respect for the variety of religious beliefs among your constituents? Should a political leader's use of religious language reflect the language of his/her religious tradition, or be more broadly inclusive? How do you balance the principles of your faith and your pledge to defend the Constitution, particularly when the two come into conflict?

When a politician speaks of herself as a Sikh or a Zoroastrian, a Buddhist or a Christian, she makes a helpful contribution to the electorate's understanding. However, to suggest overtly, or even implicitly, that political authority is enhanced by a particular religious affiliation or that decisions on matters of state will be informed primarily by the dogmas and ethics of one particular religious tradition, compromises the appreciation for diversity so integral to a healthy democracy. But the electorate needs to know the potential for such compromise.

The phenomenon of God talk in the public square is an irrefutable fact. But is this phenomenon new? Does the prevalence of God talk in today's American social-political life differ significantly from that of the past and, if so, how?

History supports the argument that national leaders always have engaged in God talk. Indeed, in his Farewell Address to the young nation, George Washington said, "Of all the dispositions and habits which lead to political prosperity, religion and morality are indispensable supports." In his First

Inaugural Address, Washington had made reference to "the invisible hand" which, he said, "conducts the Affairs of men more than the People of the United States." Confronted by an imposing crisis dividing the nation, President Abraham Lincoln often referred to and appealed to the divine name. In his heroic remarks at Gettysburg, Lincoln spoke of "the nation, under God" experiencing "a new birth of freedom." Though Lincoln elsewhere affirmed the "sacred principles" of "our ancient faith," he viewed the Declaration of Independence as "spiritually regenerative." The great civil rights leader Martin Luther King Jr. declared, "There is a creative power that works to pull down mountains of evil and level hilltops of injustice. God still works through history His wonders to perform."[17]

Religious rhetoric generally and God talk specifically are not new to the public square of the United States. Presently, however, religious rhetoric appears much more frequently, dominates public debates more pervasively, and, in substance, differs dramatically from previous occurrences of such talk.

For the most part, public leaders in the past used the language of faith to talk about affairs of the nation in a manner that transcended religious particulars/ "uniting all citizens in a single covenant."[18] Even as late as the 1960s, Martin Luther King Jr., himself a devout Christian minister, spoke of religion as a resource for enabling the nation to be true to its original vision of inclusion and to live up to its commitment of freedom and justice for all. Today, however, the great preponderance of public religious rhetoric draws from a very particular religious tradition and seeks to advance a specific partisan or sectarian point of view. This is new, different, ironic, and disturbing.

George Washington affirmed the importance of religion, but not once in the twenty volumes of his collected papers did Washington mention Christ or refer to the virtue of any particular religious dogma.[19] Though John Adams made frequent references to God, in each instance the former president related the divine name to the nation's commitment to religious liberty, peace, and justice—core values rooted in most religious traditions and affirmed as a means of building support for the common good within the nation. Numerous presidents have spoken about the divine mission of the nation, but always defining that mission broadly, challenging the nation to export freedom to other governments around the world. President Eisenhower praised the importance of religious faith and the American people, but he hastened to point out that any faith was acceptable. When speaking in the public square, Martin Luther King Jr. spoke in nonparticularistic religious language such as, "Whatever the name, some extra-human Force labors to create a harmony out of the discords of the universe."[20] In each instance, the highest level of leadership in the nation drew words and phrases from specific religious traditions but applied those terms inclusively to political and governmental initiatives.

In literature published prior to the year 2000, some scholars advanced the notion that the issue of religious pluralism in the nation had been settled with John F. Kennedy's election to the presidency of the United States. A distinct Christian Protestant language would no longer prevail among governmental leaders, so the argument went.[21] Such estimates have been proven wrong. Not merely an echo of such talk in the past, today's God talk among political leaders is far more tradition-specific. Indeed, much of the religious rhetoric coming from contemporary political leaders suggests, at least implicitly, the establishment of Christianity as the official religion of the realm.

Today the United States is the most religiously pluralistic nation in the world.[22] Every major world religion has found a home in this land, as have literally countless numbers of lesser-known religions. At the very moment when the nation is more religiously diverse than ever before and thus in need of mutual respect between religions, God talk in the nation is more religiously specific, and thus more divisive, than ever before. Inherent in these dual realities are both the potential for major problems and an opportunity for significant and promising change.

FROM PROBLEM TO PROMISE

The American public is conflicted regarding the use of religious rhetoric by politicians. A majority of people seem quite satisfied with the amount of God talk in the speeches of President Bush and other national leaders, though many Americans express real discomfort when a public figure's use of tradition-specific religious language affects them directly.[23] God talk is not without problems, however. In fact, too much God talk from the president of the United States, in the halls of government, on electoral campaign trails, and elsewhere in the public square carries with it consequences that can negatively affect both religion and the democratic process.

God talk in the public square, especially God talk employed for political purposes, *compromises the integrity of religion*. Bombarded by religious comments intended to advance political concerns, individuals lose sight of the real substance of religion. Faith becomes more a utilitarian tool for coping with civil processes than a spiritual reality of value in itself that respects and appreciates transcendence as a source for healing divisions, helping hurting people, and building a more compassionate as well as just society. Unable to disentangle the religious and the political dimensions of public speech, people judge the viability of various public policy initiatives and candidates for public office more by the persuasiveness of the religious language with which each is presented than by the actual substance of the policy in question or the qualifications for public service that characterize a candidate.

Since the inception of the United States, religions have made their greatest contributions to the public square by functioning *as religions*—speaking prophetically, offering comfort indiscriminately, clarifying values helpfully—not as bloc voters, political action groups, conduits for federal money or missions, or power brokers affiliated with partisan political parties. God talk in the public square has proven most helpful when offering comfort—calming, reassuring, and encouraging people racked by fear, stunned by terror, or grieved by tragedy—and when trumpeting prophetic discourse reminding national leaders of basic moral values, challenging the nation to remain true to the freedom-laced dream of its founders, and advocating for relentless engagement in protecting liberty, assuring civil rights to all Americans, guaranteeing justice, avoiding needless military conflicts, working for peace, respecting the rights of minorities, and providing for the general welfare. The religious rhetoric that sustained and advanced the civil rights movement of the 1960s and that inspired and instructed the forgiveness of Third World debt in 2000 stand as cases in point.

Pastors, imams, rabbis, other ministers of comfort, and would-be prophets who use the language of faith to do the work of political operatives and to advance the cause of partisan politics grievously erode the respect accorded to religious offices and seriously cheapen the value of the language of faith. Conversely, political operatives who depend on God talk to gain authority and to evoke popularity desacralize religion and turn God into a mascot for people advancing a particular brand of politics. To suggest that a person's failure to agree with them politically is a sign of the opponent's religious immaturity or, worse still, infidelity, redefines the substance and inclusive nature of religion in a most destructive manner.

God talk in the public square not only contributes to the compromise of religion but *threatens the vitality of democracy*. Not infrequently God talk has been used in attempts to shut down debate on an issue or to silence voices of opposition to an issue.

When religious rhetoric is made into a form of propaganda that establishes a specific position on a political issue as the equivalent of a moral-spiritual conviction, simple differences of political opinion can be labeled as evidence of questionable faith and of a lack of authentic spirituality. Once that point has been made, the people involved in the discussion are no longer engaged in healthy political debate for the purpose of clarifying varying points of view to achieve mutual understanding and to move toward consensus or compromise; now people are defending a religious or moral dogma about which, at least, those on one side of the debate believe there is no room for give-and-take without a betrayal of conscience. The democratic value of compromise so essential to efficient and effective legislative politics is branded a weakness (e.g., "There can be no compromise with evil!"). Morally absolutistic rhetoric shuts down political debate and diminishes the vitality of democracy.[24]

Princeton scholar Elaine Pagels understands the strategy involved in bringing moralistic language into discussions on controversial issues. This emotionally powerful language bypasses the brain and goes straight to the gut. Such language is not unlike the language of religious extremists in Islam and terrorists in the Christian Identity movement; it silences opposition and even justifies acts of violence toward its opponents.[25]

Periodically, an uncritical intermingling of political rhetoric and God talk contributes to a *level of divisiveness that heightens incivility* both in language and action. Partisan political ideas articulated by religious leaders, and sectarian religious beliefs articulated by political leaders tend to replace vigorous democratic debate with impassioned, persuasive, and uncivil rhetoric that draws sharp lines of distinction between those who are "right" and those who are "wrong" on an issue. The language of religious certitude eliminates the religious virtue of personal humility and the social virtue of public civility. The result is an environment conducive to fanaticism. Discussions quickly deteriorate into shouting matches. Fanatics consider differing political perspectives on matters as indicators that only some people are blessed by God's favor and some people are sure to experience God's disfavor. And woe to those in the public square who choose to live without religion entirely; these are people best (in the minds of fanatics) relegated to the periphery of the political process. Obviously, such divisiveness and incivility make cooperation amid diversity and the concept of community appreciative of pluralism a virtual impossibility.

So where do we go from here? Pollsters document the nation's continuing interest in religion.[26] Political consultants and pollsters agree that religion's role in the 2004 elections supercedes the importance of religion in former election cycles.[27] The correct answer to that question about how to move forward should not be a recommendation that all religious rhetoric be removed from the public square. Muting religion is not a viable response to those abusing religion.

As in this essay, so in society, the president of the nation and other high-profile leaders will significantly influence the manner in which religious language is used in the public square.[28] From the bully pulpit will come either the language of a specific religious tradition—language that threatens basic constitutional principles and social cohesiveness—or a more general religious language that appeals to the appreciation for religion that has been at the heart of this nation from its inception and that relates religion to the core values of this democracy. All who lead this nation, like all who live in this nation, should continue to draw deeply from their personal religious beliefs or freely hold to their personal convictions apart from any reference to religion, while none, either by rhetoric or action, should attempt to transform the public square into an altar for their particular religious tradition or into a realm in which only their religious beliefs prevail.

Religious rhetoric can and should continue to play a vital role in the life of the nation, exhibiting appreciation for religious pluralism and respect for various religious traditions. A serious concern for protecting the integrity of religion and its public voice can birth an appropriate restraint in speech, preventing the manipulation of religious language for political purposes and silencing references to God for the purpose of assigning ultimate value to partisan concerns. With studied effort, religious rhetoric can be a positive source of health and healing that reflects a shared commitment to values that complement the core concepts of democracy and make the public square a safe place characterized by freedom and inclusion.

2: VIEW FROM THE NEWS DESK

Law and the Middle East Media: Between Censorship and Independence

Mohammed el-Nawawy

The media in the Middle East are now being challenged and to a great degree influenced by internal and external factors flowing to the region through transnational media, namely, freedom of expression and freedom of the press. This essay will provide an overview of some of the media laws and policies that govern Arab print and broadcast media and how they are affected by the political culture of the region. It will also address the patterns of influence on freedom of the press and their impact on Arab journalists, who are mostly threatened by a censorial political culture, one that develops in an environment usually dominated by a single political party. Finally, the essay will touch on the transnational satellite networks that have been sweeping the Arab Middle East and how they have increased the pressure for change and made issues of censorship obsolete.

MEDIA AND POLITICAL CULTURE
IN THE ARAB MIDDLE EAST

The Arab world's political culture is a censorial one that directly affects the region's media operations. The term "political culture" refers to the "values, norms, beliefs, sentiments, and understanding of how power and authority operate within a particular political system."[1] The Arab media are largely government monopolies used as a political and propaganda tool, and the primary purpose of news agencies, which are government controlled, is to reflect the achievements of the many state sectors.[2]

State preservation and national security concerns are among the main reasons for the limited freedom of expression in the region. These concerns involve anything that can be considered a threat to the ruling regimes and their interests, including negative statements about social beliefs, values, and national traditions.[3]

In the foreword to the United Nation's Arab Human Development Report issued in 2003, it is mentioned that in most Arab countries, the media operate in an environment that sharply restricts freedom of the press and freedom of expression and opinion: "Journalists face illegal harassment, intimidation, and even physical threats; censorship is rife and newspapers and television channels are sometimes arbitrarily closed down."

The direct and inevitable result of the Arab governments' censorial steps against journalists is that news about several aspects of Arab politics, society, and religion is often simply not disclosed. In this restrictive media environment, oppression and the arbitrary application of media laws are not uncommon.

ARAB MEDIA LAWS AND REGULATIONS

Since the early 1960s, most Arab countries have undergone a process of modernization of media regulations; however, profound restrictions against the media still exist, and most of the media are still owned by governments.[4]

Radio and television are controlled more closely than the print media. Unlike the print media, the broadcast media can bypass illiteracy in the Arab world and appeal to mass audiences. Electronic media are absolute monopolies under direct government supervision.[5] Arab states also require approval before any broadcast or satellite channels may be carried on cable systems. Many states license or prohibit receiver dishes. In Saudi Arabia, a satellite ban that started in March 1994 to appease local religious conservatives was scarcely enforced.[6]

Because regulation rather than ownership is the mode of control for many Arab newspapers, many Arab countries require prior licensing for newspapers before they can publish. In Syria, for example, the president signed a decree in 2002 legalizing the private ownership of newspapers, but the prime minister retains the exclusive right to license newspapers. In the United Arab Emirates, as of 1999 the license is issued by a resolution from the council of ministers; in Kuwait, by the head of the Print Publications Department; and in Bahrain, by the minister of information with the endorsement of the council of ministers. Once issued, these licenses can be suspended or revoked if editors or journalists violate the laws controlling the content of what may be published.[7]

The governments of several Arab states, such as Bahrain, Qatar, Syria, Lebanon, Jordan, Kuwait, and Egypt, impose further financial requirements on their publications to guarantee their loyalty and submission. The ease or difficulty with which these requirements can be met varies considerably. For example, in Bahrain, the law requires a cash deposit of 5,000 Bahraini dinars (approximately US $13,000) at the Ministry of Information if the newspaper is a daily. In Qatar, the guarantee is 3,000 riyals (approx. US $825). There are other significant restrictions on ownership. Some countries, such as Egypt and Yemen, permit ownership of newspapers by political parties.

The penal code, press law, and publications law are the three main pieces of legislation used to govern media systems in the Arab world. The penal code stipulates fines and/or imprisonment for criticizing the heads of states, members of the government, and foreign heads of state. Both the press and publications laws are intended to provide protection against malicious or unsubstantiated reporting, but they have been used to charge journalists with libel or defamation if they cross certain "red lines" determined by the government.[8]

Many Arab states have constitutional provisions guaranteeing freedom of expression. Yet in almost all these states the constitutional freedoms can be limited "according to law," and inevitably one finds other laws circumscribing constitutional protections also on the books. Moreover, in many Arab countries the very structures of administration do not depend on formal laws. Laws may satisfy international constituencies in terms of the formulae, of worldview deployed, but they do not always depict the realities within which the media have to operate.[9]

CENSORSHIP AND SELF-CENSORSHIP

Censorship in the Arab Middle East is tolerated and even expected as a form of civic responsibility. In addition, Arab leaders, in general, are very sensitive about criticism; hence, in many cases it is prohibited to publish or broadcast criticism of the state national system, officers of the state, courts, military and security officers, and religious leaders.[10]

In many states the minister of information or minister of interior has the power to halt publication. In Egypt, for example, the minister of information has the right to prevent any publication that attacks religions in such a manner that would have the perceived effect of disturbing the public peace. In other nations, such as Jordan and Syria, broadcast media are government controlled and staffed by government employees who ensure that sensitive subjects involving the president, the army, high-level officials, security forces, and human rights abuses are not aired. The chief editors of the government-owned newspapers typically hear from senior officials about how they would like an issue to be portrayed in the media, an instruction they always take seriously.

Specific rules apply to censoring magazines or newspapers coming from abroad. In Tunisia, the minister of interior can decide to confiscate, prevent publication, or prohibit entry of any international foreign publications. In Saudi Arabia, the minister of information can confiscate any unlicensed publication and destroy it without compensation.[11]

In this setting, many Arab journalists retain a pervasive fear of the political system, consequently enhancing self-censorship. The long history of censorship in the Arab world has contributed to an inability on the journalists' part to formulate a sustained political critique or opinion. The resulting self-censorship can be attributed to fear, to a lack of confidence, or to a perceived incompetence in political matters.[12]

ANTICENSORSHIP ALLIANCES

Penal codes, emergency laws, and publication laws are all part of the legacy of a long history of state hegemony. Many of these laws are still enforced, with serious repercussions for press freedom in the Arab Middle East. What has changed, however, is that some members of the media are engaged in a collective effort to deal with this problem by forming alliances with the legal profession. The Arab Journalists' Union and the Arab Lawyers' Union cooperated on the draft of a press law for the Arab world to ensure that it avoids the pitfalls of existing laws.[13]

The draft of that law, presented to Arab leaders at a summit in Amman, Jordan, in March 2001, proposed

> abolishing prison terms for press "offenses" and called for freedom of publishing, printing, and distributing for individuals and corporations and the abolishment of the requirement of administrative licenses; the abolishment of the practice of suspension of publications by any authority other than the judiciary and the termination of any role played by political and administrative agencies in this regard; and recognition of the right of journalists to access information as well as the imposition of sanctions against individuals illegally obstructing this right of withholding information.[14]

This proposed law is part of a collective effort by many Arab journalists to create a more transparent media environment with less government restrictions. Thanks to this effort and others, more independent-minded newspapers and private satellite channels have appeared in the Arab world, challenging the iron grip of the older, state-controlled media on political opinion, news, and information.

ARAB MEDIA AND RELIGION

The concept of press freedom is fundamentally different in some predominantly Muslim states from that of its Western counterparts. In almost all Arab countries, the press must respect the state's relationship to a particular embodiment of religion. Because of radicalism or implied or attributed threats to national security, even elected governments see as essential their role in limiting the use of the media by certain groups, such as radical religious groups or groups thought to promote secession or even political opposition. In some instances, these steps are encouraged and even demanded by Western governments.[15]

"Since the rise of political Islam, journalists who defend their freedom have found themselves caught in a conflict between the government, which seeks to restrain free speech, and the religious fundamentalist leaders, who condemn those who dare to report accurately about their groups, " according to H. Y. Amin.[16] Most Arab journalists defend Islamic societies, traditions, and values; thus, freedom of expression does not include offensive or negative statements about Islam or religious beliefs.[17]

In the Arab Middle East, it is forbidden to publish or broadcast any materials that could cause disputation among different religious groups; material found to violate this precept is censored, and journalists who publish such material are penalized. In this context, the Egyptian authorities in 2001 arrested an editor of a newspaper owned by an opposition political party after he published an article alleging that a Coptic monk was engaging in sexual activity with women in a monastery. The editor was charged with "propagating false information with the aim of inciting sectarian strife and insulting a heavenly religion" and was sentenced to three years in prison. His newspaper lost its license.[18]

THE ARAB MEDIA AND GLOBAL INTEREST
IN NATIONAL SECURITY

Freedom of expression organizations, supported by Western governments, have always opposed the broad use of national security as a basis for media repressions. However, since the events of September 11, 2001, international political pressures have become more complex, pushing for democratic reforms but also encouraging many countries to ensure that terrorist-related speech is monitored, regulated, and sometimes even prohibited. Many Arab governments have made use of that situation to enforce more restrictions on their media. For example, in Jordan, tensions in the Middle East since the September 11 attacks have been cited as justifications for increased punishments for violations of press laws and for cancellation of parliamentary elections. "Civil liberties advocates have complained that Western governments have turned a blind eye to such oppression."[19]

SATELLITE TELEVISION AND PRESS FREEDOM

The Arab Middle East has been witnessing an explosion of Arab satellite networks over the past fifteen years—a phenomenon that has revolutionized the Arab media scene and challenged the Arab governments' strict control over broadcast media.

Over time, there would develop two types of satellite-television stations in the region: those that were an extension of local government's programming, and those considered "offshore," with little or no "clear" relationship to the government of a particular nation.

While controls are still in place, state media are losing their relevance and monopoly over information, and the patterns of censorship described above are now undermined. In short, an extremely important influence on state-based Arab media (and therefore the legal framework affecting them) is the expansion of relatively independent Arab satellite channels.

The independent satellite channels have set a higher standard for the Arab press by allowing more tolerance of diverse points of view and by engaging debate on Arab affairs. In the process, they also undermine those state regulatory frameworks that have put their own media at a competitive disadvantage in terms of their range of reportage. Audiences tend to be attracted to the most interesting media, as evidenced by monitoring the significant numbers who tune in to these new satellite networks.[20]

One of the direct consequences of Arab satellite networks is that several Arab countries have initiated plans to develop Free Media Zones in which full freedom of expression would be respected and no limitations placed on legitimate media enterprises. So far, three Arab countries—Jordan, Egypt, and United Arab Emirates—have Free Media Zones.[21] While offering tax incentives and guarantees of freedom of expression to attract foreign media to a country, such free regulations are not supposed to apply to the country's own journalists or media. Nevertheless, parliamentary debates in several Arab countries have started to consider more media reforms and less government restrictions on the press.

THE "AL-JAZEERA EFFECT"

Al-Jazeera, the first 24-hour Arabic television news channel beaming from Doha, Qatar, has raised eyebrows with its aggressive investigative reporting style. Since its birth in 1996, it has demonstrated dissent against regional governments and hosted volatile political debate shows.

The station's courageous talk shows, which have crossed all "red lines" set by the Arab governments and delved into all kinds of sensitive issues that have always been considered "taboo" in the Arab world, have set an unprecedented standard for journalistic professionalism in the Arab world. The station's news style and political debates have been imitated by most channels in the region. For that reason, many media observers have called the impact of Al-Jazeera the "Al-Jazeera effect." The network's immense success, with an estimated audience of 50 million viewers worldwide, has drawn attention to its brand of journalism.

The extent to which Arab states regard one another's media as extensions of the state—whether or not it is an accurate portrayal—is exemplified by the diplomatic problems and friction that have taken place between Qatar and several Arab countries because of Al-Jazeera programs. Although the Qatari government has announced repeatedly that it does not have any say over the editorial content of Al-Jazeera, many Arab countries, such as Kuwait, Jordan, and Libya, have recalled their ambassadors to Qatar over programs considered "insulting" to their ruling regimes.[22]

One of Al-Jazeera's greatest achievements in the Arab world is that its open and free debates have forced the Arab governments to adjust their rhetoric to put an official spin on the uncensored news that is broadcast, and in the process become less nation-centered and more geared to the Arab world as a whole. So in short, Al-Jazeera has contributed to an alteration of domestic media systems eager to maintain their audience and advertising revenue, and spawned imitators across the region.

STRUCTURAL PROBLEMS AFFECTING MEDIA FREEDOM

In a number of Arab countries in the Middle East, basic legal and structural problems not specifically related to the media allow governments excessive discretion and prevent effective exercise of freedom of expression. Such structural problems include the power of the executive branch to issue decrees unchecked by other branches of the government, a lack of judicial independence, and the absence of a civil society, which is not a helpful environment for the extension of human rights.[23]

In Jordan, for example, the king has the authority to issue royal decrees amending legislation, including recent amendments increasing penalties for journalists, and can suspend parliamentary elections indefinitely to prevent his decrees from being overturned. These structural problems exist in many other Arab countries and can prevent the effective application of even the best media laws.

CONCLUSION

Arab governments must see that a free press, abiding by global standards of accuracy and fairness in reporting, is the best safeguard for responsible democracy. Most rulers of the region have a different set of problems from the ones they had with the old media they easily controlled: how to keep their grip on power while some of the control over communication is out of their hands and beyond their borders. Some governments have adapted by liberalizing their media; others are facing the prospect of having their state-run media become irrelevant because of competition from pan-Arab and regional satellites.[24]

The changes made to the terrestrial television in the Arab Middle East in an effort to retain audiences who have been attracted by the more independent satellite networks is a sign of hope and opportunity for a free media. The key question here is whether these changes are cosmetic or whether they represent a decisive break with heavy-handed censorship in a region where freedom of speech is not a right guaranteed by the Constitution, but rather a privilege granted by the governments to a selected group of journalists.

Arab nations cannot afford to maintain a censorial culture in a world moving fast toward full utilization and maximization of freedoms. And today, with the existence of truly independent Arab networks like Al-Jazeera, the time has come for building a strong foundation for a civil society in the Arab world, replacing fear with responsibility and censorship with freedom.

Chapter 3

The First Amendment and the Falun Gong

Paul Moses

Journalists assigned to the religion beat find out very quickly that many of the people they cover suspect the news media are biased against them. Evangelical Christians, Catholics, Jews, and Muslims all complain that they are victims of unfair coverage. Christian broadcasters and such groups as the Anti-Defamation League, the Catholic League for Religious and Civil Rights, and the Council on American-Islamic Relations assail alleged media abuses, sometimes calling for followers to boycott advertisers or cancel subscriptions. News organizations, striving to increase ratings or gain circulation, take such threats seriously.

It's a clash between two institutions that can claim powerful rights under the First Amendment. But how far can each side go in this ongoing battle? Does freedom of the press allow newspapers to print lies that undermine the practice of a religion? Does the right to gather in worship allow believers to stop a newspaper from attacking their beliefs?

Rarely do the First Amendment rights of religion and the news media conflict more starkly than in a libel lawsuit the Falun Gong meditation movement pursued against *China Press*, a Manhattan-based daily that caters to immigrants from mainland China living in San Francisco, Los Angeles, New

York, Seattle, Chicago, Boston, Houston, Phoenix, Washington, and other U.S. cities. Members of Falun Gong, which was banned in China in 1999 after adherents dared to demonstrate outside government offices in Beijing, charged that *China Press* had poisoned the atmosphere for their movement in New York's Chinese immigrant community by publishing lies. And while *China Press* may be little-known outside the Chinese community, within it the Chinese language *China Press*, with a circulation of 120,000, is a powerhouse. The paper chose to use that power to hammer American members of Falun Gong and import the Chinese government's propaganda campaign against the spiritual movement to the streets of New York's Chinatowns.

That onslaught prompted the spiritual movement's members to seek an extraordinary remedy in the courts—an order barring future publication of articles that allegedly defamed them and their beliefs. But the Falun Gong adherents faced a steep challenge. In *Nebraska Press Association v. Stuart* (1976), the U.S. Supreme Court has viewed "prior restraint"—barring an article before publication—as "the most serious and the least tolerable infringement on First Amendment rights." But, the Falun Gong members argued, their First Amendment right to gather in worship and express their religious views was being violated.

Mainstream New York newspapers such as the *New York Times* and *Newsday* published articles portraying Falun Gong members as victims of persecution in China. While the Chinese government contended that Falun Gong was a political threat, articles in the English-language press portrayed it as a spiritual movement rooted in traditional Chinese mind-body healing methods that have been practiced for thousands of years. Although small in number, the practitioners in New York were a familiar sight in city parks, where adherents slowly stretched through breathing and relaxation exercises aimed at ensuring good health and inner peace. Nothing in the English-language press challenged that peaceful picture of Falun Gong. Yet the power of the ethnic news media often is overlooked. New York, where the lawsuit was filed, teems with dailies in Spanish, Russian, Chinese, Korean, and other languages.[1] As Falun Gong members found, these papers are an influential voice in emerging immigrant communities.

Falun Gong devotees in New York discovered that the scathing *China Press* coverage had clout among recent immigrants from the Chinese mainland. Following the lead of the Chinese government, *China Press* dutifully reported that Falun Gong members were responsible for 1,700 deaths in China, 136 suicides, and 20 murder cases. It carried undisputed allegations that Falun Gong members cut open their own stomachs and burned their children to death. According to court papers, the newspaper carried reports charging that Falun Gong induces psychosis and that practitioners engaged in "many" illegal activities in the United States and were intent on causing disorder in New York. There were more deaths because of the Falun Gong, the paper alleged, than from the Movement for the Restoration of the Ten Commandments of God, the Ugandan cult that unraveled with the slaying of hundreds of members in 2000. The newspaper even said that the U.S. government should crack down on Falun Gong as it did on the Branch Davidians, the heavily armed cult federal agents assaulted with tear gas in 1993, leading to the fiery deaths of more than eighty members in Waco, Texas.

"Some people think that the U.S. government never treats evil cults without mercy," the *China Press* wrote in an article advocating that Falun Gong members be denied the right to take part in a community parade in New York City. But, it said, "what they did to the Branch Davidians a few years ago is a very good example. That the U.S. government allows Falun Gong to act openly is inconceivable."[2] *China Press* did not note that the events in Waco have gone down as a black mark on the record of federal law enforcement.

By filing a libel lawsuit seeking to stop the unfavorable coverage,[3] Falun Gong practitioners responded in a way that bishops, pastors, imams, or rabbis who feel harried by the news media perhaps have fantasized about. The lawsuit charged two newspapers, *China Press* and the 181,000-circulation *Sing Tao Daily*, with "relentless publication of false and defamatory statements concerning the plaintiffs," according to some sixty-seven Falun Gong practitioners and an umbrella group called Friends of Falun Gong. (Although *Sing Tao* was named as a defendant, all but one of the dozens of articles at issue were in *China Press*.) The suit charged that the defendants "acted as an unofficial mouthpiece for the Chinese government in reprinting and localizing a range of propaganda intended to subject the Plaintiffs to harassment within their community and to prevent their exercise of their First Amendment privileges of association and expression." *China Press*, the suit charged, had other aims than to report news—it was deliberately violating Falun Gong members' civil rights. It did that, the suit asserted, by joining forces with the Chinese government and an "American Citizens Anti-Evil Religion Association" that was formed in New York's Chinese immigrant community with the aim of stamping out the local practice of Falun Gong.

Those familiar with Falun Gong are often surprised at the intensity of China's drive to eliminate it. The movement was founded in 1992 by Li Hongzhi, a former clerk and trumpet player in China who has since taken refuge at an undisclosed location in Queens, New York. He has said he studied with a Buddhist monk and then with Taoist masters.[4] His spiritual masters encouraged him to teach *qigong*, a traditional Chinese meditative exercise. He developed a philosophy that combined elements of qigong, Buddhism, Taoism, moral teachings, and, it might be added, his belief in aliens. According to the Master, as he is called, there is a wheel of energy within the lower abdomen that spins off a healing force. (Falun Gong means "wheel of the law.") Through exercises and meditation, followers try to cultivate this force, which Li says brings both mental and physical benefits. The idea that the connection between body and mind can improve health is hardly new in the Far East, but the focus on physical well-being helped make the movement hugely popular in China.

Practitioners say they have no interest in political power and simply want to improve their health or state of mind. They hardly seem a threat, as Erik Eckholm noted in the lead to an article in the *New York Times*: "Has it come to this: that the Chinese Communist Party is terrified of retirees in tennis shoes who follow a spiritual master in Queens?"[5]

But by 1999, Falun Gong members had become far too outspoken for the control-minded Chinese leadership. According to James T. Richardson, who has studied the Chinese legal system as a scholar at the University of Nevada in Reno, the government did not stop Falun Gong from holding a number of protests over the group's portrayal in state-controlled media. Chinese authorities even stepped in to defuse such situations.[6] The emboldened Falun Gong members then demonstrated at a student newspaper that refused to back down from its coverage. When the government would not step in, Falun Gong responded by sending 10,000 members to protest outside Communist Party headquarters in Beijing. The Falun Gong members' show of force shocked party officials.

While Li says he is not interested in political power, it should be noted that in China's past, religiously based groups did in fact seek it. The Boxer Rebellion in 1900 was begun by a secret religious society, the Fists of Righteous Harmony, whose members practiced calisthenics and martial arts (hence the nickname "boxers" in the Western press). The practitioners, who believed they had magical powers to help them in battle, sought to eliminate Christian and foreign influence from China. At first, they also sought to overthrow the Chinese dynasty. Later, they did its bidding. Many Christians, both missionaries and Chinese, were killed in the violence that followed. The so-called rebellion led to a brief, disastrous war with Western nations seeking to carve up China to serve their own imperialist interests. Such historical memories have continued to shape China's dance with the West as it seeks to benefit from the global economy while preventing what its leaders describe as foreign interference in its internal affairs.

On July 22, 1999, an alarmed President Jiang Zemin ordered what would be a brutal crackdown aimed at eliminating the practice of Falun Gong. The accompanying propaganda campaign against Falun Gong quickly spread around the world through Chinese consulates. At the consulate in Manhattan, for example, visitors were welcomed with posters featuring graphic pictures of dead bodies charred by fire, ripped open with scissors, beaten on the head with a spade, hung from a rope. Each poster had captions that blamed Falun Gong for the mayhem. The body of the man whose stomach is drenched with blood had used scissors on himself, the sign said, to try to extract the inner "wheel" Falun Gong teaches about. It is a far cry from the scenes advertised in most consulates: snow-capped mountains, sandy beaches, quaint city centers, lavish spreads of food, smiling people in native dress.

The propaganda campaign focused on the overseas Chinese community and the news media serving it. So when the *China Press* held a reception on January 4, 2000, to mark its tenth anniversary, the keynote speaker, the *charge d'affaires* from the Chinese embassy, quickly got to the point. First, Liu Xiaoming offered congratulations from the Chinese government, noting that Jiang Zemin himself had praised the paper. Then, according to an account on the Chinese consulate's Web site, he launched into the standard attack on Falun Gong:

> Numerous irrefutable facts have proved that Falun Gong is an evil cult which has committed a host of serious crimes including organizing and employing cults, obstructing justice, causing human deaths and illegally obtaining state secrets. So far, more than 1,400 Chinese citizens have died, thousands more have suffered psychologically and a large number of families have been broken due to practicing Falun Gong.[7]

By banning Falun Gong, he said, the Chinese government was "safeguarding the human rights and freedoms of the people and upholding the rule of law." He advocated a U.S. crackdown on Falun Gong, saying, "We all know how mercilessly the United States dealt with the cults on its own soil," an apparent reference to the Waco disaster.

The Chinese government continued to follow up, sending its diplomats to speak at "seminars" in New York on how to combat Falun Gong on U.S. territory. According to the Web site of the Chinese consulate in New York, Ambassador Zhu Qizhen again portrayed the Chinese crackdown as an attempt to protect human rights. "It is precisely for the sake of protecting the fundamental freedoms and human rights of its citizens and safeguarding the Chinese Constitution and other laws that the Chinese government has outlawed and cracked down on the Falun Gong organization," he said. "In handling this issue, the Chinese government has adopted a policy of persuasion and education towards the vast majority of general practitioners and punishment according to law towards only law-breaking criminals who are small in number."[8]

The editors of *China Press* work in two worlds that have far different views of human rights. They've shown familiarity with both. But they chose to make their newspaper a conduit for the Chinese government's view, despite their claim that it is "a leader for delivering accurate, balanced, in depth analysis" and that it offers "detailed reporting and impartial and insightful editorials." The Chinese-language paper is proud of its close ties to the Chinese government, noting on its Web site that it has done many exclusive interviews with Chinese leaders. "No other U.S. Chinese newspaper has gained the same privilege of unlimited access to news about Mainland China," the paper says.[9]

Thus the paper reported only the Chinese government's side of the Falun Gong story, with its increasingly bloated body count. The "accurate, balanced" *China Press* carried no hint that there is even another side to this propaganda, one that can be found with a quick trip to the U.S. State Department's Web site. There the Chinese persecution of Falun Gong is amply described in the State Department's Annual Report on International Religious Freedom. It cites "numerous credible reports that police and security personnel abused, tortured, and even killed Falun Gong practitioners." It says that on a broad scale, followers were forced to recant their beliefs or face torture, including electric shock. "Many thousands of Falun Gong practitioners are serving extra-judicial administrative sentences in reeducation-through-labor camps," the report says. Amnesty International found that torture or force-feeding hunger strikers had caused many deaths in police custody.

China Press suppressed that part of the story and claimed that reports on the Chinese government's crackdown were exaggerated. It accepted at face value the ambassador's claim that the government was merely engaging in a campaign of "persuasion and education," ignoring reports in the U.S. media of psychiatric abuses. And it failed to ask the obvious question: If crazed Falun Gong practitioners had really caused such a wave of death and destruction in China, why had that not occurred in the United States, where thousands of adherents live? In short, the *China Press* coverage was slanted in the worst way—it was propaganda, not reportage. There was, indeed, a vague undercurrent of violence in some of the coverage. One article quoted a powerful Chinatown leader saying that Falun Gong members are like "mice crossing the street, everyone yells to hit it," according to court filings.

In their lawsuit, Falun Gong members contended that bogus claims reported in *China Press* had made their lives miserable as fellow Chinese immigrants shunned them.

"I was not allowed to take care of my grandson anymore," Falun Gong practitioner Chen Zhulli, 58, an artist from Flushing, New York, said in an affidavit. Her daughter was frightened to leave the child with her because of the newspaper's reports on Falun Gong, she said.

Lam Wai Ling, 53, of Manhattan, complained about being pummeled while handing out Falun Gong literature. "I simply don't feel safe anymore practicing in public," he said. He was assailed, he said, two days after *China Press* ran an article headlined, "Strike Hard at Falun Gong."

This, the Falun Gong members alleged, is what happens when a newspaper publishes "without due consideration for the standards of information gathering and dissemination ordinarily followed by newsgathering agencies." Their lawsuit, filed in April 2002 at the New York State court in Queens, New York, alleged libel. It advanced a bold step: it sought to block the newspapers from publishing any future articles containing the repeated attacks on Falun Gong. That was necessary, the suit argued, to prevent "serious physical and financial injury."

China Press was quick to invoke its own First Amendment rights, responding in an article that the "unusually stubborn" Falun Gong was bent on "strongly interfering in the media's freedom of the press." The newspaper asserted, erroneously, that it was protected against a libel claim because it was simply reprinting articles from a news service. "*China Press* did not 'forcefully claim' anything," the newspaper said. "This is a right of freedom of press given to American media."[10]

But it should be noted that a news organization can be liable for publishing someone else's defamatory claims, even in an advertisement or letter to the editor. *China Press* had been quick to claim its constitutional rights as an American newspaper, but it overlooked its responsibility to check the facts it published. Ironically, it ended its lecture on press freedoms by telling Falun Gong that it had "better learn how things are done over here."

But *China Press* owners quickly made a savvy move: they went to attorney Floyd Abrams, a leading expert on the First Amendment, to represent them. Abrams focused on the lawsuit's request for an immediate order barring *China Press* from repeating its biting claims about Falun Gong.

This, Abrams said, would be a classic example of prior restraint. If the *China Press* were to libel the defendants, it could be punished afterward, he argued. But, he said, it was unconstitutional to muzzle the paper. Abrams speaks with great authority on that subject. He was cocounsel to the *New York Times* in the Pentagon Papers case, in which the U.S. Supreme Court issued a landmark 1971 ruling in *New York Times v. United States* that allowed the *Times* and the *Washington Post* to print classified documents detailing a secret history of the Vietnam War. The court finding that the Constitution required a "heavy presumption" in favor of freedom of the press overturned a lower-court decision that let the Nixon administration bar publication on national security grounds.

Abrams argued that a ruling in favor of the Falun Gong members would set a dangerous precedent by making it possible to silence the news media. A state judge in Queens rejected the Falun Gong members' request for a preliminary injunction. But the judge gave the Falun Gong plaintiffs a chance to provide more evidence, and they revised the lawsuit to add a new claim under federal law—that they were the victims of a conspiracy to deprive them of their civil rights. After the federal claim was added to the lawsuit, Abrams got the case transferred to U.S. District Court in Brooklyn, New York. With the case now in the federal court system, Abrams spotlighted the First Amendment rights of the *China Press*. In his version of the case, the Falun Gong members were the aggressors seeking to undermine cherished American rights. A ruling in favor of the Falun Gong adherents would hurt the entire news media, he argued.

If Abrams was right, the news media have a legal right to be very one-sided in reporting on a religion. "It is precisely in the area of criticism of religion that free speech protections are greatest," he argued in court filings.

Abrams cited the 1940 U.S. Supreme Court decision in *Cantwell v. Connecticut*. That case involved Jehovah's Witnesses member Jesse Cantwell, who took to the streets of a heavily Catholic neighborhood in New Haven, Connecticut, in 1938 with a recording that attacked the Catholic Church as an instrument of Satan. Two Catholic men accepted his invitation to listen to the record and were sorely tempted to respond with fisticuffs unless Cantwell and his Victrola exited. Cantwell left, but was arrested and later convicted of inciting others to breach the peace. The court overturned the conviction, noting that exaggeration and vilification are often part of debates over religion or politics. "The people of this nation have ordained . . . that, in spite of the probability of excesses and abuses, these liberties are, in the long view, essential to enlightened opinion," the court found.

Libel law protects expressions of opinion, a refuge Abrams also sought for the *China Press*. The problem with this defense was that the protection does not extend to erroneous facts entwined with the opinion. As the Supreme Court said in 1974 in *Gertz v. Welch*, "Under the First Amendment there is no such thing as a false idea. . . . But there is no constitutional value in false statements of fact. Neither the intentional lie nor the careless error materially advances society's interest in 'uninhibited, robust, and wide-open,' debate on public issues."

The *China Press* had reported many dubious factual claims about Falun Gong, such as the allegation that practitioners had burnt their children to death. Abrams insisted this was "the type of ideological invective routinely hurled during the course of robust public debate." The courts have protected such opinion—"ideological invective"—from libel suits so that the news media can be free to report on a wide range of viewpoints. (For that matter, it would be impossible to review a film honestly without a protection for commentary. But if the reviewer were to allege that the movie was bad because the director and star had an affair during the filming, the reviewer had better be correct on the facts.)

Another hurdle for the lawsuit was that none of the sixty-seven plaintiffs was mentioned directly in the *China Press* coverage, even though they claimed to have been damaged by it. To prove libel, plaintiffs must establish that they have been identified in the offending article. It's not necessary to be named, but it must be demonstrated that readers would reasonably be able to identify the statement with the plaintiff. The Falun Gong plaintiffs sought to overcome this barrier by filing a series of affidavits. The practitioners alleged that they had been mistreated by people who became infuriated against Falun Gong after reading the inflammatory newspaper coverage.

Abrams said that courts have always thrown out lawsuits filed by individuals who said they were the victims of slurs against their religion. Sam P. Israel, attorney for the Falun Gong members, said this case was different. Unlike Christians, he said, Falun Gong members are a small group in the United States. Inevitably, readers will associate what they read with the particular practitioners they know, he contended.

Abrams disagreed. "The courts are saying over and over again that the First Amendment protects just this sort of speech," he said in a court hearing before Judge Carol Amon. "We cannot allow people to transform speech about a movement . . . into an attack on an individual."[11]

Israel responded: "We're talking about a very specific group of people who are being targeted by these articles that are advancing not just defamatory material but are calls for people to take action against a very specific group of people."

Yet another hurdle for the lawsuit was its claim that the defendants conspired to subvert the Falun Gong members' civil rights. Abrams said that for such a claim to stand, the federal civil rights conspiracy law required that there be some failure on the part of the government (as could be claimed, for example, in a lawsuit alleging police misconduct). But no one was arguing that any level of government in the United States was responsible for the newspaper's attacks against the Falun Gong.

Even as Abrams picked apart the legal basis for the lawsuit, attorney Israel advanced some arguments with powerful emotional appeal. He created the scenario of a newspaper controlled from Germany and published in New York in the 1930s. The newspaper called for New Yorkers to join an anti-Semitic club, to harass Jews in public, and to demand that Jews not be allowed to parade. The paper constantly accused Jews of being members of a cult whose members commit random acts of murder, kidnapping, and child abuse. The parallels to *China Press* were clear and all the more chilling because, as Holocaust scholars point out, Hitler's "final solution" to eliminate the Jewish people was preceded by a gradually intensifying effort to deny their rights and to harass and humiliate them. Such a violence-tinged drive had already begun in China, and *China Press* championed it in New York.

When asked about that example in an interview, Abrams responded without hesitation. "It would be legally protected," he said. "We're the only country in the world that protects hate speech." Abrams was asked if he had read the State Department's reports on the Chinese crackdown against Falun Gong; he said he had. "You have to decide if you believe in the First Amendment or not," he said.[12]

In an opinion issued September 24, 2003, Judge Amon dissected libel down to its basic elements. But she did not go into the most basic defense against a libel claim—truth. Fortunately for the *China Press*, the newspaper never needed to argue that it had reported the truth about Falun Gong.

It is up to a jury to decide during a trial whether the news coverage is false. As is usually done in civil suits, the owners of *China Press* and *Sing Tao Daily* had asked the judge to dismiss the lawsuit before a trial could be held. The judge was limited to ruling on the law. That meant she had to accept all of the facts the Falun Gong members alleged. The suit could only be dismissed if, even after accepting all the factual allegations as true, the judge decided the laws cited could not have been violated. So truth, the most basic defense against libel, was not an issue in the pretrial phase. News organizations are eager to win libel cases at this early stage because it protects them from the uncertainty of being judged by a jury and saves them the steep legal cost of going to trial.

In her ruling in the case *Falun Gong v. Pacific Culture Enterprise, Inc.*, the judge came down on the side of the defendants on the key question of whether the articles had in any way identified the plaintiffs. "In this case," the judge wrote, "plaintiffs cannot demonstrate that any of the defendants' allegedly defamatory statements reasonably gave rise to the conclusion that they particularly reference any of the plaintiffs." The lawsuit had failed to overcome what is known as the "group libel doctrine." The generalized attacks on Falun Gong could not be taken as an attack on individual adherents. As a result, Judge Amon dismissed the lawsuit's libel claim.

The judge also dismissed the claim that the newspaper companies had schemed to deprive the Falun Gong practitioners of their right to freedom of expression. She accepted Abrams' legal argument that the federal civil rights conspiracy statute did not apply in such a case.

That left one more claim, that the newspapers had violated the plaintiffs' civil rights under New York state law. The issue here was whether the newspapers' coverage incited organizers of a parade to exclude Falun Gong participation, thus denying the practitioners' rights. The judge said there had been no showing that this was the case; more facts were needed to support such a conclusion. She added: "To find liability under this statute on the facts presented here would raise serious concerns as to the First Amendment rights of the defendants."

The case had begun with charges that extremely biased news coverage had subverted the Falun Gong members' First Amendment rights. It was ending on the note Abrams had argued all along—that the lawsuit had endangered the freedom of the press. Judge Amon dismissed the lawsuit.

Journalism students, particularly those from outside the United States, often are surprised at the freedom the American news media have—the ability to publish even classified or leaked information, for example. But it would be wrong to assume that Judge Amon's ruling dismisses the need for journalists to be fair. Careful, honest, accurate reporting is the first line of defense against libel claims or lawsuits that challenge the methods of gathering information, which can be more difficult to defend. "Any paper has a journalistic duty to be fair, but the law imposes few restraints on what newspapers can publish and does it for significant First Amendment reasons," Abrams said.

Falun Gong adherents are left with the remedy the First Amendment shelters: more speech. As Abrams said in court filings, the remedy is "the right to criticize their critics and to persuade others of the rightness of their views in the marketplace of ideas." At this the Falun Gong practitioners are adept. They have filed lawsuits against the Chinese government in many places, getting almost daily news coverage that draws attention to the persecution in

China. Falun Gong members demonstrate regularly outside the Chinese mission in New York, outside the White House, and in many other communities in North America, Europe, and Asia.

Of course, that conflicts with the conventions the *China Press* imports from China. In one *China Press* article, an official from a Chinese organization in New York referred to the Beijing protest that led the Chinese government to crack down on Falun Gong. "They would certainly be bold enough to surround the White House," he said.[13] The official did not seem aware that the protesters' trail to Washington is well worn, hallowed by such figures as the Rev. Martin Luther King Jr.

The Falun Gong case shows a need for the mainstream news media and journalism critics to take a longer and more questioning look at what is appearing in the ethnic press, which has a powerful influence in emerging immigrant communities. Reporters sometimes face coercion, at times heroically. In 1991 journalist Manuel de Dios Unanue was fatally shot in New York on the orders of a leader in a Colombian cocaine cartel because he was angered by de Dios's articles in a Spanish-language magazine on drug trafficking. Reporters in the Chinese-language press also face coercion, as Michael Powell points out in his article, "The Chinatown Clampdown."[14] Such issues rarely are covered in the English-language media, in part because of language barriers.

The value of the Falun Gong lawsuit is that it exposed an extreme example of bias in the news media. But the case wound up teaching the Falun Gong a lesson as well. As the U.S. Supreme Court said in its 1974 ruling in the case of *Gertz v. Welch*: "However pernicious an opinion may seem, we depend for its correction not on the consciences of judges and juries but on the competition of ideas."[15]

3: View from the News Desk

First Amendment and the Common Good

Peter Smith

Debates over the role of God talk in the public square have become a staple of our headlines and newscasts. First Amendment lawyers have kept busy fighting over everything from the "under God" clause of the Pledge of Allegiance, to the installation of Ten Commandments monuments in public places, to the government funding of faith-based education and social services.

Former Alabama chief justice Roy Moore made national news in 2003 and received acclaim as a near-martyr from religious conservatives for installing a two-ton monument of the Ten Commandments in the state courthouse and then defying a federal court order to remove it and being himself removed from his job. Similar battles have arisen throughout the South and Midwest, with rural counties and state governments trying to post the Ten Commandments in public places. Though few have gone as far in judicial defiance as Moore, most would echo the baffled reaction of a rural Kentucky county executive when faced with an American Civil Liberties Union lawsuit over a public display of the Ten Commandments: "Who wouldn't support God's word?" Opponents are equally baffled at why officials don't recognize the repeated court admonitions to remove such public displays. In fact, not only did the state of Kentucky lose a federal lawsuit over plans to install a Ten Commandments monument on capitol grounds, but it also had to pay

$121,524 in legal bills to the American Civil Liberties Union, which challenged the installation.

And it's not just the Ten Commandments that raise these questions about the First Amendment. In 2002, a federal court upheld a decision by Colorado school officials to prohibit religiously oriented memorial tiles at the site of the Columbine High School massacre. In 2003, the University of Louisville prohibited drama students and faculty members from including religious dedications in the playbills that accompany their productions. And of course, the December news cycle wouldn't be complete without the annual lawsuits over public displays of crèches and menorahs.

Church-state tensions repeatedly arise in the administration of President George W. Bush, the most overtly religious president in recent memory. The Rev. Franklin Graham stirred controversy by praying "in Jesus' name" at the inauguration in 2001. Bush paraphrased a gospel song when he cited the "wonder-working power" of faith-based social services, and he echoed Scripture with the phrase, "We're all sinners," to explain his opposition to homosexual marriage. When Attorney General John Ashcroft began holding early morning Bible studies at the Department of Justice, critics questioned whether the sessions, while voluntary, created an inside network for those who shared Ashcroft's beliefs (or were willing to pretend they did). Of course, critics of Ashcroft turned their attention to other matters in the post-September 11 world, but the religious stakes have only grown in this new environment. Army Lt. Gen. William Boykin launched an international controversy for giving speeches while in uniform to church groups, calling the war on terror a religious conflict between Christians and Muslims. Evangelical Christian missionary groups drew a similar international reaction for entering postwar Iraq to distribute humanitarian aid with religious literature.

One thing we can be certain of: these issues will be with us in the future. Regardless of how the U.S. Supreme Court rules on whether public-school students can use the phrase "under God" in the Pledge of Allegiance, the issue will resonate far wider than just the family of Michael A. Newdow, the California village atheist who sued over the clause. As soon as Newdow won a lower-court ruling, several members of Congress stood on the Capitol steps and recited the full pledge for news cameras. Meanwhile, a Washington State college student went to the Supreme Court, challenging the denial of government financial aid due to his theology major, a year after the Supreme Court upheld the use of vouchers in Ohio for parochial school tuition. And a potential flare-up loomed over whether a Ground Zero memorial should include a venerated pair of steel beams found in the shape of a cross in the wreckage.

Sooner or later, as in most public policy debates, questions about the invoking of God's name in the public square come down to money. Should the government be supporting social services operated by religious organizations? And should those religious organizations accept government money even when it's legal?

Just as Jesus used a Roman coin as an illustration to make his point—to give to Caesar what is Caesar's and to God what is God's—so this church-state debate plays out in two modern-day, true-to-life parables in Louisville, Kentucky, where I cover religion for the *Courier-Journal*.

In the first case, an African-American Baptist pastor launches faith-based community projects in Louisville, championing them as models of success in neighborhoods where government has failed. Yet he is also accused of being intoxicated by government funding to the point of allegedly being the toady of conservative Republicans and blaming black victims of police brutality.

In the second case, a historically white, Baptist social service agency fires a lesbian worker, drawing widespread criticism, nearly losing state funding, and spending years in court with the inevitable ACLU lawsuit. But the case takes a surprising turn when the agency pursues independence from government funding so it won't have to choose between money and principle.

That two faith-based service providers could reach opposite conclusions—one seeking Caesar's coin, the other preparing to give it back—has as much to do with race, class, sex, and money as it has to do with faith itself. It goes without saying that none of these subjects are safe dinner conversation. Yet here they are, all on the table.

A SHOOTING AND A DEBATE

In a bleak industrial neighborhood in Louisville, St. Stephen's Baptist Church launched a faith-based organization that built a gleaming new community center, featuring computer rooms, basketball courts, a café, and an exercise area. It then focused on another blighted neighborhood, buying the campus of a Jim Crow-era black college and launching still more programs. St. Stephen's Pastor Kevin Cosby likes to boast that his church sponsors the only racquetball courts in Louisville's predominately black West End. The church—Kentucky's largest African-American congregation, with 8,000 members—paid for some of these programs on its own. But it has also received more than $2 million in federal grants, and other African-American churches have received more than $5 million to launch a fleet of other faith-based social services across Louisville.

Cosby says black churches have succeeded compared with the "bureaucrats who do not live in the community and parachute solutions into the community. . . . We fulfilled an indigenous need in the black community because the black community has been deinstitutionalized, and institutions that other neighborhoods take for granted do not exist" (Cosby, personal interview).

Whether faith-based services really do out-perform their secular counterparts has largely been unexplored, though a preliminary study by Indiana University-Purdue University Indianapolis suggests they do not. Moreover, critics say black churches are muting their traditionally prophetic, liberal voice in public policy, cozying up to conservatives who critics say promote policies harmful to poor minorities.

All this came to a head in what might at first have seemed an unrelated incident: a fatal shooting in yet another blighted area of town. On the night of December 5, 2002, two white police detectives were working in the gritty Smoketown neighborhood when they heard a woman calling for help from an upstairs apartment. They rushed to the scene and confronted a 50-year-old man who had been threatening the woman. They handcuffed the man, James E. Taylor, but failed to frisk him thoroughly enough, and soon Taylor began advancing toward a detective, holding a box-cutter knife. The detective opened fire, killing Taylor with seven bullets. The episode stoked already-simmering debates in Louisville over race, police use of force—and eventually, the government funding of faith-based services.

At first even the local prosecutor said the shooting looked "so horrible." But more facts then emerged. Taylor—who had already served time for manslaughter—had been smoking crack and drinking vodka before threatening his female companion. A grand jury concluded on February 24, 2003, that the cuffed Taylor still had enough flexibility to pose a genuine threat to the cornered detective.

The explanation convinced many citizens, but others protested, with some activists calling for a temporary boycott on Louisville chain stores.

Then Cosby weighed in with a commentary in the *Courier-Journal* on March 16, 2003. He called instead for African Americans to "boycott the police"—that is, to avoid potentially lethal encounters by avoiding criminal behavior in the first place. He called for African Americans to concentrate on economic self-help and family responsibility rather than indulging the "grandstanding black activists who are caught in a time warp, trying to relive the 1960s while ignoring the problems of a new century." He added:

> It's a mistake to equate the death of blacks engaged in criminal activity with the martyrdom of people who were viciously murdered by racists. . . . Such comparisons desecrate the memory of Medgar Evers, Emmett Till, Martin Luther King Jr., James Cheney and many others. . . . It cannot be ignored that the late Mr. Taylor lived in a culture of death before he ever encountered the police on Dec. 5. . . . It is extreme hypocrisy for our people to wage protest when police bullets take someone out, but then push the mute button when one black gang member kills another, when a black person overdoses on drugs, or when black people, with our disproportionate levels of diabetes and hypertension, disregard lifestyle changes essential to promoting longevity. . . . We should be concerned about police brutality, racial profiling and injustices in law enforcement, but whatever gets you to the morgue, you're just as dead. (D1)

Some cheered Cosby's message, while others called for an apology, saying he was blaming the victim, dodging the role of racism in police violence, and pandering to the public officials responsible for the millions in government aid, particularly U.S. Representative Anne Northup, R-Louisville, a conservative congresswoman who has made a high-profile effort to channel federal grants to faith-based groups.

Although her Democratic challengers have also made appearances at St. Stephen's, Northup's appearances there have galled some black Democrats who believe such actions have tipped the balance her way in a series of bitter election campaigns.

Said the Rev. Louis Coleman, as ubiquitous a protester in Louisville as his occasional collaborator Jesse Jackson is nationally: "If [a church is] going to continue to receive those dollars, it gives up its voice of advocacy, it compromises your beliefs. If you want to step out on an issue, challenge the powers that be, you have to think twice, three times, four times before you do it, and the majority of times that step is not taken" (Coleman, personal interview). (In fact, Coleman's civil rights organization did receive a $123,000 state grant to boost minority participation in state construction projects. The state decided not to renew the contract in 2002, citing sloppy record keeping and "extremely modest" results, but Coleman contended his experience proves the government will use grant money to reward supportive ministers and to punish those, like himself, who continue to protest government policies.)

Ricky Jones, a professor of Pan-African Studies at the University of Louisville, said churches risk being exploited by a cynical government. "Governmental entities are starting to pawn off some of their problems on the faith-based community, which is very ill prepared to handle [them and which] they shouldn't have to handle," he said (Jones, personal interview).

Cosby replied that the criticism "is more of a caution—to be careful not to deny the reality of racism—and that is a justifiable critique. The fact still remains that people rise and fall based on the level of their thinking. If you think defeated, then you will be defeated, and if you think optimistic, the chances are that you can achieve tremendous things" (Cosby, personal interview).

The faith-based debate has deep roots here in this once-segregated southern border city. Cosby draws lessons from his own grandfather, his predecessor in the St. Stephen's pulpit, who earned a seminary degree despite originally being shut out by Jim Crow laws. The lesson for Cosby is to do more than just decry the racism that closes doors but to seize opportunities when the doors open.

And several other local African-American megachurch pastors told me they agreed with Cosby.

"That's what the black church has been about all along. We have a responsibility to reach folk before they become the Taylors of the community," said The Rev. T. Vaughn Walker, professor of black church studies at Southern Baptist Theological Seminary. Walker's own church, First Gethsemane Baptist Church, also receives grants for child care, tutoring, and other programs. To those who say churchgoers should do social service programs on their own dime, Walker says they are. "We pay taxes too," he said. "We can use some of the tax money to work in partnership to turn that community around." Black churches don't have the luxury of considering whether to do everything with private-sector funding, Walker said, unlike those white churches with well-heeled members "who can write any check they want to" (Walker, personal interview).

"KEEP YOUR MONEY, WE'LL STILL SERVE YOUR KIDS"

Significantly, however, white (and often wealthier) evangelical groups are rethinking the wisdom of government funding, even as they question current legal case law on church-state separation in other areas, such as school vouchers and public displays of the Ten Commandments.

The funding issue arose with Kentucky's largest private child-care provider, a faith-based organization that has taken care of needy children since the days when Civil War orphans wandered the streets of Louisville. The Kentucky Baptist Homes for Children (KBHC) has in recent years received more than half its funding from the state. But the organization reserves the right not to hire employees whose religious beliefs conflict with it, a category in which it includes homosexuals. That has left outside critics challenging the organization's right to receive taxpayer dollars, and it has left the Baptists themselves questioning the wisdom of doing so.

By all accounts, the issue arose by accident.

Alicia Pedreira worked as a supervisor at a group home for troubled youth in suburban Louisville operated by the KBHC. Pedreira kept low-key about her same-sex orientation. But in 1998 a photographer entered a portrait of Pedreira and her female partner in a photo contest in the Kentucky State Fair. In the photo, taken at a local AIDS walk, Pedreira is wearing a T-shirt depicting a map of the Aegean Sea marking the "Isle of Lesbos."

Pedreira's employers at the Kentucky Baptist Homes for Children fired her when they learned of the photo and its obvious implications. The KBHC, the state's largest private child-care provider, is associated with the state affiliate of the Southern Baptist Convention, which holds the sinfulness of homosexuality as literally an article of faith.

"My firing took away my livelihood," Pedreira said at a news conference in 2000, as the ACLU filed a federal lawsuit on her behalf, claiming religious discrimination. "My civil rights were assaulted."

In 2001, a federal judge denied her claim, saying that "civil rights statutes protect religious freedom, not personal lifestyle choices" such as homosexuality. But the judge allowed another portion of the lawsuit to proceed: a claim by seven other plaintiffs that their rights as taxpayers are being violated because the KBHC is using public money to provide services that are instilling children with Baptist values.

Bill Smithwick, executive director of the KBHC, said his organization is "not going to acquiesce to political pressure," adding that employing homosexual counselors is "not the best way to care for troubled and abused children" (qtd. in *Courier-Journal*, 18 April 2000).

But though the KBHC won its first legal round, Smithwick concedes that it may lose the war. That's why, in November 2001, it launched a fund-raising campaign with hopes of weaning itself entirely from Caesar's coin. That effort, which would have to replace more than half the organization's revenue stream, is still under way.

"We'd like to raise enough money in the next three to four years that we can tell the state: 'Keep your money, we'll still serve your kids,'" Smithwick said to the applause of delegates to the Kentucky Baptist Convention at its annual meeting in 2001.

Smithwick said he believed there are potential donors who would say, "Bill, Kentucky Baptist Homes, we commend you for standing up against the agenda of the ACLU, we commend you on your stand for holding traditional family values high" (qtd. in *Courier-Journal*, 15 November 2001).

In fact, unrelated developments are rapidly changing the context of this case, as budget cuts have forced the KBHC to lay off nine employees.

Referrals to KBHC—and other private child-care providers—have declined in the wake of the federal Adoption and Safe Families Act of 1997. That law states that children removed from their parents should be placed as promptly as possible into a foster or permanent home, rather than in group homes such as KBHC.

But Smithwick said he believes referrals are down partly because social workers are snubbing the agency over its policies. In fact, the state Cabinet for Families and Children had threatened to cut off funding to the KBHC until the governor intervened at the 11th hour in 2000, telling state workers to base placement decisions only on the best interests of children and not on KBHC's employment policies.

"We want to continue to cooperate with the state," Smithwick said later. "It's not that we're just trying to pull away." But if the courts or the state decides public funds shouldn't go to a religious agency, "and we think probably one day it will, we may have to break ranks with public funding" (Smithwick, personal interview).

Nothing would more please the plaintiffs suing the KBHC.

"Churches should get their hands out of the public till," said the Rev. Paul Simmons, a plaintiff and Baptist minister. "And government should stop trying to use churches as proxy service providers. Churches cannot and should not do social work simply as a secular enterprise" (qtd. in *Courier-Journal*, 18 April 2000, A1).

But as this case shows, even if the courts say they can, some churches may decide it's just not worth it.

Chapter 4

A Framework for Understanding Fundamentalism

Rebecca Moore

In her novel *The Handmaid's Tale*, Margaret Atwood describes a future world governed by Christian extremists. Women are subservient to men in the Republic of Gilead. Their primary sanctioned roles are as child-bearers and household managers, while their unsanctioned roles are as prostitutes for the elite. Although the leaders rely on certain types of technology—particularly to fight their wars—much of Gilead is pretechnological or preindustrial. The handmaids go to the store each day to buy necessities. These are labeled with pictures, rather than words, because reading is discouraged. Executions are public and serve as violent group exercises in acting out aggression. Biblical law provides the foundation for all of society, governing social relations between men and women and prescribing practices within the family.

While *The Handmaid's Tale* is a compelling novel, a future controlled by religious extremists probably would look entirely different. Far from being antitechnological or antimodern, this world would rely on technology and communications media to control all aspects of life and culture. Giant global corporations and satellite systems, conservative think tanks and publications, small-market radio stations, Internet chat rooms, and direct-mail campaigns would all play a role in maintaining the theocratic state.

A variety of conservative religious extremists are already successfully using these tools and techniques: from Christian Reconstructionists who want to establish a government under biblical law in the United States, to Muslim *madrasas* (schools) in Pakistan and Saudi Arabia that teach their students a militant reading of the Qur'an. Although their ideologies may appear to be antimodern, most religious extremists now depend on an array of technologies to promote their agendas in the modern world.

"Fundamentalism" has become the catch-all phrase used to characterize an assortment of movements that have arisen in opposition to the beliefs and values of the modern world. Fundamentalists are responding to what they see as the weaknesses and dangers of the world in which we live. They resist accommodation to what they believe are evil or ungodly social structures by fighting culture wars. Rather than embracing or even tolerating the pluralism endorsed by modern social and political systems, fundamentalists hold to a radical dualism in which two sides—God versus Satan—take no prisoners and brook no compromise.

George Marsden, a historian of Protestant Christianity, identified late-nineteenth- and early twentieth-century fundamentalism as "a loose, diverse, and changing federation of cobelligerents united by their fierce opposition to modernist attempts to bring Christianity in line with modern thought." Marsden emphasized "militancy against modernism" as "the *key distinguishing* factor that drew fundamentalists together."[1]

Although some analysts continue to see fundamentalism as a retreat or separation from modernity, fundamentalism today works *within* the modern world to create a new society that incorporates ancient religious values. Fundamentalists are using mass media and the latest technologies in order to realize their vision of a future based on God-given truths. They are creating cultural alternatives—such as school systems, broadcasting networks, satellite hook-ups, and Internet sites—that in appearance, if not substance, look remarkably modern. "[Fundamentalists] may reject the scientific rationalism of the West," Karen Armstrong observes, "but they cannot escape it."[2]

In fact, the nineteenth-century antimodern movement within American Protestantism as described by Marsden has changed dramatically. Today fundamentalism describes a variety of religious movements that both critique, yet remain firmly dependent upon, modern values and mores. Fundamentalists in the early twenty-first century share many general assumptions of the modern world, including a regard for the scientific method and a belief in universal norms and narratives. Using modern methods and media, they attempt to establish an idealized past within the present. They claim universality by invoking sacred origins, and they resist contemporary society by citing sacred texts. They condemn the rampant materialism, consumerism, and individualism that they see in current Western society. They criticize society's mistreatment of women, children, and families. Most significantly, fundamentalists around the world question the elimination of religion and human values from important political discussions, even as they engage in debates about important social issues. They feel that the world does not live up to the requirements of a divinely ordained social order. In short, they seek to recreate a world that reflects specific religious, rather than secular, values within the confines of modernity.

BACKGROUND

Part of the difficulty in describing precisely what fundamentalism is—and in using the expression accurately—comes from its distinctly American roots in nineteenth-century Protestantism. Responding to the twin challenges of science (i.e., Charles Darwin and the theory of evolution) and of critical biblical studies, conservative Protestants elevated the authority of Scripture, claiming that it is both inerrant and infallible. Inerrancy means that the Bible is without error and therefore is literally true. The belief that no mistakes or problems exist in the Good Book is related to the concept of infallibility, which means that the Bible is never wrong; it is a sure, reliable, and dependable guide.

The response to the threat of science and biblical criticism was not unique to Protestants. In 1869–70, the first Vatican Council of the Catholic Church adopted the doctrine of papal infallibility. This means that when the pope makes a pronouncement on issues of faith and morals *ex cathedra*—that is, from his official chair—then that doctrine is without error. It is no coincidence that the Protestant idea of scriptural inerrancy and the Catholic idea of papal infallibility arose at the same time in history. Both are attempts to reestablish the religious authority that modern science had undermined.

The term "fundamentalism" itself comes from a series of pamphlets called *The Fundamentals*, which were published in the early twentieth century. These pamphlets sought to teach correct Christian doctrine. They questioned or refuted liberal attempts to reconcile Christianity with modernity. One of the writers for *The Fundamentals*, J. Gresham Machen, went so far as to say that liberal Christians were not Christian at all, and that liberalism was an entirely different religion.

This initial phase of fundamentalism crashed to an end as a result of the Scopes Trial in 1925. John Scopes was arrested, tried, and convicted of teaching the theory of evolution in his high school biology class in Dayton, Tennessee. A celebrated trial was argued by Clarence Darrow, for the defense, and William Jennings Bryan—America's foremost spokesperson for fundamentalism at the time—for the prosecution. Although Bryan and the fundamentalists won the day, the trial discredited their cause by exposing fundamentalist beliefs to public ridicule and contempt. Fundamentalists—who at that time were indeed antimodern in the sense that they opposed compromising their religion with science—retreated from public scrutiny and essentially withdrew from the impure and corrupt society surrounding them. Although fundamentalists continued to exist, their involvement in the world outside church doors was somewhat limited.

A second phase began in the 1970s, when fundamentalists emerged from their self-imposed exile to participate in the political process in an active, and even aggressive, manner. The roots of this reemergence grew out of dissatisfaction with the U.S. Supreme Court decision on school prayer in 1962 and swelled with the court's decision on legalized abortion in 1973. Fundamentalists joined evangelical Protestants to help elect Jimmy Carter president in 1976. Although Carter was himself an evangelical—that is, a moderate Christian who was able to reconcile modern scientific findings with his biblical beliefs—his liberal social policies quickly disenchanted the most conservative supporters. Conservative political strategists, along with fundamentalist Christians, saw an opportunity to mobilize large numbers of conservative voters in support of social causes.

Jerry Falwell, the pastor of Liberty Baptist Church in Lynchburg, Virginia, was a key player in the mobilization. In 1979 he formed the Moral Majority to organize a number of different types of religious conservatives behind common causes: against abortion, for school prayer, and so on. Funded by the political right wing, the group energized traditionally apolitical individuals and encouraged them to get involved in the political process—which they did in large numbers. Conservative voters helped elect Ronald Reagan to the presidency in 1980 and again in 1984. They elected thousands of candidates to state and local offices, where they either gained control of, or found a voice on, school boards, city councils, and state legislatures. The Moral Majority had lasted for less than a decade, however, when it became clear to the religious constituency that working within the political process meant compromise on deeply held principles and beliefs. Reagan had disappointed conservatives with his lack of effort in support of a school prayer amendment to the Constitution and had outraged them with his appointment of Sandra Day O'Connor—pro-choice on abortion—to the Supreme Court. The failed presidential campaign of religious broadcaster Pat Robertson in 1988 seemed to mark a watershed, and in 1989 a newly organized Christian Coalition replaced the interfaith and interdenominational Moral Majority. Christian fundamentalists retrenched at that point, but they did not retreat.

A third phase in the development of fundamentalism had already started outside the United States, but it first came to international attention with the Islamic Revolution in Iran in 1979. A turn to reactionary forms of Islam was occurring throughout the Muslim world in the 1960s and 1970s, fueled by anti-Western and anti-imperialistic sentiment. Western observers called these movements "fundamentalist" and their adherents "Islamic fundamentalists," but there are problems with this terminology. Islamic scholars object to the word "fundamentalism" because it referred to a Christian rather than a Muslim phenomenon. Moreover, unlike their Christian counterparts, Muslim clerics were not reading their own holy texts literally. Instead, lay Islamists were the ones searching the Qur'an for passages to support their political aims and programs.

Islamists who want to promote Islamic culture and civilization, however, might well fit into a broad definition of fundamentalism provided by Martin E. Marty and R. Scott Appleby, two scholars of religion: "Fundamentalism has appeared as a tendency, a habit of mind . . . which manifests itself as a strategy, or set of strategies, by which beleaguered believers attempt to preserve their distinctive identity as a people or group."[3] This outlook can be seen from a survey of thirty-five incarcerated Middle Eastern terrorists—including twenty-one Islamic terrorists representing Hamas, Islamic Jihad, and Hezbollah—who indicated that they all felt victimized, and that they despaired about the future of their people.[4]

Fundamentalism today, then, is clearly not a monolithic movement.[5] It is instead diffuse and multifaceted. Now that some Muslims, and even a few Hindus and ultra-Orthodox Jews, are called fundamentalist, the term has outgrown its Christian connotations. It may outgrow its usefulness as well if we indiscriminately call all religious conservative fundamentalists. Certainly fundamentalists do not identify themselves in this way: it is only outsiders who call specific movements and their adherents fundamentalist.

Looking closely at two key elements of fundamentalism may help to clarify what is common to the many groups called fundamentalist today. These elements are, first, their critique of modernity; and second, their paradoxical appropriation of modernity to create alternative institutions. In other words, fundamentalists use the presuppositions of modern science and technology, of contemporary politics and economics, to redirect those same presuppositions to a divine purpose.

WHY FUNDAMENTALISTS CRITICIZE MODERNITY

Fundamentalists do not hate modernity or modern society. They embrace many aspects of contemporary life, including technology, global and capitalist economics, and a certain universalism. But there are a number of aspects of modernity that fundamentalists oppose.

The hypersexualization of society and culture alarms fundamentalists of all faiths. They believe that the media's ubiquitous use of sex to sell products, promote programs, and engage audiences objectifies both women and men. Related to the sexualization of media and society are the problems of narcissism, self-indulgence, and excessive individualism. Fundamentalists condemn the greed and self-centeredness evidenced by national figures: from sports stars and media celebrities, to corporate executives and public officials.

Fundamentalists claim that there is a general moral decline in contemporary life, largely due to the privatization of religion. God has been banished from the public schools and the public square, they argue, and the result is the breakdown of the family, the basic unit of society and the source of moral education and religious values. This disintegration can be seen in the rise in teenage pregnancies, abortions, single-parent households, and children who are neglected in a variety of ways, and in the decline of male authority as fathers and providers. As a result, fundamentalists have organized around key family issues: abortion, the Equal Rights Amendment, gay marriage, and sex education.

Globalization is also regarded with suspicion by Christian funda-mentalists. A typical story from *Awake!* the popular magazine published by the Watchtower Bible and Tract Society of the Jehovah's Witnesses, asks the rhetorical question: "Globalization: Curse or Cure?" The story notes that globalization has increased the gap between rich and poor and that "human rights and social equity have lagged far behind technical and material progress." The Jehovah's Witnesses believe that the only globalization that will work is one that hinges on the ethical standards preached by Jesus Christ, a theme repeated in Witness literature designed for the masses.

The critique of modernity also exists outside the United States in post-colonial nation-states that see the power and privilege of the United States in the world and either resent or desire it. People in the countries of the Middle East, Asia, and Africa share many of the same criticisms as American fundamentalists of the destructive nature of globalization: individualism, consumerism, sexual objectification. For example, the founder of the Muslim Brotherhood—an Islamist group that wanted the "re-Islamization" of Egypt—called upon Muslims to bring humanity the "Truth," and to free them from slavery to materialism.[6] Hassan al Banna (1906–49) exhorted Muslims to attack the "collective manifestations of immorality," which included sexual immorality and drinking alcohol.

In short, fundamentalists worldwide decry the negative side effects of modernity. Many believe that the cure for underdevelopment—the progress implicit in globalization and modernization—may be worse than the illness.

ALTERNATIVE INSTITUTIONS

The critique of the moral degeneration that has resulted from modern tolerance for deviance, and from the loss of social and/or divine controls, has not discouraged fundamentalists from enjoying the benefits of modern media technology, including e-mail and CNN. Nor have fundamentalists resisted using implements of modern warfare, from plastic explosives to nuclear devices. As a result, fundamentalists have developed alternative institutions and organizations that rely on current technology and that reshape mass culture. This is not a separation from society, but rather is the creation of an alternative society that celebrates fundamentalist religious and social values.

Christian fundamentalists in the United States have created a marketplace in which books, videotapes, and products like bumper stickers and breath mints—all with religious themes—are sold in Christian specialty stores. The marketplace extends to mass media, including radio and television stations, and record companies specializing in religious music designed to appeal to young people. A large Christian readers' niche is apparent in the best-selling "Left Behind" series by Jerry Jenkins and Tim LaHaye. Dozens of books, videos, children books, and related shirts, caps, and other spin-offs from the series show how profitable the fundamentalist vision of end times can be.

Fundamentalists also have their own schools and housing developments, their own real estate companies and brokerage firms. They have developed a number of faith-based nonprofit organizations, as have mainstream religious groups, but with a difference. These nonprofits emphasize a personal conversion to Christ as the major solution to various social problems, such as drug addiction or unemployment. Fundamentalists have established a variety of religious institutions: from "house churches," in which small groups gather for Bible study and political action, to "mega-churches" and "para-churches," in which thousands of people gather for weekly services, revivals, and a variety of social services such as marriage counseling, sports leagues, and childcare. It is important to note that not all conservative Christians are fundamentalists. Many people who take advantage of these Christian alternatives are neither fundamentalist nor Christian. This fact merely underlines the tremendous impact that some extremist groups are having on the mainstream.

Like their American counterparts, non-Christian fundamentalists have established alternative institutions. The Haredim in Israel, for example, are Orthodox Jews who believe that they must live by Torah alone. In order to do this, the Haredim have created their own enclaves, with separate schools that teach only the basics of reading and arithmetic and that focus on study of Torah and Talmud. They strictly observe the Sabbath and harshly punish violators. They may throw rocks at people driving cars on the Sabbath or even block traffic.[7] For the most part, however, the Haredim live in their own little world, removed from what they see as the immorality and depravity of the secular state of Israel. Their alternative institutions tend to be separatist and thus most resemble the earliest Christian fundamentalist movements.

The Muslim Brotherhood provides a similar example of a group building religious alternatives to secular society. Founded in Egypt in the 1930s and 1940s, the movement established a network of new mosques, schools, sports clubs, factories, and service providers that distributed free meals to the poor and needy. The idea behind the brotherhood was to create an alternative to the secularization of Egypt that was occurring under political leaders who were attempting to modernize the country. Today the Muslim Brotherhood has expanded throughout the world and has grown increasingly militant and, in some cases, violent.[8]

Another visible alternative to Western-style modernism is evident in the clothing adopted by Muslim women. When Muslim women wear the veil, they are resisting the Western definition of feminism. During the Islamic revolutionary period in Iran in the 1980s, many women adopted *hijab* as a way of rejecting Western imperialism. For some, the veil is the symbol of liberation and independence—liberation from Western-style political systems and values, that is. Wearing Western dress would indicate subservience and submission to the values of a foreign culture. Ironically, wearing *hijab* is anti-imperialist, an extremely modern political position.

Two facets of modernity especially illuminate the rise of fundamentalist alternative institutions. The first is the tendency toward classification and categorization, that is, dependence on science, or more specifically, on scientific discovery and method.[9] The second is the tendency of modernity toward universalizing narratives, that is, constructing stories that attempt to explain things for everyone, as though all humans were alike. Those narratives may state that all human beings are created equal, or they may assert that men and women were created with specific gender-defined roles. Modernists operating within the fundamentalist worldview behave like their liberal counterparts in these two respects. Where they differ is on core beliefs and values.

The tendency toward dependence on science—albeit a science directed by religious values—as well as the tendency toward universalizing narratives exist in the alternative institutions that have arisen. The various fundamentalist movements are not merely reactions to modernity, but rather are embedded within modernity. Fundamentalists take a modern stance to attack liberal forms of modernity. Using the mass media and all the resources of modern science and technology, contemporary fundamentalists seek to impose a universal narrative on the world, whether it is the Islamic idea of *ummah* (the universal community of the faithful), or the Christian idea of the Lordship of Christ. These alternatives stand against the prevailing modern trust in science and reason, which distrusts religious faith and belief.

We live today within the presupposition that science can address almost every question and problem, from biological to psychological. Certainly the scientific method has influenced society at all levels, especially in universities, where research and debate follows the protocols required by science and reason. We can call this faith in the reliability of reason "scientism": the belief that the scientific method can and ultimately will answer all our questions. Scientism requires a faith in reason and in the rationality of human beings. As a worldview, it also demands certainty and is unhappy with ambiguity.

Not surprisingly, scientists and fundamentalists have a lot in common. Both are looking for certainty in an uncertain world. Both seek particular truths. Both reject the language of myth, metaphor, and figure. The literalism of fundamentalists is not so very different from the literalism of scientists: if it's not factual, it has no meaning. Scripture must be historically, literally, and factually true to satisfy fundamentalists. God created the world in six, 24-hour days, say Christian fundamentalists. God wrote on two stone tablets and gave them to Moses, say Jewish fundamentalists. God spoke directly to Muhammad through the angel Gabriel, and Muhammad accurately remembered and recited God's words, say Muslim fundamentalists. Scientists dismiss the validity of Scripture on exactly the same grounds: they are not satisfied unless something is historically, literally, and factually true.

HOW FUNDAMENTALISTS USE MODERNITY

While differences exist among and between fundamentalists, most share the modern affinity for the scientific method and adopt the modern idea of universalizing narratives. From the Institute for Creation Research, to religious broadcasters and political organizations, to Web sites on the Internet, fundamentalism reflects a "modern" mindset.

The Institute for Creation Research is a think tank in San Diego which promotes creation science as an alternative to the "uniformitarian dogmatists" who teach evolution in public schools. The institute is Christian and bases its theology on the creation and redemption story in the Bible, but it also attempts to use science to show that what the Bible says about the universe and creation is factually accurate. The institute has on the premises a museum that marries science and the Bible in an informative and educational way. The museum presents a six-day creation and a six-thousand-year-old earth, claiming that the earth's geologic features were fashioned rapidly, by catastrophic processes. Graphic displays indicate that mutation and natural selection could not have brought about the present complexity of living organisms.

What is most interesting about the museum is not its attempt to reconcile contemporary science with the Bible but the questions the researchers from ICR raise about current scientific assumptions. They note the weaknesses in a number of theories, from the big bang creation, to stair-step, or punctuated, evolution. In other words, they attempt to use science—their science—to challenge the dominant scientific explanations. For example, the tremendous explosions and volcanic eruptions of Mount St. Helens in 1980 provided ICR researchers with the proof they needed to say that the Grand Canyon could have been formed in a matter of years, rather than over eons.[10]

By the end of the nineteenth century, religion had to be rational to be taken seriously.[11] It had to respond to modernity in one way or another. Using science against science is a modern and rational thing to do. The creationists at ICR could have rejected science entirely and adopted the approach: "God said it, I believe it, that settles it." Instead, ICR is engaging in the debate by poking holes in the weakest areas of our current assumptions. It is scientism at its best—or worst. Arguing that the diversity in the universe is an argument for a creator God, one of the displays at the museum asserts: "It is more reasonable to believe that God created every star with its own characteristics, just as He has created billions of human beings, each one different from all others." While we might disagree over what is and is not reasonable, the fact that the creationists are using reason—rather than faith or belief—demonstrates their commitment to, and dependence on, the very presuppositions they attempt to undermine.

Although the museum at ICR is the most visible part of the Institute's program, it may well be the smallest part. ICR has a national radio ministry that airs "science, scripture, and salvation" on dozens of radio stations around the country. It also offers advanced degrees in science, awarding the Master of Science in astro/geophysics, biology, geology, and science education. These programs are aimed at primary and secondary school science teachers and provide participants the "opportunity to break away from current scientific dogma and think creatively," according to a promotional brochure. "ICR Graduate School pushes past the bias of humanistic evolutionary dominance, and explores alternatives informed by creation thinking." ICR also offers "creation tours" to the Galapagos Islands and to Yellowstone National Park. In addition, ICR sponsors research that will support its creationist perspective, especially studies that corroborate or authenticate biblical accounts of natural history, such as a worldwide flood.

Pat Robertson and other Christian broadcasters provide another example of how fundamentalists are using modern methods to communicate their message. Robertson is a minister in the Assemblies of God, and founder of the 700 Club and the Christian Broadcasting Network. His Web site depicts him as a friendly, folksy multimillionaire whose favorite hobby is starting up corporations (http://www.patrobertson.com). Although he is not the first Christian broadcaster, Robertson is certainly one of the most successful. His telecommunications network produces, markets, and distributes programs through a combination of vertical integration and converged technologies, supported by advertising commercial products.

In 1997 Pat Robertson sold his cable outlet, *The Family Channel*, to media mogul Rupert Murdoch for $1.9 billion. The corporation was renamed International Family Entertainment, or IFE; the channel was renamed *Fox Family Channel*; and Robertson remained chairman of the board, while his son Tim Robertson stayed on as director and CEO of IFE. As part of the basic cable package, IFE reaches 95 percent of all cable households and 63 percent of all television households.[12]

What the corporate story of IFE tells us is that, far from being separatist or isolationist, fundamentalism and its promotion of a particular type of family values is both popular and lucrative—at least for people like Pat Robertson and his family. The entire subculture of Christian media presents an alternative vision of modernity and its values. At the same time, it functions well within the values, considerations, and requirements of modern technology and capitalism. Indeed, Christian fundamentalists part company with Jewish and Muslim fundamentalists over the issue of capitalism, since the latter see it as a major part of the problem of globalization and Western-style democracy.

Another successful Christian broadcaster is Bud Paxson, the cofounder of the *Home Shopping Network*. Paxson founded *PAX-TV* in 1998 to counter the "moral manure" found on commercial TV after he received a religious revelation in a Las Vegas hotel room.[13] The network airs reruns of family favorites like *Dr. Quinn, Medicine Woman*, *Highway to Heaven*, and *Eight is Enough*, as well as original programming like *Woman's Day with Phyllis George*. Unlike the *Fox Family Channel*, *PAX-TV* is more overtly sectarian, promoting a Christian message throughout the day. But first things first: five hours of infomercials air every morning on *PAX-TV*, direct from the *Home Shopping Network*.

While the original fundamentalists may have withdrawn from political activity, the new fundamentalists are well-organized activists who are determined to bring government policies into conformity with their vision of modern society. Perhaps most indicative of its recognition of how politics work in this country is the Traditional Values Coalition, a religious lobbying organization which encourages political activism among its members. It is necessary to Christianize the country through political action, and TVC pursues this goal. Working within the system, it endorses a number of extremely conservative political causes. Its Web site has a link to the site Conservative Petitions Dot-Com, which promotes a number of conservative issues (http://www.conservativepetitions.com). The top five petitions on the site during July 2003, for example, included support for a school prayer amendment; for a $1000 educational tax credit for parents with school-age children; and for Senator Rick Santorum, who had compared homosexuality to bestiality, pedophilia, polygamy, and incest. This last petition commended the Republican's strong stand for family values and berated Democratic Senator John Kerry for "deceitfully" comparing homosexuals' push for "special rights" with the black struggle for "civil rights." Antigay and anti-Muslim language permeate these and other petitions.

Two final examples of the fundamentalist appropriation of modern techniques and devices come from the Middle East, and the world of Jewish and Muslim extremists. Two Web sites demonstrate both the sophistication of technological use and the explicit commitment to using technology to advance the cause. A Jewish group called the Temple Mount Faithful seeks to rebuild the temple in Jerusalem. Their Web site calls upon Jews worldwide to support this religious—but extremely political effort (http://www.temple-mountfaithful.org). Video and audio clips at the site provide graphic evidence of the sophisticated use of current technology. The audio for the song "Your Enemies Are My Enemies," is available on the site, and visitors to the site can also download a music video for the song:

Your enemies are my enemies.
Your foe is my foe.
You are the One who can set me free.
Deliver Your servant . . .

Search Your Land and deliver her.
Make us warriors in Your Kingdom.
Search Your Land and deliver her.
Make us warriors in Your Kingdom.

Make Us Warriors In Your Kingdom.
Deliver Your Holy Hill.

While not an explicitly fundamentalist site, the Islamic World Web site does state that science and technology will combine to make a "fully and truly Islamic World" possible within a generation (http://www.islamic-world.net/). The site's authors say they will use the most "sophisticated information technology" to disseminate knowledge of Islam. Included in a clear statement of plans, the group says it will "utilize the motivational and educational potential of the Internet" to empower and join together the entire Muslim *ummah*, or community of the faithful. The plans will:

- Encourage the wide use of modern knowledge and technology by Muslims on behalf of Islam.
- Use powerful motivational techniques from the social sciences to encourage Muslims to unite and participate in the creation of a fully and truly Islamic world.
- . . . [S]how how modern science and its philosophical implications have reached a point where they are consistent in all ways with the revealed truths and essence of Islam.

The Web site explicitly states that it hopes to unite Muslims to fight against the "devastating power of the onrushing wave of secular materialism poised to crush the Islamic way of life."

SUMMARY

Fundamentalism has traveled far from its roots in an isolationist American Protestantism. Elements of fundamentalism appear today in a variety of global religious movements that are using science and technology to universalize their messages and to take them into the mainstream.

There are, of course, many ways in which fundamentalists still remain on the periphery. They believe that they are, in fact, the majority and that their majority views have been marginalized and pushed to the side by evil forces. Those evil forces might be the homosexual lobby, the Great Satan of the

United States, or Arab fanatics. Fundamentalists have a dualistic worldview in which the forces of good battle against the forces of evil. This sense of being embattled affirms their conviction that we are living in a time of crisis, which calls for extreme measures and immediate action. Because they believe that their individual, familial, and collective identity is being threatened, fundamentalists are willing to make a number of great sacrifices on behalf of their ideology. Their justification is based on selective memory of past theological doctrines that many in the modern world would deny.

Will Christian, Muslim, Hindu, or other religious extremists be successful in extending their vision throughout society and the world? Fundamentalists view current events and politics as the battleground between God and Satan—between good and evil—and believe that God is on their side. Their sophisticated use of technology may give fundamentalists a competitive edge over their opponents in the battle for hearts and minds.

4: VIEW FROM THE NEWS DESK

Modernity and Fundamentalism in Mongolia

Corey Flintoff

Six months in Mongolia is either way too much or not nearly enough. I was there from June through December of 2001. Much of my work consisted of teaching basic journalism and broadcasting at small radio stations in dusty provincial towns. I learned how the legacy of totalitarian government can subvert the practice of journalism long after the government itself is gone.

I found that reporters who spent the formative parts of their careers in a climate of repression had a hard time adopting the international journalistic standards of independence, enterprise, and accuracy. They stuck to the practices of totalitarian reporting as true believers might cling to the rituals of a failed religion, mocking themselves even as they did so. The experience showed me how difficult it can be to introduce modern standards of journalism in areas where repressive regimes or religions have held sway. It may foreshadow the problems of establishing independent journalism in Iraq and Afghanistan, but it also points to some directions that journalists can take toward independence.

I had a lot of help from the Mongolian Foundation for Open Society (the Soros Foundation), and from the Gobi Initiative, an assistance program for nomadic herders and small business people funded by USAID. Both of these organizations have helped fund radio stations in rural areas with a view to promoting civic responsibility and grass-roots capitalism. They've achieved some success in towns such as Dalanzadgad, in the south Gobi Desert, and in Khovd, in far western Mongolia. Both places have FM radio stations that are the equivalent of community licensees in the United States. They are controlled by community boards and are independent of the local government.

It may be well to set the scene here, to talk about what's meant by expressions such as "rural" and "town" in a country where more than half the population still gets around on horseback. Mongolia is a country of about 2.4 million people. Much of the land is desert and steppe, with little in the way of resources, other than the sparse grass that supports herding families and their livestock. A typical provincial town has fewer than 30,000 residents, many of whom live in felt tents clustered around a few administrative buildings, a small hospital, some apartment blocks and schools. Few people have telephones, and newspapers from the capital are usually a day or two old, so radio is important.

Mongolia's primary religion, Tibetan Buddhism, was ruthlessly suppressed under the Communist regime. During the 1930s, most of the nation's Buddhist monasteries were razed, and tens of thousands of monks were slaughtered because they refused to abandon their beliefs. Communism was proffered as a scientific and practical replacement for religion, and the communications media were essential for spreading its message. I think that part of the reluctance of older Mongolian journalists to abandon the old ways is because the ideology they supported had much of the force of religion in their lives. Several people told me that it wasn't Communism that failed; the failure was theirs. They believed that they had failed to put enough of their faith, intelligence, and energy into the task of making Communism work.

The most effective radio stations were those with young staff members who hadn't worked in journalism or broadcasting during the Communist era. They saw their work as public service, whether they were giving the all-important weather forecasts or challenging the way local government was run. The station in Dalanzadgad actually changed the local economy by broadcasting the daily market prices for cashmere wool and other animal commodities in Ulaanbaatar and Beijing. Before the price reports, local herders were at the mercy of the traders because they didn't know the market value of their products.

At the station in Khovd, on the edge of the western mountains, my students succeeded in making their town government more responsive to citizens by reporting on local problems. In one case, people were seriously injuring themselves by falling into unmarked utility trenches. The town had no street lights, and the administration never bothered to announce when it would be digging up the streets for utility work. Unmarked trenches just appeared. My young reporters did several stories on the problem, including a hospital interview with an 8-year-old who broke his arm in a fall. The reports triggered a public protest and forced the town officials to adopt basic safety procedures. It should be noted that the officials weren't easily won over; the local governor frequently threatened to cut off the station's electricity, but they could never muster the political support to get away with it.

These small radio stations have not yet gained the stability or experience to do the kind of investigative reporting that might expose government or business corruption, but they're gradually building their credibility and raising the expectations of their listeners.

The modern nation of Mongolia was created after the Communist revolution in 1921. Russian Bolsheviks fought side-by-side with the "Red" Mongols, and because of that, Mongolia was always dear to the Russian heart. The Russians were anxious to make sure that Mongolia's Communist regime appeared successful, even if that meant providing big subsidies for Mongolian industries, health facilities, and schools.

Here's a story I heard in the rusting industrial town of Dharhan. It takes place during the Communist era, when some Russian dignitaries were getting a tour of the town from the head of the local Party committee. "Over there," says the local apparatchik, "is the power plant that was built for us by our comrades from East Germany. Next to that is the flour mill that was built for us by our comrades from Ukraine. There you see the hospital that was built by our comrades from Hungary, and beyond that is the technical school built by our comrades from Bulgaria." Finally the Russians interrupt their tour guide. "But comrade," they ask, "what are the Mongols building?" The local Party leader smiles proudly. "We are building Socialism."

One important result of this subsidized life was that Mongols had a very-high rate of literacy (more than 90 percent) for an essentially rural society. Most educated Mongols spoke Russian, and many had studied in Russia, Ukraine, and eastern Europe. Even nomadic herders who lived in felt yurts without electricity and running water were literate and were great consumers of information, from newspapers and books to state-run broadcasting.

The Soviet government underwrote a powerful broadcasting system, centered in Ulaanbaatar, the capital city, and relayed all over the country by regional transmitters. This system was so well-engineered and solidly built that it still functions, more than a dozen years after the withdrawal of Soviet support. The national broadcasting company, Mongol Radio and Television, still survives and produces daily programming. The current government has pledged to make the system independent, but it has yet to give up control.

Mongol Radio was wired directly into buildings in provincial towns. You can still see the speakers on the walls of people's apartments. They're a powerful symbol of totalitarian radio, because they have only one knob, a volume control. Since there was no choice of stations, there was no need for a tuning knob. I suppose if they were a *perfect* symbol of totalitarian radio, there'd be no volume control, either.

The totalitarian model still persists in parts of Mongolia, especially in the so-called "Red" provinces of the southwest and the west, where former Communist political machines still hold power. I visited a radio station in Altai, in the southwest Gobi, where the local party boss appointed the station manager. That worthy happened to be a well-connected trader in cashmere, the luxurious wool of Mongolian goats. The Gobi Initiative, which set up the network for cashmere price information, was concerned that the station frequently failed to broadcast the market prices, especially at those times of year when local herders were most likely to sell their wool.

Although the station was fully staffed, it produced only two hours of local programming each week. Most of the time it simply repeated the programming of Mongol Radio. I worked with the station's four reporters, men in their mid-50s who'd learned their craft under Communism and had no interest in doing things any other way. They read the local government's news releases in authoritative voices, they droned through pages of statistics on agriculture production, and they devoted a lot of time to speeches by local officials. Most of the day, we sat around their battered studio, where they smoked incessantly and cracked jokes about the town's politicians. The reporters had worked out a system whereby they took turns producing each week's news programming, leaving themselves more free time to pursue other activities that supplemented their meager salaries. One was a musician and songwriter. The others seemed to be involved in small-time trading in the town's open market. They were masters at doing what people in totalitarian states do best: evading the authorities.

On my second morning, as I came into the station, one of the reporters informed me that a village mayor had been carried off by a *yeti*. The yeti is a hairy, man-like creature that apparently originated in Tibetan folklore. It's best known in the supermarket tabloids as "the abominable snowman."

The story had it that the mayor had been riding through the desert in a Russian jeep with some friends and that he'd been snatched when he stopped briefly to relieve himself by the side of the road. This was a cause for some hilarity in the newsroom, but the reporters tracked this story more avidly than anything they'd done in months. Most of their information was gleaned from calls to the single phone in the village where the missing man was mayor, although a second-hand version came from a desert trucker who'd passed through the village on his way from the Chinese border.

By noon we had learned that the mayor in question was very drunk at the time of the incident, as were his companions. Nevertheless, the companions said they searched for him diligently when he vanished, and could only conclude that he'd been snatched by a yeti. By evening, the reporters had learned that the mayor was, in fact, so drunk that he had fallen down in the sagebrush and passed out while he was on his little errand. His companions were so drunk they couldn't see him, so they made up the yeti story and drove home. The mayor wasn't recovered until the following day, when his companions retraced their steps and found him, pretty much where they'd left him, and in remarkably good shape, considering the circumstances.

Apart from the comic aspects, which the Mongol reporters thoroughly appreciated, there were at least a half-dozen angles from which this story might have been usefully reported, not the least of which were drunken driving, criminal negligence, and misuse of a government vehicle. My colleagues at the station did everything but report this story, because that's what news people did in totalitarian days. They didn't report. They repeated. They passed on what they were told to pass on, and everything else was just jokes and gossip.

When we discussed this story later, the reporters justified their lack of action in several ways. On the one hand, they said that since the mayor was recovered and there was no harm done, the matter was trivial and shouldn't have been reported. Although the story involved malfeasance, they maintained that reporting it would undermine the authority of government. To the suggestion that perhaps the authority of some government officials should be undermined, they replied that proper respect for the government was more important than the follies of individual office holders. At no point did the reporters suggest that they feared that they'd lose their jobs or get into other trouble because of covering the story, and I had the impression that they really were acting on their own. Although these men mocked the local power structure in private, they saw themselves as part of it and believed they had a stake in upholding it.

When all was said and done, I didn't change anyone's mind at that station. I did obtain copies of several of the station's news programs, after telling the reporters that I intended to use them as examples in future teaching situations. I didn't disguise the fact that I didn't consider them good examples, but my hosts seemed to feel that their work would stand up to scrutiny from their colleagues in other parts of the country. In fact, the reception it got was overwhelmingly negative among young staffers at independent stations. They perceived it as old-style Communist broadcasting, and it prompted many good discussions about ways to break away from that mold. The station eventually lost the financial support of the Gobi Initiative, in part because of its failure to report timely market prices for cashmere.

The progress that's being made toward independent news media in Mongolia appears to be happening outside the former state-run news organizations. Mongol Radio and Television are still organs of the government. Independent newspapers are struggling but surviving in the capital, though they have relatively little impact in the provinces. Independent television has gained a foothold in Ulaanbaatar but doesn't have the resources to extend its reach around the rest of the country. Independent radio is the only medium that's currently having much success in the countryside, but its viability will depend on whether it can build an advertising base and/or audience support in a region where most people are living near the subsistence level.

Cash flow is the single biggest concern of independent radio stations in Mongolia. They can expect only limited support from the aid organizations that helped them get established, and they must start supporting themselves. Salaries for radio journalists are very low. An announcer/reporter in Dalanzadgad normally works seven days a week for the equivalent of 25 to 35 dollars a month—not a good salary, even by Mongolian standards. The shortest joke in Mongolian is "I live on my salary," because almost no one can afford to do such a thing. Almost everyone is forced to work other jobs, and that exposes journalists to all sorts of potential temptations and conflicts of interest.

Mongolia can move toward the kind of independent, public service media that help support democracy, but the process is apt to be a slow one. I believe that simply privatizing the former state-run media is not the answer. I saw a lot of dead wood at those organizations: staffers who are still attached to the old beliefs, inappropriate relationships with the government, and disputes over former state property. It's easier to start from scratch with new operations and new personnel. Even then, independent news outlets will need time to educate themselves and their audiences about what people in a free society can expect from their governments, civic institutions, and businesses. They'll have to build credible reputations for honesty and impartiality. And they'll have to support themselves, either as businesses or nonprofit organizations, in such a way that they won't be vulnerable to financial pressures. My experience of the Mongols is that they are a resilient, resourceful, hardworking people with a great fund of national pride and an abiding sense of humor. I think they can do it.

Chapter 5

Biblical Prophecy and Foreign Policy

Paul S. Boyer

Does the Bible foretell a nuclear World War III, a regime change in Iraq, Israel's vast future expansion, and the rebuilding of the Jewish temple on a site sacred to Muslims? Do divinely inspired scriptures prophesy a future economic and political dictatorship that will control the entire globe? Is the United Nations the forerunner of this new world order? Is Islam an evil religion whose destruction has been foreordained by God himself?

Millions of Americans at the beginning of the twenty-first century answer all these questions with a resounding yes. For many Bible prophecy believers, President George W. Bush's go-it-alone foreign policy, hostility to the United Nations, suspicion of Europe, preemptive war in Iraq, and tacit acceptance of the expansionist policies of the extreme right-wing in Israeli politics are not simply actions in the national self-interest or an extension of the war on terrorism, but are part of an unfolding divine plan. Without close attention to the prophetic scenario embraced by millions of American citizens, the current U.S. political climate cannot be fully understood.

PROPHETIC BELIEF IN CONTEMPORARY AMERICA:
PERVASIVENESS AND KEY THEMES

Abundant evidence makes clear that millions of Americans—upwards of 40 percent, according to opinion polls—believe that Bible prophecies detail a specific sequence of end-time events. The most rapidly growing sector of American Protestantism from the 1970s through the early twenty-first century has been evangelical, fundamentalist, and Pentecostal denominations such as the Assemblies of God, along with burgeoning community churches and fellowships in which biblical literalism and an intense interest in Bible prophecy loom large. In the nation's largest Protestant denomination, the sixteen-million-member Southern Baptist Convention, anticipation of the imminent second coming of Jesus Christ after a period of growing wickedness is a bedrock belief. Religious bodies such as the Seventh-day Adventist Church, Jehovah's Witnesses, and the Church of Jesus Christ of Latter Day Saints (Mormons) offer particular prophetic interpretations of the end times.[1]

The most popular prophetic system in contemporary America, premillennial dispensationalism, was formulated by the nineteenth-century British churchman John Darby (1800–82), a founder of the sect known as the Plymouth Brethren. An avid student of the Bible, Darby derived his end-time scheme by assembling and arranging prophetic and apocalyptic passages found throughout the King James Bible, including the books of Daniel, Isaiah, and Ezekiel in the Old Testament; and, in the New Testament, the Gospels, the Pauline letters, and above all, Revelation, or the Apocalypse of John, with its memorable evocation of a final eschatological confrontation between the forces of good and evil, the destruction of the wicked, and the ultimate triumph of the righteous.[2]

According to Darby's system, a series of last-day signs will signal the approaching end of the present epoch, or dispensation, which he called the Church Age. These signs include wars, rampant wickedness, bizarre natural phenomena, and the emergence of an anti-Christian world system. This bleak prospect derives in part from Jesus' answer to his disciples, as recorded in Mark 13 (with variants in the other gospels), when they asked what signs would alert people that the end was near. Jesus responded with a grim catalog of false prophets, rampant immorality, and "wars and rumors of wars," together with earthquakes, falling stars, and other disruptions in the natural order. As in the days of Noah (when God sent a flood that destroyed nearly all creatures on earth because of human wickedness), Jesus says, "so also shall the coming of the Son of man be." But the end will also come amid fervent missionary activity, Jesus adds, "when the gospel must first be published among all nations" (Mark 13:7-10, 28; Matt 24:37-39).

According to this interpretive scheme, the end stage of human history will also witness the return of the Jews to the land promised by God to Abraham, Isaac, Jacob, and their descendants.[3] The Zionist movement that arose in the

1890s (strongly supported by Christian prophecy believers), Israel's founding in 1948, and the Israeli army's capture of Jerusalem's Old City in 1967 were all interpreted by successive generations of prophecy believers as key end-time signs.

As the Jews reestablish themselves in the Promised Land, dispensationalists believe, its borders will expand to the boundaries specified in Genesis 15:18: from "the river of Egypt" to the Euphrates. Some biblical interpreters believe "the river of Egypt" refers to the Nile; others, to a smaller river, the Wadi-el-Arish, separating the Sinai Peninsula from Egypt. Whatever the precise western demarcation line, the boundaries of future Israel as foretold in Scripture will clearly be vast, encompassing not only the West Bank and Gaza, but all or parts of present-day Lebanon, Jordan, Syria, Iraq, Kuwait, Saudi Arabia, and possibly Egypt.

Dispensationalists also believe that in the last days the Jewish temple in Jerusalem, sacked by the Romans in A.D. 70, will be rebuilt. This belief is based on prophecies that when the Messiah comes, he will reign in a restored temple. In the Christian version, the Messiah is Jesus Christ, who, upon his triumphal return, will be hailed by Jews as the promised one and will reign for a thousand years in the rebuilt temple (Rev 20:6). For Orthodox Jews, the Messiah is yet to appear. Both groups thus anticipate the restoration of the temple, though they differ on who will occupy it. Dispensationalists are thus deeply interested in, and supportive of, ultra-Orthodox Jewish groups in Jerusalem such as the Temple Mount Foundation that are actively preparing for the rebuilding of the temple and the revival of ancient rituals.

Temple Mount, of course, is also sacred to Muslims as Al-Haram al-Sharif, or Noble Sanctuary, on which are situated the Mosque of Omar (the so-called Dome of the Rock), from which Mohammed is believed to have ascended to heaven, and the eighth-century Al-Aqsa Mosque. Dispensationalist writings are replete with speculation about how these Islamic shrines may be eliminated to make way for the rebuilt temple. Some writers envision an earthquake; others rather implausibly speculate that the two mosques might be taken apart piece by piece and reassembled in Saudi Arabia. Still others foresee their destruction in a war between Israel and its neighbors. (During the first Persian Gulf War, when Saddam Hussein lobbed missiles toward Jerusalem, some prophecy believers waited with bated breath to see if one of them might strike Temple Mount.)

In Darby's system, the present dispensation will end with the Rapture, when all true believers will join Christ in the air, creating panic and chaos among those left behind.[4] Next comes the Tribulation, mentioned by Jesus in his end-time sermon to the disciples. By complicated calculations involving various time sequences mentioned in the Bible, dispensationalists believe the Tribulation will last for seven years. The specific events of the Tribulation, supposedly foretold in Daniel, Ezekiel, Revelation, and other portions of the

Bible, are particularly important for an understanding of how dispensationalist ideas influence the shaping of U.S. foreign policy.

According to Darby's scenario, the Tribulation will see the rise of a charismatic but satanic figure, the antichrist (1 John 2:18), referred to in Revelation as "the Beast." Arising in Europe, in the lands that once comprised the Roman Empire, antichrist will first rule over a ten-nation European confederacy, a revived Roman Empire, but will soon extend his rule worldwide. An eloquent orator, antichrist will initially present himself as a man committed to world peace and to ending the warfare between Israel and its enemies. But halfway into the Tribulation, he will reveal his demonic purpose as the servant of Satan. Establishing a brutal global dictatorship, he will impose his universal tyranny under the dread sign "666" (Rev 13:18).

Antichrist will also launch a murderous campaign of extermination against the Jews, whom he hates because they are God's chosen people. Dispensationalists see this persecution foretold in Ezekiel 38, in which a mysterious northern ruler, Gog, from "the land of Magog," joined by "Persia, Ethiopia, and Libya," as well as other rather ill-defined groups, invades Israel and wreaks terrible destruction before his army and those of his allies are in turn destroyed by fire from heaven. Citing a passage in Zechariah, some prophecy interpreters predict quite precisely that *two-thirds* of all Jews will perish in this final and most horrendous Holocaust.[5]

The dispensationalist view of the Jews is thus highly ambivalent, not to say schizoid.[6] On one hand, as we have seen, dispensationalists firmly believe that God's promises to Abraham will be literally fulfilled at the end of time, including Israel's expansion to include the vast territory mentioned in Genesis. They also anticipate the restoration of the temple on a site sacred to Muslims. On the other hand, dispensationalists not only foresee a mass slaughter of the Jews by antichrist during the Tribulation, but have also traditionally taught that anti-Semitism and Jewish persecution in the present age, including the Nazi Holocaust, are a part of God's "chastisement" of his chosen but wayward people for their rejection of Jesus as Messiah and their role in his crucifixion. In the past, such views sometimes edged over into overt anti-Semitism. Hal Lindsey's *The Late Great Planet Earth* (1970), a slangy popularization of dispensationalism that became a runaway bestseller, deals with the Holocaust in a section breezily entitled "God's Woodshed."

Historian Yaacov Ariel of the University of North Carolina has summed up this ambivalence concisely:

> Motivated by a literal reading of the Bible, and adhering to the messianic faith, many evangelical Christians view contemporary Jews as heirs to biblical Israel and the object of prophecies about a restored Davidic kingdom in the messianic age. At the same time, evangelical Christians insist that only those persons who are "born again in Christ" can be saved and promised eternal life. As the Jews have not accepted Jesus, they are spiritually and morally deprived. This dualistic view of the Jews

forms the basis for the complex and at times contradictory evangelical views on the Jewish people.[7]

Darby's scenario, like the Book of Revelation on which it was partially based, ends with a series of awesome and cataclysmic events. After the seven-year Tribulation, Jesus Christ—a warrior king on a white horse, wearing a blood-drenched white robe, a flaming sword proceeding from his mouth—returns to earth with the raptured saints. Christ annihilates antichrist's armies at Armageddon (Har-Megiddo, an ancient battle site near Haifa). Antichrist is cast into a lake of fire, his followers are destroyed, and Christ, enthroned at last in the restored temple in Jerusalem, inaugurates his millennial reign of peace and justice. At the end of the thousand years comes the Last Judgment, when Christ, seated on a great white throne, consigns everyone who has ever lived to either heavenly bliss or eternal punishment. The old earth is destroyed, a new heaven and a new earth arise, and human history, having begun in the Garden of Eden, reaches its foreordained end.[8]

This system of prophetic interpretation, which Darby spread through his copious writings and tireless evangelistic tours, including several transatlantic trips, was popularized in the United States by expositors like Cyrus Scofield, whose reference Bible, with notes based on Darby's scheme, became a bestseller and remained so for many decades. More recently, dispensationalism has been promulgated by radio evangelists; paperback popularizers; TV luminaries like Jerry Falwell, Pat Robertson, Jack Van Impe, and James Hagee; and many thousands of fundamentalist and Pentecostal pastors in storefront churches and vast suburban megachurches across the land.

Lindsey's *The Late Great Planet Earth* became the nonfiction bestseller of the 1970s. But even Lindsey's book was eclipsed by the "Left Behind" series, a multivolume fictional treatment of dispensationalism by Tim LaHaye and Jerry B. Jenkins, which sold nearly sixty million copies from the time the first volume appeared in 1995 through 2003. Volume 10, *The Remnant* (2002), topped the *New York Times* bestseller list; Volume 11, *Armageddon*, appeared in April 2003 with an advance printing of 2.5 million copies. In 2003 the publisher of the series, Tyndale House, launched a radio serial based on the novels that aired on 350 stations nationwide.[9] The "Left Behind" novels and hundreds of other prophecy paperbacks are readily available through Internet outlets such as Amazon.com and mass-market distributors, such as Wal-Mart, Barnes & Noble, and Borders.

Prophecy popularizers appear frequently on Christian radio stations and Christian television networks such as Pat Robertson's Christian Broadcasting Network (CBN) and Paul Crouch's Trinity Broadcasting Network (TBN), beaming their message worldwide via communications satellites. Supplementing dispensationalism's global diffusion through the print and electronic media, thousands of fundamentalist and Pentecostal missionaries spread end-time prophecy belief across vast swaths of Latin America and sub-Saharan Africa in the late twentieth century and beyond.

This dispensationalist message has also been promulgated by movies such as *The Omega Code* (1999) and its sequel *Megiddo* (2001); by multimedia organizations such as Midnight Call ministries of Columbia, South Carolina, with its annual prophecy conferences in leading resort hotels, its glossy monthly magazine *Midnight Call*, and a publication program featuring scores of prophecy paperbacks. The prophetic word is also spread by videotapes offering end-time dramatizations and sermons by leading prophecy preachers. The Internet is alive with prophecy Web sites and chat rooms. In 2003 a search for the keywords "Rapture," "antichrist," and "Armageddon" yielded some 17,000 hits.

Rapture kitsch abounds. One can buy comic-book versions of the "Left Behind" novels and "Don't Be Left Behind" T-shirts. Also available are placemats featuring an artist's rendering of the Rapture, complete with crashing cars and airplanes, and a wall display with a videotape behind glass and the message "When the Owner of this Video Suddenly Disappears, Open Immediately and View the Tape Within." The video, of course, is a sermon explaining the Rapture and warning the viewer to reject the antichrist at all costs.

Prophecy expositors have always used the latest communications technologies and visual imagery to convey their message. Hildegard of Bingen (1098–1179) recounted her prophetic visions in manuscripts enlivened by vivid and colorful illustrations. In the Reformation, Protestant artisans produced woodcut broadsides for popular distribution, portraying the pope as the Beast of Revelation. In America, the followers of William Miller, who calculated that Christ would return on October 22, 1843 (later adjusted to 1844), used the new high-speed printing presses of the day to produce a flood of cheap periodicals and charts of King Nebuchadnezzar's dream of a great statue, described in the Book of Daniel, that supposedly offered a key to the cycle of world empires that will culminate in the rule of antichrist. Preachers and popularizers of the late twentieth and early twenty-first centuries simply carried on this long tradition of using the most up-to-date communication technologies to spread the prophetic word.

WORLD EVENTS IN THE LIGHT OF BIBLE PROPHECY: THE COLD WAR AND BEYOND

Prophetic belief merits close attention not only because it is so widespread in contemporary America but also because it plays a significant role in shaping believers' views of world events. During the Cold War, Hal Lindsey and other prophecy gurus focused on the Soviet Union, interpreting Magog, the northern realm mentioned in Ezekiel 38, as Russia. They also found portents of a thermonuclear World War III in prophetic passages foretelling the earth's fiery destruction.[10] From their vantage point of prophetic certainty, they typically dismissed efforts to ease Cold War tensions or to negotiate nuclear arms control treaties as doomed to fail, since Russia's ultimate destruction and indeed the incineration of the earth itself were, in their view, so clearly foretold in Scripture. Typically, too, they viewed the United Nations and other international organizations, multinational corporations, the global economy, and the worldwide communications grid facilitated by satellites and eventually by computers as providing the organizational and technological infrastructure for antichrist's world rule.[11]

After 1990 the end of the Cold War, the collapse of the Soviet Union, and the diminished fears of a global thermonuclear holocaust required a reconfiguration of the end-time scenario. Prophecy interpreters have always shown great ingenuity in adapting to shifting world realities, and once again they rose to the challenge. Playing down (without entirely abandoning) the Russian theme, popularizers in the 1990s and beyond concentrated even more insistently on the rise of an interlocking global system led by the United Nations, the World Bank, the International Monetary Fund, the World Trade Organization, and other international agencies, together with global financial institutions, media conglomerates, and multinational corporations. Pat Robertson's *The New World Order* (1991) viewed over two centuries of Western history as a vast and sinister conspiracy, from the Bavarian Illuminati and the Rothschilds to the Federal Reserve Board and the Beatles, pointing inexorably to antichrist. This world system, they preached, faces ultimate destruction, represented in Revelation 18 as the fiery devastation of wicked Babylon, the embodiment of earthly vanity and greed. One impressively designed prophecy Web site featured a vivid animation (with a throbbing audio adding a sinister note) of New York City in flames, with "BABYLON" emblazoned on one skyscraper and "666" on another. In the foreground a wanton, nearly naked woman, the "Whore of Babylon," performs a lascivious dance for a loathsome, lizard-like creature—the Beast, the Evil One.[12] The post-Cold War prophecy popularizers also highlighted growing environmental hazards—air and water pollution, acid rain, global warming, the thinning ozone layer—as well as cloning and genetic manipulation as anticipations of the ecological and cosmic catastrophes and bizarre creatures foretold in the Bible: earthquakes, deadly hailstorms, rivers and streams becoming "as the blood of dead men," a darkened sun and bloody moon, horrible sores afflicting people's bodies, and monstrous insect-like beings crawling from the earth.[13]

Just as they dismissed efforts to promote world peace or nuclear disarmament, dispensationalist writers saw little point in international efforts such as the Kyoto Accords to reduce atmospheric pollution and other environmental hazards, since biblical prophecy makes clear that the environment will become increasingly degraded as the end approaches. In Hal Lindsey's 1996 prophecy novel *Blood Moon*, Jesus quickly solves the environmental crisis when he returns to earth, in the process discovering and destroying all weapons of mass destruction:

> The radioactive waste, the hazardous chemicals and biological warheads He had already cleaned up. Jesus said: "I have [. . .] completely renewed the ecological balance of nature to the pre-sin standards. All of the climate changes have been reset to ideal conditions. The whole earth will now have a mild climate, and almost all of the earth's surface will be suitable for agriculture. (338)

THE MIDDLE EAST IN BIBLE PROPHECY

As the Middle East increasingly dominated attention in the 1990s and beyond, and particularly after the terrorist attacks of September 11, 2001, prophecy popularizers shifted their emphasis accordingly.[14] The lands of the Bible have always loomed large for prophecy interpreters, and this predilection now became even more intense. Prophecy writers interpreted the growing number of Jewish settlements in the West Bank (a process that had begun after the 1967 war), the efforts to make Jerusalem an entirely Jewish city, and the speculation by ultra-Orthodox groups about reoccupying Temple Mount and rebuilding the temple as steps in God's unfolding plan.

The more hard-line and expansionist groups in Israel, including Likud Party leaders, welcomed this unwavering support. When Prime Minister Benjamin Netanyahu visited the United States in 1998, he called first on Jerry Falwell, and only afterwards met with President Clinton. In 2000, Ariel Sharon addressed a large delegation of Christian prophecy believers in Israel—a meeting reported in the *Jerusalem Post* under the headline "Sharon Dazzles Christian Zionists."[15] (The Holocaust-as-chastisement motif, antichrist's slaughter of Jews, and the conversion of the surviving remnant to Christianity—central dispensationalist themes in the past—were downplayed as enthusiastic and uncritical support for Israeli hard-liners became the rule.)

On the basis of these beliefs, dispensationalists opposed any scaling back of Jewish settlements in the West Bank or Gaza, since these areas lie well within God's grant to Abraham. They also denounced any proposals for shared governance of Jerusalem. As the Rev. James Hagee, pastor of a 16,000-member church in San Antonio, Texas, wrote in *Final Dawn Over Jerusalem* (1998):

> Christians and Jews, let us stand united and indivisible on this issue: There can be no compromise regarding the city of Jerusalem, not now, not ever. We are racing toward the end of time, and Israel lies in the eye of the storm. . . . Israel is the only nation created by a sovereign act of God, and He has sworn by His holiness to defend Jerusalem, His Holy City. If God created and defends Israel, those nations that fight against it fight against God. (131, 150)

In this apocalyptic scenario, the Islamic world is allied against God and faces annihilation in the last days. This is actually an ancient theme in Christian eschatology. As Islam spread across the Middle East and North Africa and even threatened Christian Europe itself, late medieval and early modern prophecy expositors saw it as the demonic force whose doom is foretold in Scripture. As Richard the Lionhearted prepared for the Third Crusade in 1190, the famed prophecy interpreter Joachim of Fiore assured him that the Islamic ruler Saladin, who held Jerusalem, was the antichrist, and that Richard would defeat him and recapture the Holy City. (Joachim's prophecy failed: Richard returned to Europe in 1192 with Saladin still in power.) Later interpreters cast the Islamic Ottoman Empire, which by the mid-sixteenth century extended from Hungary in the west to present-day Iraq in the east, and southward to include Egypt, as the realm of antichrist.

This theme faded somewhat after 1920 with the final collapse of the tottering Ottoman Empire and the emergence of the Soviet Union as the new focus of evil. The anti-Islamic strand never disappeared entirely, however, even at the height of the Cold War, though it was usually subordinated to the Russia-as-Gog theme. "The Arab world is an Antichrist-world," wrote the Rev. Guy Duty in *Escape from the Coming Tribulation* (126). Arthur Bloomfield in *Before the Last Battle* declared bluntly: "When all the Jews return . . . in complete fulfillment of the prophecies . . ., Arab power will be destroyed. . . . God says he will lay the land of the Arabs to waste and it will be desolate. . . . This may seem like a severe punishment, but . . . [t]he terms of the covenant must be carried out to the letter" (65).

After 1990, with the Cold War over and tensions rising in the Middle East, Islam and its prophetic significance returned to center stage. Prophecy popularizers not only fervently supported the most hard-line groups in Israel but also demonized Islam as irredeemably evil and destined for destruction. James Hagee in *Final Dawn Over Jerusalem* invested the Middle East's tensions and hatreds with eschatological significance: "The conflict between Arabs and Jews goes deeper than disputes over the lands of Palestine. It is theological. It is Judaism versus Islam. Islam's theology insists that Islam triumph over everything else. . . . Muslims believe that it is the will of God for Islam to rule the world" (141). (Hagee's dispensationalist eschatology, of course, insists on precisely the same thing: the forces of antichrist—presumably including all Muslims—will be annihilated, and Christ will rule the world.) Bringing Moscow back in the picture, Hagee argued that the Bible foretells that Russia will ally with the oil-rich states of the Middle East and, as part of the deal, agree to command "a massive pan-Islamic military force" to invade Israel. Yet it will not be Israel that will be destroyed, Hagee goes on, but rather the Muslim invaders and their Russian allies, as foretold in Ezekiel and Revelation (144–48). In Lindsey's *Blood Moon*, Israel, in retaliation for a planned nuclear attack by a fanatic Muslim extremist, launches a massive thermonuclear counterattack that destroys "every Arab and Muslim capital

. . . along with the infrastructures of their nations" (312). Genocide, in short, becomes the ultimate means of prophetic fulfillment.

Anticipating President George W. Bush, prophecy writers of the 1990s quickly zeroed in on Saddam Hussein. If not the antichrist himself, they suggested, Saddam could well be a forerunner of the Evil One. In full-page newspaper ads during the Persian Gulf War, the Jews for Jesus organization declared that Saddam "represent[s] the spirit of Antichrist about which the Bible warns us."[16]

Prophecy believers found particular significance in Saddam's grandiose plan, launched in the 1970s, to rebuild Babylon on its ancient ruins.[17] The fabled city on the Euphrates south of Baghdad, one of the seven wonders of the ancient world, owed its splendor to King Nebuchadnezzar, the same wicked ruler who warred against Israel and destroyed Jerusalem in 586 B.C., for which impiety, according to the Book of Daniel, he was driven mad and condemned to the ignominy of eating grass in the fields.

In Revelation, Babylon embodies all that is corrupt, "a great whore . . . with whom the kings of the earth have committed fornication" (Rev 17:1-2). It stands as the antithesis of Jerusalem, the city of righteousness, and Revelation 18 prophesies its annihilation by fire "in one hour." Dispensationalists who see the "Babylon" of Revelation as the actual ancient city rather than as an allegorical representation of the entire antichrist system viewed Saddam's ambitious public-works project as an essential step toward this key prophetic fulfillment.

Charles Dyer's *The Rise of Babylon: Sign of the End Times* (1991) elaborated this theme. Along with the emergence of modern Israel and the European Union (another building block of antichrist's empire), Saddam's restoration of Babylon signals the approaching end and offers "thrilling proof that the Bible prophecies are infallible," wrote Dyer. "When Babylon is ultimately destroyed," he continued, "Israel will finally be at peace and dwell in safety" (20). He asked: "If Babylon will be destroyed in the end times, who will destroy it? The United States? Will Americans wipe out Iraq? . . . [T]he United States is a major world power—how could it *not* play a major role in the last days?" (165–66). Such speculation flowed naturally into musings about Saddam's overthrow. Indeed, the cover illustration of Dyer's book juxtaposes Saddam and Nebuchadnezzar. Well before the Iraq War, Americans attuned to the latest speculation in prophecy circles were primed for its coming.

All the major themes of the post–Cold War dispensationalist scenario converge in the "Left Behind" novels. As the plot unfolds, the antichrist, global media mogul Nicolae Carpathia, becomes secretary general of the United Nations. ("I've opposed the United Nations for fifty years," boasts coauthor Tim LaHaye, a veteran activist on the religious right.) Carpathia moves the UN from New York to a rebuilt Babylon, laying the groundwork for the simultaneous destruction of *both* the organization that will spearhead antichrist's satanic world order and the city that in the schematic and rigidly polarized realm of dispensationalist thought represents absolute evil and defiance of God's prophetic plan.

Speculation about the prophetic significance of events in the Middle East reached a fever pitch early in George W. Bush's presidency, particularly after the attacks of September 11, 2001. To be sure, some Bush administration policies troubled prophecy believers. The expansion of Washington's surveillance powers after 9/11 under the USA-PATRIOT Act (led, ironically, by Attorney General John Ashcroft, darling of the religious right) struck some as another step toward the antichrist's global dictatorship. Counterbalancing this, however, other key administration positions—its hostility to multinational cooperation and to international agreements on the environment and arms control, its barely concealed contempt for the United Nations and what Defense Secretary Donald Rumsfeld dismissed as "old Europe," its muted response to growing Jewish settlements in Palestinian territory, its unrelenting focus on Saddam Hussein, and in 2003 its war on Iraq—struck dispensationalists as wholly in harmony with God's prophetic plan.

After 9/11, prophecy writers' strident anti-Islamic tone and fervent backing of Israel's expansionist hardliners intensified. In 2002, Hal Lindsey's Web site featured a cartoon of a military aircraft emblazoned with a U.S. flag and a Star of David and carrying a missile with a label targeting "Saddam." The caption quoted the prophet Zechariah: "In that day I will seek to destroy all nations that come against Israel." In June 2002 *Midnight Call* magazine warmly endorsed an attack on Islam by the Rev. Franklin Graham (Billy Graham's son) and summed up Graham's view in stark terms: "Islam is an evil religion" (10). Jerry Falwell implied much the same thing, characterizing Mohammed on *Sixty Minutes* as a "terrorist," and endorsing a fellow Southern Baptist preacher's description of Islam's founder as "a demon-possessed pedophile."[18] (Under a hail of criticism, Falwell issued a partial apology.) In November 2003 *Midnight Call* praised dispensationalists "for their outspoken dedication to seeing that the God-ordained borders in Israel are restored and the land returned to it's [sic] rightful owners, the Jews" (3).

In 2003, as the war against Saddam Hussein unfolded, prophecy writer Michael D. Evans in *Beyond Iraq: The Next Move* called for an expansion of the conflict to a full-scale holy war against Iran, Syria, and ultimately Islam itself. Evans denounced the U.S. road map to peace in the Middle East, with its call for compromises by both Israel and the Palestinians, as a betrayal of Israel's divinely sanctioned claim to the West Bank and Gaza. Only when Israel fully occupies these territories, he argued, can the next stage of the prophetic timetable unfold.

The apocalyptic perspective is hardly new. Indeed, it shapes the mythic writings of the oldest Mesopotamian civilizations. The Greek word *apokalypsis* literally means "an unveiling of that which is hidden." What the early apocalyptic writers unveiled was the reality underlying all existence: a battle of order against chaos, light against darkness, purity against corruption, righteousness against evil. Apocalypticism penetrated learned Jewish thought in the second and first centuries B.C.E. and from there flowed into early Christian writings. Benjamin Beit-Hallahmi of the University of Haifa has concisely summed up this worldview in its Judeo-Christian form:

> The essential ingredients of the apocalyptic dream are first a total destruction of the evil world as we know it at present, and then a birth of "a new heaven and a new earth" for the elect, who are only a remnant of humanity. [. . .] Millenarian groups promise imminent collective salvation for the faithful in an earthly paradise that will rise following an apocalyptic destruction ordained by the gods.[19] (173)

The apocalyptic mindset reinforces a longstanding tendency among Americans to view their history and the nation's world role in religious terms. Jonathan Edwards believed that the Great Awakening of the 1740s would soon spread to England and beyond. Many colonial preachers saw the American Revolution in biblical terms. One identified the hated Lord Bute, who had been born on a Scottish island, as the "beast from the sea" prophesied in Revelation.[20]

Julia Ward Howe's great Civil War anthem "The Battle Hymn of the Republic" is steeped in biblical imagery and is explicitly apocalyptic, with the marching Union armies carrying out God's plan for purifying the nation. In 1917 President Woodrow Wilson, a devout Presbyterian, assured Americans that the nation's entry into the European war would lead to an era of universal peace, justice, and righteousness.[21] American evangelists from Dwight Moody to Billy Graham have carried their message of salvation to Europe and, in Graham's case, around the world.

From the 1940s through the 1980s, not only prophecy writers but American leaders in general interpreted the Cold War conflict with "godless communism" in quasi-religious terms. "[F]orces of good and evil are massed and armed and opposed as rarely before in history," declared President Dwight D. Eisenhower in his first inaugural in 1953. A year later Congress, in a flurry of piety, added "In God We Trust" to the nation's currency and coinage and "under God" to the Pledge of Allegiance, making clear that God's purposes and the nation's purposes were as one in the Cold War struggle. President Ronald Reagan was simply echoing these religious pronouncements thirty years later when he denounced the Soviet Union as "the focus of evil in the modern world."

During the first Gulf War, President George H. W. Bush called for a national day of prayer and intoned: "One cannot be president of our country without faith in God—and without knowing with certainty that we are one nation under God. . . . God is our rock and salvation, and we must trust him and keep faith in him."[22]

The horror of 9/11 added urgency to this religiously inflected view of the nation's destiny, with "terrorists" replacing "communists" as evil incarnate.

George W. Bush's call for an open-ended "crusade" against terrorism, and his subsequent launching of a preemptive war to overthrow Saddam Hussein intensified the apocalyptic aura in Washington and the nation. *Washington Post* journalist Bob Woodward, after a long interview with Bush in the run-up to the war, left the Oval Office convinced that "the president was casting his mission and that of the country in the grand vision of God's master plan."[23] Garry Wills wrote of a White House "honeycombed with prayer groups and Bible study cells." In this climate, interest in the dispensationalists' end-time scenario flourished.

The most explicit articulation of the powerful undercurrent of Christian apocalyptic thinking in high government circles was that of Lt. General William G. Boykin, deputy undersecretary of defense for intelligence and a confidant of Defense Secretary Rumsfeld. In sermons in evangelical churches and talks to prayer groups in 2002–03, Boykin, resplendent in full-dress uniform, repeatedly voiced his basic message: terrorists hated America "because we're a Christian nation, because our foundation and roots are Judeo-Christian and the enemy is a guy named Satan."[24] Boykin dismissed Allah as an "idol" and "not a real God," and reported his boast to a captured Muslim warlord in Somalia: "You underestimated our God."[25]

Confronted with angry protests from Muslim leaders and domestic critics, Bush distanced himself from Boykin and described Islam as "a religion that brings hope and comfort to good people across America and around the world."[26] But despite the critical fallout, the White House and Pentagon resisted demands that Boykin be fired or reassigned. In fact, the general was simply expressing openly what millions of Bush supporters firmly believed, on the basis of their reading of Bible prophecy. Indeed, Falwell, Graham, Hagee, the editors of *Midnight Call*, and many other prominent dispensationalists had already said as much.

James Madison in 1785 warned citizens of the new republic against deploying "religion as an engine of civil policy." Nearly 220 years later, religious belief and foreign policy at times seemed almost indistinguishable. Garry Wills observed in March 2003, as the administration pursued the war against "evildoers" and prepared for war in Iraq, that "no matter how much Jefferson and Madison tried to [keep] religion out of official government actions, it has kept sneaking back in, beating down attempts to contain it."[27]

The interaction between popular prophetic belief and the tendency of U.S. leaders to cast world issues in apocalyptic terms constitutes a vicious circle. On one hand, the upsurge of grassroots prophetic interest from the 1970s on encouraged the propensity in official circles to portray America's international relations in apocalyptic terms. On the other hand, the apocalyptic pronouncements emanating from Washington reinforced many ordinary Americans' inclination to interpret world events from a perspective of biblical prophecy, thus helping shape the climate of opinion within which U.S. foreign policy was formulated and the way those policies were sold to the public. When key leaders themselves share this religious worldview, or when their political base includes vast numbers of voters who hold these beliefs, as in the administration of George W. Bush, the role of the apocalyptic mindset in shaping the nation's diplomacy looms even larger.

The apocalyptic outlook that gripped so many Americans in the early twenty-first century was matched in the Muslim world by radical Islamists (as well as by ultra-Orthodox Jews and Hindu fundamentalists). The anthropologist Henry Munson has emphasized the religious roots of Muslim anger over America's tacit support of Israel's hard-line expansionists and the heavy (though recently reduced) U.S. presence in Saudi Arabia with its Muslim holy sites. "Islamists like [Osama] bin Laden articulate such grievances in archaic terms of evil infidels oppressing virtuous believers," he writes. "To dismiss the resentment of Western domination articulated by Islamists like bin Laden as mere xenophobia would be a mistake."[28] The upsurge of apocalyptic and fundamentalist worldviews in this "clash of civilizations"[29] is accompanied by global economic trends and advances in communications that increasingly throw competing religious worldviews in direct confrontation—a dangerous and volatile combination.

THE APOCALYPTIC WORLDVIEW: LARGER IMPLICATIONS

Academics and citizens in general urgently need to pay more attention to the role of religious belief in American public life. Indeed, the global rise of fundamentalist movements grounded in apocalyptic readings of history demands scrutiny. Scholars in the humanities and social science disciplines (often situated in university settings far more secular than the rest of country) have generally ignored or underestimated the influence of religious belief in America and have rarely sought to understand its structure and the sources of its appeal. As society and popular culture seemingly grew increasingly secular, it was tempting to assume that religious belief, particularly in its literalistic and fundamentalist forms, would gradually fade.[30] Instead, from the 1970s on, fundamentalist and evangelical churches grew by leaps and bounds while the more liberal mainstream denominations hemorrhaged members.

As the political clout of religious believers became unavoidably obvious, academia belatedly paid attention. In 2003, for example, *Dædalus*, the journal of the American Academy of Arts & Sciences, published a symposium in which thirteen scholars (plus Thomas Jefferson) weighed in on the subject of "Secularism and Religion." In his contribution, theologian and historian Martin E. Marty wrote: "We need a new model for describing the world that we actually inhabit. It is neither exclusively secular nor exclusively religious, but rather a complex combination of both . . . , with religious and secular phenomena occurring at the same time in individuals, in groups, and in societies around the world."[31] For the American version of this messy interpenetration of religious and secular, I can think of few more useful areas to examine than the influence on U.S. politics and foreign policy of biblically based end-time beliefs that are promulgated by the latest communications media available in our "secular" and technologically advanced society.

In another essay in the *Dædalus* symposium, Jean Bethke Elshtain, the Laura Spelman Rockefeller Professor of Social and Political Ethics at the University of Chicago Divinity School, calls for a greater tolerance of religiously based ideologies in the public sphere:

> One enters political life as a citizen. But if one also has religious convictions, these convictions naturally will inform one's judgments as a citizen. My religious views help to determine who I am, how I think, and what I care about. This is as it should be. In America, it makes no sense to ask people to bracket what they care about most deeply when they debate issues that are properly political.[32]

Fair enough, but how should one respond when the beliefs that people "care about most deeply" lead them to expect—and indeed to welcome—a final showdown between cosmic forces of good and evil, a showdown that cannot be avoided because it is ordained by God himself, and that will end in the mass extermination of most of the human race? And how should one react when these citizens form their opinions about current political and foreign policy issues on the basis of these beliefs and work actively to translate their apocalyptic worldview into public policy? And what if these beliefs are amplified and endlessly pumped into the public arena by high public officials, by prominent religious figures who wrap their pronouncements in the mantle of prophetic authority, and by all the instruments of persuasion available to the masters of our contemporary mass media? Such a situation is, of course, simply a description of the reality of American public life today, and the dilemma is not merely a theoretical one.

The dilemma becomes all the more crucial because the apocalyptic worldview underlying the dispensationalist interpretation of Bible prophecy shapes not only believers' interpretation of specific events but their understanding of history itself. Apocalyptic thought assumes radically polarized oppositional forces, with no middle ground or shades of gray. From this perspective, conflicts and disagreements among nations or groups are not seen as the normal ebb and flow of international relations to be addressed through compromise and negotiation, but rather as manifestations of history's underlying dynamic: the struggle between good and evil that is unfolding according to God's predetermined plan. From this perspective, all human efforts to ameliorate conflicts among nations are futile since the only ultimate resolution will come in the final apocalyptic struggle when evil will be eradicated by supernatural means. As the Rev. Arno Froese wrote in the February 2004 issue of *Midnight Call*: "Whatever type of peace the world may achieve is based upon deception, and it is temporary" (10). Lest there be any doubt about his point, this excerpt from Froese's essay was highlighted in boldface and illustrated with a photograph of the United Nations Security Council.

For the prophecy believer who foresees an apocalyptic end to history, the goal in the present age is not to seek to reduce the level of violence and conflict between nations or within societies, or to ameliorate the human suffering these struggles bring in their wake, but to discern how these realities fit into the eschatological timetable revealed in the Bible. The believer's sole duty is to make sure that he or she is on the correct side, to win others to an acceptance of biblical truth through evangelism and missionary effort, and to confidently await the ultimate triumph of the righteous and the destruction of the wicked. It's a breathtakingly simple—and therefore enormously powerful and appealing—way of viewing the modern world's maddening complexity. The dispensationalist, possessing knowledge hidden to nonbelievers, either withdraws into passivity as crises unfold, awaiting the preordained outcome, or (as seems increasingly the case in early twenty-first-century America) plunges into the fray on the "good" side, eager to hasten the apocalyptic denouement that will finally fulfill God's plan.

What is to be done? The First Amendment obviously protects the right of those who hold this worldview to inject it into the public discourse by any means at their disposal, from mass-market paperbacks and communications satellites to DVDs and Internet Web sites. But given the prevalence of this belief system in contemporary America and its influence in shaping believers' worldview and thus, indirectly, in shaping U.S. foreign policy and civic discourse, I believe it becomes incumbent on those who do not share such a deterministic and nightmarish vision of humanity's fate to subject these "faith-based" beliefs, however sincerely held, to the most searching possible critical scrutiny and public debate.

5: View from the News Desk

Post-9/11 Media and Muslim Identity in American Media

Aslam Abdallah

In an article in the *New Statesman*, a prominent Muslim scholar, Ziauddin Sardar, suggests that "the West's hatred of Islam stems from, more than anything else, the denial of its true lineage. The Western world as we understand it is a child of Islam. Without Islam, the West—however we conceive it today—would not exist. And, without the West, Islam is incomplete and cannot survive the future."[1] Consequently, a sizeable number of people perceive Islam as a dangerous faith capable of destroying their social and individual lives. Concurrently, journalists and media professionals are beginning to define Islam, not as an Arab religion, but as an ethnically diverse one with local roots. For centuries, historians and academics have portrayed Islam as a foreign, exotic religion, but they have begun to see how Islam might be recognized in Western countries. While media professionals have produced several stories about American Muslims and cultural diversity since 9/11, it was the media coverage of the 1992–95 war in Bosnia and the genocide in Kosovo in 1999 that demolished the myth of Muslims as a Middle Eastern community. These two conflicts shattered the idea of a monolithic Islamic world in Western eyes. The Serbian campaign of ethnic cleansing directed at Bosnian Muslims shocked people into realizing that there are blond, blue-eyed Muslims and European Muslims—and that Muslims can be victims as well as perpetrators.

Perceptions of Islam and Muslims still resonate with old stereotypical images drawn from medieval Europe, however. A recent survey by the Pew Foundation found that more Americans are distrustful of Islam than ever before. To them, Islam is not peace or humility; it is violence and bloodshed. Americans are getting such information from their news media. They think they know what *jihad* is because they have been told they're watching it live on FOX News. American audiences are "witnesses" to people who call themselves Muslims fighting and killing in the name of their religion.

The fact is that what they see is not true. Rather, what they are witnessing is in fact the confusion, hatred—and in some cases, ignorance—of terrorists and extremists. These terrorists and extremists have turned Islam's ideal of peace and harmony on its head. Pundits featured in such media reports rarely mention that such actions are not sanctioned by the religion and have no place within Islam.

While jihad indicates bloodshed and tyranny to American media consumers, to the majority of Muslims, as Karen Armstrong explains, "the primary meaning of the word jihad is not 'holy war' but 'struggle.' It refers to the difficult effort that is needed to put God's will into practice at every level—personal and social as well as political."[2]

Islamic scholars have challenged those who believe jihad is holy war in the Qur'an. The term does not exist there. A quotation rarely seen in the American media is of the prophet Muhammad telling his companions as they return home after battle: "We are returning from the lesser jihad [the battle] to the greater jihad." This "greater jihad" refers to the far more vital and crucial task of extinguishing transgression from one's own society and one's own heart.

So how did jihad evolve from its peaceful beginnings to what the American public sees on TV? The way jihad is projected in the American media and expounded by some Muslim extremists has an immediate impact on Islam's negative portrayal. The present manifestation of jihad by terrorists has great audience appeal. It allows room for media twists and dramatic flourishes that bode well for the ratings. The negative portrayal of Islam influences Muslims all over the world. Because of the actions of a handful of disillusioned individuals, Islam is viewed as a deadly disease and its followers as carriers about to infect the rest of the world. It is apparent that the current portrayal of Islam is deeply embedded in the conflicts and military confrontations between the West and Islam dating back to the seventh century and running through the Byzantine Empire, the Crusades, the Spanish Reconquista, the fall of Constantinople, the eras of colonialism, and national independence.

Many Westerners have tried to understand Islam in a way that is analogous to Christianity. Since Christ is the foundation of Christian faith, it was assumed—quite incorrectly—that Muhammad was to Islam as Christ was to

Christianity. Hence, the polemic name "Mohammedanism" given to Islam and the automatic epithet "impostor" applied to Muhammad. According to this line of reasoning, Islam was just a misguided version of Christianity. A large body of literature appeared that intensified the Christian picture of Islam. In the *Chanson de Roland*, the worship of "Saracens" (Muslims) is portrayed as embracing "Mohamet" and Apollo! "Moametto" turns up in canto 28 of Dante's *Inferno*. Experts speaking on Islam through today's media still tend to rely on historical and literary images evoking medieval Europe. The experts often view Muslims and the West in the context of an ongoing conflict between Islam and Judeo-Christian ideals, although Muslims are now citizens of the United States, an integral part of the West—including large Muslim communities in Europe and Australia.

The vast majority of Western media rely on a limited number of "experts" in Islam and the Muslim world. The absence of diverse sources of information tends to lock common people into an immutable mode of understanding Islam, leaving self-styled experts the opportunity to inculcate ordinary minds with their concerns. For example, Samuel Huntington, a Harvard professor often consulted by media, has said, "The underlying problem for the West is not Islamic fundamentalism. It is Islam, a different civilization whose people are convinced of the superiority of their culture and are obsessed with the inferiority of their power."[3] The view of such advocates presumes that the sudden emergence of any contrary position to the secular culture of the United States (not only an Islamic one) would produce massive international instability and global anarchy.

Countering these arguments with a different perspective about Islam, also heard frequently in the popular media, is a move toward creating a dialogue between opposing views on Islam and Muslims. However, both sides of the argument appear to be inaccurate generalizations that still appear in the media regularly, giving substance to Muslim fears that the media is a conspirator in damaging Islam's reputation.

Despite these fears, the national discourse seems encouraging, since it gives Muslims the chance to understand the pluralistic diversity of America while the media simultaneously explore the diversity of Muslims as well. Some terms—Islamic terrorist, Muslim fundamentalist, Wahabi zealot, Shia extremist, Sunni bomber, Islamic Jihadi, Arab killer, Islamic suicide bomber—while used extensively in American media, are not as old as Islam or Muslims are. Relatively new, such terms are often used to describe a variety of violent actions or extremist statements attributed to people associated with Muslims. Since September 11, 2001, these terms have entered the popular vocabulary as both the print and broadcast media have increased their usage exponentially. The headlines on CNN, FOX, CBS, or MSNBC, and news reports or opinion columns in the *New York Times* or *Los Angeles Times*, have succeeded in creating a public perception of Islam that is directly contradicted by Muslim denunciations of terrorism, and the reality prevalent in the Muslim world. The American public sees Osama bin Laden and his cronies on TV and confuses their identity with that of true ambassadors of Islam.

No single region or religion has a monopoly on violence. In the absence of a universally accepted definition, the term "terrorism" can be applied loosely to almost every act of violence or killing. However, those who control sources of information have an edge over others since they often decide and determine the extent, nature, and scope of coverage to be given to the perpetrators and victims of violence and terror.

Almost every religious community has produced its own terrorists, violence mongers, hate-speech promoters, and extremists. During the last five decades, hundreds of thousands of acts of violence have occurred all over the world. These incidents involved Tamil Tigers professing Hinduism, Sinhale retaliators embracing Buddhism, Shiv Sena and Bhartiya Janata Party workers invoking Brahmanism (domination of the upper-caste religious clergy), the Irish Republic Army involving Catholics, Ulster Union followers practicing Protestantism, and Jewish Defense League members proclaiming Judaism. In these cases, however, American media rarely used terms such as Hindu terrorist, Catholic killers, Protestant violence mongers, or Jewish extremists to report events that involved the followers of these religions. When members of any of these groups carry out violent acts, one does not see discussions in the media about the relationship between violence and religion, or debates on religious scriptures' treatments of terror. Where is the scholarship linking the Tamil Tiger's act of suicide bombing to early Hindu warriors who promoted violence against people belonging to lower castes?

Latin America, too, has witnessed a long and sustained period of bloodshed and violence. In many of these incidents, religious clergy and institutions were involved in conflict; yet the terms used to describe incidents of violence were not "Christian" or "communist terrorism" but "liberation theology."

Violence or terror is not the only issue where Muslims and Islam have been designated as villains. On issues pertaining to women, human rights, child welfare, relations with non-Muslims, patriotism, and democracy, the media has also given Islam and Muslims disproportionate criticism, often compromising objectivity and fairness. Since 9/11, Islam has been projected in the media as a faith that needs to be changed if it is to exist in the modern world. Neither Christianity, Judaism, Hinduism nor Buddhism has ever been exposed to such harsh criticism, even if the members of these communities were involved in violent acts directed against Americans or the Western world in general.

Since September 11, 2001, the media have seemingly become more conscious of Muslim critiques of the media. Since then, the significant change that took place in the media's coverage of Islam and Muslims was the presence of diverse ways in which Muslims voiced issues that concerned their religion. The *New York Times*, the *Los Angeles Times*, the *Boston Globe*, and the

Washington Post have included more Muslim writers in their op-ed pages than ever before. Similarly, FOX, CBS, NBC, PBS, CNN and MSNBC have given space to voices representing Muslim centers and organizations on their shows.

In some newspapers, such as the *Washington Post* and the *Los Angeles Times*, there has been improvement incoverage in the past two years. Journalists in these papers are much more reluctant to label everyone a fundamentalist or extremist, or to make gross generalizations about Islam and the Muslim community. They are beginning to differentiate between the acts of individuals and the teachings of the religion itself. Monolithic misconceptions are subsiding as the nature of the Muslim community worldwide gains more attention.

The media have also begun to realize the presence of a diversified Muslim community that abhors terrorism as much as other Christian or Jewish communities do. Stories about Muslim communities and their contribution to America in general have helped Muslims gain a degree of respect.

The media coverage of Islam and Muslims post–September 11, 2001, generally can be categorized into five different styles: informative, appreciative, accusative, provocative, and offensive. Every media outlet has published all five styles since 9/11. Almost all American media have tried to develop an accurate understanding of Islam. The difference among them is in the scope and nature of the coverage. They have tried to inform their readers and viewers of what Islam is and what its tenets are. Several media outlets, such as the *Washington Post*, the *New York Times*, ABC, CNN, and MSNBC, have used Muslim experts to explain Islam and Muslims. Others have used Christian or Jewish scholars.

Informative articles by and large were neutral. They presented a textbook-like description of Islam and Muslims. *Appreciative articles* focused more on groups and institutions that were strong in their condemnation of terrorism or violence. The coverage ranged from small Muslim groups in Los Angeles to large organizations in Pakistan or Egypt. The media outlets gave several Muslim writers and intellectuals the space to voice their concern over the problem, and explain their version of Islamic teachings on violent killings.

On the other hand, the *accusative articles* focused on raising doubts about the real intention of Islam and Muslims. Writers who belonged to a special interest group, or whose hostility toward Muslims was well known, contributed articles in this category. Most of these articles discussed Islam's vulnerability to violence. The *provocative articles* focused on intellectual challenges Muslims face in defining their religion in the modern world. Islam's so-called incompatibility with democracy, human rights, and equality of genders was the subject of articles in this category.

Articles in the last category proved more controversial and questionable. One must ask: Why were those offensive articles published and what was, or is, behind the poor, subjective, imbalanced, and often unfair coverage?

American audiences have a lot to discover about Islam before any sound opinion can be formed. Such a discovery is possible, provided the media move away from the stereotypical images of Islam, and the American public thinks critically about how the media portray religion—especially religions practiced by immigrants to the United States.[4]

Chapter 6

Last Words: Death and Public Self-Expression

John P. Ferré

In *Western Attitudes Toward Death,* Historian Philippe Ariès called it "forbidden death"—the state of death denial that dominates American culture. Just as Americans have become unaccustomed to witnessing death firsthand, they have been discouraged from thinking about it and talking about it. There are professionals to care for the dying and the dead, and the bereaved are encouraged to get over their grief and get on with their quest for happiness. Death in America has become taboo.

It wasn't always this way. A hundred years ago Americans witnessed a lot of death and dying. Most Americans lived in small towns or on family farms, where the experience of death was both common and immediate. Infant mortality was high, children died more frequently, and adults were not expected to live much past fifty. People who became ill seldom went to a hospital because there was no hospital nearby. Instead they stayed home, where children and adults tended them. And when they died, they died at home in full view of both children and adults, who were likely to be present at the deathbed.

When someone died, the doctor left and the undertaker came in with his bottles of chemicals and his cooling board. Working as quickly and as unceremoniously as possible, the undertaker embalmed the body in the home so that it could be displayed for the wake in the parlor at the front of the house. Children were not spared funerals any more than they were spared the deaths of family members. There was no choice but to deal with death as frankly as one's psychology and faith would allow. Death was a familiar part of the home. People knew the sound of the death rattle, and they talked about the life that was and the life that was to come.[1]

The immediacy of death waned in the second half of the twentieth century as people moved to metropolitan areas rich with medical institutions and professional caretakers. Improvements in medical care extended life expectancy so much that after World War II few people experienced the death of an immediate family member before they reached adulthood. The very ill were no longer cared for in their own homes. They went to a hospital or a nursing home, and when they died, they were likely to die there. By the end of the century, four out of five Americans died in hospitals, not in their homes, and their bodies were no longer prepared and mourned at home. Professionals removed them, embalmed them, boxed them, and buried them. From the hospital or nursing home, the corpse went directly to a funeral home, where the wake, and maybe even the funeral, would take place. In less than a century, families lost most of the responsibility they once had for caring for the dying and the dead. The immediate experience of death has largely given way to second-hand experiences and, of course, the vicarious experience in television and movies, mostly of violent death. It is much more common today for people to *watch* a conversation about death and dying than to have one themselves.[2]

Americans have a greatly diminished ability to discuss—and hence to think about—the meaning of death and dying because they relinquished responsibility for caring for the dying and the dead in the twentieth century. But not everyone is content with turning over every dimension of funerals to professionals. Physical remains may be given to funeral workers, but mourners are going to greater lengths to reclaim symbolic ground where they can come to terms with death. Their desire to make meaningful public statements is reasserting itself in personalized obituaries, roadside memorials, and online memorials.

PERSONALIZED OBITUARIES

Had Cinderella Laughridge died in the late twentieth century rather than in the late nineteenth century, she would have been remembered much differently in the newspaper account. Here is how her late twentieth-century death notice might have appeared:

> Cinderella E. Laughridge, 34, died yesterday at her home. She was a
> native of Virginia and a member of the First Baptist Church of Kansas
> City. Survivors include her husband, John; three children; her mother;
> two brothers; and a sister. Funeral services will be held at 11 a.m. Tues-
> day at the First Baptist Church. Burial will be in Perpetual Gardens.

Except for her young age, everything in this death notice seems normal,
even routine. And that is the point. By the end of the twentieth century, most
daily newspapers devoted a page or two to obituaries and death notices, so
there was little space that could be devoted to any particular death. To be fair,
newspapers printed the barest of facts in every death notice: name, age, place
of death, identifying feature (often occupations for men and volunteer associations for women), immediate family, and funeral and burial information.
The reports were as sterile as they were factual.

What a departure from the newspaper report that actually appeared in the
Louisville, Kentucky, *Courier-Journal* in 1874! The article describes a devout
Christian woman who first confessed her faith at the age of 15 and who was
baptized by the Rev. Dr. Warder in Maysville, Kentucky. She married John
Laughridge when she was 20 and had three children. By the time she was 26,
though, Cinderella Laughridge had become bedridden. "Only occasionally
was she able to visit friends and attend church," her death notice reports.
After three years of Cinderella's chronic suffering, the Laughridges moved to
Kansas City, where they joined the church of the Baptist minister of her
youth. Her health never improved though, and she died five years later. Her
last words, spoken to family and friends gathered at her deathbed, were
"Meet me in heaven."[3]

Such a death report would not appear a century later because daily newspapers had committed themselves to verifiable factuality and had distanced
themselves from most religious expression. The 1874 report, which included
several passages of poetry, described Laughridge as "rich in the grace of God"
and said that "her sufferings were made the means of her preparation, in a
remarkable manner, for another life, better and purer than this one, so full of
trial." It also said that when Laughridge "fell asleep in Jesus" that "the side of
her death bed was a place that seemed very near God's paradise." Such language is gibberish to people who separate verifiable fact from religious sentiment, so it disappeared from death reports in the twentieth century. People
simply died; they did not pass away or meet their savior. And the things they
said, believed in, and hoped for were left for family lore, far from the widely
read obituary pages.

But death reports lost more than their religiosity; they also lost their character. To keep death notices manageable, daily newspapers stripped them
down to their barest essentials. To be sure, these brief reports still notified
readers of the deaths of neighbors and friends and supplied crucial information about visitations and funerals. But people whose deaths were reported

had become little more than ciphers. There was no telling detail, no indication of what made those who had died individuals. Newspapers simply stopped reporting why most people who died would be missed.

Although most people who die in this country will rate a death notice in a local newspaper, only a fraction of them will receive an actual obituary. "Many are called," say the Gospels, "but few are chosen." *New York Times* obituary writer Alden Whitman listed four characteristics of persons whose death would prompt an obituary in a metropolitan daily newspaper: fame, infamy, eccentricity, and controversy. On the other hand, he said, "The poor, those who work in an occupation not high on the prevailing scale of social values, or who belong to one of the lesser regarded ethnic groups, or have never previously been in the news for good or ill, are unlikely to make it in death."[4] That means, of course, that most people will not rate an obituary when they die. Occasionally a reporter will build a reputation by writing obituaries of the rank and file, but they are exceptions who prove the rule.[5]

For many newspaper readers, shrinking death notices signify the increasingly impersonal nature of news. "I get vicarious pleasure from reading about somebody, whom I don't know, but who obviously has led a good and fulfilling life," a reader wrote to the editor of the *Courier-Journal*. "Please reconsider your obituary policy. Personalize them, again."[6]

Many papers have responded to the pleas for longer and more personal death notices by moving the obituary page from the news department to the advertising department. Death notices treated as news put newspapers in an untenable position. Increasing populations mean greater numbers of death notices, but profit-minded editors have been loath to increase the space available for them because there is a limited amount of advertising available for the obituary page. One solution is to print more death notices by shrinking the size of the print, but small type frustrates the large number of older people who read the obituary page. Another solution is to print death notices with less and less information, but that too is frustrating to families and readers who want to read memorials rather than census entries. A third solution, one that is becoming increasing popular, is to treat death notices like classified advertising: survivors get to say whatever and how much they want about family members who die, as long as they are willing to pay for the column inches. When the Cedar Rapids, Iowa, *Gazette* started charging for death notices, it said, "Many families and funeral homes repeatedly suggested they would be willing to pay for obituaries if they could control the information that appeared in the death notice or obituary."[7] For the sake of propriety and to reduce the possibility of hoaxes, newspapers accept only those death notices faxed to them from funeral homes. That policy lets family members in charge of the funeral say what they want.

The result is immediately noticeable. No longer are death notices all the same. Some, for instance, include a photograph, sometimes recent, sometimes from long ago. People continue to die, but now they also pass away, depart this life, go to be with the Lord, or enter into eternal rest. The major difference, though, is biographical material—sometimes lots of it. Death notices still include surviving family members (occasionally with commentary, such as "survivors . . . will miss her dearly"), but much more space is now devoted to the individual's accomplishments and hobbies. Death notices often report cause of death, but seldom when the cause of death is seen as shameful, as with suicides and AIDS. In short, death notices are more and more coming to reflect what family members want to say about their loved ones for the record.

The measure of the meaningfulness of the new policies is evident in the increased length of death notices. Grieving families want to tell more about their recently deceased family member than they used to have the opportunity to do. They want to say why they miss the individual, and doing that takes column inches that they are willing to buy.

There are, however, drawbacks to the increased responsibility that families now have for the death notices that appear in daily newspapers. The first drawback involves omission. Some feuding families are tempted to leave out the names of individuals who they believe do not deserve to be named in connection with the deceased. Other facts that are less than flattering—a failed marriage, perhaps, or a telling cause of death such as cirrhosis of the liver—may be best left untold, according to surviving family members looking to put the best spin on an ambiguous life. The other drawback is falsification. It may be comforting to refer to a sexual partner as a husband, or to being fired from a job as a change in vocation, but such dishonesty may reinforce a refusal to face dysfunctional family dynamics in the present as well as provide miscues to progeny trying to write a family history.

However it might be misused, the increased freedom to write obituaries is on balance positive. Something needed to change. Newspapers had begun to publish the most scaled-down death notices possible, notices that did little more than give the time and place of funeral services. Families now have the ability to step in and state for the record why an individual's death has caused them to grieve. That is what good obituaries do.

ROADSIDE MEMORIALS

Traffic fatalities—there were 43,220 in the United States in 2003—leave families with the pain of unexpected loss. In this circumstance, the normal routine of a wake, funeral, and burial is sometimes not enough to meet the need of those who grieve. So every year, thousands of people who have lost loved ones to traffic accidents take matters into their own hands—literally. They fashion crosses, gather keepsakes, and return to the site of the fatality to memorialize the person whose life was cut short at that place. Only through such participation do they feel satisfied with their response to the needless and unforeseen death.

Roadside memorials do more than mark the locations of traffic fatalities; they serve as sites for rituals that surviving family members develop over time. Sondra Edwards has spent numerous hours meditating at the roadside memorial on Cummings Skyway northeast of San Francisco that marks the place where her son Chris died in a car accident during a school field trip. "It's not the same feeling as when I go to the cemetery," Edwards says. "With the quietness, I can get in deep thought. I can't explain it. It's closer to the feeling that's in my heart every day."[8] Patsy Juliano's experience is similar. She visits the site in Revere Beach, Massachusetts, where her son Joey died in a car accident. "This was the last place Joey was alive, the place where his spirit left this world. We come here for birthdays, baptisms, at Christmas. We say prayers, light candles, and leave flowers. We can't imagine going anywhere else—no other site would hold any meaning for us."[9] The experiences of Sondra Edwards and Patsy Juliano show one reason that roadside memorials have become so plentiful in the last few decades: The places retain their significance because they mark the spot where the person died. As another woman who visits the cross that marks the spot of her daughter's fatal traffic accident says, "I know they pronounced her dead at the hospital," but the scene of the accident "is where you leave your spirit. That's where she was last. I can go there and pay my respects and talk to her."[10]

The typical roadside memorial is a homemade wooden cross painted white and decorated with flowers, balloons, candles, photographs, notes, and personal mementos such as teddy bears. They are put up shortly after the death and sometimes remain in place for years, being tended regularly and redecorated on holidays such as Christmas or Easter. People put them up out of a deeply felt need to create something to mark the person's life that ended tragically and without warning. They are a form of direct action: there's no funeral director or minister to go through, no set time, no protocol. People feel free to put them up when they want and decorate them however they want.[11]

Their meaning is more specific than the meaning of monuments in cemeteries. Cemetery monuments mark the site of burial and tell visitors who died and when that person lived. Roadside memorials, by contrast, tell passers-by that somebody died in a traffic accident right here and that travelers should consider that fatality and beware. There is an urgency to roadside memorials that cemetery monuments do not have.

That roadside memorials might serve as a warning to drivers and thus help to reduce traffic fatalities has been a theme since as long ago as 1953, when American Legion posts in Montana began their Highway White Cross Program of placing crosses at the sites of fatal traffic accidents on state highways. Although people place wreaths and other decorations on the American

Legion crosses, the monuments are placed on the sites of fatal accidents to promote highway safety; they are public service messages that remind drivers to drive carefully.[12] Roadside markers for purposes of public education rather than memorialization include the "X Marks the Spot" campaign in Colorado of Mothers Against Drunk Driving. The idea is to put markers at the site of every alcohol-related traffic fatality.[13] Others see this same message in the roadside memorials placed by grieving friends and relatives. "Any message that gets out to the public that somebody lost their life on a highway helps make people be more aware of their driving," says Cliff Kroeger of the California Highway Patrol.[14] Omaha resident Steve Nastase says that white crosses along highways have helped him stay alert on trips between Nebraska and Texas: "It's kind of like they're saying, 'Wake up, it could happen to you.'"[15]

Ironically, roadside memorials can themselves be hazards. Located at dangerous intersections, hairpin curves, steep embankments—places other drivers failed to navigate safely—they can provide distractions to drivers who should be vigilant. A week after four teenagers died in a fiery car crash after hitting a flood wall near New Orleans, for instance, three cars crashed because drivers were looking at the crash site covered with written messages, bandannas, flowers, and T-shirts.[16] The Florida Department of Transportation has taken this hazard seriously. Since January 1997 it has removed homemade roadside memorials as a matter of policy because they can distract drivers, interfere with roadside maintenance, and endanger people who park on the side of highways as they visit these memorials. Instead, friends and family members can request an official marker, a circle that bears the name of the deceased and the message "Drive Safely."

Roadside memorials may be illegal in most states, but police and highway departments are usually lenient about enforcing these laws. Sympathizing with those who are coping with the loss of loved ones in traffic accidents, they typically leave the markers alone, sometimes for years, unless the markers pose their own dangers, as is the case with ones set in concrete close to the road. A Kentucky Transportation Cabinet spokesperson said, "Our policy is to use sensitivity in this matter, but first and foremost our priority has to be the safety and convenience of motorists."[17]

Filling out paperwork so that the state will eventually install a standard, nonreligious marker at the site of the fatal accident goes directly against the impetus for creating roadside memorials. As expressions of people who need to do something themselves to work through the deaths of friends and family members, they are supposed to be homemade, religious, and idiosyncratic in their decoration. Just as importantly, they are supposed to be placed by family or friends soon after the fatality. Roadside memorials are spontaneous and personal, and although their creators may hope that others will see them and drive more carefully, they are seldom created with a public service announcement in mind. Rather, people make them to proclaim that somebody important died at this particular spot. If they are created as reminders, then they are reminders to their creators of the loved one whose life ended suddenly and brutally.

Crosses may be a recognizable sign of memorials, but they are also Christian signs, and that fact angers some people who object to religious symbolism on public property.[18] When Florida began removing homemade roadside memorials, the state offered to replace them with standard markers with a cross like the Red Cross uses. This gesture offended Jewish groups, so Florida redesigned the markers in the shape of a circle.[19] Likewise, the Freedom from Religion Foundation complained to the Wisconsin Department of Transportation about roadside crosses along I-43.[20] Although some people have responded by denying the cross's religious connotations, most people do not debate the issue. Roadside memorials are erected without permission anyway, so arguing about the meaning of the cross seems superfluous to people who want to erect them. Erecting roadside memorials satisfies an emotional need to mark the site where spirit was unexpectedly torn from flesh, and religious symbolism seems particularly fitting for that.

Experience confirms that roadside memorials can be therapeutic. Guy Fino put a cross at the intersection near Tampa where his best friend Alvin Burgos died in a motorcycle accident. He says, "Putting the cross out there was a bit of closure for me. It really helped me get through a rough time." Not far away, Mike Lavin regularly drives by the cross he used to mark the spot where a pickup truck killed his 15-year-old son Kevin as he rode home on his bicycle. "It was hard at first," Lavin says, "Then it became almost like you're saying hello during the day."[21] Similarly, Diane Burke, who lost her 4-year-old daughter Jamie Lee Burke in a fiery pileup in Louisville, finds comfort when she drives by the small white cross with a laminated picture of Jamie that marks the spot where she died. "I relate more to that cross than to her grave at the cemetery," she says. "I used to cry when I went by there," she said. "But now, I drive down the street, see her beautiful face there, and I just smile and say, 'Hi, Baby.'"[22]

Roadside memorials matter more than just to the people who put them there. They sometimes function as community shrines, places where neighbors can mourn traffic fatalities, particularly of children. In Omaha, a 6-foot-high wooden cross was erected for high-school senior Kelly Allen. The cross was adorned with a stuffed bunny in a yellow dress, a woven basket filled with plastic Easter eggs, plastic flowers. Across town, the memorial for another high school crash victim, Josh Brockington, included an Altoids mints tin, a Scooby-Doo doll in a Santa hat, and a commencement cap tassel. Neighbor Steve Nastase says, "Kids put things on there that you wouldn't put in your front yard, but it's their grief, so you go with it." Meanwhile, across town at the Pleasantview Homes public housing development, neighbors added items to the homemade memorial for 8-year-old Shannon Ventry, who died after a car hit him on his bicycle. "It seems like every time I drive by there, I see different things," said Taniqua Ventry, Shannon's 18-year-old sister. "I notice someone put a cross there, or more flowers. To me that helps a lot, to know that no one forgot about him."[23]

Just as persons who construct roadside memorials are unlikely to feel the same about a standard state marker, many people who have lost friends and family members to traffic accidents are unlikely to be tempted to order ready-made markers. But that does not stop people from trying to sell them. Road-sidemarkers.com, for instance, offers "four beautifully designed crosses . . . [that] accommodate the name, birth date and day of passing. . . . They come finished in white with grey design accents and all lettering is in black." For $129.50 plus $15 shipping, Roadsidemarkers promises a "lasting tribute for many years to come." A marker bought with a credit card and the click of a mouse is not the same as one made with hammer, nails, wood, and glue. Of course, however people obtain their crosses, they erect them and embellish them on their own without the help or the guidance of professionals.

ONLINE MEMORIALS

The World Wide Web is providing another venue for people to express their grief on their own with little or no assistance from professional middlemen. The Web is an attractive medium because it can accommodate much more material than ordinary newspaper obituaries can. Besides text, it can display numerous photographs and even sound recordings. It can also accommodate new text, so that people who want to contribute to the site after it is up can do so indefinitely. The Web is increasingly proving itself to be a useful medium for people who need to express themselves in ways that traditional obituaries cannot accommodate.

Perhaps the need to come to terms with death is no greater than immediately following a calamity. That certainly seemed to be the case after TWA Flight 800 exploded above the coast off Long Island in 1996, killing all 230 aboard. Conspiracy theories swirled through the Internet and ultimately through print media, casting doubt on the government's conclusion that a design flaw allowed a spark to ignite a fuel tank.[24] Family members and friends read these accounts with great interest but without solace. For that, they turned to each other and to the World Wide Web.[25]

More than seven years after it first appeared, the Web site of Families of TWA Flight 800, the nonprofit group formed to facilitate communication among the friends and families of crash victims, is still running. Hosted by the Long Island newspaper *Newsday*, it provides copious information about TWA Flight 800, resources for coping emotionally and physically after an aviation tragedy, and legal information for surviving family members. But the most moving parts of the Web site are the memorials and tributes. In addition to hymns and psalms, people contributed poems, such as "The Rabbi

Prayed," by Bernadette Cioch, an emergency medical technician who described a rabbi praying over the bodies in a temporary morgue. Here is the third verse:

> Many hours had passed
> No relief at last
> Backpacks and teddy bears
> God, please dry our tears
> Parents without children
> Children without parents
> And the Rabbi prayed.

Another poem, "Quietly Thinking" by Liskula G. Cohen, ends with the following lines:

> Some weeks go by slowly,
> like a rainy Monday.
> I wait for the weekend,
> so I can relax.
>
> Meditation's not possible,
> So, I'll just wait for the facts.

The memorials are likewise moving. The memorial to passenger Courtney Elizabeth Johns of Clarkston, Michigan, quotes Pastor Doug Trebilcock's observation: "This is not God's will. God weeps."[26]

The Web sites created to memorialize the victims of TWA Flight 800 were forerunners of the sites dedicated to the victims of 9/11. In fact, so many Web sites were created about 9/11 that the Library of Congress commissioned the September 11 Web Archive to maintain a comprehensive record of them. The archive of thousands of memorial sites, tribute pages, survivor registries, solicitations for charity, news sites, and government sites adds up to more than five terabytes of data.

Of course, these sites are experienced one at a time, and their communicative power lies in their ability to convey how much friends and family members miss those who perished in the terrorist attacks.[27] One method of communicating this sense of loss was to post letters to the deceased on Web pages devoted to individuals who lost their lives. Cantorfamilies.com—a site that pays tribute to employees of eSpeed, Cantor Fitzgerald, and TradeSpark, who died in the World Trade Center—has numbers of such letters. Following are selections from letters written by three friends:

> Hey Deb [Bellows],
> GOD BLESS YOU, on your second anniversary in heaven!! You are still always in my thoughts. I will never forget you!
> Love, Claudine [Morales]

[To Edward DeSimone III]
I find myself, I'm sure like others, asking God how & why? But I also thank Him for the wonderful gift of you. I am so lucky to have had the chance to know you & to have had you as a friend for 12 years. I will always pray to Him to give your family strength and to watch over them.
Cabrina Caruso

Hey! Charlie [Waters]. I was always late even to say thanks. I was having problems in the Department I was in and you took me in. In a short time that I knew you, you made a difference in my life. You gave me the opportunity to move on and make a new life when my life was in the toilet. You are a great friend because you still inspire me. Your family should be proud to carry your name. God Bless the Waters.
Jose Pichardo

"We all have a need to go somewhere and just sit and be with our loved one. A lot of us do that on the Web," says Tracy Orr, whose husband, Alex Steinman, died in the World Trade Center but whose body was never recovered. Online memorials permit persons who lose loved ones in large-scale tragedies to come to terms with their deaths by participating as a community in the making of tributes.[28]

Online memorials put up after national tragedies may receive the most hits, but memorial Web sites created by individuals after individual deaths are just as heartfelt. The motivations for making these Web sites are the same. Building a virtual memorial—or contributing to one—can be cathartic. Making a Web page with tributes that show why one individual will be missed can help those who put their grief into words, not just by the contemplation required to articulate feelings, but also by the social act of communicating meaningful information to others.

ArriveAlive.com is a site dedicated to the life of Robert Thomas Church, who died in a drunken-driving accident at the age of 20. Written by Robert's father, it provides an illuminating biography of the handsome and popular young man from a small Texas town who enjoyed working with his hands and who hoped to start his own air conditioning business after finishing his classes at Texas State Technical College and working for a few years in Waco. It also tells the story of Robert's troubles with alcohol, including his being convicted of possessing alcohol as a minor and later of driving while intoxicated. The biography ends when the drunken Robert drives off a gravel road and his pickup truck overturns in a pool of water at the bottom of a steep culvert. The site includes various photographs of Robert growing up and includes photographs taken at the scene of the accident.

Most of the site, though, is broader information about alcohol abuse, including links to sources on alcohol, underage drinking, and DWI. Robert's father is using the World Wide Web to make his son's death into a lesson for other parents and their children. "My God has told me not to beat myself up over the past, but to learn from my mistakes and share my testimony with others, so they might learn from those mistakes," he writes. "Despite God's assurance that I should not beat myself up over mistakes of the past, realizing that I had no idea at the time how my actions were influencing Robert, they are nonetheless regrets that I will carry to my grave. Please don't expose yourself to similar regrets."[29]

Another online memorial is dedicated to Noah Allen Gray, who was born lifeless in a California hospital on September 21, 2002. "Born An Angel," the Web site proclaims. "Our beautiful son . . . left to be with Jesus before we got that chance to hear his precious cries," writes his mother, Stephanie Gray. "He is truly an Angel from above and he was just so perfect and beautiful in every way, the only thing he didn't have was a heartbeat." Like many other online memorials, this one is very personal, even intimate. It tells about the parents' marriage and their desire to have children. It details the day Stephanie's doctor said, "I'm sorry but your baby didn't make it." It offers recollections from the funeral service and explains why the parents disinterred the ashes and had them moved home, where they are displayed in an urn under a spotlight surrounded by Precious Moments figurines. There are links to information about stillbirth and links to sites of other children who died at birth. Throughout the site are photographs of Noah, usually cradled in the arms of his mother or father. The site is both a public presentation about the experience of stillbirth and a conversation with a son whose voice his mother never heard.[30]

Of course, most experiences of death in this country are not of stillbirths or traffic fatalities. The leading causes of death are heart disease, cancer, and stroke; and life expectancy is 77 years, not 0 or 20. These deaths are what we think of when we think of death due to "natural causes," and they probably account for the majority of online memorials. These memorials typically include an obituary, photographs, and tributes from family members and friends, but they seldom have the bigger message that Web sites created after unexpected tragedies often have.

New ideas are not around long before they are packaged and sold to the public, and this principle certainly holds true for memorial Web sites. Dozens of companies such as lifefiles.com, memorypost.com, and partingwishes.com, offer online memorial packages with setup wizards that help the bereaved create a virtual memorial by guiding them through a simple protocol. Such packages make sense because many people who would like to memorialize their loved ones on the Web are unable to build Web sites on their own. These people are willing to pay the sometimes hefty setup and maintenance fees to online memorial services, which are increasingly being offered through funeral homes. Such online memorials have the additional appeal of genealogy. "You can keep a legacy of your family alive down through the generations," says Monte Hoffsommer, vice president of CompuTech Business Solutions, which sells Time Honored Tributes. "Memories aren't going to get lost in some shoe box somewhere."[31]

CONCLUSION

As acts of communication, personalized obituaries, roadside memorials, and online memorials are efforts to influence what Barbie Zelizer calls collective memory. Just as individuals remember certain things and forget others, society also remembers and forgets. And just as personal memories affect how individuals act in the present, so collective memories affect contemporary society. Zelizer explains that understanding collective memory requires that we answer four questions: "Who remembers? Why remember? How does one remember? And for whom is remembering being accomplished?"[32] These four dimensions of collective memory highlight processes by which shared meanings and remembered images are created.

People who erect roadside memorials or write extended tributes for newspapers and the World Wide Web do so in part out of a sense that traditional rituals are necessary but insufficient means of coming to terms with the death of a loved one. Under the control of physicians, ministers, and funeral directors, death rituals often fail to allow more than passive compliance from mourners. Many people are left feeling as if not enough has been done, that the life that has ended requires greater acknowledgment. A common theme among people who participate in memorial making is their need to do something more than simply follow brief mourning rituals. So they search for public ways to mark the lives that ended, reclaiming symbolic space lost in the twentieth century as life's passages became dominated by specialized professionals. They write or they build because they feel compelled to create something—an essay, a tribute, a marker—anything to express the significance of their loss. Their activity is cathartic; it helps satisfy their need to create something in the aftermath of a death they were powerless to prevent.

Although personal, these creations are by no means private. Just as Americans in past generations wore mourning clothes to signify their grief to the community at large, these memorials are public proclamations. They are meant to be read in the newspaper, seen on the roadside, and visited on the Web. And like the mourning signifiers of old, these memorials are meant to last long after the casket has been lowered into the grave. The obituary will be laminated and reread, the roadside marker will be passed day after day, and the Web site will be visited from time to time in perpetuity.

These contributions to the collective memory have moral dimensions. Most memorials are created for people to be remembered because of who they were—trusted coworkers, loving family members, humorous friends. They express the goodness of people who illustrate cherished character traits. Other memorials—such as crosses on the roadside—are created as warnings. Be sober! Drive carefully! Don't become another object lesson! Whether created to inspire or to warn, memorials stand as testimony that individuals mattered and are missed. They spring from populist impulses that insist that everyone has the right to be remembered because memory, like power, should be democratic. Drivers should remember the teenager who died on the highway; newspaper readers should acknowledge the loss of a community member; and the Web should have space for persons who lived their lives beneath the radar of the popular media.

Personalized obituaries, roadside memorials, and online memorials show that people in mourning need opportunities for nonscripted public expressions that satisfy their need to articulate their most heartfelt experiences. Contributing to the collective memory requires individuals to express their anguish and thus deal with death squarely and personally. Memorial making allows people to speak for themselves and to be heard by others. Running counter to the culture's short-sighted and dishonest denial of death, it gives people the dignity to mourn and to remind the community that their loved ones mattered.

6: VIEW FROM THE NEWS DESK

Comedy and Death in Media Space

Mark I. Pinsky

According to recent polls, an increasing number of Americans—including those identifying themselves as Christians—believe that it is possible to communicate with the dead. A dead character appeared to great effect in an episode of the 1980s hit series *Family Ties*, according to Father Andrew Greeley, the Catholic priest, sociologist, pollster, and novelist. In his book *God in Popular Culture*, Greeley said that watching at least two episodes of well-written situation comedies like this one starring Michael J. Fox, or others of the period, like *The Cosby Show*, should excuse viewers from listening to a Sunday homily or sermon in church. Greeley was moved by a special, hour-long episode of *Family Ties*, which he said was an example of "a modern version of the medieval morality play" and a "practically perfect Good Friday/Easter story." In the episode, a good friend of Fox's character, Alex Keaton, dies, "and Alex himself must die to his old self to put on the new man." The friend is:

> as kind and as self-effacing as Alex is just the opposite. A friend from the earliest days of grammar school, he died in an auto accident at a time when Alex was supposed to be with him. Alex had refused to join him because of pure selfishness. Hence he felt guilty not only because his friend had died and he hadn't, but also because his life was purchased

143

by the selfishness of which his friend seemed incapable. After the funeral, Alex returns to the Keaton family house but continues to see his friend whenever the rest of the family leaves the room. Typically, the friend is perfectly willing to forgive Alex. Just as typically, Alex is as hard on himself as he is on others.

Greeley writes that, in this context, Alex's conservative, acquisitive character is unwrapped: he finds his identity through a *metanoia*, a conversion. Greeley laments that too few "homilists and catechists in America comprehend what wonderful instructional resources these programs are," nor do many clergy see "sermon material" in family programs like this one.[1] One might also ask how many members of the viewing public "get religion" from the death of fictional characters.

Characters die all the time in complete, discrete media, like television movies and mini-series and big screen features, songs, and novels. It's expected, and sometimes welcomed. Yet it is when a beloved (or at least well-liked) character in a hit, prime-time series dies that most Americans think about the jarring and lasting intrusion that death can mean. It is, literally, like a loss in the family. A face you are used to seeing, a voice you are used to hearing on the same night of the week, is suddenly missing. There's a vacuum, and at the same time, a need to make some sense of it.

There are a variety of reasons why fictional characters on popular shows "die." Actors demand more money or want to leave the series because they have lost interest in the part or have other, more creative or lucrative opportunities. In 1956 Jean Hagen left Danny Thomas's *Make Room for Daddy*, and her character, the family's wife and mother, died offscreen. McLean Stevenson, who played Col. Henry Blake in *M*A*S*H*, left the show in 1975 for a starring vehicle (the first of several failures). His character was dispatched when his plane crashed in the Sea of Japan. Jimmy Smits left NYPD Blue in 1998 for a short-lived movie career, which led the show's writer to kill off his character, Detective Bobby Simone, in a shattering episode. In 2000, in the wake of a salary dispute with the actress who voiced her animated character, Maude Flanders of *The Simpsons* died in a freak accident, providing a moving crisis of faith for her husband Ned, a devout evangelical Christian.

Producers of hit shows in doldrums may think a "death" will shake up the creative mix by eliminating characters. Others, struggling with big budgets and middling ratings, simply take an ax to the cast. Or an actor will actually die suddenly or become terminally ill, like William Frawley, who played the grandfather in *My Three Sons*, did in 1966. Later, memorable deaths following real deaths in ensemble shows included Michael Conrad, who played the beloved Sgt. Phil Esterhaus in *Hill Street Blues*, and Nick Colasanto, the equally endearing Coach on *Cheers*. "Death on television can have a number of different impacts on the overall chemistry of the fictional family, as well as the people who are vicariously participating in that family," said Robert

Thompson, director of the Center for the Study of Popular Television at Syracuse University, in an interview with the author. Sometimes removing a character through death can change the dynamic of a show and reinvigorate it. In that sense it can mirror real life. When someone who is part of a real family goes away, it allows the family to change and to evolve in new and sometimes healthy ways. However, death can also be disturbing. "Most American viewers, perhaps 80 percent, turn to television for anesthesia, which means that in the end television is for the most part a medium profoundly incapable of actually dealing with the entire range and impact of emotion that comes with death," Thompson said. "The whole point is, most of the time we are watching television, we are watching it to forget bad things—and death is the worst of bad things."

For more than a decade, veteran television critic Hal Boedeker has written with depth and insight about the portrayal of death in network series. In a February 17, 1991, column for the *Miami Herald* entitled "Will Death Breathe Life into *Thirtysomething*?" Boedeker discussed the killing off one of the ABC series' main characters the previous week. The fatality followed months of discussions among the producers and writers over which of the seven angst-ridden, Philadelphia yuppies to dispatch. After four seasons, the show was adrift creatively and was dropping in the ratings. Boedeker reported that the leading candidate to go had been a female character who had been operated on for ovarian cancer. Ann Lewis Hamilton, one of the show's writer-producers, said the character of Nancy Weston was ruled out "because of the reaction to the cancer shows. . . . The mail and phone calls we got were so amazing," she told Boedeker. "People who worked with cancer patients begged the producers to save Nancy. The show wanted to present the disease without melodrama and without making the patient a paragon of bravery. It's like you can get cancer and move on," Lewis explained. "You realize the disease doesn't always turn into death."

Instead, the writers and producers settled on a character named Gary Horton, killed in a traffic accident while riding his bicycle. Gary's death in one episode, and his wake in another that followed, provided an opportunity to examine how a tight-knit group of friends in their thirties deals with sudden, unexpected death. Hamilton described the wake episode to the critic as intentionally "Swedish," what Boedeker described as "the heavy, meditative style of Ingmar Bergman's films." One character, Melissa, had had a big fight with Gary, and the two had not reconciled. Nancy, the cancer survivor, had to deal with "survivor's guilt." Hamilton told Boedeker that she guessed that Gary would not reappear in later episodes as an apparition—but that is exactly what he did, helping his best friend Michael deal with the loss. In CBS's *Cold Case*, a hit of the 2003–04 season, long-dead murder victims appear on screen at the close of each episode and smile at the investigator who solved their case, as if in gratitude.

As a longtime crime, cops, and courts reporter turned longtime religion writer, I have written a good deal about death over the past thirty years, albeit from different perspectives. Along the way, I've noticed some curious things about the way mortality is depicted and considered through North American media. Older people tend to read the daily, local obituaries—for obvious reasons. When political figures or celebrities of broader societal interest pass on, they are the subjects of considerable coverage and often of in-depth profiles. In the case of people from the arts and entertainment world, an essay called an "appreciation" is sometimes written. Like local obituaries, these too are well read, especially those dealing with the poignant or courageous manner in which the departed faced their ends. The AIDS epidemic, which for a time took so many people in the prime of life, compelled an intimate consideration of the meaning of loss. For similar reasons, the short obituary profiles of 9/11 victims published by the *New York Times* and *Newsday* were riveting. Yet regular day-to-day reporting on death resulting from crime, disease, illness, and accident has a tendency to blur into abstraction. The same is true of coverage of executions in those states that have instituted death by lethal injection; accounts written by observers are alike to the point of monotony. The procedure is sterile, and thus, perhaps by design, it lacks atmospheric drama beyond the obvious. For example, in early November 2003, Timothy Keel was put to death at Central Prison in Raleigh, North Carolina. There was so little interest that the *News & Observer*, the city's daily newspaper, did not send a reporter, and the Department of Corrections spokeswoman, Pam Walker, did not come out to read an official statement. From time to time, controversies erupt over the "right to die," like the Karen Ann Quinlan case in New Jersey in 1985 and Nancy Cruzan in Missouri in 1990. After Florida Governor Jeb Bush pushed through a law in 2003 allowing him to order a feeding tube into a comatose young woman named Terri Schiavo against the wishes of her husband, a statewide poll found that nearly two-thirds of those surveyed opposed such a law. While these cases do focus editors' and readers' attention on death, this interest is usually transient.

Outside of their own personal losses, I believe that most North Americans experience death's sense of loss and its deepest emotional and intellectual dimension elsewhere in media, beyond broadcast news reports and the printed pages of newspapers and magazines. Given the growing intersection of religion and popular culture, it is not surprising that when people consider mortality, this engagement is most likely to be through its fictional manifestation—that is, in entertainment media—and in one form in particular: popular, long-running, commercial, network television series. Current fascination with death runs the gamut from the two highly rated *Crime Scene Investigation* series and their imitators, to the HBO television series *Six Feet Under*, which is set in a family-owned funeral home in Los Angeles. Both *Six Feet Under* and *CSI* deal profoundly with the issues of death and mortality. However, in *CSI* episodes, like in those of *Quincy* before them, the victims are already dead before the narrative begins. And *Six Feet Under*, a pay-cable, limited-run series in which characters become corpses in the first few seconds of each episode, reaches just a fraction of a network hit's audience. Death was a character named Andrew in the religion-centered series *Touched by an Angel*, played by an actor named John Dye, a coincidental irony. In his column, "The Pop Gospel," published in the July 19, 2003, *Calgary Herald*, Canadian cultural critic David Buckna wrote:

> Dye said in an interview that "death is the biggest change we can imagine. It's the great unknown. Even with the faith of Job, there is probably a bit of fear for every person because it is the unknown." Because Andrew is the angel who takes people to heaven, Dye wanted to portray him as "the most compassionate, caring, gentle, accepting face I could possibly put on him. I wanted to make Andrew as welcoming and as strong as possible." Andrew's character changed over the run of the series, becoming more of a caseworker. "With all the audience response, Andrew expanded accordingly," notes Dye. "Now, when I appear [on screen], it doesn't necessarily mean someone is going to die. They may or may not. It adds to the drama of the show."

Hal Boedeker, now with the *Orlando Sentinel*, returned to the subject of "Death on the Airwaves" in a May 9, 2002, story pegged to the death from a brain tumor of a central character in the top-rated NBC medical drama, *ER*. "Dr. Greene has been the center of the show for so long," executive producer Jack Orman told the critic. "We thought it was important to give the audience a strong goodbye, and given the fact he's dying, there were some things he needed to get in order. He's always been bugged by difficult relationships." In order to understand why these events have such a great impact on the real lives of millions of viewers, Boedeker spoke with Greg Limongi, director of spiritual care and bereavement services at Hospice of Orange and Osceola counties in Central Florida. "There's a new honesty in looking at the complexity of death and our emotions that doesn't fit any stereotypes," Limongi said. "We are most affected by what is most intimate to us," he says. "The reading of the letter [about Greene's death] makes it personal. It doesn't try to make it global. It makes it specific. Then that becomes universal." For context, Limongi reached back to the death of Col. Blake on *M*A*S*H*, which Boedeker said still reverberates with fans. "You saw that death entirely through the experiences of survivors," Limongi told him. "I'll never forget seeing Radar's face," referring to the character Radar O'Reilly, played by Gary Burghoff. "Sometimes you can convey more through understatement."[2]

Limongi then cited the death of Chuckles the Clown, one of the most famous episodes of *The Mary Tyler Moore Show*, which presented a humorous side of death that the culture usually shies away from. "During the first part of the show," Boedeker wrote, "Mary Richards castigated colleagues for their lighthearted reactions to the ridiculous circumstances of Chuckles' death: Dressed as a peanut at a circus parade, he was crushed by an elephant. But then she laughed uncontrollably at his funeral," which Limongi said was understandable. "We're raised to believe death is only serious and somber," he said. "Humor is one of the most powerful releases. You're sharing something so emotional. At a hospice, we laugh at things others wouldn't. It's not being irreverent." When Boedeker interviewed Mary Tyler Moore, the actress called the Chuckles episode "her favorite." She remembers that she was fearful about the unusual subject matter, and that the regular director, Jay Sandrich, passed on doing it because the script made him nervous. "We were dealing with the humorous aspect of death," she says. "As so much in comedy does, it reminds us that nothing is written in stone in terms of your feelings and your ways of expressing them. Everything is legitimate."[3]

Others in the television industry agreed. "Death has become a major part of the television narrative," said Ron Simon, curator of television at the Museum of Television and Radio in Manhattan. "There's so much about death being a major character in the new century. It's not a taboo subject anymore." Tim Brooks, coauthor of *The Complete Directory to Prime Time Network and Cable TV Shows*, explained it this way to Boedeker: "Television is a very personal medium," Brooks told the critic. "Viewers see TV personalities as friends. It's almost like a death in the family. Many tears are shed on both sides of the screen."[4]

The death of subsidiary characters, particularly in dramas, can be weathered. Jim Davis, the actor who played Jock Ewing, the patriarch in *Dallas*, died in 1981, providing the show with a plot twist as his legacy. More recently, Richard Crenna and his character died in *Judging Amy*, as did Lynne Thigpen in *The District*. *The Sopranos*, another HBO series, violently dispatched numerous characters through the seasons and then wrote into the show the death of Tony Soprano's mother Livia, following the death of the actress Nancy Marchand. (Tony had earlier tried to smother her, believing she was trying to have him killed.) The award-winning and highly regarded drama *St. Elsewhere*, set in a hospital—where death is a common occurrence—eliminated six main characters during its seven-year run in the 1980s, without ill effect. But the sudden loss of a central character through death can be fatal to a series. The light-hearted Western *Alias Smith and Jones* lost momentum after the 1971 suicide of costar Pete Duel. And this phenomenon seems to be magnified, perhaps for psychological reasons, when the series is a comedy—whether or not it is acknowledged onscreen. *Chico and the Man* did not long survive Freddy Prinze's 1977 suicide, even though his character's absence was explained as a sudden move. Redd Foxx's 1991 death was acknowledged in CBS's *The Royal Family*, but the new show lasted only one season. Similarly, *NewsRadio* made it through just one more season following the 1998 murder of Phil Hartman.

The most recent national experience with the death of a popular television character in comedy was doubly tragic. John Ritter, the star of ABC's emerging success, *8 Simple Rules for Dating My Teenage Daughter*, died suddenly of an undiagnosed heart ailment on September 11, 2003, at the age of 54. He was on the show's set, shooting an episode, when he fell ill. In business, life, and art, Ritter's passing provided an opportunity for the larger world to grapple with the meaning of death. ABC had built its hope for the season around *8 Simple Rules* and was already banking on its continued success. Ritter, who played a stay-at-home sportswriter named Paul Hennessy, acknowledged this reality in an interview published after his death in the September 13, 2003, *Los Angeles Times*. During a break in the shooting, the actor joked that Michael Eisner, chairman of the Walt Disney Company, which owns ABC, "is in my dressing room right now, waiting to give me a deep-tissue massage."

Production on the show was closed down immediately following Ritter's death as ABC decided how to proceed, with executives remaining close-mouthed until after his September 15 funeral. "The first few days we really didn't talk about the show," Lloyd Braun, chairman of the ABC Television Group, told Bernard Weinraub in the October 7, 2003, *New York Times*. "People were emotional messes. Everyone was grieving. We knew it had to be one day at a time." ABC executives like Braun and Susan Lyne, president of ABC Entertainment, were quickly made aware of how much Ritter's death had shaken viewers, according to the *Times*. "We were getting so many e-mails and calls and letters about John, a lot of people sending in their own stories about losing a family member," Lyne said. "There's this thing about television, particularly television comedy and family comedies. You're in somebody's living room and bedroom. You're in people's lives in a powerful way. You do feel close to these television families. It's different when the father in a family comedy dies than when an actor on a show dies."

Lyne, Braun, and others considered a spectrum of ways to handle the death, from ending the show to replacing Ritter's character—both of which were rejected. The actor's widow, Amy Yasbeck, was brought into discussions about the series' future, and through ABC, the actress issued a statement saying that Ritter "believed in this show and its message that a strong family can get through anything." Ultimately, the decision was made to continue the show after a decent interval, incorporating Ritter's death into the plot. "Everyone felt that dealing with the tragedy on-air was the right thing to do, creatively and cathartically," Stephen McPherson, president of Touchstone Television, which produced the show for Disney, told the *New York Times*. "It seemed to be the best choice."

In the meantime, a one-hour special, *John Ritter: Life of Laughter*, drew an audience of 14 million viewers when it aired September 16 in the series' regular time slot. Ritter's death reverberated beyond ABC. The September 21 broadcast of the 55th annual Emmy Awards, which normally emphasized comedy, presented the next opportunity for public mourning for Ritter and other stars who had died during the year, from Bob Hope to Richard Crenna. Don Bellisario, producer of CBS's *JAG* and *Navy NCIS*, told the *Los Angeles Times* on September 20 that the award ceremony could integrate the mourning and the celebration. "I don't think this will dampen the awards completely," he said. "Obviously there will have to be tributes. But I think everything will be put into perspective. Death is part of life. It grabs all of us. John would not have wanted his death to dampen the ceremony. He would have wanted the opposite."

As other Disney executives said earlier, there was now a purpose beyond ratings for the show's episodes dealing with Ritter's death. Susan Lyne told the *Los Angeles Times* on September 17, 2003, "We will have an opportunity for people to get to know the Hennessy family in a very unusual way, in a way that television rarely does. We will let viewers in on the journey this family will take." The final new episode starring Ritter aired October 7 and drew an audience of 17.45 million viewers. When the special, one-hour episode dealing with Paul Hennessy's death was broadcast on November 4, 2003, nearly 21 million North Americans were watching. Alessandra Stanley wrote in the November 5 *New York Times* that the show "was done as tastefully as television permits, blending scenes of sorrow with wry touches of comic relief." And religion played a role in the way the family dealt with their grief. Hennessy's wife Cate, played by the actress Katey Sagal, lay awake in her bedroom, railing at God for taking her 46-year-old husband. But her mother, portrayed by Suzanne Pleshette as being very religious, tried to argue that God was not to blame for Paul's death. At another point, Pleshette's character snapped at James Garner, portraying her ex-husband, for bothering Paul's widow to find his last, unpublished sports column. Garner, capturing the wildly mixed feelings that often attend death, replied acidly that he was sorry for assuming that trying to fulfill a posthumous professional obligation was not nearly as important as what Pleshette was doing—freezing leftovers from the wake. Stanley of the *New York Times* cited some of the episode's shortcomings for teaching life lessons:

> The half-hour sitcom format is almost ideally unsuited for depicting profound loss and raw wounds. Even in this longer episode, some things seemed too neatly contrived. All three children reacted differently to the news, but by episode's end, all three had rallied, found some measure of peace and were able to provide one another and their mother with loving support. But children do not always bounce back and find their better natures after a death, particularly a parent's premature one. Anger, guilt, fear and sorrow surge up in all sorts of untidy, destructive ways that do not fit a 22-minute arc.[5]

Unlike life on the other side of the small screen, by custom and practice the dead on television shows are rarely spoken of after their passing. However the absence of major characters is explained, they are rarely referred to on the show thereafter. Writers, said Boedeker in an interview, "don't want to dwell on something that will bring the viewer down. They need to move on. If you keep looking backward, you can't move on." Also, syndicated episodes are often shown out of sequence, so there is a continuity problem. But, the critic said, Ritter "may be an exception, since he was so central to the show."

Robert Thompson agreed that Ritter's death was different, for a constellation of reasons that would probably prove fatal for the series. As he said when I interviewed him, there were "parallels between the death of a fictional character and the impact on the fictional family; with the death of a real actor and the impact on the profession; as well as its impact on the viewers who were vicariously a part of that family. Those things are a lot harder to survive." The key to the survival of a show like *8 Simple Rules* after the death of an actor and character like Ritter is

> the ability to get past the sorrow of the "Very Special Episodes" and be funny again. It's got to do that pretty quickly, or it becomes the kind of program that is the antithesis of what people turn to a sitcom to see. Whereas, with real death, the loss of a family member or close friend is always with you. The show cannot continue to be darkened by that event. In life, a death doesn't just get settled in a "Very Special Episode." It's something that colors the rest of the lives of the people around them, and it does it in a color that is not on the palette of entertainment television.

But in a sense, Thompson said, "television in fact conquers death. In reruns, Lucy is still a young woman, John Ritter is still tripping over a sofa on *Three's Company*. We watch those shows and, in perpetual syndication, we see the closest thing to immortality this side of the afterlife."

Chapter 7

Collective Memory, National Identity: Victims and Victimizers in Japan

Richard A. Gardner

What has come to be known as "the Aum Affair" illustrates many of the issues that have arisen in recent years concerning the relation of media and religion, including how media coverage of religion is inextricably linked with questions concerning national and cultural identity.[1] Following the release of sarin gas on the Tokyo subway system on March 20, 1995, it was discovered that members of the new religion Aum Shinrikyô were responsible not only for this act of terror but also for a series of crimes and murders in prior years. As the extent of Aum's crimes became clear, Japan faced a sort of identity crisis. Throughout the spring and summer of 1995, great attention was given to the question of whether Aum was somehow a mirror of Japan. Nearly every dimension of culture, society, tradition, and recent history in Japan was examined and questioned as to whether it might somehow account for the rise of Aum and its turn to violence. How the story of Aum was told, reported, and analyzed was related, either explicitly or implicitly, to fundamental questions concerning national, cultural, and religious identity in Japan. To appreciate this dimension of the ways narratives of Aum were constructed in Japan requires giving special attention to two additional, interrelated topics: history, and the relation of victims and victimizers.

In considering the relation of media and religion in Japan and elsewhere, history is important. In the case of Japan, many postwar Japanese institutions and practices, including freedom of the press and freedom of religion, were founded on an explicit rejection of Japanese institutions, laws, and practices of the war period.[2] Debate has also continued, both within and without Japan, about whether Japan has really been able to free itself culturally and politically from what is sometimes referred to as the emperor system, or the feudal dimension of Japanese society. Such issues were particularly on people's minds in 1995 because the year marked the fiftieth anniversary of the war's end and brought with it hope that the postwar (and thus the wartime legacy as well) was at an end.

Discussions and narratives of Aum were almost invariably structured by a sharp opposition between victimizers (*kagaisha*) and victims (*higaisha*).[3] In many respects, the notions of victims and victimizers have also played a central role in discussions of Japanese identity in the postwar period. Critics both within and without Japan have continued to question whether Japan has sufficiently reflected on, apologized for, or made redress for its actions during the war period. Attempting to reverse the role of victims and victimizers, some nationalists and conservatives have argued that Japan was a victim, forced into war by Western colonial powers. For many in Japan, as in other parts of the world, stories of the past and present continue to be cast in terms of an unresolved opposition of victims and victimizers.[4]

IMPERIAL JAPAN

Following the collapse of the Tokugawa regime, the restoration of the emperor, and the establishment of the Meiji state in the 1870s, Japan witnessed an incredibly rapid process of modernization, industrialization, social transformation, and development. Japan's military was developed and modernized to the point that it was able to defeat China in the Sino-Japanese War of 1894–95 and consequently acquire Taiwan. Then, to the astonishment of the West, Japan defeated Russia in the Russo-Japanese War of 1904–05 and as a result was able to annex Korea in 1910. Participating on the side of Britain in World War I, Japan was also able to acquire some of Germany's concessions in China. Japan was so successful in following Western models that it had come to rival the Western nations in economic and military power and had become a colonial power in its own right. Though the Taishô period (1912–26) showed some increasing signs of liberalism, it was also marked by the government increasingly promoting the divinity of the emperor. The Shôwa period (1926–89) witnessed a growth in imperial and colonial ambitions resulting in the invasion of Manchuria in 1931 and, at least according to some, a continual period of war until surrender in 1945. Following its defeat, Japan was occupied until 1952 when it was granted formal independence.

The relation of media, religion, and the state was of such importance throughout this period that one might well write its history in terms of the relation of the three.[5] In charting their course toward modernity, Meiji period leaders reached the decision to place, however symbolically, the emperor at the center of national, political, and religious life. Though legally and politically understood in various ways throughout the period, the emperor was the center of the Japanese state, and the state itself was understood as a religious entity. Though freedom of religion was at least nominally granted, largely as a result of pressure from Western nations wanting the right of Christian missionaries to proselytize, the state exercised fairly strict controls on religious organizations and required citizens to participate in activities defined as nonreligious but involving veneration of the emperor.

As part of its drive toward modernization, the government also encouraged the growth of media and journalism. The publication of newspapers, magazines, and journals developed rapidly in the Meiji period, and radio broadcasting began in 1925.[6] While encouraging the growth of a modern mass media, concerted efforts were made throughout the period to control and censor the media. The nature and degree of control and censorship naturally fluctuated. Katô Shûichi provides a succinct overview of the government's stance toward newspapers: "It [the government] encouraged their founding; then imposed strict censorship and police control; then adopted a more liberal attitude, if not *de jure*, at least *de facto*; then in the era of military domination, exerted direct control over all means of expressing opinion."[7]

Though not usually described as such, all acts of censorship throughout this period had a religious dimension.[8] Given that the state was defined in religious terms, the censorship of any views concerning political issues inevitably, if only implicitly, involved a religious aspect. Censorship was also frequently connected, however, to more explicitly religious issues. Publications about the emperor or imperial family were strictly controlled and censored, based on the assumption that the emperor was a sacred personage. Religious groups were also under various forms of social control, extending to censorship, throughout the period.

Government control of religious groups was particularly strict when they were perceived as somehow undermining or offering alternatives to the model of national and cultural identity centered on the emperor. Newspapers also frequently joined in campaigns directed against suspect new religions. At least in Japan, "cult controversies" are not new. Throughout the Meiji and Taishô periods, newspapers carried discussions of new religions reminiscent of the discussion of cults to be found in the media in both Japan and the United States in recent years. The most prominent example of the suppression of a new religion was that carried out on Ômotokyô in 1921 and especially 1935 when its leaders were arrested and its facilities destroyed.[9] As will be suggested later, the case of Ômotokyô is not without relevance to discussions of Aum.

Throughout the war years, the state's supervision and control of religion and the media increased to the point that it is difficult to untangle the three. Members of religions or the press who questioned the war effort were quickly intimidated or imprisoned. Government leaders and newspapers explicitly portrayed the war as a holy war being fought for the emperor. As John Dower has extensively documented, however, Japan was not the only country to wage a war of propaganda, largely directed at its own people, portraying the war as a holy war. In both Japan and the United States, wartime propaganda had an explicitly racist and religious dimension.[10] Both countries fought with "God" on their side.

As already suggested, images of Japan during the war years still play a role in shaping perceptions of Japan within Japan, the West, and Asia. In the simplest of terms, the dominant image of wartime Japan is that of a people indoctrinated into blind obedience to the emperor to the point of being willing to fight to the death and inflict unnecessary suffering on others. However, despite the concerted efforts made by the government to censor the media and indoctrinate the population in the ethos of the emperor system, Japan is not best thought of, even during the war period, as a monolithic culture, state, and society with everyone thinking and acting like.[11] Japan is better understood as a complex set of tensions between competing centers and various peripheries. Seen from the perspective of some in the United States and elsewhere, however, the Japanese are still not infrequently portrayed in both the mass media and some more scholarly presentations as bound to an unusual degree by the shackles of tradition, group mentality, or culture.

POSTWAR JAPAN

The American occupation and the enactment of Japan's new constitution were meant to reestablish Japan as an open, democratic society and to eradicate from Japan all traces of its feudal past that were responsible for the military's rise to power and Japan's actions during the war years. As already noted, many postwar Japanese institutions, laws, and practices (such as freedom of religion, freedom of the press, and limits on the power of the police and military) were thus founded on a rejection of those of the war years. In addition to phenomenal economic growth in the postwar period, Japan also witnessed a rapid growth and expansion in the mass media as well as the appearance and rapid growth of many new religions. Japan's wartime actions, however, have left an unresolved legacy. Underlying almost all discussion of Japan in the last sixty years, indeed, has been the question of whether Japan has actually managed to free itself of its past, as well as continued reflection on the relation of victims and victimizers.[12]

Both in the mass media and in academic works, questions have continually been raised about whether Japan has a true democracy, whether the press is really free, whether the educational system stifles individualism and creativity, and whether Japan's religious institutions offer anything of spiritual value. These questions are almost invariably raised as part of a larger question: Has Japan managed to break free of its past? The negative forces of the past are characterized in a variety of ways, including feudalism, groupism, authoritarianism, the legacy of Confucianism, or the emperor system. These forces and structures are also almost invariably seen as having most clearly manifested themselves in the militarism of the war years.[13]

Much of the discussion of Japanese religion in the postwar period has been shaped by this wartime legacy. Because of their close association with the war effort, the emperor and the major Buddhist and Shinto organizations were discredited in the eyes of many.[14] To those of a conservative orientation, however, this loss of trust in traditional religious organizations, as well as the postwar separation of religion and state, has resulted in the loss of cultural, religious, and national identity. While some new religions present themselves as alternatives to traditional religious organizations, others present themselves as embodiments of traditional values, with some even promoting reverence of the emperor. Evaluations of the new religions are mixed. While some view them as providing a healthy diversity of religious orientations opposing the pressures to conform, others view them critically as somehow perpetuating Japan's feudal past. Though for different reasons, thinkers of both a conservative and a more liberal persuasion have viewed religions in postwar Japan as never having developed mature and meaningful orientations. In this view, religions in Japan have yet to recover from the trauma of the war years. In reflecting on the Aum Affair, many commentators linked the emergence of Aum to a "spiritual vacuum" existing in postwar Japan.

Issues related to the war legacy are also reflected in debate on the mass media as well as in the Japanese media's coverage of religion in the postwar period. While some have celebrated the Japanese mass media, others have questioned whether it is not simply a tool of the government and thus a sign of the lack of true democracy in Japan.[15] How the past creates ambiguities in the coverage of religion can be seen most clearly in the media's coverage of the emperor and imperial family. As is well known, the media voluntarily refrains from certain types of reporting on the emperor and the imperial family.[16] This gives rise to criticism, of course, that the "emperor system" still holds sway. At the same time, the media has often been subjected to criticism from conservatives and to harassment and even violence by right-wing groups because of its commentary concerning the emperor or the war.[17] Because of its inevitable connection with the emperor, as well as with the spirits of the war dead, any critical discussion of the war in the media has a religious aspect for at least some. Simply put, casting the emperor in the role of victimizer offends the Right, while downplaying the role of the emperor and the Japanese military as victimizers offends those of a more liberal orientation.

Though a simple characterization is difficult, the media's coverage of religion in the postwar period is also marked by the wartime legacy. There have been cases of critical and sometimes sensationalized coverage of religion, particularly new religions, in the news media. The most prominent case, aside from Aum, is that of Sōka Gakkai, which was criticized for aggressive proselytizing in the 1950s and 1960s, especially after it took the step of forming its own political party.[18] In a sense, Sōka Gakkai opened itself to criticism, at least in the eyes of some, by attempting to undo the strict separation of state and religion and thus recalling Japan's wartime past. At the same time, there has also been reluctance, especially on the part of the major newspapers and television networks, to be too critical of religions. To be aggressively critical of religions, it is feared, would be to recall if not repeat the persecution (in which the major newspapers participated) of religions that took place during the war years. One of the fears expressed following the Aum Affair was that the media, because of Aum's crimes, now felt a new confidence not only in criticizing but in offering sensationalized coverage of new religions.[19]

Aside from occasional controversies involving new religions, news coverage of religion in postwar Japan has tended to focus, both within and without Japan, on issues directly linked to the legacy of the war years. Both Japanese and Western news media gave extensive coverage to the death and funeral of Emperor Shōwa, as well as to the enthronement of the new emperor Akihito.[20] The death of Emperor Shōwa gave rise, of course, to extensive discussion of the emperor's role in the war and the question of whether Japan had adequately atoned for its actions in the war and colonial past.[21] For at least the last twenty years or so, the annual controversy generated by the visits of Japanese politicians to Yasukuni Shrine, where Japan's war dead are enshrined, seems to have received almost yearly coverage in newspapers in Japan, Asia, and the West. Whether explicitly or implicitly, the coverage inevitably gives rise to questions such as the following: Has Japan sufficiently apologized and atoned for its actions during the war? Is Japan properly respecting the separation of religion and state? Are nationalism and militarism on the rise in Japan again?

The continued reflection on Japan's wartime past and the way it is reflected in the present can also be seen in the legal fallout resulting from the Aum Affair.[22] In December of 1995 the Religious Corporations Law, originally enacted in the early postwar years to ensure freedom of religion, was revised. The revision sparked considerable debate and opposition, with some suggesting the revision would mark a return to the mentality of the war years. Controversy also surrounded efforts to apply the Anti-Subversives Activities Law to Aum. This law was also enacted in the early postwar years and was aimed primarily at communists and leftists. Though enacted, the law has never been applied. Too many have deemed it unconstitutional as well as reminiscent of laws concerning national security enacted during the war years. Because of strong opposition, the law was not applied to Aum. A new law, especially designed to apply to Aum, was enacted and applied instead.

MEDIA AND THE RISE OF AUM

Issues concerning the relation of religion and media play a major role in accounts of the rise and development of Aum Shinrikyô from the early 1980s to 1995.[23] It can be argued, indeed, that such issues, along with concerns about the relation of victims and victimizers, are inextricably linked with the development of Aum and its turn to violence.

Not long after its founding in 1984 as a yoga group, Aum Shinsen no Kai, Aum began developing its own forms of media. In 1986 the group began publishing books by its founder, Asahara Shôkô, and other Aum leaders, and the monthly magazine *Mahayana* was launched in 1987. Beginning in the late 1980s, Aum also began developing a range of other forms of media: manga and anime, promotional videos, music recordings, and theatrical productions. In the early 1990s, Aum began weekly radio broadcasts from Russia. At some point in the 1990s, Aum also established its own homepage on the Internet. In addition to using these various forms of media for proselytizing, the group made use of its audio and videotapes as part of its regimen of ascetic practices and relied on technological metaphors (e.g., the input and output of data) to explain its teachings concerning the working of the human mind.

The years 1989 and 1990—crucial for understanding the history of Aum—witnessed a major confrontation with elements of Japanese society, including the news media, which played out as a debate between victims and victimizers.[24] In the spring of 1989 the journalist Egawa Shôko introduced concerned parents of Aum members to the lawyer Sakamoto Tsutsumi, and the Association of Aum Shinrikyô Victims was formed.[25] Despite having received complaints from citizens about Aum, the Tokyo metropolitan government approved its application for legal status as a religious group in September of 1989. The laws regarding religious groups, quite liberal to avoid a repeat of the victimization of religions that occurred in the war years, gave no grounds for denial.[26]

Criticism of Aum in the media intensified in the fall. From October through December, the weekly magazine *Sande Mainichi* (Sunday Mainichi) ran a series of articles highly critical of Aum entitled "The Insanity of Aum Shinrikyô." In response, Aum published a book refuting the charges. In the process of preparing a case against the group, Sakamoto also spoke out against Aum on the radio. The Tokyo-based television network TBS was also preparing a program on the Aum controversy in which Sakamoto was to appear. TBS allowed leaders of the group to preview the program and then decided not to air it after the leaders threatened a lawsuit. In early November, Sakamoto and his family disappeared from their home in Yokohama.[27] Suspicion centered on Aum, and Egawa began writing a series of articles and books critical of the group and attempting to link it to Sakamoto's disappearance. The police investigation of the disappearance led nowhere.[28] In January of 1990, media attention turned to Aum's participation and total defeat in the Diet elections. A subsequent Aum retreat in Okinawa that spring found Asahara preaching a more pessimistic apocalyptic vision, and the retreat itself was disrupted by hordes of journalists.

Though a new controversy arose in the fall of 1990, Aum was able to gather outside support in its efforts to portray itself as a victim of persecution. After acquiring land and establishing a commune near the small village of Namino-son in Kumamoto Prefecture, an anti-Aum movement drawing on the rhetoric of the anticult movement arose among locals, and several Aum leaders were arrested on charges concerning fraud in the group's acquisition of land there. As Watanabe Manabu has noted, a number of lawyers, scholars of religion, and citizen movements came to Aum's defense, claiming the dispute involved the violation of human rights and the suppression of religion.[29] One scholar of religion, Ikeda Akira, drew parallels with the government's suppression of Ômotokyô during the war period. This seems to be the inspiration of Aum's later claims that it was a victim of state suppression of religion such as occurred during the war period. Throughout the early 1990s a number of public figures, including scholars of religion Shimada Hiromi and Nakazawa Shin'ichi, wrote sympathetically of Aum or published dialogues with Asahara in popular publications. Aum made use of such positive evaluation of itself by prominently recycling such accounts in its own publications. Views of Aum were thus, for the most part, polarized. Drawing on the language and concepts of the anticult movement in the United States, anti-Aum activists saw it as a dangerous cult, mind-controlling and victimizing its members. Defenders of the group tended to support, either explicitly or implicitly, its claim to be a victim.

Given its history of confrontations with the media, it is not surprising that the media came to play an increasingly larger role in Aum's vision of the dangers facing the world and the possibility of a coming apocalypse.[30] Aum had long discouraged its members, particularly those who renounced the world to live in Aum facilities, from reading newspapers and magazines and watching television. Some members eventually developed an explicit theory of the mass media as an instrument of mind control. In this view, the mass media was being manipulated by those, such as Freemasons and Jews, who were conspiring to control the world. To explain the influence of the media, the language of computers was borrowed: the media, as well as the surrounding culture in general, controlled people by inputting bad "data" into their minds. In addition, the media was also presented as making extensive use of subliminal images to control thoughts and feelings. Aum's teachings and practices were even presented as being a mirror image of the media; they allowed for the input of good data and deletion of bad data. By 1995 the media had come to be viewed, at least by some Aum members, as a central part of the evil forces threatening the world.[31]

It should also be noted that some in Japan in retrospect blamed the mass media for the rise of Aum and its turn to violence.[32] Some pointed to the influence of apocalyptic manga and anime that were popular in the 1970s and 1980s when many members of the group were coming of age.[33] Others pointed to the boom in interest in supernatural powers in the 1980s when Japanese television and popular publications gave extensive, sensationalized, and at times sympathetic coverage to the topic. Such publications and programs, some argued, helped render Asahara's claims to supernatural powers plausible. Still others have suggested that aggressive media attacks on Aum, such as that by *Sande Mainichi*, only helped alienate Aum further from mainstream society. The discovery in 1995 that TBS had allowed Aum members to preview its program on Aum before Sakamoto's disappearance and then failed to inform the police of this following the disappearance also gave rise to criticism that TBS had a role in precipitating, and then withholding relevant information about, acts of murder. Rather than a neutral observer, TBS was thus cast in the role of abetting victimization.[34]

MEDIA COVERAGE FOLLOWING THE TOKYO SARIN ATTACK

Following the sarin attack in Tokyo on March 20, 1995, there was nearly constant media coverage of Aum until the arrest of Asahara on May 16, 1995. In many ways the media, particularly television, continued to play an active role in the Aum drama rather than being a simple objective reporter of the news. Attention here will be focused on how television coverage of Aum at times became an active participant in the unfolding drama as well as shaped public perceptions in the way it presented and told the story of Aum.[35]

In some senses, television coverage of Aum represented an intensification of the "war" between Aum and the media as well as a "war" between the private broadcasting networks for viewer ratings.[36] In the coverage of early raids on Aum facilities aired on television, members were frequently shown filming with video cameras both the police and television crews covering the raids. Aum leaders held press conferences denying their involvement in the attack, claiming that they indeed had been victims of attacks with sarin and suggesting that they were victims of a conspiracy. Aum also opened up some of its facilities to television crews for tours and interviews. In the days following the sarin attack, Aum members were soon handing out pamphlets on the street, claiming to be victims of state suppression of religion as was Ômotokyô in the war years.[37]

Television coverage of Aum was extensive. Programs on Aum made up the top twenty television shows in April and May and roughly seven hours a day were being devoted to the topic. Regular news programs, now devoted almost entirely to coverage of Aum, were supplemented by a daily array of extended news programs, news specials, and documentaries. In addition, morning and afternoon talk shows (called "wide shows" in Japan), usually aimed at housewives and focused on the lives of entertainers and media personalities, devoted their airtime almost exclusively to Aum. Producers and hosts who had honed their skills covering for the most part the ups and downs of the lives of entertainers now turned their attention to Aum. The results were predictable and met with not a little criticism in Japan. Much of the television coverage was responsible in the sense that it provided extensive background information of the history of Aum and a fairly close account of the police investigation. Much of the coverage of Aum, however, was sensationalized, focusing on all that was strange and bizarre. At times television simply seemed desperate to fill space with stories about Aum and Asahara, as suggested by detailed reports about "gluttonous" meals Asahara had eaten at restaurants.

What did most, perhaps, to shape television coverage was the decision made by the major private television networks in Japan to allow Aum officials to appear on television to answer the questions of, and debate with, journalists and anti-Aum activists. For at least several weeks, mainly in April, members of Aum appeared on television nearly daily. The most prominent were Jôyu Fumihiro (Aum's official spokesperson), Murai Hideo (Aum's minister of science), and Aoyama Yoshinobu (Aum's main lawyer as well as member of the group). Most prominent in opposing them in the debates was Egawa Shôko, who was often on television from morning to night appearing on several channels in the same day. While images of the deceased lawyer Sakamoto and of the in-hiding Asahara were repeatedly broadcast as a way of representing the conflict between Aum and Japan, the most visible, live confrontation between the two played out as an ongoing debate with Egawa and others opposed to a handful of Aum leaders. The major participants in these debates became more widely known, it seems, than all but the most prominent of Japanese politicians and government officials.

The most dramatic instance of how the media coverage helped shape and then became entangled in the unfolding events is the murder of Murai Hideo on April 23, 1995. Returning to Aum's Tokyo headquarters in the evening, Murai was forced to enter through the front door because the mass of television and newspaper reporters blocked access to a side entrance. As Murai approached the front door, he was stabbed by a man angry with Aum (but whose motivations are still unclear), and he died later that evening at a hospital. The stabbing was not only filmed in graphic detail by television crews but was also repeatedly broadcast on several channels. There was some criticism of both the police and media for failing to preserve access to Aum's headquarters and thus, to an extent at least, creating a situation in which the stabbing was possible. There was also considerable criticism of television stations for repeatedly airing film of the stabbing. There was an additional furor when it was later discovered that one television network, TBS, had inserted subliminal messages in its film of the stabbing in a subsequent documentary.[38] This is one of the major instances in which news about the coverage of Aum became a central part of the story of Aum.

A standard narrative soon emerged to explain the group: Aum was a "cult," and its members had been "mind-controlled" by Asahara. The words "cult" and "mind control" had earlier been taken into the Japanese language as *karuto* and *maindo kontorōru* as the result of the influence of the anticult movement in the United States on the opponents in Japan of religious groups such as the Unification Church.[39] Those with experience in opposing groups they regarded as cults were soon in demand to appear on television. At some point in her years of opposition to Aum, Egawa had also adopted the language of the anticult movement. Though a range of Japanese intellectuals and scholars attempted to complicate if not simply reject the notions of cult and mind control, few if any did so on television, and their writings, even if published in major newspapers, seem to have had little impact.[40]

To some degree at least, the language of cults and mind control also served to distance Aum from Japan. As noted, the word "cult" had been introduced relatively recently into Japanese and, in addition, had been most prominently used in relation to the Unification Church, a new religion perceived by many in Japan as being non-Japanese. To an extent, cults were also associated with new religious movements in the United States. Some even claimed that cults, by definition, were non-Japanese and largely a Western phenomenon. Aum's use of quasi-Indian dress and the language of Tibetan Buddhism provided other rationale for perceiving Aum as somehow being more of a foreign cult than Japanese. Aum was understood by many, in other words, not so much as a product of Japanese culture, society, and religion, but as a result of foreign influence. This use of the term "cult" to understand and distance Aum from Japan, however, was soon at least somewhat undermined by those claiming that Japan itself had been a cult and its people mind-controlled during the war years.

The narratives generated by the notions of cult and mind control were supported in some ways by the appearance of Aum members on television. While Aoyama, Murai, and Jōyu put on impressive performances and at least seemed to hold their own in some debates at times, they frequently made implausible claims and arguments. They also continued to deny that the group was in any way involved, when it was becoming increasingly clear that at least some Aum members were involved in a number of crimes, including the Tokyo sarin attack. Aside from the Aum leaders, a number of members who had left the group or whose loyalty was wavering also appeared on television. Almost invariably, their voices were distorted and their faces hidden by mosaics in order to hide their identities. This helped create the impression that they were not quite normal, if not outright bizarre. Not a few of the ex-members also claimed that they had been mind-controlled.

The language of cults and mind control was also bound up with a sometimes explicit and sometimes implicit sorting out of Aum members into victimizers and victims.[41] Asahara was clearly a victimizer and responsible for numerous crimes in addition to having mind-controlled his followers. Ex-members could present themselves and be presented as victims because they had been mind-controlled. In the case of other members, sorting them out into victims and victimizers was not so simple.

While measuring and documenting the influence of television on people is notoriously difficult, it does seem to me that coverage of Aum on television (whether it was creating, reflecting, or interacting in complex fashion with public views) provides a fairly good index of the views of Aum held by many in Japan. Though a simple point, it is important to remember that the television coverage did not, at least in any simple fashion, represent the views of many people in Japan. From almost the beginning the coverage of Aum on television was extensively criticized by scholars, intellectuals, journalists, and writers of various sorts in major newspapers as well as in a range of magazines and journals, including many to be found at any train station kiosk or bookstore in Tokyo. There is little if anything in non-Japanese or outsider critiques of the media coverage that is not to be found in Japanese critiques of the media coverage.

The media coverage of Aum was also subject to considerable ridicule and parody in many popular magazines.[42] Criticism of the media coverage can also be seen in the collection of *senryū* (satiric verse) composed by readers and appearing almost daily in major Japanese newspapers:[43]

> Wide shows hiring lousy detectives as part-timers.[44]
> Television stations offering religious contributions for television appearances.[45]
> Television has put headgear on us.[46]
> Former Aum members, treasured by the mass media.[47]

Given the degree to which television coverage of Aum was subject to criticism and the sort of popular ridicule reflected in *senryū*, it is thus difficult to conclude that the influence of television was total.

A TABOO ALTERNATIVE VIEW OF AUM AND THE MEDIA

Two of the most remarkable and important accounts, not just of Aum, but of the interaction of Aum, the media, and Japanese society, are the documentaries *A* and *A2* made by Mori Tatsuya. Both the content of the films and the reaction to them in Japan illustrate how concern with the relation of victimizers and victims has structured accounts, narratives, and understandings of Aum in Japan.

A freelance producer of documentaries for television at the time, Mori found himself dissatisfied throughout the spring of 1995 with the televised news coverage and documentaries about Aum.[48] Mori eventually decided that he wanted to make his own documentary of the group with, as he has written, the aim of undermining the sense of understanding Aum created by the constant use of the words "mind control."[49] In the fall of 1995, he wrote letters to members of Aum's public relations staff asking for their cooperation in making a documentary of the group. As discussions with representatives of the group continued throughout the fall and winter, Mori also submitted a plan of the documentary to a television station and had it approved. Just before he was to begin filming in earnest in the spring of 1996, the project was canceled and Mori dismissed, at least partially because he refused to include prominent anti-Aum activists in the film.[50] Mori decided to make the film on his own, using a rented, hand-held camera, and eventually he enlisted Yasuoka Takaharu as producer.

Filmed between the spring of 1996 and 1997, the film shows in many ways the opposite of what was shown on television about Aum. For the most part, the film focuses on Araki Hiroshi, the group's new spokesperson, as he goes about his daily life, deals with members of the media, and attempts to explain Aum to the public. There is no narrative, commentary, or explanation in the film beyond a few written statements identifying the date and location of the scenes to follow. The film simply documents Aum members' interaction among themselves, with Mori, and with the outside world. The intent seems, indeed, to present viewers with a riddle or puzzle rather than an explanation.

Part of the power of the film is that it shows Aum members as they had never been seen before. It seems evident that over the course of the year some of the members, particularly Araki, grew comfortable with Mori's presence.[51] While Mori's questions are sometimes probing and direct, he is not confrontational. Aum members are shown expressing differences of opinion, doubts, and uncertainties. Some profess belief in supernatural powers, others dismiss them. Some clearly still consider Asahara to be of great importance, others downplay his significance. Though some are hesitant to address the topic, others discuss their growing realization that some fellow members do seem to have been involved in the crimes they are accused of. Mori's refusal to use mosaics to hide members' faces or to electronically distort their voices also contributes to rendering them somehow more normal.[52] Viewers are thus shown, basically for the first time, members of the group looking relatively normal and less "mind-controlled."

The film also offers a stunning reversal of perspective and shows something else not shown before. With Mori frequently filming Araki's interaction with representatives of the media, viewers come close to viewing the media from Aum's perspective. Mori also includes here many scenes that the media filmed but never broadcast and never thought to broadcast: media representatives negotiating with, cajoling, badgering, and sometimes even attempting to deceive Araki in an effort to get permission to film inside Aum facilities or interview Aum members. The behavior of some of the television crews is such that viewers may be forgiven if they find themselves, if only for a moment, somewhat sympathetic with Araki. In the course of his negotiations with the media, Araki also grows more strident and tense than in other scenes. The film reveals, in other words, how the media's acts of gathering information and reporting transform, in sometimes subtle but important ways, the people it seeks to report on.

The power of the film derived also from the way it muddies the clear-cut opposition of Aum as victimizer and the rest of society as victim. As suggested, it is difficult not to sympathize at points with Araki and other Aum members. Another scene, in which Mori films five or six police officers stopping Araki and two other believers on the street and questioning them at length, muddies the waters even more. The scene ends with the officers falsely arresting one Aum member for obstructing a police officer. Mori's filming of this incident then becomes part of the film. Though initially reluctant, Mori gives a videotape of the incident to a lawyer Aum has engaged when he realizes it is the only chance of the arrested member being released. The Aum member is released almost as soon as the police are informed by the lawyer that he has a film of the arrest. When the police asked Mori whether he was a member of Aum as he filmed the incident, Mori said, no, he was a freelance director. For the police, it was unthinkable that any member of the media would turn over to Aum or make public film damaging to the police. Though it did not get prominent coverage in the news, Aum later sued the police over the incident and won damages.

Filmed throughout 1999 and 2000, A2 focuses on the daily life of Aum members and their relations with members of the surrounding community in which they live.[53] Aside from reports on the progress of trials of Aum members and government efforts to monitor Aum, the major news regarding the group in the last several years has concerned the efforts of local governments and citizens to expel Aum members from their communities. Members have been denied the right to legally register their residency in a number of communities, their children have been denied the right to attend schools, and citizens groups have maintained constant surveillance of Aum residences. Japanese courts, nevertheless, have consistently upheld the rights of Aum believers to reside where they wish and for their children to attend local schools.

Here again Mori is able to show us something that television and Japanese newspapers have rarely if ever shown. Coverage of tensions between Aum members and surrounding communities on television inevitably portrays a situation of sharp opposition, with local communities united in their desire to expel Aum members. At points in *A2*, however, members of Aum are shown talking amiably and even laughing together with the local residents manning the stations set up to monitor the group. One of the local citizens admits that though at first he was always yelling and screaming at them, he has gotten to know them and will even miss them in some ways now that they have decided to move. In one scene, Aum members and local residents take a commemorative photo of themselves together. A television crew chancing upon the scene is forced to ask which ones are Aum members and which ones local residents. One Aum member says, correctly, that such scenes of believers and local residents getting along are never aired on television. This too, it seems, would inappropriately blur the boundary between victims and victimizers.

The reaction to the films in Japan is also revealing. Despite being widely praised by commentators and film critics in some major newspapers and magazines, and winning awards in foreign film festivals, the films have been little seen in Japan. Though they were shown at a number of small art theaters in a few large cities, none of the large cinema chains were interested in the films. This perhaps is not so surprising. Though a few short clips from the films were aired on television, television stations have also declined to broadcast the films, even after midnight when more controversial works and programs are often shown. In addition, until 2003 no company could be found that was willing to distribute the films in video or DVD format.[54] Negotiations with such companies usually broke down on orders from executives who had never seen the films. Rumors circulated that Mori was a member of Aum, had taken money from Aum, or was even an Aum official.[55] Some scheduled showings at Japanese universities were canceled when officials received calls saying that Mori was an Aum member. Two prominent anti-Aum activists, one seemingly without having seen the film, stated on their homepages that *A* was too sympathetic if not outright supportive of Aum. The explanation for the scant attention the films received, especially for the first, which appeared when concern with Aum was still very strong, is simple. As suggested, both of the films tend to undermine the understanding of Aum in terms of a stark opposition between good and evil, victims and victimizers.[56]

OTHER VIEWS OF AUM

Though the portrayal of Aum as a "cult" was widely echoed in major newspapers and popular magazines, an incredible range of interpretations appeared in newspapers, popular magazines, scholarly journals, and books. With varying degrees of explicitness, such interpretations invariably raised issues concerning national and cultural identity in Japan. The emergence of Aum was related, indeed, to nearly every aspect of recent Japanese history, culture, and society: the continued influence of the emperor system, the loss of the emperor system, the educational system's failure to provide moral training and to develop individualism, the influence of Western and especially American values, political corruption, the spread of consumer society, the failure of traditional religions, the continued influence of traditional religions, a spiritual vacuum, and so forth.[57] Most if not all of these interpretations of Aum can be linked to issues regarding the relation of postwar Japan and Japan of the war years or, in other words, to the question, Who are we as Japanese?

As noted earlier, a number of intellectuals and scholars of religion, particularly Shimada Hiromi and Nakazawa Shin'ichi, had written or spoken favorably of Aum or taken part in discussions with Asahara later published in popular magazines. Following the Tokyo sarin attack, Shimada also frequently appeared on TV attempting to explain, if not explicitly defend, Aum. As Aum's involvement in a series of crimes became clear, criticism grew of those perceived as sympathetic to or even supporting the group.[58] Criticism of Shimada reached the point that he was forced to resign his university position. To an extent at least, the motivation of scholars such as Shimada and Nakazawa was linked to the wartime legacy. They perceived Aum and other new religions as offering alternatives to mainstream Japanese society and as being potential victims of what they understood to be the pressures to conform in Japanese society. Their potential victims, however, were revealed to be victimizers.

Though members of Aum cast themselves as victims of state suppression of religion such as occurred during the war years, a number of prominent intellectuals, most of whom had come of age during the war or in the early postwar years, drew parallels between Aum and Japanese militarism of the war years.[59] Included here were Maruyama Masao, Katô Shûichi, and Tsurumi Shunsuke. Though it was not given prominent coverage, some major newspapers reported that Arima Akito, former president of the University of Tokyo and minister of education at the time, within a week or so of the Tokyo sarin attack had made a statement likening Aum to the Japanese state during the war years. Following the death of Maruyama Masao, the foremost postwar critic of the emperor system, on August 15, 1996, NHK produced a two-part documentary on the life of Maruyama that aired in December of 1997. The documentary opened and closed with Maruyama's comments on the similarities between Aum and Japan of the war years. Such views were given little if any coverage, however, on private television networks.

Intellectuals of a more conservative orientation, however, traced the origin of Aum to the loss rather than the persistence of traditional values. Writing in a widely read conservative monthly journal, the scholar of Confucianism Kaji Nobuyuki identified the breakdown in the unity of religion and state centered on the emperor as the source of the current malaise that had made religions such as Aum attractive to Japanese youth.[60] Though not calling for a restoration of the unity of religion and the state as Kaji, Yamaori Tetsuo (a well-known scholar of religion writing frequently for popular publications) argued that the forced separation of religion and state and the encounter with Western values had helped create a situation in which a religion such as Aum could appear.[61] Such views, however, were also rarely voiced on private television networks.

Some of the foreign accounts of Aum, particularly those written with little direct access to Japanese sources, at least implicitly portrayed the group as somehow being a result of Japan's unresolved past. As part of an explanation of Aum, David E. Kaplan and Andrew Marshall's *The Cult at the End of the World: The Incredible Story of Aum* (the title itself should give pause) portrays contemporary Japan as, among a long list of other undesirable things, a country devoid of individuality.[62] This view of Japan, of course, owes much to images of wartime Japan and treats the Japanese as basically mindless victims of themselves, a trait presumably not shared with citizens of more enlightened nations. Though a much more serious and substantial work, Robert J. Lifton's *Destroying the World to Save It* also tends to portray Japan as a victim of its unresolved wartime past.[63] Lifton gives extended discussion to parallels between Aum and the imperial cult in wartime Japan, possible (though not clearly explained) causal links between the two, and Japan's failure to seriously reflect on the war. What is stunning and wildly misleading about Lifton's account is that it gives no indication that these issues were widely and extensively discussed in Japan. The impression created by Lifton is that people in Japan are still victims of some sort of thought control and are incapable of reflecting on the war years or worrying about possible links between the present and the past.

Though much of the debate concerning the relation of Aum to the war years did not appear on television or in prominent publications, the topic was given extensive discussion in *Sensôron* (Debate on the War), a best-selling collection of manga writer Kobayashi Yoshinori's writings on the debates concerning Japan's role in the war. Responding to critics who had likened Aum to Japan of the war period, Kobayashi argued that it was not wartime Japan but postwar Japan that was mind-controlled. In this view, Japan of the war years was as much victim as victimizer, and postwar Japan was a victim of mind control that could be traced, largely, to the American occupation of Japan. Kobayashi's work also illustrates how the language of the anticult movement had also come to be applied to discussions of Japan's past and present.

There are scholarly works in both Japanese and English, however, that have presented more nuanced and complicated interpretations of Aum. "The Evolution of Aum Shinrikyô as a Religious Movement," an essay by Shimazono Susumu, professor of religion at the University of Tokyo, is exemplary. Opposing the reduction of Aum to the notion of "cult," Shimazono argues that Aum was a religion and that precedents for most aspects of Aum could be found in Japanese religious history. In addition, Shimazono suggested that the reasons for the rise of Aum as well as for its turn to violence were to be found in contemporary Japanese society as well as in forces and trends at work throughout much of the world. What Shimazono did not offer, however, was a story or explanation that could be reduced to a simple format and presented as having offered a clear, unambiguous explanation. Works such as Shimazono's, in other words, do not reduce the story of Aum to a clear-cut opposition of victims and victimizers.

CONCLUSION

The aim of this essay has not been to argue that Japan is struggling with a unique set of problems or a set of problems that other nations, peoples, or cultures have somehow resolved or overcome. The aim has been, rather, to suggest that the opposition of victims and victimizers is at the heart of most if not all issues and controversies regarding the relation of media, religion, and national or cultural identity. For examples, one need only think of Northern Ireland, South Africa, the dissolution of Yugoslavia, the Middle East, Korea, or the current "war on terror." Whether involving the confrontation of groups within nation-states, the dissolution of nation-states, or confrontations between nation-states, there are few if any controversies and crises involving religion and identity that are not experienced and construed in terms of a sharp opposition between victims and victimizers and, at least at times, a sharp opposition of good and evil. The opposition of victims and victimizers presents scholars and journalists alike with a number of challenges and dilemmas. By way of conclusion, I will simply note a few of these challenges and suggest how they might be related to crises outside of Japan.

As the case of Aum illustrates, the past can have a significant influence both on how current events unfold and on how they are interpreted. The legacy of wartime Japan shaped not only reactions to Aum before the Tokyo sarin attack but also subsequent interpretations and reactions to Aum in a variety of ways. The way the past shapes the present, however, is not always readily apparent: an appreciation of its influence requires more than a basic knowledge of the past and of the peoples in whose lives it is present. In addition, the meaningful past often stretches back not merely sixty or seventy years but centuries. The Holocaust, for instance, cannot be understood without an awareness of nearly two thousand years of Christian understanding of Jesus as a victim of Jewish victimizers. Within the Muslim world, the opposition of Shiites and Sunnis is nearly fourteen hundred years old and involves, among other issues, radically different evaluations of victims and victimizers in the political struggles within early Muslim communities. The power of the past in the relations between Christians and Muslims can be seen in President Bush's description of the war on terror as a "crusade" and in Muslim reactions to the description.

Most current conflicts and controversies shaped by the opposition of victims and victimizers involving religion, the state, and identity also have deep roots in the often traumatic history of the emergence of modern nation-states in the last two centuries. Different groups within modern nation-states and different modern nation-states have, of course, often radically different understandings of that history. Two basic stories, with nearly endless permutations, are frequently told here. Those in a position of at least relative power tend to tell a story of heroic sacrifice in which victimizers were overcome, a just order established, and the relation of victims and victimizers resolved (or simply suppressed, forgotten, or not acknowledged as having existed). Those who see themselves as having unjustly suffered in the past and present tend to tell a story of an unresolved opposition of victims and victimizers. The heroes of the first narrative are not infrequently cast in the role of victimizers in the second type of narrative. Both types tend to be structured around a clear and unambiguous opposition of victims and victimizers.

The ways in which the past is alive in the present pose particular problems and challenges for journalists (though their identities and activities often overlap with those of scholars). In contrast to scholars, journalists usually face extraordinary limitations in terms of time and space. Stories often must be written relatively quickly, and space usually allows for only brief, if any, reference to history. Given these limitations (which are particularly acute for newspaper and television news), "news" becomes almost by definition something occurring in the present with little of any meaningful relation to the past. This erasure or downplaying of history, however, can at least implicitly support and encourage a particular view of history. This is the view that past oppositions between victims and victimizers have been politically, morally, or legally resolved, or are simply part of a distant past no longer relevant to the present.

Both scholars and journalists face a twofold challenge in attempting to construct their own narratives of the stories people tell. The first is the simple problem of giving appropriate weight, space, time, and nuance to the often radically different views of history and of the relation of victims and victimizers involved in what we think of as "current" events. The second involves the difficulty of constructing narratives that do not, either intentionally or unintentionally, embody yet another clear-cut opposition of victims and victimizers. The difficulties here are hard to overestimate. Even if it is not an innate human disposition, there seems to be a widespread expectation that stories should not only involve a clear opposition of right and wrong, good and evil, and victims and victimizers but that they should also offer clear explanations as well as satisfying resolutions.

Though there are seemingly endless cases of peoples having been subjected to unwarranted persecution and suffering, much of history, human experience, and current events is not, however, easily susceptible to simple explanation, satisfying resolution, and a black-and-white allotment of people into the roles of victims and victimizers. As suggested by the reaction to Mori Tatsuya's films *A* and *A2*, many are ill at ease with stories that offer no simple explanations and that blur clear-cut distinctions between victims and victimizers. It may well be, however, that it is just such complicated and ambiguous narratives that are needed for people to be able to begin to move beyond the simple narratives of victims and victimizers that have done so much to structure history and human experience.

7: VIEW FROM THE NEWS DESK

Religious Contradiction and the Japanese Soul

Teresa Watanabe

At first glance, Japan seems to be a land riddled with religious contradictions. It appears to be one of the most spiritual places in the world, with sublime Zen rock gardens and sacred forest groves, enormous Buddha statues and hundreds of thousands of temples and shrines. Every year, millions of people throng to the shrines to ask for divine blessings over the New Year, during travels, pregnancies, and test-taking. Many homes, at least those of the older generation, feature both Buddhist and Shinto altars, which are kept refreshed with flowers and offerings of rice. According to official government statistics, 94 percent of Japan's 127 million people identify themselves as Shinto, 72 percent as Buddhist, and 84 percent as both.

Japan also appears to be highly secular. With some exceptions, traditional religious organizations do not generally play a major role in the lives of most Japanese. Most Japanese do not attend weekly religious services or follow a daily regimen of prayer or meditation. Colleagues who have worked with each other for years confess they have never had one conversation about each other's faith beliefs; fear of creating differences in this culture of harmony and consensus has, in many quarters, somehow shelved religion as a common conversational topic.

And what about all of those self-identified Buddhists and Shinto follow-ers? Evidence suggests that the affiliations, for many, are nominal. According to an independent survey by the Study of Christianity in Japan, a Tokyo-based research organization, 65 percent of those surveyed said they actually believed in nothing. Such data are reinforced by personal surveys conducted by people like the Rev. Dickson Yagi, a Southern Baptist minister who taught university students in Japan for twenty-six years. He says that 70 percent of students he surveyed every year said they believed in no religion at all. In a 1999 survey by Kokugakuin University, 65.8 percent of 4,000 students sur-veyed said the word "religion" was scary.

Religion seems everywhere, and nowhere, in Japan.

As a Tokyo correspondent and bureau chief for the *Los Angeles Times* dur-ing the 1990s, I had a chance to explore Japan's fascinating spiritual land-scape. I chronicled the modern-day struggles of traditional Buddhist temples, the dynamism of so-called new religious movements, the spiritual longings of those who flocked to shamans, seers, and American New Age gurus. Reli-gion was in the news during those years, too. In 1995, a religious group named Aum Supreme Truth was accused of releasing sarin nerve gas on a Tokyo subway in an attack that killed 12 and injured more than 5,000. That same year, the political party of Japan's largest Buddhist organization helped a fledgling opposition party win an upset electoral victory over the ruling Liberal Democratic Party, sparking fierce debates over church-state separa-tion. In 1993, offering a veiled glimpse into one of the biggest Shinto rituals of the century, the Crown Prince of Japan, heir to the 2,600-year Chrysan-themum Throne, wed Masako Owada, a foreign ministry diplomat, before Amaterasu, the sacred sun goddess and mythical matriarch to the Imperial Family.

"I'm not religious, I'm spiritual." That self-description is popular among a growing number of Americans today. It is not far afield of describing what many Japanese might say about themselves, too.

Traditional religion is, by most accounts, in decline. Buddhism, first intro-duced to Japan via China and Korea 1,440 years ago, once played an irre-placeable role as the community's spiritual core, acting as schools, medical clinics, nursing homes, administrative offices and recreational centers. Today, however, it suffers from a dark image as a religion preoccupied with funerals and death. In a practical division of labor, Shinto priests got the marriage business and Buddhist monks got the funerals. Many monks spend far more time performing pro forma memorial rites for ancestors than teaching their flocks about Buddhist ideals and how to live them out. Chiaki Kitada, a Tokyo writer, remembers watching her father, a university professor, quiz a monk about Buddhist concepts when he visited their Kyoto home to perform a memorial rite for her grandparents. The monk could not answer her father's questions—an experience she says raised skeptical questions for her about the tradition's vitality.

Some Buddhist experts say an inability of monks to transmit the tradition's essence and relevance is a widespread problem. "Its dogmas have become unintelligible to the public, and few people show an active interest in the religion," Hajime Nakamura, one of the nation's foremost Buddhist scholars, wrote in an analysis for the *Encyclopedia of Japan*. "The Buddhist ideals of human life have been forgotten."

For some monks, one problem is economics. With Japan's high cost of living, a growing number must moonlight to make ends meet, cutting down time for religious study. Sects such as Soto, Shingon, and Shinshu Otani have reported that one-quarter to one-third of their priests work on the side. Yasuo Sakakibara was one of those moonlighters.

During a visit to his Kyoto temple some years ago, Sakakibara confessed he was far more capable of explaining statistical analysis than Buddhism. He took over the temple from his father as a family duty, but to make ends meet, he moonlighted as a professor of economics—a greater passion, he said. Sakakibara said his father used to read sutras every morning, pray before each meal, and hold more memorial services, usually one hour, in strict accord with Buddhist ritual. In contrast, the son said he neither meditated nor read sutras daily, had pared back service time to 35 minutes and, aside from presiding over funerals, generally celebrated only four major festivals. "I'm a bad priest," he laughed.

But at least he chose to be a priest. Especially in rural areas, a growing number of temples are closing because they can't attract a priest or sustain a congregation as people flock to the cities for work.

In an attempt to revitalize the tradition and attract more youthful followers, the Soto branch of Buddhism—one of Japan's two major Zen sects—began efforts at social justice: launching a program to eradicate discrimination against the untouchable class known as *burakumin*, holding workshops on women's rights, and sponsoring Cambodian refugee relief efforts. The Soto branch also opened an education office in the United States in 1997 to serve as a conduit of ideas and contacts between the Zen communities in both nations. The Rev. Taiken Yokoyama, who served in the office at the time, said Soto leaders were intrigued by such American Zen programs as street retreats with the homeless—innovations that might attract Japanese youth.

Japanese Buddhism cannot catch young people's hearts, in Yokoyama's view, but once in the U.S. culture, "young people can find good ideas relevant to Japanese Buddhism."

The life-affirming rituals of the Shinto tradition, by contrast, still seem to attract millions of Japanese, at least on the surface. Every New Year's Day millions of people visit Shinto shrines to pay respect—and contributions—to the gods in hopes of winning divine favor for the year. Millions more flock to colorful Shinto festivals featuring men in loincloths carrying *mikoshi*, divine palanquins transporting the local deities between shrines. Young and old visit shrines to purchase protective amulets or write petitions to the gods for good health, marriage, success at university entrance exams. And Shinto weddings are de rigueur for many young couples.

But many experts, such as Rev. Yagi, argue that such rituals have lost much of their religious meaning and become little more than cultural events or gestures as essentially playful as making wishes before throwing coins in a fountain. Do people make their New Year's pilgrimage to Meiji Shrine in Tokyo because they deeply believe that the gods will hear their petitions? Or because everyone else goes?

In addition, some Japanese remain wary of affiliating too closely with the Shinto tradition because of the way it was used by militarists to promote a cult of emperor worship and mobilize the nation for the disastrous wars of the 1930s and 1940s.

This is not to say that the Japanese people feel no deep spiritual hunger or lack the means to feed it. Dogma, doctrine, and organized services may not appeal to many Japanese, but spirituality is palpable in this nation, often expressed toward ancestors and nature. And modern religious movements, although somewhat damaged by fallout over the Aum affair and financial scandals, boast a dynamism largely absent in many traditional temples.

The Soka Gakkai lay Buddhist organization, for instance, is Japan's largest religious organization with millions of members in Japan and 115 countries around the world. The group owns Japan's third-largest newspaper, *Seikyo Shimbun*; it has started an art museum, cultural programs around the world, and an education system that includes Soka University in Southern California. Soka Gakkai also launched a political party, Komeito (Clean Government Party), which was known mainly for pacifism and promotion of welfare before coming under widespread attack in 1995 for helping an opposition party topple the ruling Liberal Democratic Party in upper house Parliamentary elections.

In preparing a 1996 profile of Soka Gakkai leader Daisaku Ikeda, I remember being taken aback by the virulence of the attacks against the organization. Critic after critic, including then LDP Secretary General Koichi Kato, declared that Ikeda would seek to control all of Japan. Some predicted he would remove the current separation of church and state and declare his Buddhist sect the state religion. Others imagined tax harassment, and one writer baldly claimed Ikeda would kill his enemies. All of these charges, and worse, were reported in Japan's media with little restraint, a frenzy that reminded me of the attacks on Aum Supreme Truth and anyone faintly suspected of complicity with the group. In a rare interview, Ikeda denied the nefarious charges and reminded people that Soka Gakkai was one of the few religious organizations that resisted Japan's Shinto-based militarism of World War II; its founders were persecuted for it. Why on earth, he asked, would the organization repeat those sins and use the power of government to persecute others?

It amused me, a few years later, to see the LDP embrace Komeito as a partner in the ruling coalition that now governs Japan. For the record, Ikeda did not kill his enemies, make his Buddhist sect Japan's state religion, or launch campaigns of tax harassment after the party gained power.

Another glimpse of a modern Buddhist organization came when my relatives introduced me to Shinnyoen. The group of 765,000 members with branches around the world, was founded in 1936 as an offshoot of the esoteric Shingon Buddhist sect. After so many experiences with temples in decline, I was astonished to visit the Grand Holy Temple in Tachikawa, a Tokyo suburb, and see hundreds of followers filling the grounds to pray, chant, watch videos of lectures and, later, meet with spiritual advisors. The group offered three kinds of spiritual consultations: one for acute crises, another for minor problems, and still another for yes-or-no decisions on such questions as whether to marry a particular person or make a certain investment. I decided to investigate further.

At one meeting, after an hour-long chanting session and video, followers gathered in a circle in a large room as *reinosha* (spiritual guides), moved around and offered each person a few minutes of advice channeled, they said, from the spirit world. I was told the reinosha were mirrors that would reflect my true nature back to me and illuminate what needed to be corrected. Open yourself, I was told, and follow everything the reinosha says so as to attain my Buddha nature.

Over a few meetings, I would be told to practice the Buddhist path with an obedient heart, reach out to the teachings to receive mercy, be a good listener, and dedicate myself to others. At one session, the reinosha told me she could sense that ancestors on my mother's side were lonely and needed me to console them. At another session, another reinosha told me that he saw an ancestor on my father's side.

"He sits in *gassho*, hands together, pleased that you have entered this path," the reinosha said. "He lived a long time, was very gentle, and people could rely on him. You are like that. You are a responsible person. Your mission is to seek spiritual enlightenment and advancement not only for yourself but also for your ancestors and those around you. But you must make more effort."

I stopped attending the meetings after I learned that the extra effort entailed climbing a training ladder to become a reinosha myself. Since that required various fees, plus bringing in new followers at each level ascended in what seemed to me a spiritual pyramid scheme, I politely declined.

The experience was a telling glimpse at the power that ancestors have over the Japanese soul. And there were many other similar experiences. Japan is filled with those who make a business out of ancestor veneration. Once a woman came to my apartment door and invited me to a meeting about ancestors. Curious, I tagged along and found an entire organization built around solving people's personal problems based on analysis of the lives of your ancestors. The group offered general lectures on such topics as "This World and That World" and "The Mystery of Family Lineage," then charted out your entire lineage, offering spiritual and psychological analysis of it. When they started asking questions about the size of my bank account, I stopped attending.

I also traveled to Mt. Osore (Mt. Dread), one of the eeriest places in Japan in the northern prefecture of Aomori. The desolate mountain, featuring a volcanic lake and strong smells of sulfur, is regarded as one of the three best peaks in Japan to commune with the dead. During certain months, blind shaman women called *itako* gather there for festivals where people come to communicate with ancestral spirits.

During a reporting trip to the region, I visited one itako named Mayama Take, who lived in a small brown house in Aoyama City. She was a small woman, with hair dyed brown, who said she had worked as an itako for sixty years, since the age of 19. Curious to see her in action, I asked her to contact an ancestor named Shiratori Juro, a feudal lord who was assassinated more than three hundred years ago. She lit a candle, asked for his date of death, shook a string of heavy wooden beads decorated with animal teeth and other charms. Then she attempted to enter a trance.

A few minutes later, Take said she couldn't call him down so would instead try to reach my mother, who had died three years earlier. After another shake of her beads, she announced a connection had been made. Through the shaman, my mother told me I was doing a good job at work but needed to settle down and start a family. It sounded like Mom.

Despite the tomfoolery in some of these schemes, the reverence for ancestors is deep and triggers many of the religious formalities that Japanese people do engage in. My sister-in-law, Yuko, has never been religiously observant and, unlike her parents, has never placed either a Buddhist or Shinto altar in her home. But she says she expects to put a Buddhist altar in her home once her parents die, to respect and remember them. She also believes in a higher power, which she calls *kamisama*, and says she expects to visit a Shinto shrine in the New Year to purify herself of the bad luck of the past year.

The Japanese religious sensibility is found in such impulses, not in the formal dogma or required rituals common to other faith traditions. Indeed, many experts call Zen Buddhism a "religionless religion" and Shinto not a religion at all but a communal way of life. Shinto, Japan's indigenous faith tradition, has no founder, no dogma, no holy scripture. As Rev. Yagi notes, it is experienced through the mystical stillness of sacred forest groves, the crunch of pebbles underfoot, the chirp of birds, the smell of trunks and leaves, the gurgle of a running mountain stream. It is expressed through a heart of gratitude—for a good harvest, for good health, for family and friends. Shaped by such ancient traditions, it is no surprise that Japanese experience spirituality and glimpse the divine through the senses and heart far more than the intellect.

In reporting an article about the Japanese search for meaning amid unprecedented material affluence, I spoke with one woman about her deepest spiritual longings. "I want to go to a faraway temple that no one knows about, sit in a bamboo forest with moss-covered rocks and drink tea from a beautiful Japanese cup," she said.

That is the Japanese soul.

Chapter 8

Appalachian Regional Identity in National Media

Howard Dorgan

Perhaps the first thing that should be said, in this essay on mass media and Appalachian religion, is that these mountain churches deserve every ounce of any honor, esteem, and respect shown to the institutions of any of America's religions. In other words, if we are to start with the assumption that all faiths deserve some base level of deference that must be awarded to religion per se, then we can't restrict that treatment solely to mainline religions—assuming, of course, that no practice being followed by the nonmainline groups is unlawful.

This nonjudgmental equality in treatment hasn't always been the case. If we judge a religious faith to be in any way less enlightened in its theological dogmas and worship practices—and we need to seriously evaluate how we come to such conclusions—we are prone to grant fewer rights of privacy, tactful handling, and general reverence than we would automatically grant to religious institutions that we place on some higher level of culture, erudition, or historical prestige.

Usually American values give religion and its practices some higher level of respect than the institutions of politics, commerce, and perhaps even education; however, it seems that such a tendency breaks down when we make some negative cultural judgments about the respective denominational base. Is there, nevertheless, some core base of homage that should be paid to all religious orientations, especially by the mass media?

After beginning my Appalachian religion research in the summer of 1971, I went on to spend thirty-two years, by the time of this writing, traveling throughout southern and central Appalachia and studying the wonderfully rich indigenous religious traditions of these regions. Because I was trained in the field of speech communication when I began this ethnographic study, my first scholarly attentions were directed toward the dynamically rhythmical chant/song preaching patterns that developed along the Appalachian frontier during the last half of the eighteenth century.[1] This rhythmical pattern was greatly influenced by the field preachers of the "First Awakening" (roughly 1726 to 1756), furthered in its maturation in style by the camp-meeting evangelism of the "Great Western Revival" that took place primarily in the frontier regions of Kentucky and Tennessee from 1797 through 1805, and then continued throughout the South as a movement of summer or fall camp meetings.[2] However, I also had some schooling at Perkins School of Theology at Southern Methodist University and quickly broadened the horizon of my study of Appalachian religion to include not only the theologies of the various "Old-Time" Baptist faiths to which I was being introduced, but also all of the numerous worship traditions that Appalachian congregations had preserved from the eighteenth and nineteenth centuries. In this work I immediately took note of the strongly held sensitivity in these churches regarding outsider visitations, but the more these congregations warmed up to me and the more I learned of the histories of their faiths, the more I understood the reasons for that sensitivity. I'll touch on four regional circumstances that worked to create this cultural attitude of distrust for the outside observer, not only in relation to religion but also concerning most areas of the region's socioeconomic conditions. The first of these circumstances did not concern media per se, except as religious journalism of the period tended to report the events—happenings that emerged from a period that American religious historians refer to as the "Missionary/Antimissionary Split."

During this era of religious turbulence in America, our nation rushed rapidly into the throes of our imperialistic age, quickly finding ourselves, along with other Western colonial powers, in control of native Pacific cultures, and thus shouldering what many historians have labeled as the "white man's burden" to "civilize and Christianize" the native peoples of the Pacific northwest, Hawaii, American Samoa, the Marina Islands, the Philippines, and elsewhere. At the same time, home missionary work intensified with all of the American Indian tribes, driven by a multitude of denominational missionary societies centered on our eastern seaboard.

Such evangelistic activities quickly disturbed the Calvinistic elements of American Christianity who believed that "God calls, not man" and that if God wanted "heathens" added to the redeemed peoples of the world, "He would do so at his own good time." Thus, between 1800 and 1840—and even beyond—Appalachian churches that were mixed in their theologies between Calvinism and Arminianism split to the "missionary side" or the "antimissionary side" and, among the Baptists, forged the "Missionary" and "Old School," or "Primitive," subdenominations. This reality became even more the case when missionary societies began to send workers to the Trans-Allegheny regions of the American frontier, either to raise money for missionary efforts or "to correct" the perceived heretical beliefs and practices of Appalachian religious institutions.

Baptist churches in such early associations as Elkhorn (founded 1785) and Holston (established 1786) had already survived as long as one hundred years as frontier fellowships before these eastern missionaries arrived "to set them right"; therefore, these congregations took great offense at the missionary assumptions that Appalachian churches needed re-Christianizing. Consequently, the first half of the nineteenth century became the first significant period during which these mountain cultures were persistently stung by the judgmental intrusions of outsider forces. During this period the region's religious institutions and practically all other cultural concerns drew inward, developing severe distrust for eastern movements aimed at "helping" or "correcting" them. Why weren't their physical churches, their theologies, and their worship practices sufficient to the spiritual needs of their frontier region?

During the next century and a half, this initial cultural wariness for the outsider was never removed from the Appalachian mind, causing difficulties for all the missionaries, educators, and social workers who orchestrated the great settlement school movement that followed, and then even complicating the "War on Poverty" period of the 1960s and 1970s by promoting negative feelings that southern and central Appalachians continued to hold for "busybody lowlanders." Hard feelings about these "outsiders" were again inflamed as the region once more found itself under an all-encompassing critical scrutiny as the national media sought to provide evidence of the region's social and economic needs. Swept into this sudden swarm of interest in the region's poverty during the Kennedy and Johnson administrations, mountain folks found themselves surrounded by media crews that were filming every scene that looked backward, ugly, or impoverished economically, intellectually, or culturally. Indeed, Appalachians began to feel that they didn't have a chance to show anything good about themselves and that the total impact of this activity was to support demeaning stereotypes about the region. Even when scenes were being filmed that had significant social or historical meanings and that cried to be explained to genuinely sensitive audiences, the opportunities for such deeper cultural understandings were dropped into an environment of blame-the-victim judgments that reeked of general disdain for helping Appalachia. The region's inhabitants didn't know whether the intent of the mass media was to help them or to harm them.

More often than not, the latter was the conclusion, especially when such tags as "Yesterday's People"[3] were applied to the mountain folk in general.

In 1991, when I was working on my book *The Airwaves of Zion*, I spent some time in Welch, McDowell County, West Virginia, visiting the Sunday broadcasts of several live religious programs aired over radio station WELC. While in that town I also interviewed the mayor of Welch, Martha Moore, who was concerned about the images of her town that I would capture in my book. Mayor Moore told me that she had been queried by many journalists (newspaper and television) who had come to Welch to report on the industrial decay that had been left in the Tug River Valley by mining companies that had closed down their operation in the area and left their debris behind. "Invariably," she said, "When the reporters write their articles or produce their television documentaries, they make it sound like the decay present in our valley can be blamed on character flaws present in the people of this town and county. . . . The biggest problem that we have to overcome is the stigma that has been laid upon us, that all of this is the result of some deficiency in our own character. That is simply not the case. She added, "Persistently, these critics suggest that only a little more get-up-and-go is needed in the spirit of our people to make all of this industrial ruin go away and become replaced by newer, cleaner, higher paying, and less environmentally destructive enterprises than coal extraction has been for us."

During her tenure in office, Mayor Moore's municipal crews have maintained clean and flower-decorated city streets even when those thoroughfares run past blocks of empty storefronts. Moore has also worked with civic leaders in Welch and McDowell County, notably the wife of Sam Sidote, owner of Welch's AM/FM station WELC, to organize volunteers to clean up all of the waterways connected to the Tug River. They have removed years of debris deposited in these streams by the almost yearly floods and by the multitudes of small businesses that have left the county as the mining interests themselves pulled out, invariably leaving their own abandoned and decaying structures to mark their flights from the economic depression that settled over the region at the close of the World War II era. Wartime industries had placed the demand for West Virginia coal at its zenith, but what is left of this once-thriving coal industry is only the occasional strip mine, destructive to the environment and minimal in its requirements for a well-paid labor force.

"It is so hard for the outsider to come to our county," says Moore, "and see all of the old crumbling mining facilities and to envision economic hope for our region. Those companies that bled us of a natural resource when there was so much money in coal extraction took all that capital and went elsewhere, leaving only crumbling structures behind to cast a shame on us, a shame that we don't deserve. Do you wonder why we get nervous when any writer comes with notepads and cameras?"

The Martha Moores of Appalachia appear to be caught in a "catch 22": invite the media in to document and dramatize regional needs, and then suffer the ignominy that an affluent nation occasionally dumps on those regions of the country that have not maintained the acceptable levels of affluence apparently demanded of all regions in the realm. This is not unlike the shame and embarrassment that seems always to attach itself to poor relatives of any household.

The next circumstance relating to Appalachian cultural sensitivity touched directly on religion and on outsider attitudes that derived from much of the early social science scholarship published in the 1960s and 70s, including Weller's work, *Yesterday's People*; a book by Joseph Finney, *Culture Change, Mental Health, and Poverty*; and an especially offensive short piece of scholarship by Nathan L. Gerrard, "Churches of the Stationary Poor in Southern Appalachia," among others. Although Gerrard was addressing the Pentecostal Holiness traditions in Appalachia, his highly negative judgments seemed to sweep across most of the indigenous religious traditions in southern and central Appalachia, suggesting connections between this region's religious movements and the causes of social decay: educational deprivation, an absence of societal enriching values, a multitude of innate character flaws (including sloth and a lack of self-improvement motivation), a general absence of the morality and ethics that is traditionally associated with all religious institutions, and finally, with a Calvinistic fatalism that stood in the way of any faith in economic and social progress. Unfortunately, much of the outside world took Gerrard's indictments as the general rule for Appalachian religious cultures. Thus—in sharp contrast to the attitudes that currently prevail in publications of the Appalachian Studies Association—many of these early scholarly evaluations of mountain culture fell far short of being supportive of, or protective of, Appalachian traditions and values.

By the mid-1970s this battery of none-too-flattering scholarly treatments of Appalachian religion had become so pervasive that Loyal Jones of Berea College contributed an article to *Mountain Review*, "Mountain Religion: The Outsider's View," that ultimately had a profound impact upon this situation. Jones won a number of writers over to a more positive approach to their mountain subject matter.

Jones charged that much of what had been written, especially by social scientists, fell into the genre of broad generalizations that ignored the great diversity present in the mountain religious phenomenon while leaning heavily on demeaning stereotypes. This criticism, he felt, was especially true for the writings of Weller and Gerrard.

Jones also attacked the "blame the victim" approach that he said was being used in examinations of Appalachian socioeconomic problems and countered the argument that Appalachian churches promoted no social gospel. In doing so, he detailed a number of the activities of mountain religious leaders who had fought the environment-destroying practices of the strip-mining movement and the horrible wrongs inflicted upon so many mountaineers through black lung illnesses.

However, the most influential argument that Jones advanced had to do with the tendency of Appalachian religion critics to adopt the Karl Marx rationale that religion is the "opiate" of the common man, serving almost exclusively to deaden the pains of poverty and social destitution. Jones complained that these mountain faiths were being examined solely as "crutches" that enabled believers to survive severe economic and socially crippled states that otherwise could not be endured. Thus, this charge suggested that by promoting a tolerance for social injustice rather than the appropriate methods for fighting the respective wrongs, Appalachian faith did more harm than good.

Later, this last argument by Jones was expanded by Melanie Sovine and Deborah McCauley to say that Appalachian religion should be studied as religion, not as socioeconomic consequence. Here the judgment became that the study of any religion solely as a sociological development that has arisen to meet the hardship needs of a people is innately demeaning to the faith.[4] For the last two decades, this last ethic has constituted the prevailing approach by Appalachian religion scholars, bringing far more cultural respect to the movement, and certainly making the faithful feel better about their faiths.

"We're in a far better situation today than we were thirty or forty years ago," said Elder Unice Davis, "when so many writers started off with the assumption that Appalachian theologies could not possibly be studied with the same degree of scholarship as might be directed towards an understanding of the Cumberland Presbyterian faith or even the beliefs of the original Methodists. Because we feel like we are more respected than we once were, we don't fear the visitations of the outsider and his media as much as we once did."[5]

SERPENT HANDLING

While serving as the "religion consultant" to the Evening Star Production Company of Akron, Ohio, which in May 2004 aired a four-hour PBS documentary *The Appalachians*, I attended the 2001 Labor Day weekend homecoming services of The Church of the Lord Jesus, in Jolo, West Virginia, a serpent-handling congregation. In an attempt to regulate the national media's excessive attention to their practices, this fellowship now opens the doors to their services only one weekend a year, and that happens to be their "homecoming" weekend—Friday, Saturday, and Sunday evenings.

The crowded attendance for these 2001 Jolo services was typical for what has become this annual event, with still, video, and movie cameras present in every corner of the small facility, so much so that I personally was ashamed of being part of this throng of camera-holding observers. I didn't like being what I feared would be perceived as a "gawk," even though I recognized the importance of the documentary team of which I was a part. Indeed, after thirty years of Appalachian religious ethnographic study, this became the first visit I had paid to a serpent-handling service, not because I had felt I would be in danger, but because I believed very strongly that the national media had devoted a disproportionate degree of attention to this one Appalachian religious phenomenon, with the consequence that many outside observers seemed to believe that this practice was the religious norm in central Appalachia. Such is far from the truth, given that serpent handlers in America have been estimated to be only approximately 2,500 in number, including fellowships not only in southern and central Appalachia but also in the lower and upper Midwest, along with a moderate number of churches in the Middle and Deep South.[6] In addition, the field seemed not to need another serpent-handling scholar, since three major book-length works had been published since 1991,[7] along with a wide range of journal articles.

I wanted to see some of the other, less sensational Appalachian faiths receive their due in terms of deserved attention, so I had determined that I did not want to be a part of the usual frenetic focus on the sensational serpent manipulations themselves, thus giving the impression of circus media coverage, playing to the dangers of the practice while ignoring the actual doctrines of faith. Indeed, my first advice to the Evening Star Production Company was that the documentary's coverage of serpent handling be extremely respectful and sensitive, centering strongly on interviews that probed the meanings of the faith and the depths of commitments to doctrine enjoyed by the various practitioners—commitments that could precipitate wonder and inspiration if approached with the right frame of mind.

My final concern had been fostered by criticism I frequently heard of serpent handling. The critics in question would say something like this: "It's all about showmanship. Away from audiences and cameras, few people would handle those poisonous snakes. If you believe that faith actually is the primary motivation for this practice, then take away all those cameras and see how many people will be inspired by a within-the-closet pursuit of this persuasion."

My response to this argument had always been that it seemed unfair to single out only the serpent handlers for this criticism when it appeared entirely possible for any religious practice to be tarnished by such a very human motivational weakness. Nevertheless, this assigned rationale for serpent-handling behavior touched me directly, since as an outside observer in so many Appalachian worship services I had occasionally wondered about the impact of my own presence on the practice of these old-time rites. Therefore, in relation to serpent handling I suspect that I attitudinally "hedged my bet" by limiting the consequences of my own possibly poor behavior.

Still, the situation in which I found myself at Jolo wasn't at all like the ones I had experienced for over thirty years during my work as a religious ethnographer, sitting quietly in various "Old-Time" Baptist or Pentecostal Holiness congregations and absorbing the emotional intensity of the services developing around me. In the past, only rarely had I employed any media device other than a still camera devoid of a flash unit, and only then with the consent of the leaders of the church. Only twice had I taken a laptop computer into a service, quickly recognizing that it became a congregational distraction, particularly to children in the church.

Nevertheless, there were a number of congregations that got to know me so well that they actually asked me to record their services by still camera and/or mike and tape recorder. But typically I captured far more photographs of outside-the-church events such as baptisms, dinners on the ground, and graveyard memorial services. Inside-the-church religious dynamics—feetwashings, "carried out" preaching services, and emotional coming-to-the-altar "salvation" scenes—demanded more sensitivity on my part. In short, the use of media in any form complicated my work as an ethnographer. I felt safer relying on my skills in providing rich verbal descriptions of the scenes I witnessed. When I did take photographs, I made it a point on my next visit to take a portfolio of my pictures back to the church so that the membership could view the events that I had captured. Frequently I was asked if I would make a copy of a picture for some individual.

Common sense should tell the sufficiently sensitive person when a moment has become too delicate for the employing of a camera. Such a circumstance occurred in 1986 at the annual meeting of the Union Association of Old Regular Baptists when, concerning the splitting of one of the member churches, it was charged that the moderator of the respective church had committed adultery. The evidence for that charge was presented during the business meeting of the association, and the resulting debate became very personal, embarrassing, and heated.[8]

However, while there at Jolo the only restriction I imposed upon myself was that of not using flash photography, for fear of how a sudden bright light might impact the behavior of the snakes. During those Labor Day weekend services at Jolo, I relied on very fast black-and-white film, 400 ASA and up. I could live with some slight graininess in the photography better than with being the cause of someone's being bitten.

Mass media productions, however, not only gravitate to such high-drama and sensational Appalachian religion events, but these production teams do so with little concern for what stereotypic images of the region are produced by such heavy diets of this sensationalism. The constant coverage of these dynamic services without a broadening historical, cultural, and theological perspective cultivates an Appalachian image that is out of balance with reality. What we must first remember is that the events that generated a serpent-handling tradition in Appalachia are less than one hundred years old,[9] and that they lack far less of the heart-of-the-region's spiritual characteristics than do the "Old-Time" Baptist traditions that sprang directly from the colonial and immediate postcolonial environments of the First and Second Great Awakenings.[10] To be in greater parallel with the historical, cultural, and spiritual nuances of central Appalachia, these outsider perceptions should not focus almost exclusively on serpent handling but on the spirited eighteenth-century-like traditions of the "Old-Time" Baptists: lined singing; chanted or sung improvisational preaching; "living water" baptisms; touchingly emotional feetwashing services and other highly tactile worship exchanges (constant embracing and handshaking); congregational shouting, crying, and hollaring; still noticeable gender separations (especially the two doors on the front the church); starkly simple, white, wood-framed churches, with unfinished wooden pews smoothly polished by decades of use.

Nevertheless, during my work with certain "Old-Time" church groups such as the Old Regular Baptists of the Primitive Baptist Universalists, I have occasionally heard stories about media groups that barged in on "Old Baptist" services, showing little or no sensitivity for the privacy rights of congregations. Such was the case when during my eight years of studying the Old Regular Baptists, primarily in eastern Kentucky and southwest Virginia, I became especially disturbed by a story told to me by the congregation of the Dunham, Kentucky, Old Regular church.

Dunham is a bygone mining town just southwest of Jenkins, Kentucky, and the only structures that remain there as evidence of the town's former glory are the old company store, now used for various forms of storage; the old railroad depot, which now serves as the church for the Dunham Old Regular congregation; and a number of rusting structures that were part of a coal transportation tipple. Since Dunham is very much a coal mining ghost town, a television production crew from Lexington or Louisville visited the site one weekend to do a short documentary on this old coal industry location. There was a sign on the side of the old depot indicating that the structure was at the time being used as a church, but the production crew either missed the sign or decided to visit the service in session as part of the total story of the spot. As a result, the crew stumbled into the church unannounced, cameras running. The congregation was horrified by the intrusion. The scene was not unlike many of those televised intrusions into West Virginia, Kentucky, and elsewhere during the days of the War on Poverty.

It doesn't take long for the insults of a Dunham, Kentucky, media treatment to spread throughout the Appalachian religious culture, and these happenings make all scholars, no matter how sensitive, fraught with fears of rude treatment from outsiders. My own work with Central Appalachia religious groups has been heavily complicated by these histories of thoughtlessness. I usually have to spend at least five or six years with an Old Baptist sub-denomination before they trust me sufficiently to allow any video recordings of their services, and that trust can be weakened quickly by any loss of sensitivity on my part.

I spent far longer than that with the Old Regular Baptists before an Appalachian State University colleague of mine, Kevin Balling, and I coproduced As the Ages Roll On, a documentary of an Old Regular family memorial that received seven airings on KET (Kentucky Educational Television), that state's PBS affiliate. The film captured the 1991 annual family memorial of Elder Raymond Smith, staged at the Smith home on Straton Fork of Meat House Creek, Pike County, Kentucky. Elder Smith is the moderator of Lonesome Dove Old Regular Baptist Church, which sits only about one hundred yards down Straton Fork from the family's home. Part of the memorial service was held in the church, but we had to restrict our filming to events occurring at the home. Nevertheless, that allowed us to capture a great amount of Old Regular preaching and singing, plus the part of the event that was the most culturally rich, the Old Regular practice of calling out all of the names of deceased family members who are being memorialized, usually going back at least three generations, and sometimes as many as five. Traditionally such memorials begin on Friday night with preaching and singing in the home, progress to a Saturday morning business meeting and service in the church, followed by a noon meal at the house for all church members and family members who have by that time arrived at the event. Then there is the Sunday morning service at the church, the large dinner-on-the-ground at home, and finally the closing out that afternoon, first with the ceremony involving the naming of deceased family members, accompanied by emotional oral histories of the family lineage, and concluding with another round of preaching and singing that usually goes on until at least mid-afternoon. Such family memorials attract many members who have long ago moved from the region. Thus attendance may represent at least six or eight states.[11]

CONCLUSION

The national media need to adopt ethics that spell out what a minimal base of respect should be for nonmainline religions. I recommend the following: (1) congregations, or at least the leaders of these churches, should be given a reasonable chance for informed consent before any type of electronic media is introduced into these churches; (2) whenever possible, individual members of these congregations should be able to exclude themselves from the films, videos, and other forms of recording; and (3) when a particular segment of the film or video is especially embarrassing to one or more members of the congregation, those individuals should be given a chance to place some restrictions on the use of the respective footage. Concerning this third standard, I have one set of footwashing photographs that one Old Regular Baptist family gave me oral permission to take, with the understanding that the prints could be housed among the archival holdings of Appalachian State University's Appalachian Collection, but that they should not be included in the publications without the permission of the individual celebrant for the individual publication. Probably I will never include these photographs in any published manuscript, but the agreement comforted two members of the family.

The final code that I recommend is that special care be taken with photography so that the prints in question are always decorous. My best example in this regard concerns the photographing of the "women's side" in footwashing services. In these services "Old-Time" Baptist usually restrict the ritual to same-sex pairings and even go so far as to arrange a segment of pews—for the women's side—that circle in toward each other and thus provide an extra degree of privacy. The reason for this is simply that when washing a woman's feet, a dress may be pulled up a little higher than is normally comfortable for that woman. Therefore, the photographer may need to watch carefully the angle and closeness of the shot. I am thankful to an Old Regular elder who years ago confided his concern for my footwashing photography after looking at some of my pictures. I doubt that one of the church women would have told me this.

The use of media in these churches reveals some areas of sensitivity that must be carefully examined at all times. Some of what I have learned, I have discovered the hard way, and that is in spite of the fact that as an ethnographer I have been conditioned to be especially watchful for all possibly offensive behaviors on my part. Media film crews, on the other hand, seldom have been introduced to courses of study that assist them in dealing with the many areas of Appalachian sensitivity.

8: View from the News Desk

The Reporter as
Participant-Observer

Adam Phillips

For two decades, it has been my regular challenge and joy to produce sound-rich, human-interest radio features that explore religious and spiritual experience within complex cultures. Reporting has taken me to South Africa, the United Kingdom and Ireland, the Middle East, South Asia, and into other foreign cultures. More often, the religion beat has meant covering the spiritual experience within American borders—from the Blackfoot Indian Reservation in Montana, for example, to the southern Appalachian Mountains, south central Los Angeles, and New York City, where I live.

More than a pervasive social force, religion and spirituality are the expression of seemingly hardwired inner needs, and as such, they affect practically every facet of human existence. They can provide guidelines for seemingly pedestrian matters such as daily diet and provoke the most exalted cultural and ethical achievements; they are used to inspiring and justifying almost every kind of human behavior. As a result, religion reporting offers an endlessly deep trove for a curious reporter.

Conducting research and interviews where inner *experience* is the primary subject matter requires a deeper level of empathy and responsiveness on the reporter's part than is usually necessary with stories where objective "facts" drive the story. Also, writing stories about people and ideas within spiritual and cultural traditions that differ markedly from one's own requires a willingness to "cross over" to other perspectives in order, first, to understand them, and then to put them in context for the readers or listeners who, one hopes, can connect those perspectives and insights to their own worlds. In that sense, a good religion reporter must be both participant and observer. Even more, he must be willing to have his worldview altered, suspended, or even changed by encountering other viewpoints.

Religion reporting differs both in subject matter and approach from most mainstream reporting in several ways. Most religion reporting is news, and as such, it is primarily concerned with events, especially their "who, what, where, when" aspects. Features reporting should focus particularly on the "how and why." And questions of how and why, of course, are also fundamental to the religious and spiritual life.

Event-based mainstream religious reporting is often a subcategory of political reporting that tends to focus on certain kinds of stories: ideological and doctrinal conflicts among or within religious or faith-based groups; political or cultural developments that affect the way religions are practiced or suppressed; the fallout when the ideals of a religion or tradition have been violated by its caretakers or leaders; economic and territorial stories where religious people are the primary actors or where religion is linked to a specific ethnic group in conflict.

Mainstream religion reporting tends to cover such stories from a news perspective. It describes how the pieces on the board originally looked and how they are being, and may yet be, "shifted around." This kind of religion reporting is less interesting to me than the *experience* of religion and spiritual matters and the underlying drives they embody and express.

The broad issues that religions raise and attempt to explain are equally fascinating: issues of meaning, purpose, and connection, of ethical and moral coherence. It is my personal belief that these concerns and goals are as basic to human nature as the drive for power, status, and material goods, and that the quest for them helps to determine the shape of a culture. Because the needs for these sorts of meaning are hardwired, they are as important to my listeners as they are to me (even if, like me, they are essentially secular in their day-to-day lives). This is true regardless of the cultural context.

For example, in the early 1990s I spent about six weeks traveling down back roads in the West of Ireland, where Gaelic is still an everyday language, in search of remnants of the old pre-Christian fairy beliefs and folkways. I spoke with old people and children, often in cottages without electricity, who said they had either seen leprechauns or fairies, or heard the wail of the *ban shee* (a female death spirit) or knew someone who had. Now most people are familiar with similar ideas from childhood bedtime stories and the imaginative worlds of play. That's how they can have experience relating to these stories. Most dismiss them as fantasy when they grow up.

However, sophisticated and distinctly spiritual attitudes had developed from continued belief in the "Other Side" among some adults in the West of Ireland, including a conviction that everything in nature has its own spirit, purpose, and personality, which can interact with and affect the fortunes of humans for better or worse—depending on how it is treated. From this develops an ethic of respect and stewardship for the land and its power to bless or curse, and a sense of continuity between nature and the human world. By highlighting these values, a reporter can help make a bridge between the values of a folk religion and the values of a more modern, ecologically based perspective.

In Ireland, evidence of belief in what some rural people call the Other Side is hardly ever as overt and obvious as, say, belief in Catholicism, which is apparent in every village from the many churches. Some people are even embarrassed to admit a faith in the old stories, or they remember a time when they were punished or ostracized for practicing the old folkways. So to find my interview subjects, I'd simply take long walks or hang out in small country pubs and get the conversation around to the old ways, then gently inquire as to who in the area might still know or remember them. For these stories (and many others), I always sought out the old and wise members of the community. When I'd get to their homes, I would be straightforward about my ignorance and express my questions in an open and honest way; my sincerity, curiosity, and respect would come through to them. I was not afraid to be emotional. Once people had a sense that my "heart was in the right place," they would usually open up, and I gathered some of the best interviews (and experiences) of my life. This is very different from political reporting, in which the people being interviewed are often accustomed to speaking about their views and eager to put them forth publicly.

Religion and the stories that are the expression of religious belief often translate themselves into political passions, even violence. For example, reporters often refer to the conflict between Palestinian Muslims and Israeli Jews as a "religious" one, and leave it at that. Typically, they then proceed to report body counts and reprisals, domestic politics, negotiations, and the "peace process." When I lived in Jerusalem, I was determined to take the religious dimension of the conflict seriously in its own right. Using the violence at the Al Aqsa Mosque/Temple Mount as my point of departure, I set out to ask religious scholars from each tradition to cite, and then to explain, the actual scriptural sources (for the Muslims within the Koran, and for the Jews within the Torah) underlying their group's assertion that they alone were the inheritors of God's promise to give the land of Israel/Palestine to their group.

How the teachings in sacred texts are transmitted to ordinary citizens who support and wage their conflicts based on literal scriptural interpretations is a fascinating cultural study in itself. However, it is a fact that religious Jews and Muslims *agree* that both peoples claim common descent from Abraham (traditionally considered the first monotheist), yet vehemently *disagree* as to which of his sons, Isaac (from whom Jews claim direct descent) or Ishmael (from whom Arab Muslims claim descent) received Abraham's divine inheritance to the land. I believe that, without this background, anyone wishing to understand the present-day conflict—either its apparent intractability or its potential for "internecine" reconciliation—is at a crippling loss.

As a responsible journalist, I try to take an evenhanded approach that will make my role as an observer authentic and meaningful. But like any journalist—especially a features journalist—I am a *storyteller*, and I attempt to bring a measure of wit and artfulness to my work in ways that will engage, not just the mind, but the imagination of my listeners. The religion reporter is at a special advantage on this score exactly because the essence of a religion is almost always conveyed to believers in the form of stories and myths.

Indeed, because religious narratives are constructed to talk about origins, distant history, and the future, and they purport to explain the unseen world or relate transcendent truths, there must be a "once-upon-a-time" quality to the way faiths frame their imagination of their identity. A religion reporter can make excellent use of such religious narrative while remaining completely faithful to the sense of the religion's self-expressed purpose. Because everyone has the ability to suspend disbelief and listen to a story and be absorbed as if a story were true (even jokes make constant use of and depend on this faculty), stories from even the most exotic worldviews can resonate with listeners who have very different religious or spiritual paths, or who have no spiritual path, or who are simply curious about how others understand the world—which is, after all, fundamentally the *same* world that they inhabit, too.

A religion reporter who casts himself in the ethnographic mode, in a dual role of participant and observer, is different from a reporter who is trying to investigate possible wrongdoing within a faith tradition, or even a philosopher or theologian who wants to arrive at some ultimate "answer," or to be skeptical or critical regarding the credibility of a religious worldview or set of claims. The primary raw material for my sort of journalism is the lived faith experience itself.

This can be a complex balancing act. On the one hand, the features journalist is somewhat relieved of the burden of "objectivity." There must be a willingness on the part of the journalist—and by extension, the listener—to go along with the storyteller because the focus in religious and mythic stories is inner experience or social realities based on inner needs, not objective facts. This is not exactly the same as suspending one's disbelief. On the other hand, it is inappropriate for the journalist to advocate any religious position, and the conscientious reporter works hard to avoid even the appearance of proselytizing, or reading into the story for purposes other than the telling. Perhaps what I do is more akin to entering the world of art, or even fine entertainment, where the canvas is the human heart.

Sometimes religious stories from other cultures can seem quite strange indeed, but they can be a vital part of the deep background a reporter must have in order to understand a story. For example, in 1996 I spent some time among the Zulus of South Africa, a highly traditional herding people whose ancient and richly differentiated cosmology includes a belief that the stars we see from below are actually scuff marks left by celestial cattle as they roam above the skies in a supernal light. Now I wasn't doing a story on Zulu religion per se; I was the originator and lead producer of a Carnegie Corporation-sponsored project that explored conflict resolution and the psychological roots of violence and peacemaking. My special interest in South Africa was the post-Apartheid "truth and reconciliation" process that had been designed to incorporate, among other views, both white European-based concepts of justice and punishment, and African-based traditions that hold that only by a full airing of grievances before one's entire community—and especially those one has wronged—can forgiveness and healing occur. These were deep issues. But it was impossible to get a feeling for the actual emotional and psychological context for the positions and attitudes of many parties and stakeholders unless I became familiar with their spiritual beliefs and stories, and their bearing on South African politics at the time and the overall nation-building process.

While relating people's sacred stories is a powerful tool in helping the listener to understand a culture "from the inside," so are sacred music and liturgical texts or chants. They allow a mood to be created for the listener in keeping with the nonrational dimension of the spiritual life. Hearing sacred music tells a listener a lot that words cannot say. Simply put, if the heart is open (by music or whatever means), the information will enter more easily.

I like the phrase "Nothing human is foreign to me" and try to remember it in the field. Without wishing to sound grandiose, I take it to mean that for both better and worse, I embody within myself the common heritage of all of humanity and share equally in its potential to create both light and shadow. I integrate this knowledge into my approach to my work as a religion reporter. I must do so because *nothing human is foreign to the listener either*, and I take it as a given that what moves me, and what is meaningful in the lives of one group of people, will probably, if sensitively and artfully presented, move others.

Identifying with others is a common theme in my stories, which are written for an extremely diverse international audience. The reports are constructed in ways that will invite the listeners to find common ground with others unlike themselves, by identifying with the way the same human longings and yearnings they are hearing about are felt and expressed within their own cultures. Indeed, by enlarging their understanding of others and by connecting human interests, listeners enrich their understanding of their own cultures and humanity, and may even broaden their sense of group identity to include the other, the erstwhile stranger.

One way I have done this is to link secular or civic holidays with an underlying spiritual impulse that finds expression in a variety of seemingly unconnected religions. Last year, when the annual call to reporters went out for Thanksgiving stories, and not wishing to do another soup kitchen or Norman Rockwell style Americana story, I took a moment to think somewhat "outside the box," and began to reflect on what gratitude and the giving of thanks (the ostensible reasons for the holiday) *really* are. It occurred to me that while the Puritan Pilgrims were Christian, every other religion and spiritual tradition also posits gratitude as a spiritual value and says, in some way, that to give thanks for a good received is in turn good for you. So I spoke to articulate leaders from four major faiths (Jewish, Sufi Muslim, Christian, and Buddhist) and asked them to tell me what their respective traditions had to say about gratitude and thanks-giving and why.

An opposite tack in pursuing a religion story is sometimes the better approach. Instead of finding the *unifying* thread in several religions, I focus on a particular religious or spiritual tradition as a singular response to fairly disparate experiences (without, of course, advocating the truth or debating the actual merits of a specific path). For example, in a feature about a coed Zen Buddhist monastery for Americans in New York, I would not attempt to investigate the truth or falsehood of Buddhist doctrines concerning suffering, or the path to liberation, or even the spiritual advisability of meditation in a life well lived. Rather, I'd want to get a sense of the range of the experiences and conditions that have led many different sorts of Americans to take an active interest in a Buddhist path. Such people might include a Wall Street lawyer who wants to escape his high-stress lifestyle; a young person in a crisis of faith who seeks an alternative to the restrictive fundamentalist Christian beliefs in which she had been raised; or an Asian American raised as a Buddhist who desires an Americanized (nonritualistic, nonhierarchical) version of the religion she was born to. Most importantly, personal interviews provide the core of the stories where religion is concerned.

The responsible religion reporter must also know when to stand back, to offer historical context, and provide balance and perspective, even nonpatronizing skepticism. Yet the interview itself is not the time for critical detachment. That comes later, in the writing and production process. The interviews themselves should be true dialogs, where it is easy (perhaps even advisable) to "forget" that one of you is a journalist and the other is a source. That is, a reporter must be willing to "show up" as a human being, and even further, to be moved, or even changed, by the interview. This process is one of the most rewarding aspects of the work.

I am interested in wisdom, and I love to ask people—anyone!—how they think and feel about the ultimate issues and values in their lives and the various challenges they encounter. Whether I am asking the Dalai Lama to explain the spiritual basis for his advocacy of nonviolence as a strategy for dealing with the Chinese, or a suburban witch is telling me over tea how feminism, the reverence for nature, and the pull of the erotic join together in her spiritual beliefs and practices, I feel fascinated and, frankly, privileged to be there.

Now just as there is a political dimension to almost any story that deals with organized religion, there is a potential spiritual dimension to most of the seemingly everyday stories one hears. For example, the love of sports can be viewed "under the skin" as a desire for transcendence, or fraternity, or connection to a greater whole. News of airplane crashes and earthquakes touch the fear of death and the fundamental insecurity of health and life, and their transience. Politics itself—especially national and international politics—often touches the sphere that is the traditional province of religion through symbolism, civic ritual, and the leader and warrior archetypes.

Our public life becomes a stage where we can see the constant creative tension between good and evil, order and change, the individual and the greater whole, played out. All this is the stuff of good drama. At its best, religion reporting can help expose the deeper themes inherent in these public dramas—the "wiring under the boards" as it were. Features reporting is sometimes dismissed as "soft" or "fluff" by hard-news people, but to my mind, a good case can be made that these murky yet powerful psychic tendencies are the *real* story. World War II, for example, was more than a series of battle reports and news reports. Fundamental forces were at work, and such forces are what religion and religious discourse are about.

Some stories are so powerful that the spiritual and the political dimensions of a story seem to give rise to each other seamlessly. September 11, 2001, was such a story. As soon as the planes hit, I was ordered to leave Washington and head for New York, my old hometown, and report on the human dimension of the aftermath.

In the following days, this human dimension was the real story, it seemed to me: from the hush and grief that pervaded the city; to the stunned and sacred sense that surrounded Ground Zero itself; to the compassion for the victims and their families and the heightened sense of value, mutual protectiveness, and support everyday New Yorkers extended to each other; to the makeshift people's altars of flowers and candles, impromptu poetry, the photographs of the missing that seemed to exalt ordinary people to the level of near-sainthood, where their very ordinariness became something to be valued and cherished in itself—all this afforded an incredible wealth of stories to an observer who was seeking out the human truth underneath the headlines. But it was my role as a *participant*—an average New Yorker who suddenly experienced up close the wounds of the city he was raised in and loved—that led me to the very people I needed to interview and provided the rapport that helped them open up to me and share their stories and travails. The ways that my own perspective and experiences became entangled with theirs were a nearly constant leitmotif in the stories I filed during the early aftermath of September 11.

Now because of the scale of that event, and even more so because of the scale of the *reaction*, the deep underlying connections between New Yorkers (and, in widening circles, between Americans and even world citizens) were writ large; ordinary time and routine were suspended (a significant universal component of all religious ritual), the cultural veneer was somewhat stripped away, and the ancient underlying universal processes of grief, anger, compassion, heroism, and the externalization of a common enemy were all inspired by the event. Precisely because it cut so deep and across so many separate lines of affiliation, the September 11th story entered realms that normally are the province of religion. So at least at first, before the sacred hush morphed (as it had to) into a political tangle—the nationalistic outrage and the calls for war, and later, the controversy over what to build on Ground Zero, and what sort of memorial there should be—we were dealing with a spiritual event, and I reported it as such.

Maybe it's no coincidence that the largest story in our nation's recent memory was also the one that linked spiritual ideas to the news, because the fundamental, underlying story—the one that has endured, not just as a continuing human-interest saga but also a political one—was and is taking place in the lives of people, and not just in their outward economic and political personas, but in their inner core as well. And for many, that inner core is also a place of the spirit.

Chapter 9

The Virgin of Guadalupe
as Cultural Icon

Virgilio Elizondo

Nowadays we realize that religious symbols, which theologians have labeled as "popular" religion and have looked upon as a species of pagan practice, do not have to be rejected, but need to be reinterpreted. In past decades the tendency of rational theology was to consider symbols as fantasies, to underline their ambiguity, and therefore to speak of them only in negative terms. This leads to an opposition between the religion of the people, which is not looked upon as true faith, and faith in Christ, which appears as the religion of the intellectual elite. A closer view of reality leads to a different understanding.[1] Even though to the theologian popular devotion appears ambiguous, nevertheless, it is the way the people relate to the God of Jesus. Therefore, from the pastoral as well as from the theological point of view, we have to try to answer the following question: What is the meaning of popular symbols, and how do they function in relation to the gospel? I will try to clarify the problem by considering one of the most important living symbols of the Catholicism of the Americas: Our Lady of Guadalupe.

If Our Lady of Guadalupe had not appeared, the collective struggles of the Mexican people to find meaning in their chaotic existence would have created her. The cultural clash[2] of sixteenth-century Spain and Mexico was reconciled in the brown Lady of Tepeyac[3] in a way no other symbol can rival. In her the new *mestizo* race,[4] born of the violent encounter between Europe and indigenous America, finds its meaning, uniqueness, and unity. Guadalupe is the key to understanding the Christianity of the New World[5] and the Christian consciousness of the Mexicans and the Mexican Americans of the United States.

HISTORICAL CONTEXT OF THE APPARITION

To appreciate the profound meaning of Guadalupe it is important to know the historical setting at the time of the apparition, when an exterior force, the white men of Europe, suddenly intruded on the closely knit and well-developed system of time-space relationships of the pre-Columbian civilizations.[6] Neither had ever heard of the other, nor had any suspicion that the other group existed. Western historiographers have studied the conquest from the justifying viewpoint of the European colonizers, but there is another perspective, that of the conquered. With the conquest, the world of the indigenous peoples of Mexico had, in effect, come to an end. The final battles in 1521 were not just a victory in warfare, but the end of a civilization. At first, some tribes welcomed the Spaniards and joined them in the hope of being liberated from Aztec domination. Only after the conquest did they discover that the defeat of the Aztecs was in effect the defeat of all the natives of their land.[7] This painful calvary of the Mexican people began when Cortez landed on Good Friday, April 22, 1519. It ended with the final battle on August 13, 1521. It was a military as well as a theological overthrow, for their capital had been conquered, their women violated, their temples destroyed, and their gods defeated.

We cannot allow the cruelty of the conquest to keep us from appreciating the heroic efforts of the early missionaries. Their writings indicated that it was their intention to found a new Christianity more in conformity with the gospel, not simply a continuation of that in Europe. They had been carefully prepared by the universities of Spain. Immediate efforts were made to evangelize the native Mexicans. The lifestyle of the missionaries, austere poverty and simplicity, was in stark contrast to that of the conquistadors. Attempts were made to become one with the people and to preach the gospel in their own language and through their customs and traditions. Yet the missionaries were limited by the socioreligious circumstances of their time. Dialogue was severely limited, since neither side understood the other. The Spaniards judged the Mexican world from within the categories of their own Spanish world vision. Iberian communication was based on philosophical and theological abstractions and direct, precise speech. The missionaries were convinced that truth in itself was sufficient to bring rational persons to conversion. They were not aware of the totally different way of communicating truth, especially divine truth, which the native Mexicans believed could only be adequately communicated through flower and song.[8] Even the best of the missionaries could not penetrate the living temple of the Mexican consciousness.

This was also the time of the first *audiencia* of Guzmán, which was noted for its corruption and abuses of the Indians. During this period the church was in constant conflict with the civil authorities because of these authorities' excessive avarice, corruption, and cruel treatment of the natives. The friars were good men who gradually won the love and respect of the common people. However, the religious convictions of generations would not give way easily, especially those of a people who firmly believed that the traditions of their ancestors were the way of the gods. As the friars tried to convert the wise men of the Indians by well-prepared theological exposition, the Indians discovered that the friars were in effect trying to eliminate the religion of their ancestors. The shock of human sacrifices led many of the missionaries to see everything else in the native religion as diabolical, whereas the shock of the Spaniards' disregard for life by killing in war kept the Indians from seeing anything good or authentic in the conquerors' religion. This mutual scandal made communication difficult.[9] Furthermore, the painful memory of the conquest and new hardships imposed upon the Indians made listening to a "religion of love" difficult. Efforts to communicate remained at the level of words but never seemed to penetrate to the level of the symbols of the people, which contained the inner meanings of their world vision. For the Indians, these attempts at conversion by total rupture with the ways of their ancestors were a deeper form of violence than the physical conquest itself. Christianity had in some fashion been brought over, but it had not yet been implanted. The Indians and missionaries heard each other's words, but interpretation was at a standstill. Many heroic efforts were made, but little fruit had been produced. The missionaries continued in prayer and self-sacrifice to ask for the ability to communicate the gospel.

THE APPARITIONS AND THEIR MEANING

In 1531, ten years after the conquest, an event took place whose origins are clouded in mystery yet whose effects have been monumental and continuous. Early documentation about what happened does not exist, yet the massive effect that the appearance of Our Lady of Guadalupe had and continues to have on the Mexican people cannot be denied. The meaning of the event has been recorded throughout the years in the collective memory of the people. Whatever happened in 1531 is not just past history but continues to live, to grow in meaning, and to influence the lives of millions today.

According to the legend, as Juan Diego, a Christianized Indian of common status, was going from his home in the *barriada* near Tepeyac, he heard beautiful music. As he approached the source of the music, a lady appeared to him. Speaking in Nahuatl, the language of the conquered, she commanded Juan Diego to go to the palace of the bishop of Mexico at Tlateloco and tell him that the Virgin Mary, "Mother of the true God through whom one lives," wanted a temple to be built at Tepeyac so that in it she "can show and give forth all my love, compassion, help and defense to all the inhabitants of this land . . . to hear their lamentations and remedy their miseries, pain and sufferings." After two unsuccessful attempts to convince the bishop of the Lady's authenticity, the Virgin wrought a miracle. She sent Juan Diego to pick roses in a place where only desert plants existed. Then she arranged the roses in his cloak and sent him to the bishop with the sign he had demanded. As Juan Diego unfolded his cloak in the presence of the bishop, the roses fell to the ground and the image of the Virgin appeared on his cloak.

The Mexican people came to life again because of Guadalupe. Their response was a spontaneous explosion of pilgrimages, festivals, and conversions to the revelation of the Virgin. Out of the meaningless and chaotic existence of the postconquest years, a new meaning erupted. The immediate response of the church, however, ranged from silence to condemnation. Early sources indicated that the missionaries, at least those who were writing, were convinced that it was an invention of the Indians and an attempt to reestablish their previous religion. Yet gradually the church accepted the apparition of Guadalupe as the Virgin Mary, Mother of God. In 1754 Pope Benedict XIV officially recognized the Guadalupe tradition by bringing it into the official liturgy of the church.[10]

To understand the response of Juan Diego and the Mexican people it is necessary to view the event, not through Western categories of thought, but through the system of communication of the Nahuatls of that time. What for the Spanish was an aberration was, for the conquered and dying Mexican nation, the rebirth of the Indian people. In reading the legend, the first striking detail is that Juan Diego heard beautiful music, which alone was enough to establish the heavenly origin of the Lady. For the Indians, music was the medium of divine communication. The Lady appeared on the sacred hill of Tepeyac, one of the four principal sacrificial sites in Mesoamerica. It was the sanctuary of Tonantzin, the Indian virgin mother of the gods. The dress was a pale red, the color of the spilled blood of sacrifices and the color of Huitzilopochtli, the god who gave and preserved life. Indian blood had been spilled on Mexican soil and fertilized mother earth, and now something new came forth. Red was also the color for the East, the direction from which the sun arose victorious after it had died for the night. The predominant color of the portrait is the blue-green of the mantle, which was the royal color of the Indian gods. It was also the color of Ometéotl, the origin of all natural forces. In the color psychology of the native world, blue-green stood at the center of the cross of opposing forces and signified the force unifying the opposing tensions at work in the world.

One of the prophetic omens that the native wise men interpreted as a sign of the end of their civilization was the appearance, ten years before the conquest, of a large body of stars in the sky. The stars had been one of the signs of the end, and now the stars on the Lady's mantle announced the beginning of a new era. Being supported by heavenly creatures could have meant two not necessarily contradictory things. First, she came on her own and therefore was not brought over by the Spaniards. Second, the Indians saw each period of time as supported by a god. This was recorded by a symbol representing the era being carried by a lesser creature. The Lady carried by heavenly creatures marked the appearance of a new era. She wore the black band of maternity around her waist, the sign that she was with child. This child was her offering to the New World. The Lady was greater than the greatest in the native pantheon because she hid the sun but did not extinguish it. Thus, she was more powerful than the sun god, their principal deity. The Lady was also greater than their moon god, for she stood upon the moon, yet did not crush it. However, great as this Lady was, she was not a goddess. She wore no mask as the Indian gods did, and her vibrant, compassionate face in itself told anyone who looked upon it that she was the compassionate mother.

The fullness of the apparition developed with the Lady's request for a temple. In the Indian hieroglyphic recordings of the conquest, a burning, destroyed temple was the sign of the end of their civilization and way of life. Therefore, the request for the temple was not just for a building where her image could be venerated, but for a new way of life. It would express continuity with their past and yet radically transcend that past. One civilization had indeed ended, but now another one was erupting out of their own mother soil.

Not only did the Lady leave a powerful message in the image, but the credentials that she chose to present herself to the New World were equally startling. For the bishop, the roses from the desert were a startling phenomenon; for the Indians, they were the sign of a new life. Flowers and music to them were the supreme way of communication through which the presence of the invisible, all-powerful God could be expressed. As the apparition had begun with music, giving it an atmosphere of the divine, it reached its peak with flowers, the sign of life beyond life, the sign that beyond human suffering and death there was something greater-than-life in the dwelling place of the wonderful giver of life.[11]

The narration as it exists today does not appear to be historical, at least in the Western scientific understanding of the word. It is not based on objective, verifiable, written documentation. However, it is a historical narrative to the people who have recorded their past through this specific literary genre.[12] Furthermore, popular religion has often been too easily labeled by outsiders, especially sociologists and theologians of the dominant groups, as alienating and superstitious. Popular piety is not necessarily and of itself alienating; in fact, for a defeated, conquered, and colonized people, it serves as a final resistance against the way of the powerful. Popular religion becomes alienating when agents of religion use it to legitimize and maintain the *status quo*. However, it becomes liberating when used as a source of unity and strength in the struggle for dignity and subsequent change against the powerful of society. It is the collective voice of the dominated people crying out: "We will not be eliminated; we will live on! We have been conquered, but we will not be destroyed."

In the first stages, popular religion gives meaning to an otherwise meaningless existence and thus a reason for living. As the triumphant group has its way of recording history, so those who have been silenced by subjugation have their interpretation of the past. Their accounts exist in an even deeper way. For the defeated and powerless, history is recorded and lived in the collective memory of the people: their songs, dances, poetry, art, legends, and popular religion. For the powerful, history is only a written record; whereas for the defeated, history is life, for it is the memory that keeps telling them that things are not as they ought to be. This memory cannot be destroyed or opposed by the powerful because they do not understand it. Accordingly, it is not surprising that in the history of Mexico there is no place for the Tepeyac tradition. Guadalupe, the most persistent influence in Mexico, is found only in the folklore and popular religious practices of the masses.

At the time of the apparition, the Spanish were building churches over the ruins of the Aztec temples. The past grandeur and power of Tenochtitlán-Tlatelolco (the original name of the present-day Mexico City) was being transformed into the glory of New Spain. Juan Diego dared to go to the center of power and, with supernatural authority (as the Lady commanded), demanded that the powerful should change their plans and build a temple—a symbol of a new way of life—not within the grandeur of the city, in accordance with the plans of Spain, but within the *barriada* of Tepeyac in accordance with the desires of the people. The hero of the story is a simple conquered Indian from the *barriada* who is a symbol of the poor and oppressed refusing to be destroyed by the dominant group. This story's purpose was to convert the bishop, the symbol of the new Spanish power group, and to turn the attention of the conquering group from amassing wealth and power to the periphery of society, where the people continued to live in poverty and misery.

The narration is only a wrapping for the continuing struggle of the masses for survival and liberation from the imposition of the ways of the powerful, a struggle that has been going on for nearly five hundred years. Through unceasing struggle, a dynamic tradition has emerged from the primitive story. This tradition has come to stand for the dignity, identity, unity, personal and collective emancipation, and liberation movements of the Mexican people.

Miguel Hidalgo fought for Mexican independence under the banner of Our Lady of Guadalupe. Emiliano Zapata led his agrarian reform under her protection. César Chávez battled against one of the most powerful economic blocs in the United States under the banner of Our Lady of Guadalupe and succeeded in his struggle for justice against all human odds.

This tradition was relegated to the area of fable or legend, not because it was lacking in historical veracity, but precisely because its living historical veracity cannot be fully accepted by the powerful political, economic, educational, sociological, or religious elite of any moment of history. The full truth of Tepeyac is the obvious disturbing truth of the millions of poor, powerless, peripheral oppressed of our society. Guadalupe's significance is the voice of the masses calling upon the elite to leave their economic, social, political, and religious thrones of pseudo-security and work with them—within the *movimientos de la base*—in transforming society into a more human place for everyone.

It was through the presence of Our Lady of Guadalupe that the possibility of cultural dialogue began. The missionaries' activity had won a basis of authentic understanding, bringing to a climax their work of preevangelization. As at Bethlehem, when the Son of God became man in Jesus and began the overthrow of the power of the Roman Empire, at Tepeyac Christ entered the soil of the Americas and began to reverse the European domination of the people in those lands. Tepeyac marks the beginning of the reconquest and the birth of Mexican Christianity.

It is from within the poor that the process of conversion is begun. The poor become the heralds of a new humanity. This critical challenge of our compassionate and liberating Mother to the powerful of any moment and place in the Americas continues today; it is the dynamic voice and power of the poor and oppressed of the Americas groaning and travailing for a more human existence. Her presence is not a pacifier but an energizer that gives meaning, dignity, and hope to the peripheral and suffering people of today's societies. Her presence is the new power of the powerless to triumph over the violence of the powerful. In her, differences are assumed and the cathartic process of the cultural-religious encounter of Europe-America begins, but it has a long way to go. Nevertheless, it has begun and is in process. This is the continuing miracle of Guadalupe—the Mother—queen of the Americas. Now the dream of the early missionaries, a new church and a New World, has definitely begun. The new people of the land would now be the *mestizo* people—*la raza*—and the new Christianity would be neither the cultural expression of Iberian Catholicism nor the mere continuation of the pre-Cortez religions of indigenous America, but a new cultural expression of Christianity in the Americas.

Today, theologians cannot afford to ignore the function and meaning of popular religion for the masses.[13] A theologian's task is not the canonization or rejection of the religious symbols of the people, but a continuous reinterpretation of them in relation to the whole gospel. In this way popular religion will not be alienating, but it will help to lead people to a deeper knowledge of the saving God. It will not be alienating or enslaving, but salvific and liberating. Popular religion which is regenerated (not eliminated) by the gospel becomes the invincible and efficacious power of the powerless in their struggle for liberation.[14]

For millions of Mexicans and Mexican Americans of the United States, Our Lady of Guadalupe is the temple in whom and through whom Christ's saving presence is continually incarnated in the soil of the Americas, and it is through her mediation that

> He shows strength with his arm.
> He scatters the proud in the imagination of their hearts.
> He puts down the mighty from their thrones,
> and exalts the oppressed.
> He fills the hungry with good things,
> and the rich he sends away empty handed.
>
> Luke 1:51-52

Desert Religions

Richard Rodriguez

The Catholic priest is under arrest, accused of raping altar boys. The Muslim shouts out the name of Allah as the jetliner plows into the skyscraper. The Jewish settler's biblical claim to build on the West Bank is supported by fundamentalist Protestants who dream of the last days.

These have been months of shame and violence among the three great desert religions—Judaism, Christianity, and Islam—the religions to which most Americans adhere. These desert religions are sister religions in fact, but more commonly they have been brother religions, united and divided by a masculine sense of faith. Mullahs, priests, rabbis—the business of religion was traditionally the males. It was the male's task to understand how God exists in our lives.

Judaism gave Christianity and Islam a notion both astonishing and radical, the notion that God acts in history. The desert religions became, in response to this idea, activist religions, ennobled at times by a sense of holy purpose, but also filled with a violence fed by the assumption that God is on my side and not yours. The history of the desert religions, oft repeated by old men to boys, got told through stories of battles and crusades, sultans and emperors.

But within the three great desert faiths there was a feminine impulse, less strong but ever present, the tradition of absorption rather than assertion,

209

assertive rather than authoritarian, of play rather than dogmatic servitude. Think of the delicate poetry of the Song of Songs, or the delicacy of the celebration of the maternal represented by the Renaissance Madonna, or the architectural lines of the medieval mosques of Spain, light as music. And yet the louder, more persistent tradition has been male, concerned with power and blood and dogmatic points.

Now on the evening news, diplomats come and go, speaking of truces and terrorists and the price of oil. In truth, we are watching a religious war, Muslim versus Jew—a war disguised by the language of diplomacy. In decades and centuries past there have been holocausts and crusades and violence as fierce among the leaders of a single religion—for example, Catholics contending with Protestant and Eastern Orthodox over heresies and questions of authority. Yahweh, God, Allah, the desert deity rarely expressed a feminine aspect as in Hinduism.

The men who interpreted the Bible or the Koran rarely allowed themselves a sense of unknowing or paradox as in Buddhism. And not coincidentally, I know many Americans who are turning away from the desert religions or are seeking to moderate the mass unity of the desert religions by turning to the contemplative physics of yoga and play of the Zen koan.

Meanwhile, in my own Catholic Church, there is the squalor of sexual scandal—men forcing themselves on boys. One hears conservative Catholics who speak of ridding the seminaries and the rectors of homosexuals. As one gay Catholic, a single man in this vast world, I tell you pedophilia is no more an expression of homosexuality than rape is an expression of heterosexuality. Pedophilia and rape are assertions of power. Polls indicate that a majority of American Catholics are more forgiving of the fallen priests than they are forgiving of the bishops and cardinals who have treated us like children, with their secret meetings and their clutch on power, apologizing but assuming no penance.

Polls indicate also that Catholics continue to go to church. We go to church because of the sacramental consolation our religion gives. All of us now in our churches and synagogues and mosques—what knowledge unites us now in this terrible season? Are we watching the male face of the desert religion merely reassert itself? Or are we watching the collapse of the tradition and the birth of—what?

I think of the women of America who have become priests and rabbis. I think of the women of Afghanistan who came to the school door the first morning after the Taliban had disappeared. I think of Mother Teresa, whose name will be remembered long after we have forgotten the names of the cardinals in their silk robes. I think that we may be at the beginning of a feminine moment in the history of the desert religions, even while the tanks rumble and the priest is arrested and the girl, unblinking, straps explosives onto her body.

Chapter 10

Reporting Complexity: Science and Religion

Jame Schaefer

When covering issues that intersect religious and scientific thinking, media professionals face the difficult task of producing reports that are fair and comprehensive. An initial approach may be to include conflicting views by representatives of religion and science. However, religion-science issues are usually more complex than news stories indicate. Polls generally show that American adults do not think that religion and science conflict,[1] though a minority maintains that position.[2] One in-depth poll conducted in the wake of the recent controversy in Kansas about teaching the theory of evolution in public schools indicates that approximately 16 percent prefer to have biblical creationism taught in science class instead of evolution, while 13 percent want creationism taught along with evolution in science class.[3] Another poll shows that 44 percent believe that God created the human "pretty much" in the present form sometime within the last 10,000 years, 39 percent believe that God guided the evolutionary process out of which the human developed over millions of years from less advanced forms of life, and 10 percent believe that the human species developed over millions of years from less advanced forms through a process in which God had no part.[4] Other polls indicate that 70 percent of American adults don't see any conflict between religion and science, but instead think that the quality of religious beliefs or spiritual practices is important to guide and inspire science and technology.[5] These surveys point to the need for reporters to consider several diverse views when covering religion-science issues.

The purpose of this essay is to facilitate the management of many views on religion-science issues so that reports on them can meet the high standards of the profession. In the first part, some examples of statements frequently quoted in the media are delineated, and assumptions behind them are explored from an historical to contemporary perspective. Basic characteristics of the natural sciences are identified subsequently. Six categories for thinking about the religion-science relationship are outlined to enable the recognition of other views that should be sought. In the final part, groups and other sources of readily available information are identified.

ASSUMPTIONS PAST AND PRESENT

Recall if you have encountered any of the following statements when reading, listening to, or watching media coverage on a natural disaster, a patient's healing, or the special creation of the human: It was God's will. Thank God for sparing our neighborhood. God cured his cancer. God must have had a reason for allowing this to happen. I will never go to church again because God did not answer my prayers. God created humans in their present form within the last 10,000 years.

Inherent in these statements are beliefs that God directly wills natural acts, that God uses natural processes to reward some and punish others, and that God's way of acting in and on the world is by interfering with its natural functioning. Similar statements can be found from ancient times, long before the advent of scientific methodology, when little was known about the physical world other than what could be experienced or observed directly. Attributing natural phenomena to God's direct activity, some ancients speculated on God's purposes, often to their own benefit or to the detriment of others. Some refused to be presumptuous about knowing God's purposes (for example, see the biblical Book of Job). Polytheistic cultures treated the forces of nature as deities who took their wrath out on people for failure to worship or act appropriately.[6] As Greek philosophical traditions developed, the orderly operations of the world were described apart from divinities through qualitative observations and mathematical computations.

Christian theologians from the patristic through the medieval periods reflected variously on the world as designed and sustained in existence by God. In the thirteenth century, Thomas Aquinas provided the most thorough and systematic treatment in which he described the cosmos as a hierarchically ordered unity of diverse beings created and empowered by God to function in relation to one another according to divinely established natural laws.[7] Muslim natural philosophers considered the world an integral whole willed into existence by God, totally contingent upon God for its continued existence, revelatory of God, and held in trust by humans.[8]

Aquinas, his teacher Albertus Magnus, and other medievalists distinguished between natural philosophy, through which knowledge about the world was obtained by human reasoning, and theology, which attends to knowledge revealed by God. However, they perceived a unity of knowledge and lauded their God-given gifts of rationality that distinguished them from other creatures. William of Ockham and John Duns Scotus advanced the separation of religious faith and reason by questioning the ability of human reason to prove their beliefs with any certainty.[9] Though astronomers Galileo Galilei and Johannes Kepler, biologist John Ray, and other prominent scientists explained their religious motivation for studying God's world at the dawn of the scientific revolution, this practice ebbed as scientific inquiry became increasingly specialized and reason was touted as the only means for establishing truth.[10] As the eighteenth century drew to a close, Immanuel Kant provided the rationale for maintaining separate realms for science to attend to natural phenomena, and religion to attend to the moral life in relation to ultimate reality.[11]

During the early scientific age, cosmologist Isaac Newton thought about the laws of nature as expressions of God's will.[12] Unfortunately, he invoked God's intervention to explain phenomena that couldn't be explained through these laws. For example, Newton asserted that God occasionally adjusted the motions of the planets to keep them in parallel orbits and somehow prevented the stars from collapsing together under gravitational attraction.[13] When scientists were eventually able to account for planetary motion and other phenomena through more accurate observations and calculations, God's role was reduced to the initial design of the world machine that operated with mechanical regularity. Chemist Robert Boyle thought that "a God who could create a mechanical universe . . . was far more to be admired and worshiped than a God who created a universe without scientific law."[14]

Scientists' use of the mechanics and other design features of the world as the basis for thinking about God proved perilous. Newton's influential argument that universal mechanics supply the foundations of both geometry and Christianity loomed large in the elimination of theological concerns from the scientific quest. As Michael Buckley explains in the use of scientific foundations for theological reflection spurred the onset of modern atheism, since "religion was implicitly confessing its own intrinsic lack of warrant, confessing that it did not possess the proper resources to deal with the existence of God" from within its own data.[15]

Other concerns surface when God's activity is invoked to account for gaps in scientific knowledge, a practice that eventually was dubbed "God of the gaps." Believing that God intervenes in the universe's functioning assumes that God created a world that needs adjusting and that God didn't know what God was doing when creating the world. Traditional beliefs about God as all-wise, all-knowing, and all-powerful, as professed within the Abrahamic religions, are difficult to reconcile with a god who has to adjust the world in order to make it function properly.

Thinking that God tinkers with the laws of the universe or intervenes in its internal functioning also poses a problem for science. The reliability of data and verifiability of theories cannot be tested with any degree of confidence. Though quantum physics qualified the Newtonian confidence in the predictability of phenomena,[16] any degree of predictability would be impossible when professing faith in a tinkering God.

Attributing to God actions that privilege some but not others is also problematic for religion. Though a sense of gratefulness and utter relief can be expressed for having been "saved" from a natural phenomenon or a disease, an explanation for why another has not been saved indicates belief in a deity who acts arbitrarily—a god who is fickle, unreliable, not trustworthy. An arbitrary, fickle, and unreliable god contrasts with the radically trustworthy God of the Psalms, the Gospel of John, and the *Qur'an*.

When interviewing people who talk about God's activity in relation to the world, reporters need to be alert to the basic assumptions about religion and science behind their statements and to discern problems inherent in their assumptions. Having a firm grasp of the characteristics of religion and science facilitates this task.

DEFINING RELIGION

Religion may be defined broadly as an organized way of knowing and orienting our lives to ultimate concerns. Some religions are loosely organized, while others are highly institutionalized. Some are more local, while several qualify today as "world" religions according to their number of adherents and shared commonalities, including historical heritage, doctrines, and practices. Among the most prominent are the three monotheistic religions that trace their heritage to Abraham—Judaism, Christianity, and Islam. When studying the relationship between religion and science from their perspectives, the appropriate working definition for religion is *an organized way of knowing and orienting our lives to the mystery of God in thought, word and deed.* Theology is the discipline dedicated to thinking critically about how a religious community expresses its faith in God. Each of the Abrahamic religions has specific data, methods, and purviews from which theologians reflect.

The primary data of Judaism include the experiences of the ancient Israelites with God, the stories they told about their experiences of God as recounted in the Hebrew Bible (*Ta'anach*), and the rituals they developed and practice today. The Torah, the first five books of the Hebrew Bible, are considered the most inspired of all Judaic texts because they recount the ancient Israelites' direct communication with God. The historical books of Joshua, Judges, Samuel, and Kings are deemed less inspired, while Prophets, Psalms, Proverbs, Job, Daniel, Ezra, Nehemiah, and Chronicles are believed to have been written by humans who were inspired by God. Other important data include the *Mishnah*, a digest of all the Jewish laws and practices compiled in 200 C.E.; the *Talmud*, which records the teachers' discussions on the Mishnah; and *Midrash* which are interpretations of the Judaic scriptures by eminent rabbis on legal, moral, and spiritual issues.[17] Rituals associated with the weekly Sabbath identify the Jews as God's partners in making the world a better place who rest from their weekday endeavors and leave the running of the universe solely to God. On Rosh Hashanah, Jews make resolutions to lead better lives in the year ahead and proceed for ten successive days to examine their lives, to resolve to undo any harm done, and to joyfully accept new responsibilities. Yom Kippur follows as the most sacred day of the year for a majority of Jews, when they atone for their sins through concrete acts, fasting, and prayer.[18]

The primary written data for Christianity are the thirty-nine books of the Hebrew Bible and the stories about the first Christians' experiences of Jesus the Christ that appear in the twenty-seven books of the New Testament. Roman Catholics and some Eastern Orthodox Christians accept seven additional books beyond the Hebrew Bible that altogether constitute their Old Testament. They consider post-biblical teachings by leaders, councils, and eminent theologians of the Catholic Church as part of the "tradition" upon which to base the formulation of doctrines and moral norms. Writings by founding theologians of Christian denominations established during the Reformation period are highly valued within those denominations. Among the rituals practiced by Christians are: the celebration of the Eucharist in commemoration of the gift of Jesus' body and blood for the salvation of all; the triduum recalling the passion, death, and resurrection of Jesus during Holy Week, which culminates in Easter Sunday; and a varied number of "sacraments" selected by each denomination according to its established criteria.

Islam's most important written datum is the Koran (*Qur'an*), which Muslims believe Mohammad, the prophet of Islam, recorded from an angel's dictation of God's words. When Muslims pray the verses (*ayat*) of the *Qur'an* in mosques, they are chanting God's words and thereby giving glory to God. Next in importance for Muslims is the *Hadith*, a vast and diverse collection of reports about the teachings and actions of the prophet and his companions. The codes of conduct and laws in the Hadith are considered legally binding. Among the rituals are the five pillars of Islam: praying to God five times a day using God's words; fasting during the month of Ramadan; paying a purifying tax (*zakat*), which is distributed to the poor and needy; and making once in one's lifetime a *hegira*, a pilgrimage from Mecca to Medina to commemorate the prophet's flight from persecution. That flight occurred during the year 632 C.E., which is cited in scholarly works as the date that Islam was officially established.

Theologians use various scholarly methods when reflecting on the Abrahamic religions. Since theology is a discipline dedicated to thinking critically about a particular religion as expressed by its religious community, theologians use many skills to explore a tradition from its data. The religious community's cherished texts, rituals, doctrines, codes of conduct, and reflections by eminent theologians over time provide the bases for theological examination. Anselm's description of theology in the twelfth century as "faith seeking understanding" broadly encompasses the theological quest. Highly honed tools of analysis, logic, and synthesis are required in all fields of theology—biblical, historical, systematics, and ethics.

Theologians strive to meet at least four criteria for reflections on data and statements of faith professed by a religious community: (1) agreement with the community's most significant data; (2) coherence with other data in the tradition, allowing room for reinterpretation and reformulation; (3) consistency with broad scientific findings as well as other sources of knowledge and aspects of personal and social life; and (4) capacity to effect personal transformation and inspire a positive way of living.[19]

In theological discourse and practices, the language used about God is metaphorical. Words are inadequate to describe God and God's activity. Metaphorical models are constructed imaginatively to try to talk more cogently about God in relation to the physical world of more-than-human constituents. Scholars have identified historical shifts in modeling God in relation to the world. For example, Barbour describes the model of God as the ruler of the world kingdom that was prevalent in theological reflections from the patristic to medieval periods.[20] As the scientific revolution was underway, a shift occurred to modeling God as the designer of a law-abiding world who remains distant from its machine-like operations while remaining engaged with human persons. These shifts demonstrate the contextual nature of religious language and the role that knowledge about the world plays when attempting to talk about God in relevant and meaningful ways.

Biblical scholars apply special methods when trying to determine the meaning of ancient texts when they were written. Scholars begin with the texts as recorded in ancient languages. They examine and compare various manuscripts of a text to find the most complete and reliable ones to translate. Recently discovered manuscripts like the Dead Sea scrolls provide new opportunities to check the accuracy of translations and their meaning. Among the methods used to discover the meaning of the texts are the historical-critical method of identifying the context and circumstances of the time in which they were written, the source or sources, the genre or literary type of the text, if and how a text was edited to convey meaning, and the narrative flow of the story.

Islamic scholars study the *Qur'an* as God's sacred words communicated to Muhammad. While a minority of scholars in the Islamic tradition apply historical-critical methods to the *Qur'an*, they do so from the devout faith perspective that they are studying God's exact words, not human words inspired by God, as scholars of the Hebrew and Christian scriptures contend.[21] However, various methods of scriptural criticism are applied to the Hadith, which scholars subjected to an extensive process of authentication and translation into legally binding codes of conduct and laws.[22] Nasr ranks the Hadith equivalent to the Bible, leaving the *Qur'an* in a classification of its own.[23]

Some groups do not ascribe to scholarly criticism of the primary texts of their religious community. For example, Louis Jacobs points to the majority of Orthodox Jews, who reject all biblical criticism, especially of the Pentateuch, as "destructive of faith." They wonder where questioning of the traditional view of a text will end if one begins.[24] Christian and Islamic "fundamentalists" adhere to the belief that their revered texts are God's exact words that are inerrant and must therefore be taken literally as scientific and historical fact. Scripture scholars and theologians view the inspired texts in more dynamic terms as God's self-communication that is received and responded to by the faithful in their quest for God over long periods of time.

Overall, the purview of religion is to provide a vision and pattern for living in the world. As Barbour explains:

> "[Religion] encourages ethical attitudes and behavior. It evokes feelings and emotions. Its typical forms are worship and meditation. Above all, its goal is to effect personal transformation and reorientation (salvation, fulfillment, liberation, or enlightenment)."[25]

Religion also provides a larger framework of meaning and purpose for living. Religion addresses questions of ultimate concern: Who am I? Why am I here? Why does the universe exist? Why am I motivated to act morally? What is my destiny?

DEFINING SCIENCE

The natural sciences are disciplines dedicated to describing the physical world and its phenomena from publicly observable and reproducible data that are obtained by humans from the world in which they live. Physics, chemistry, biology, and the other natural sciences are particular ways of knowing about the world. John Haught characterizes science as "a modest but fruitful attempt to grasp empirically . . . some small part of the totality of reality."[26]

The data of the sciences consists of observed or experienced natural phenomena collected to test the accuracy of a theory. These data are *partial* descriptions of physical reality. They are publicly observable, collected, and organized in natural categories through human interpretations. They are also reproducible.[27]

Theories underlie all steps of the scientific method—the selection of the phenomena to study, the choice of the variables to measure, the type and form of the questions asked, assumptions about the mode of testing, the operation of the testing equipment, and the process of observation.[28] The observation process is particularly problematic when investigating ecological systems and the quantum world, since scientists are not detached observers, but rather, are part of the interacting phenomena. When the observer is part of the process observed, purely objective findings and unquestionable predictions are not possible.

Scientists use their creative imaginations when developing theories. They construct metaphorical models for thinking about phenomena that cannot be observed directly. The Bohr model of the atom, the wave and particle models used in quantum physics, and the billiard ball model for thinking about gas diffusion are examples of models that generate promising theories to test by four criteria that roughly parallel those used by theologians to assess religious beliefs. The most important criterion for scientists is the extent to which the theory agrees with the data and successfully makes predictions. Consistency with other theories acceptable to the scientific community, applicability to a wide range of other relevant variables, and ability to facilitate future research are the other major criteria.

Scientists develop and test theories through the scientific method. Over time, the scientific enterprise has become increasingly reductive when aiming to reach the lowest possible denominator of empirical phenomena. The ongoing genome research in microbiology and fundamental particles in quantum mechanics exemplifies the methodological reductionism that prevails in scientific circles.

The realm of physical reality is science's purview. Scientists address primarily "how" and "limited why" questions about sensed phenomena, their functioning internally and relationally, and other aspects of the physical world. Answers to "how" and "limited why" questions are based on the reproduction of prior tests and measurements from similar data. Through these endeavors, scientists can understand the world better with some degree of accuracy. Scientific findings are open to revision when new data and more probing theories are imagined and tested.

While science provides answers to questions about physical reality, it does not address why the universe exists, its ultimate purpose, or its meaning from a metaphysical perspective. Nor does science provide knowledge about the ultimate purpose or meaning of humanity. These and other "ultimate why" questions belong to religion.

When scientists claim that the scientific method is the *only* route to knowledge about reality, they have moved beyond their disciplines to the realm of metaphysics. Metaphysical reductionism constitutes a belief system that is popularly referred to as *scientism*. Scientism is not science in the sense of the bona fide discipline that is dedicated to studying the physical world.

RELIGION IN RELATION TO SCIENCE

Barbour, Haught, Bube, and Peters have identified some of the principal ways in which people think about the relationship between religion and science.[29]Six categories appear most helpful to guide media professionals in their quest to cover issues comprehensively: conflict, conflation, contrast, conversation, combination, and confirmation.

Conflict

The image of conflict between science and religion is conventional in the media today. Coverage of a story is more dramatic when extreme views are highlighted while more subtle positions go unreported. When journalists write about religion and science in conflict on issues, the "experts" they interview are usually partial to one side or the other. Those who think that the scientific method is the *only* reliable path to knowledge about the world paint science positively as objective, rational, public, and based on solid observational evidence that is tested by experimentation. They describe religion negatively as subjective, emotional, based on traditions or authorities that contradict one another, and founded on a priori assumptions that are untestable by experimentation and exempt from public scrutiny. Those who are hostile to science and technology but value religion consider science a spiritually corrosive force in the modern world and believe that technology has lamentably diminished the value of the human person and caused widespread ecological destruction. As Haught contends, these antitheses add up to an insuperable hostility between science and religion.[30]

Because the Intelligent Design movement argues against the facts and theories of evolution, it seems to fall within the conflict category of the relationship between religion and science.[31] Either one accepts that the process of natural selection results in the formation of new species or, the Intelligent Design advocates argue, one believes that there are some irreducibly complex entities that would not otherwise occur unless they were intelligently designed. Though proponents of Intelligent Design avoid equating the subject of their theory with the God worshiped by Christians, Jews, and Muslims, reaching that conclusion is compelling.

Conflation

Another slant on the relationship of religion and science is their conflation to the point that they cannot be distinguished as distinct human endeavors.

Religion and science are confused in this way of thinking about the disciplines. Falling into the conflation category are "scientific" materialists, creation "scientists," and "God of the gaps" advocates.

Those who subscribe to the scientific method as the only route to reliable knowledge about the world have moved beyond science to epistemology, the philosophy of knowing. Their fundamental belief is in science. Unlike scientific research, however, the epistemological assertion of scientism cannot be tested.

Usually accompanying scientism is the belief that matter and energy constitute the fundamental reality of the universe,[32] and that only science will disclose this reality. Proponents of this view have moved beyond science to metaphysics, the philosophy concerned with the nature of reality. Accompanying this metaphysical position are various forms of reductionism, one of which claims that all sciences are reducible to the laws of physics and chemistry, while another claims that all phenomena will eventually be explained in terms of their material components. These metaphysical reductionists also move beyond science due to philosophical assertions that cannot be tested.

Biblical literalism and creation science are examples of the conflation of religion and science.[33] Going against Roman Catholic and most mainline Protestant denominations, which hold that the scriptures are human works inspired by God, biblical literalists contend that the Bible is God's word and is therefore without error. The Bible contains scientific and historical facts that must be believed. Creation scientists contend that there is scientific evidence for the creation of the world within the last six thousand years and that humans were created in their current state within that span of time and did not evolve from lower primates. Much of this purported scientific evidence was considered dubious by the U.S. District Court, which in 1982 overturned an Arkansas law that allowed the same amount of time for teaching the creationist theory as allotted for evolution.[34]

Another example of the conflation of religion and science is the practice of attributing to God's activity natural phenomena that cannot be explained scientifically. Newton demonstrated "God of the gaps" thinking when claiming that God adjusted the solar system, since the actions of the planets did not follow planetary laws identified during his time. Of course, this approach is very risky for religion. If belief in God is limited to God's miraculous interventions, faith in God diminishes when science fills the gaps. "God of the gaps" mentality is also a risky practice for science, which requires reliable data and reproducible testing of theories based on data.

Prompted by a human craving for a unified understanding of the world, conflationists confuse religion and science. Unfortunately, conflation and conflict proponents are too often the spokespersons for religion and science in print, audio, and visual media.

Contrast

One way to avoid conflict and conflation of religion and science is to view them as totally independent and autonomous ways of knowing. Each is valid only within its clearly defined sphere of inquiry. Each should be judged by its own standards and not by the other's because they are radically different in the questions they ask, the languages they use, the tasks they tackle, and the authorities they follow.[35] As Haught explains, advocates of this approach emphasize that science examines the natural world empirically, while religion addresses the ultimate reality that transcends the empirically known world:

> Science is concerned with *how* things happen in nature, religion with *why* there is anything at all rather than nothing. Science is about *causes*, religion about *meaning*. Science deals with solvable *problems*, religion with unsolvable *mystery*. Science answers specific questions about the *workings* of nature, whereas religion expresses concern about the ultimate *ground* of nature.[36]

When this approach is followed, however, the human craving for coherence is unsatisfied because the realms of knowing are so disparate, disconnected, departmentalized, and cut off from one another.

When in the contrast mode, the primary data of a religious tradition are taken seriously, but not literally. The Bible is understood as a fallible human record that gives witness to the ancient Israelites' and earliest Christians' experiences of God. The locus of God's activity is in the lives of persons and communities who experienced and responded to God's self-communication, and not the dictation of a text as literalists contend. The scriptures are accepted as diverse interpretations of God's self-communication, and responses by believers in the contexts of their times. Scholarly methods of biblical exegesis are applied to determine the meaning of the texts when they were written.

Conversation

As the rapid growth of religion-science literature over the past twenty years and the plethora of courses now offered on campuses throughout the world indicate, many theologians and scientists recognize that they cannot compartmentalize their ways of knowing. They realize that they have something to say to one another on issues at the boundaries of their disciplines (e.g., origins and nature of the universe, of life, of the human being, of consciousness) that can provide a more complete understanding. They yearn to unify their diverse ways of knowing, as Pope John Paul II encourages.[37]

Following theologians who reflected on topics informed by knowledge about the world that was current during their times, contemporary theologians are discovering that their discourse can be more comprehensive, relevant, and meaningful when informed by scientific findings of our time.

Scientists who profess religious faith are also discovering that they can move from their scientific endeavors to a deeper meaning of their faith, that they can reflect on their purposes as scientists in the world, and that they can draw from their faith's tenets to guide their ethical behavior.

Media professionals will recognize that theologians and scientists avoid conflating and confusing their disciplines when they are in conversation with one another. Their contact proceeds from a commitment to their disciplines' data, methods, and purviews. They recognize the limitations of their disciplines. They acknowledge where their expertise ends, and they move beyond their disciplines. They appreciate the contributions each of the disciplines makes to richer and deeper ways of understanding issues. They welcome the assistance of philosophy to bridge their conversation so their terminology is clearly understood, concepts are analyzed, and possible syntheses are explored systematically. They realize that their constructs are tentative as they explore plausible approaches to issues at their disciplinary boundaries.

Combination

When theologians move beyond conversation to reformulate religious beliefs informed by contemporary scientific findings, they have entered the mode of integrating religion and science. This does not mean that they have confused or conflated the disciplines, however. When in the combination mode, theologians begin with a particular doctrine that has been developed from a particular religion based on its privileged data, and they reconstruct the doctrine in light of scientific knowledge.

For example, theologians start with the doctrine of creation, which stipulates that God willfully created and sustains the universe in existence and that it would not exist if God had not willed its existence and continuance. Theologians consider the context of the times and understanding of the world when the doctrine was established and embellished. They proceed to consider the doctrine today in light of cosmological findings about the early universe and its development over billions of years. They rework the doctrine so that it is meaningful and relevant for the believers. The reformulated doctrine expresses faith in God who willed the universe into existence, empowered its self-development over the vastness of time and expanding space without interference, and self-communicated to beings who emerged out of the cosmological-evolutionary process with the capacity to hear and respond. This expression of the doctrine of creation is regarded as tentative and open to revision as new substantive findings become available. Nevertheless, the basic meaning remains intact—the world is radically contingent upon God for its existence and continuation.

Barbour discusses other modes of combining religion and science. They include a systematic synthesis of the two endeavors within a comprehensive metaphysics of process philosophy. He cautions, however, that care must be

taken to avoid too much reliance on philosophy and science so the religiosity of the combination remains prominent.[38]

Confirmation

In this final mode of relating religion and science, religion is understood as
fueling the *quest* for scientific knowledge and as guiding the moral behavior
of scientists in their quest. Haught used the term "confirmation" to describe
the religious vision of reality that fortifies the drive to explore the physical
world in its micro- to macrocosmic dimensions. Reality is "a finite, coherent,
rational, ordered totality" of diverse entities grounded in the ultimate love of
God with a "promise" of a future yet to unfold. The trustworthy God of the
Abrahamic traditions upholds this totality. Faith in the orderly totality of the
world grounded by God's love and promise for the unfolding world provides
the incentive to pursue knowledge through scientific exploration. Faith in
God's love and promise also guides scientists toward acting in morally
responsible ways as the world unfolds, for which they are accountable ultimately to God.

The confirmation approach was demonstrated in part by some of the most
prominent scientists who launched the scientific age in the seventeenth century. As mentioned in the first section of this essay, Galileo, Kepler, and Ray,
along with Francis Bacon, the "father of the scientific method," and
renowned others explained that they were engaging in the exploration of
God's book of nature. Bacon and Kepler insisted that their scientific studies
of physical phenomena gave glory to God.[39] In *Mysterium Cosmographicum*,
Kepler explained that the task of a Christian is to acquire a "greater awareness of creation and its grandeur" which is "our magnificent temple of
God."[40] Ray described in *The Wisdom of God Manifested in the Works of the Creation* his faith-filled incentive to pursue the study of biology.[41]

This confirmation approach to relating religion and science also resonates
with the Islamic tradition. Throughout the *Qur'an* and Hadith are found references to the physical creation as God's self-disclosure, which should be
read and understood. Nasr points to a sacred saying in the Hadith in which
God speaks through the prophet: "I was a hidden treasure; I wanted to be
known." The study of God's *ayat* as displayed in the cosmos is the Muslim's
obligation and privilege. Knowledge about God's cosmic book leads to
knowledge of God and some of God's immediate purposes. As Nasr cautions,
Muslims are not presumptuous enough to think that they should search for,
or could begin to know, God's ultimate purpose for the universe, since God's
purpose is known only to God.[42]

Media professionals are wise to avoid thinking that this mode of relating
religion and science confirms scientific *findings*. That is not the role of religion or the discipline of theology. Religion does not confirm scientific findings, nor does religion embrace any particular scientific theories. In the

confirmation way of thinking about the religion-science relationship, religious faith fortifies the quest for scientific knowledge about the world. Theologians and scientists value this way of relating their purviews as an affirmation of the scientific quest and how scientists should function responsibly when pursuing knowledge about physical reality.[43]

CONCLUSION

Covering issues that intersect religion and science is a complicated and difficult task. Having a firm grasp of the definitions, data, methods, and boundaries of religion and science will help media professionals deconstruct assumptions, postures, and positions in statements people make when they are being interviewed. Discerning how people generally view the relationship between religion and science as conflict, conflation, contrast, conversation, combination, or confirmation will aid the journalist in identifying other views that should be sought. Seeking readily available sources of information will facilitate more in-depth reporting.

10: View from the News Desk

Fairness and Pressure Advocacy in Controversial Science

Joe Williams

If a dog bites a man, it's not a story.

If a man bites a dog, it could be a story, but only if you've got a picture, or "art" to go along with it.

But if a man bites a dog and you can find quotes expressing outrage from the dog's lawyer and the National Association of Canines, you're probably sitting on a front pager.

These days, it seems that every good news story is supposed to have conflict—Democrats vs. Republicans; labor vs. management; Britney Spears vs. Justin Timberlake, Creationists vs. Evolutionists, Religious Right vs. stem cell researchers, and so forth. The controversy phenomenon—the need to frame news within conflict—drives coverage to an extent unknown to most of the American public. Conflict reported by working journalists spills over to radio and television talk shows on the airwaves twenty-four hours a day.

One of the oldest conflicts in the history of journalism—if not the history of the world—is the theoretical battle between religion and science. Former Cornell University president Andrew White in 1896 described as "warfare" the clash between the two forces and argued that scientific progress was being held back by theology. Such tension continues to play out today. This commentary will address how the mainstream press covers that conflict in front-page issues like cloning, stem cells, and creationism.

My purpose here is not to focus on any one particular reporter, editor, or news outlet, but to point to the culture that has inhabited newsrooms for years. Sometimes significant pressure comes from religious groups or the scientific community over how an issue is covered in a newspaper. By pressure, I mean everything from writing angry letters to the editor to flooding newspaper phone banks with calls (usually in response to something on a talk radio program or Internet chat room). Sometimes the pressure takes the form of boycotts of publication or intimidating advertisers. It's my experience that outside pressure has a more profound impact on smaller newspapers in smaller cities, but all newspapers feel the heat from time to time—a natural form of publishing accountability.

While journalists should always strive to be fair in overall coverage, controversial topics are often approached from an overly defensive perspective. By that I mean that too much of the consideration is placed on how to avoid offending the warring parties involved rather than on advancing stories to provide new information. That kind of "fairness," if it dulls what is included in news coverage on controversial issues, is ultimately unfair to readers looking to arm themselves with information they can use to form their own opinions.

From a practical perspective, any journalist would want to limit the number of complaint calls from organized groups. Understandably, it is possible to spend more time dealing with the aftermath of stories than in gathering data, checking sources, and writing and editing the articles in the first place. It can be a frustrating use of time, and the thought of how easy it could be if only the hard questions had never been raised can be appealing. The idea of fairness should extend beyond those whose views are covered to include what is fair for independent readers who are hungry for information on a particular topic.

For working journalists, the conflict that arises between religious beliefs and scientific research plays a tremendous role in what reporters and editors consider "newsworthy." Candidly, the conflict gives life to an otherwise data-intensive, complex, or difficult story and gets it into the newspaper and before the eyes of readers.

The same conflicts that get stories headline play in newspapers and lead story in broadcasts around America also let journalists off the hook far too easily by allowing them to produce stories that often don't provide enough of the kinds of information that readers can use to draw solid conclusions.

I refer to the way general news reporters cover topics involving science and religion. Science beat reporters are theoretically better acquainted with the academic and research issues on which they report. Given the economics of newspapers, though, the real difficulty may be too few specialized reporters trained in science: my experience at several newspapers of varying sizes is that few modern newsrooms even have science as a regular beat anymore.

The phenomenon of the disappearing science beat reporters is itself a problem that has been and will continue to be addressed within the journalism community, so I won't suggest our profession is unaware of the need. One could argue that the problem is compounded by the belief that many news outlets prosperous enough to have specialty beats like science or medicine appear to be asking them to produce fluffier "news you can use" type stories about health and fitness, as opposed to regular analytical reporting on hot-button issues. The shrinking "news hole" for hard news is a real issue, for many news reporters find they have less and less space to present sometimes complicated stories to readers. I do not refer to a weekly science section or feature, of course, because it is the front-page stories in newspapers across the nation every day that tend to dominate discussion of current events in the public square and that may in turn influence the shape of science public policy.

By devoting so much space to "conflict as news," journalists too often do too little to help readers and viewers reach solid conclusions about which side of the conflict is actually right. Perhaps even worse, journalists and editors sometimes define "fair and balanced" in a way that sheepishly steers clear of taking a stab at any sort of informed conclusion. Too often, newspaper reporters and editors base fairness on whether equal time was offered to each side. In this quest for fairness, completeness is sometimes sacrificed, particularly when it comes to stories involving complicated subject matters.

Imagine, for example, how the modern press might cover the outrageous political and ideological battles between Galileo and Pope Urban VIII in the seventeenth century. The debate was whether the Earth was the center of the universe, a notion the Catholic Church treated as fact until more recently, or whether the sun was the center of the universe, a theory advanced by the Polish astronomer Copernicus in 1514.

An Italian philosopher, physicist, and astronomer, Galileo thought there was some scientific merit to the Copernican theory, and at a time when the Roman Catholic Church was the controlling political machine, his writings exploring the topic were considered blasphemy. In 1633, Galileo was interrogated by church officials for 18 days and imprisoned. He later apologized to the pope, but he remained under house arrest until his death in 1642.

How might the modern press have handled this story? Here's one pessimistic guess:

Pope to Galileo: Drop Dead

ROME—Extremist astronomer Galileo Galilei was imprisoned yesterday for continuing to suggest that the sun might be the center of the universe, Catholic Church officials said.

"This guy is so far out there we intend to give him extensive drug testing when he is in lock-up," said one church law-enforcement official, speaking on condition of anonymity.

A spokesman for Galilei, simply called "Galileo" by his followers, said sound scientific evidence suggests that Earth revolves around the sun and not the other way around.

"It may take the Church 350 years to come to terms with basic scientific reasoning, but Galileo is not the crazy one here," said the spokesman, who declined to give his name out of fear that church officials would throw him in the slammer too.

Pope Urban VIII issued an official statement blasting Galilei for "merely trying to sell books" with his foolish arguments against "what everyone understands to be fact, namely that the Earth is the center of everything created by God."

"This isn't just the church talking," the pope's statement said. "This so-called Father of Modern Philosophy thinks he knows more than Ptolemy and Aristotle as well as all of the other educated and God-fearing Catholics across the land. I think common sense speaks for itself."

Prominent scientists in Rome, all of whom run think tanks that are heavily subsidized by the church, either declined to comment or expressed support for the pope.

"If the pope says the Earth is the center of the universe, that's good enough for me," one researcher said.

The "story" on the Galileo imprisonment—which I admit is on the hyperbolic side—quoted people on both sides of the issue but generally accepted the establishment church's starting point and ultimately did nothing to try to take an independent stab at whether this "conventional wisdom" was accurate or not.

Unfortunately, my wild example is often not far from reality when modern-day journalists take up issues of scientific/religious conflict. More often than not, by the time these issues hit the newspapers, they have been reduced to political stories that don't ultimately encourage or empower readers to take a side.

While remaining nonpartisan is often admirable for news outlets covering politics, the fact that so many news stories about hot-button issues like human cloning end up as political stories and not science stories means readers are being robbed of any perspective that tries to scratch at the truth of the matter.

Imagine the job a free press could have done in the 1600s if it could have independently attempted to determine whether it was the Earth or the sun that was the center of the universe. It is the press's role to prepare and examine evidence that the public could use to come to more accurate conclusions on its own.

Society will (and ultimately did in the case of the Copernican theory) decide for itself once a critical mass of information sways a majority of individuals to conclude that a theory is correct. The press can and should play a pivotal role in creating that critical mass of information.

In the case of Galileo, even the Catholic Church eventually had to respond to the critical mass of verified information. Pope John Paul II in 1979, for example, actually appointed a commission to review Galileo's condemnation, and in 1992 declared it an error resulting from "tragic mutual incomprehension."[1]

Yet sometimes these scientific and religious clashes are covered as political issues because they are, in fact, political issues. My critique is not that these issues of politics are covered this way, but that oftentimes much of the coverage that makes the front page of the newspaper involves the politics and not the substance of the issues.

A typical example of the "conflict as a political story" can be found in a November 6, 2003, Associated Press story on a vote by the United Nations to delay any treaty that would ban human cloning. Written by AP's UN reporter, Edith Lederer, the story describes in typical political style the details surrounding the controversial vote. It quotes spokespeople on both sides of the issue and clearly defines terms like *cloning* (an exact copy made up of biological material like DNA segments) and *stem cells*. It also includes this boilerplate explanation for the religious/scientific conflict over the matter, paragraphs that appear in similar fashion in most political accounts on the issue:

> "Scientists who support cloning to produce human embryos for medical purposes say they hope to use stem cells from the embryos to find cures for Alzheimer's, Parkinson's and other debilitating diseases."
> "Stem cells can divide and turn into any kind of cell in the body—raising the possibility of 'growing' replacement organs for sick people."
> "The Roman Catholic Church and anti-abortion groups say stem cell research is tantamount to murder because it starts with the destruction of a human embryo to recover the cells."[2]

The political and philosophical debate on stem cells and human cloning figures to be a contentious issue in our modern society for the foreseeable future, and as such, it will continue to produce deservedly good news stories. The role of the press should be to arm the public with as much information as possible so as to enable more thoughtful discussion in the public square, rather than merely making sure both sides of an issue are contacted for comment.

Another hot-button issue that has dazzled reporters, editors, lawyers, and the public at large for much of the last century is the controversy over whether creationism should be taught in public schools.

In 1925, long before the days of 24-hour cable television news shows, a media circus took over Dayton, Tennessee, for the John Thomas Scopes "monkey trial." Scopes, a teacher who challenged a state law banning the teaching of evolution, would likely have been a modern-day media darling, appearing on all the big, news talk-shows, pitted against a fundamentalist minister type. This is the exactly the kind of conflict the media loves.

Nearly a century later—and four decades after the U.S. Supreme Court ruled that the teaching of creationism in public schools is a violation of the separation of church and state—heated battles continue to break out over whether textbooks and school curriculums should include theories about evolution and/or creationism.

In the fall of 2003, the state of Texas played host to a dramatic political battle in the state board of education over whether to officially approve its list of permissible science textbooks. Religious conservatives argued strenuously that many textbooks on the list treated theories of evolution as a clear-cut fact rather than as a working theory to be considered along with others like creationism. Despite intense lobbying and politicking, the Texas Board of Education voted in early November to keep the books on the list, a move that was seen as rebuke of the far right.

Much of the local coverage of the vote fell into the "conflict as a political story" genre, and predictably it treated the subject as a political issue, making good-faith efforts to quote experts and critics on both sides. Because textbooks selected by Texas tend to dictate what is used in many other parts of the country (Texas is second only to California in terms of the number of textbooks ordered in a given year), the story was covered by media outlets outside of Texas.

One account of the textbook vote, in particular, shows that it is possible to take a political story and provide heavy doses of background and analysis for readers. Los Angeles Times reporter Scott Gold, chief of the California paper's Houston bureau, wrote: "The vote, like the differences between evangelicals and evolutionists, was marked by tension, passion and drama."[3]

Writing for a newspaper that was far away from the action, Gold shows in his account of the vote what can be done when reporters are free from the kinds of local pressure that come from the parties involved in a big story. While the story's lead deals with the politics of the vote, the body of the story goes into great detail about the positions of each side of the battle, but doesn't read like a mere he-said, she-said account.

The story clearly differentiates the varying opinions of different religious leaders, rather than lumping all religious groups into one amorphous group; it quotes a statement from a group of scientists who argue that theories of evolution have been tested and verified, and provides analysis, not just of the politics behind the vote, but of the issues themselves.

Gold clearly defines, for example, a biological theory known as the "Cambrian explosion," a period about 500 million years ago in which existing species appeared to change too quickly to support all of the theories of evolution. He also describes, again in clear language, the "Intelligent Design" theory that says biological mechanisms are too complex to be attributed to evolution alone.

Most readers of Gold's story would consider it fair to the parties involved, but unlike many stories of its kind, he goes further by clearly providing some meat on the issue itself upon which readers can chew.

In a different story that previewed the vote, Gold profiled William Dembski, a scientific researcher at Baylor University who also happens to be an evangelical Christian. Going back to this essay's original contention that conflict and news are inseparable, Dembski is the personification of that conflict.[4]

Describing Dembski as a supporter of the Intelligent Design theory, which argues that some sort of divine or intelligent force had to have played some role in the evolution of man, Gold is able to branch out to again describe the politics and the substance in a way that journalists, myself included, should be shooting for on a regular basis.

It has been said that the best way to ruin a good party is to steer the conversation toward politics or religion. Conflicting theories in these areas can get messy. But news outlets love these kinds of issues, for obvious reasons. They get people's pulses going and generate a buzz in the community.

As technology and science continue to move forward at warp speed, and as theology and religion remain vibrant forces among the public, conflicts between science and religion will continue to play out in newspapers and newscasts around the country. That much is certain. The only question that remains is whether news outlets will rise to the challenge and regularly attempt to provide good, solid, and thoughtful information to help readers come to their own conclusions over time.

Chapter 11

Vatican Opinion on Modern Communication

Paul Soukup, S.J.

Of the world religions, Christianity has probably paid more attention than any other to communication. Evangelical churches cite the "Great Commission"—Jesus' command to the disciples, "Go to the people of all nations and make them my disciples. Baptize them in the name of the Father, the Son, and the Holy Spirit, and teach them to do everything I have told you" (Matt 28:19-20, CEV)— as a rationale. And as a "religion of the Book," Christianity depends on the Bible; it therefore has an interest in copying and printing the Bible, making it available to as many people as possible. These two imperatives led to and continue to foster an ongoing alliance between Christianity and communication media: the Bible was the first book printed on Gutenberg's press; within a year of the invention of motion pictures, filmmakers produced Bible films and continue to do so;[1] early radio featured church services; Marconi himself set up Vatican Radio; a Catholic bishop, Fulton J. Sheen, stands among the pioneer television personalities in the United States.

Besides this practical interest, Christian churches also show a theoretical interest in communication. Such an interest appears, first, in the writings of many individual pastors who seek either to teach people how to make appropriate use of the media (which programs to watch, which to avoid, etc.) or to influence public policy. Second, the concern appears in official statements from those churches that have a fixed public or hierarchical structure; these often address the same concerns as the local pastors, teaching congregational members and addressing public policy. Churches with fixed organizational structures that coordinate their comments on communication include the World Council of Churches,[2] the National Council of Churches of Christ (1992), and the Catholic Church.

Of the Christian churches, the Roman Catholic Church has most actively commented on communication. More likely than not, this results from the organizational structure of the Church itself. With a permanent bureaucracy in the Vatican (as well as local offices for each bishop, and national support structures), the Catholic Church has offices to address the whole range of Christian living. For example, the Vatican today has nine top-level "congregations" responsible for such things as doctrine, worship, evangelization, education, and clergy; eleven councils, which address laity, Christian unity, the family, justice and peace, inter-religious dialogue, culture, and communication; and seven commissions, which supervise everything from biblical theology to archaeology. The communication office's rank as a midlevel council indicates its stature and the importance that the Vatican places on communication.

This chapter reports on the Vatican's statements on modern (mass) communication, particularly those issued in the last forty years. Before addressing the statements themselves, the chapter will provide a brief history of Vatican interest in communication and then outline the Roman Catholic theology that establishes the context for those statements. Finally, it will introduce the statements themselves, highlighting repeating themes.

SOME HISTORICAL BACKGROUND

The very existence of a full-time office and staff for communication explains the consistency of both output and opinion of the Vatican's statements on communication. Since its establishment in 1964, the Pontifical Council for Social Communication has issued eleven documents on communication in its own name, three of them extensive and influential. In addition, it has prepared thirty-seven shorter statements for the pope's promulgation. This is a marked increase—the previous thirty years saw only four statements by the pope on communication, most of them on film, and only two of them extensive. Typically, when individual popes wrote about the media in the 1930s, 40s, and 50s, they responded to particular issues, such as commending the American Legion of Decency that sought to influence the morality of film content.[3]

Recognizing the power of the cinema, radio, and television, Pope Pius XII issued a major encyclical letter on these mass media. In *Miranda Prorsus*, the pope claims a twofold Church interest in mass media: their influence on people, and the possibility of their use in proclaiming the gospel to all nations. The letter itself aims for a comprehensive treatment. After examining the potential Church use of the media, Pius XII reviews the following: the prosocial and antisocial effects of the media; the freedom of communication and its errors; the role of public authority in its interactions with the entertainment industry; news; mass education; proper education for youth; and the role of Church communication offices. Then he turns to each specific medium, writing in turn about film, radio, and television and the various social actors involved in each—producers, exhibitors, audience members, and so forth. Though he addresses the letter to bishops and other Church leaders, his content speaks also to all who come in contact with the mass media. The overall tenor of this letter is one of concern for the dangers to Christian faith and morals posed by the media; despite this, the pope urges greater Church involvement with the media.

About ten years earlier, in 1948, Pius XII had established a standing Vatican committee for film. With its name and membership changing several times over the next few years, it formed a key advisory body in the preparation of the encyclical letter. After his election as pope in 1958, Pope John XXIII appointed within this committee a "Preparatory Secretariat for the Press and the Entertainment World" after he had summoned the Second Vatican Council. This subcommittee received the charge to assemble materials on communication for the approaching Council. More specifically, it was this Secretariat's task "to identify the problems raised by the press and the audiovisual media and, while recognizing the individual character of each sector, to assemble all this material into a single study which would yet leave room for future developments in which the different instruments of social communication, as they were called from then on, would find their proper place and receive due consideration within the Church's renewed ministry" (Pontifical Council, n.d., par. 11). The work of this secretariat led to the 1963 Vatican Council Decree on the Means of Social Communication, *Inter Mirifica* (Vatican Council II, 1963; henceforth *IM*).

The Second Vatican Council, a worldwide meeting of Catholic bishops and church leaders, with observers from other Christian churches, met from 1962 to 1965. As articulated at the beginning of its second session by the then recently elected Pope Paul VI, the Council had four purposes: "to define more fully the nature of the Church, especially as regards the person of the bishops; to renew the Church; to restore unity among all Christians . . . ; and to start a dialogue with contemporary men."[4] The dialogue with the contemporary world plays a large role in the various statements of the Council and in the subsequent work of the Pontifical Council for Social Communication.

Meeting in regular sessions in the fall of 1962, 1963, 1964, and 1965, the bishops of the Second Vatican Council debated schemata and proposals prepared by the working committees, which met throughout the year. By the end of its sessions, the Council had approved sixteen major statements, addressing topics ranging from the nature of the Church itself, the Church in the modern world, relationships with other Christian churches and with non-Christian religions, revelation, the roles of various groups within the Church (bishops, priests, laity, members of religious congregations), worship, missionary work, education, religious freedom, and the mass media.

In *Inter Mirifica* (the decree on communication), the Council acknowledges the ongoing importance of mass communication in the contemporary world and identifies several thematic areas: the right to information; the relationship between the rights of art and moral demands; public opinion; and the uses of the mass media in civil society and by the Church. To promote ongoing reflection on these and other communication issues, the Council established an annual "communication day" in each diocese and mandated the creation of the Pontifical Commission (later, Council) for Social Communication. This commission of bishops and lay communication experts would promote and coordinate Catholic thinking about communication. Finally, the Council added this charge: "The Council expressly directs the commission of the Holy See referred to in par. 19 to publish a pastoral instruction, with the help of experts, from various countries, to ensure that all the principles and rules of the Council on the means of social communication be put into effect" (*IM*, par. 32).

The commission fulfilled that mandate eight years later with the publication, in January 1971, of *Communio et Progressio*—the lengthy "pastoral instruction on the means of social communication." This document, the first of the commission, sets the direction for the next thirty years of Vatican opinion on contemporary communication.

THE THEOLOGICAL CONTEXT

Clearly, all of this Vatican thinking and writing about communication emerges from the Roman Catholic theological tradition. The most explicit exposition of the theological grounding for reflection on mass communication occurs in the introductory sections of *Communio et Progressio*. After a brief introduction, we read: "The Church sees these media as 'gifts of God' which, in accordance with his providential design, unite men in brotherhood and so help them to cooperate with his plan for their salvation" (*Communio et Progressio*, henceforth, *CP*, par. 2). This states the theme of the entire document: communication exists for increasing human communion, unity, and progress. This (and indeed all) communication, we read, results from God's love. God "made the first move to make contact with mankind at the start of the history of salvation. In the fullness of time, he communicated his very self to man" (*CP*, par. 10).

Setting this claim within the larger context of Catholic theology highlights more clearly the themes that will appear in the Church documents on communication. The theologian Richard McBrien concludes his magisterial introduction to Catholic theology and practice by identifying three key foci of the Catholic tradition:

> No theological principle or focus is more characteristic of Catholicism or more central to its identity than the principle of *sacramentality*. The Catholic vision sees God in and through all things: other people, communities, movements, events, places, objects, the world at large, the whole cosmos. The visible, the tangible, the finite, the historical–all these are actual or potential carriers of the divine presence. Indeed, it is only in and through these material realities that we can even encounter the invisible God. . . .
>
> A corollary of the principle of sacramentality is the principle of *mediation*. A sacrament not only signifies; it also causes what it signifies. Thus, created realities not only contain, reflect, or embody the presence of God. They make that presence effective for those who avail themselves of these realities. Just as we noted in the previous section that the world is mediated by meaning, so the universe of grace is a mediated reality: mediated principally by Christ, and secondarily by the Church and by other signs and instruments of salvation outside and beyond the Church. . . .
>
> Finally, Catholicism affirms the principle of *communion*: that our way to God and God's way to us is not only a mediated way but a communal way. And even when the divine-human encounter is most personal and individual, it is still communal in that the encounter is made possible by the mediation of the community.[5]

Each of these three elements (sacramentality, mediation, and community) appears as fundamental to the Vatican ideal of mass communication. McBrien identifies other Catholic elements, which will appear in greater and lesser degrees in the documents: "[Catholicism's] corresponding respect for *history*, for *tradition*, and for *continuity* (we are products of our past as well as shapers of our present and our future); its conviction that we can have as radical a notion of sin as we like so long as our understanding and appreciation of *grace* is even more radical; its high regard for *authority* and *order* as well as for *conscience* and *freedom*."[6]

Applying these ideas to what several others have called the Catholic imagination, film critic Richard Blake finds some further specifications of Catholic theology in the practice of Catholic communication. He identifies a love for the physical and for devotional activities (extensions of sacramentality), a love for saints and for mentoring (kinds of mediation), a respect for conscience, a fondness for moral narratives, and a tendency to think in hierarchies (all flowing from the reality of community).[7] These elements, or variations of them, will appear in the Vatican statements on communication.

Communio et Progressio draws on this Catholic tradition and presumes its way of thinking. For example, its emphasis on Jesus as the Incarnate Word of God calls attention to both the sacramental nature of communication and to the centrality of mediation:

> When by His death and resurrection, Christ the Incarnate Son, the Word and Image of the invisible God, set the human race free, He shared with everyone the truth and the life of God. . . . As the only mediator between the Father and mankind He made peace between God and man and laid the foundations of unity among men themselves. . . .
>
> While He was on earth Christ revealed Himself as the Perfect Communicator. Through His incarnation, He utterly identified Himself with those who were to receive His communication and He gave His message not only in words but in the whole manner of His life. He spoke from within, that is to say, from out of the press of His people. . . .
>
> Communication is more than the expression of ideas and the indication of emotion. At its most profound level it is the giving of self in love. Christ's communication was, in fact, spirit and life. In the institution of the Holy Eucharist, Christ gave us the most perfect and most intimate form of communion between God and man possible in this life, and, out of this, the deepest possible unity between men. Further, Christ communicated to us His life-giving Spirit, who brings all men together in unity. The Church is Christ's Mystical Body, the hidden completion of Christ Glorified who "fills the whole creation." As a result we move, within the Church and with the help of the word and the sacraments, towards the hope of that last unity where "God will be all in all." (*CP*, par. 10–11)

This passage, which addresses "basic points of doctrine," calls attention to Christ's role as mediator as well as to the Church's role in continuing that process through the sacraments. Implicit here too is that respect for the created world, of which the mass media are parts. They are, in the words of Vatican II, "marvelous technical inventions" (*IM*, par. 1).

Finally, the passage also highlights the goal of communication: unity among people. Such teleology, which in *Communio et Progressio* also gives rise to the communion/community so typical of Catholic theology, becomes one anchor point from which the document will evaluate all communication. The other anchor point, which also appears here, comes from the example of Christ: true communication is the giving of the self in love. This theological preference for personalism encourages, in turn, a bias toward the individual, even in the world of mass communication. The themes built on this theology run through all subsequent Vatican opinion on contemporary communication.

THEMES IN VATICAN STATEMENTS

The Pontifical Council for Social Communication has published eleven documents since its establishment following the Second Vatican Council. They are *Communio et Progressio* (1971), *An Appeal to All Contemplative Religious* (1973), *Guide to the Training of Future Priests Concerning the Instruments of Social Communication* (1986), *Pornography and Violence in the Communications Media: A Pastoral Response* (1989), *Criteria for Ecumenical and Inter-religious Cooperation in Communications* (1989), *Aetatis Novae* (1992), *100 Years of Cinema* (1995–96), *Ethics in Advertising* (1997), *Ethics in Communication* (2000), *The Church and Internet* (2002), and *Ethics in Internet* (2002).

With the exception of *An Appeal to All Contemplative Religious* and *Criteria for Ecumenical and Inter-religious Cooperation*, the Vatican statements on communication media address both public communication and Church use of the mass media (for preaching, teaching, and internal organization); the same principles animate both discussions. To keep things simpler, this chapter on the Vatican thinking on communication will focus primarily on the public communication issues rather than those of Church communication. When the Pontifical Council addresses "the means of social communication," it begins with the press, radio, cinema, and television, but it also includes every other form of modern communication.

Because the media have as their proper purpose the building up of human community, the documents emphasize, on the one hand, those things that build community and, on the other, defenses against the things that harm the community. These comments from the introduction to *Ethics in Internet* give a clear sense of the two poles of discussion of this theme. One pole is shown in *Communio et Progressio*, which states that "media have the ability to make every person everywhere 'a partner in the business of the human race'" (par. 9). John Paul II reaffirms this statement when he says:

> This is an astonishing vision. The Internet can help make it real—for individuals, groups, nations, and the human race—only if it is used in light of clear, sound ethical principles, especially the virtue of solidarity. To do so will be to everyone's advantage, for "we know one thing today more than in the past: we will never be happy and at peace without one another, much less if some are against others. ("Address to the Diplomatic Corps," par. 4)

Ethics in Internet, however, offers the other pole to the use of the Internet: "The spread of the Internet also raises a number of other ethical questions about matters like privacy, the security and confidentiality of data, copyright and intellectual property law, pornography, hate sites, the dissemination of rumor and character assassination under the guise of news, and much else" (par. 5–6). The line of thinking appears clearly here: the theologically "Catholic" characteristic of communion leads to the principles of unity and solidarity. On the one hand, communication media can foster these virtues and thus achieve a certain fulfillment; on the other hand, each individual communication medium can threaten these virtues in ways particular to it.

This pattern, as it appears here in a form refined during the 1980s and 1990s, begins with *Communio et Progressio*.

Where pre-Vatican II Council documents tended to address moral issues at length and as their primary focus, the Pontifical Council for Social Communications prefers to highlight the potential contributions of the media to human growth first and only later identify moral issues. Thus, *Communio et Progressio* treats communication media first in their role of creating and shaping public opinion. Here they establish a "great roundtable" for humanity (*CP*, par. 19) and offer the possibility of an end to the isolation of individuals and nations. Because of the importance of such communication, the document declares that people have a right to information, a right to inform, and a right to access the channels of information. From these rights flow protections against propaganda, manipulation, and deception in public affairs (*CP*, par. 33–48).

The Pontifical Council returns to this defense of the right to communicate in *Communio et Progressio*'s 20th anniversary document, *Aetatis Novae* (literally, "a new era"; henceforth, *AN*). The defense has shifted somewhat: where the 1971 document saw the greatest threats to the right to information originating in government activity, this 1992 document also warns against making people's right to communicate contingent upon "wealth, education, or political power" (*AN*, par. 15). Connecting this right to the right to religious freedom, *Aetatis Novae* urges that the Church step in to defend human rights against political, legal, educational, or corporate limits.

This overarching theme of communication for the common good, for solidarity, for peace, for human unity, and the defense of access to communication as part of this human community finds a place in many of the Vatican statements, either centrally or as a presumption to specific actions. For example, the Pontifical Council mentions it in the documents *Ethics in Advertising* (par. 16–17), *Ethics in Communications* (par. 6, 20), and *The Church and Internet* (par. 3), as well as in those already cited. Pope Paul VI makes thematic reference to it in the annual World Communication Day addresses in 1968, 1971, and 1976, as does Pope John Paul II in 1983, 1986, 1988, and 2003.

A second theme—one not at all surprising in the light of the Vatican's concerns with the media—involves the effects of communication media on individuals, groups, and societies. *Aetatis Novae* summarizes the issues:

> [T]oday's revolution in social communications involves a fundamental reshaping of the elements by which people comprehend the world about them, and verify and express what they comprehend. The constant availability of images and ideas, and their rapid transmission even from continent to continent, have profound consequences, both positive and negative, for the psychological, moral and social development of persons, the structure and functioning of societies, intercultural communications, and the perception and transmission of values, world

views, ideologies, and religious beliefs. The communications revolution affects perceptions even of the Church, and has a significant impact on the Church's own structures and modes of functioning. (*AN*, par. 4)

The overarching sense of the power of communication media appears also in the document *Pornography and Violence in the Communications Media: A Pastoral Response*, though in that document the Pontifical Council includes both moral and psychological media effects, including sin, desensitization to violence, confusion about appropriate sexual behavior, and psychological acting out. The ethics trilogy—*Ethics in Advertising* (1997), *Ethics in Communications* (2000), and *Ethics in Internet* (2002)—categorize the effects of the communication media in economic, political, cultural, and religious terms and recognize both positive and negative effects. Most of the World Communication Day addresses at some point accept the influence of mass communication and seek either to moderate that influence or to call attention to its power.

The acknowledgment of media effects seems natural to the Pontifical Council, since it flows easily from the theological principle of sacramentality. Just as material objects, people, and the events of one's life mediate one's experience of God, so too the communication media can filter and mediate all manner of human experience. For a group that believes so strongly in the reality and power of mediation through physical reality, the means of communication appear particularly important.

However, such a view does have its drawbacks. Too strong a focus on mediation when it writes about the means of communication leads the Pontifical Council "to a kind of optimistic or idealized view of these media which sees them in instrumental terms and not as social structures."[8] In other words, by principally seeing mediation and sacramental efficacy, the Church documents tend to miss some of the other paths of influence and operation of modern communication.

A third theme in the Vatican documents on communication identifies typical problem areas associated with the media. Some, like the relationship between the freedom of artistic expression and the limits of the moral law, have roots that extend well before the Second Vatican Council and find an expression in *Inter Mirifica* (par. 6). Other issues, like the social responsibility of professional communicators also appear in *Inter Mirifica* (par. 9–10). *Communio et Progressio* continues these debates and opts for freedom of expression (which it joins to the rights to information and communication) as opposed to censorship (par. 54–58). In the attempt to balance the defense of free expression with the responsibilities of communication for the social good, *Communio et Progressio* stresses the moral virtues of truth and human dignity, together with an ethics of solidarity. This yoking of freedom, responsibility, truth, and ethics appears in many subsequent documents, particularly the ethics trilogy (*Ethics in Advertising*, par. 1, 5, 17; *Ethics in Communications*, par. 20; *Ethics in Internet*, par. 12–14) and in the

Communication Day talks of Paul VI (1972, 1976) and John Paul II (1981, 2003). Rather than resolve the issues, the documents highlight the need to balance the competing goals of free expression and social responsibility.

Other Vatican documents identify specific problems in communication, problems that trigger a moral response. Given the sense of media effects outlined earlier, the Pontifical Council makes less of an attempt at balance in discussing specific problems. These problems include pornography and violence—which merit a specific document (*Pornography and Violence*)—deception (*CP*, par. 30, 60), consumerism (*Ethics in Advertising*, par. 10), undermining democratic processes (*CP*, par. 29–30, 37–41; *Ethics in Advertising*, par. 11), the protection of cultural diversity (*CP*, par. 51; *AN*, par. 16), and intrusions on privacy (*CP*, par. 42). This problem identification approach picks up the theological touchstone of community as well as Catholic theology's recognition of the tension between authority and the demands of conscience. The latter categories rest on the theological touchstone of mediation.

A characteristically Catholic response to these problems constitutes a fourth general theme in the Vatican documents: media education. Where communication media prove troublesome or morally threatening, the Vatican eschews religious or governmental censorship or restrictions; instead, it encourages the greater education of those who read, view, or utilize the mass media. Building on the much older idea of educating people for the new media (see, for example, Pius XII, *Miranda Prorsus* 1957), the Pontifical Council encourages educational responses to the media in *Communio et Progressio* (pars. 64ff). Then, beginning with the 1986 *Guide to the Training of Future Priests* (par. 9), it embraces the media-education movement as a way to "inoculate" recipients against questionable media content. The same recommendation appears in the document on pornography and violence in communication (par. 25), *Aetatis Novae* (par. 24)—where media education is encouraged for each diocese—*Ethics in Communication* (par. 25), and the *Church and the Internet* (par. 7). The majority of the publication *100 Years of Cinema* consists of media education units prepared by communication scholars and community activists from around the world (1995–96). Media education encourages personal responsibility in the face of media content, as one would expect from the Catholic emphasis on conscience and authority. At the same time, media education highlights the role of what Blake identified as mentoring—a kind of mediated approach to learning.

Consistent with this emphasis on individual responsibility and cooperative practice, the Vatican documents also stress the responsibilities of various individuals and groups who participate in mass communication. Such a widening sphere of responsibility again manifests the Catholic consciousness of mediation and community. Just as communication reaches individuals through the work of others, both individually and collectively, so the response to communication must similarly come through a kind of mediation of the community. An added motivation for those involved in improving communication arises from Christ's example of love. So the whole of the second part of *Communio et Progressio* focuses on the responsibilities of recipients, whether these be teachers, children, young people, parents, or other adults (par. 64–70; 81–83), and communicators (par. 71–80). The rest of this second part focuses on the roles of civil authorities (par. 84–91), nations (par. 92–95), and "all Christians and men of good will" (par. 96–100). This kind of approach, which calls attention to the responsibilities of groups, occurs frequently. It appears in the document on pornography and violence, where we read about the duties of communicators, parents, educators, youth, the public, public authorities, and the Church (par. 23–29). *Ethics in Communication* highlights the duties of professional communicators, audience members, parents, teachers, civil authorities, and the Church. (pars. 23–26). Over the years the papal addresses have similarly called attention to particular groups. Paul VI singled out families (1969), youth (1970), and receivers in general (1978); John Paul II has focused on the child (1979), the family (1980, 1994), the elderly (1982), youth (1985), and women (1996).

Among all these groups, the Pontifical Council has also looked to professional communicators (writers, editors, producers, directors, all those working in the communication industries). These bear particular responsibility, because they "preside while the exchange proceeds around the vast 'round table' that the media have made. Their vocation is nobly to promote the purpose of social communication" (*CP*, par. 73). The Church therefore wishes to provide them with "spiritual help to meet the needs of their important and difficult role" (*CP*, par. 104). Indeed, *Communio et Progressio* continues, "the Church is very willing to undertake a dialogue with all communicators of every religious persuasion. She would do this so that she may contribute to a common effort to solve the problems inherent in their task and do what is best for the benefit of man" (par. 105). This theme of moral and spiritual help continues in the Vatican documents. The "Appeal to Contemplative Religious" asks these monks and nuns to pray particularly for those working in communication, and *Aetatis Novae* sets the pastoral care of "communications personnel" as one of four pastoral priorities for the Catholic Church. The reasoning here bears out the Pontifical Council's reliance on a theology of mediation:

> Media work involves special psychological pressures and ethical dilemmas. Considering how important a role the media play in forming contemporary culture and shaping the lives of countless individuals and whole societies, it is essential that those professionally involved in secular media and the communications industries approach their responsibilities imbued with high ideals and a commitment to the service of humanity.

> The Church has a corresponding responsibility: to develop and offer programs of pastoral care which are specifically responsive to the peculiar working conditions and moral challenges facing communications professionals. Typically, pastoral programs of this sort should include ongoing formation which will help these men and women—many of whom sincerely wish to know and do what is ethically and morally right—to integrate moral norms ever more fully into their professional work as well as their private lives. (*AN*, par. 19)

Because their work influences so many others, the Church wishes to help them. The priorities elucidated here inform the later writings on the Pontifical Council, especially the ethics trilogy.

Among all of these concerns for individuals and groups and kinds of communications, the Pontifical Council never loses sight of the possibilities that communication media offer to the Church itself in its duty to proclaim the gospel. Precisely as media, the means of communication fit nicely into the Church's theological understanding of mediation. So it makes perfect sense for the Church to encourage its members to use all communication media possible to spread the news of Jesus Christ. The Church devotes as much attention to this theme as to any other in the various documents. *Communio et Progressio* specifically discusses how the Church can use the mass media, both under the rubric of "the use of the media for giving the good news" (*CP*, par. 126–34) and as a part of a much longer discussion of "the active commitment of Catholics in the different media" (*CP*, par. 135–61).

Most of the subsequent documents also lay claim to the media for the gospel. Part of the appeal to contemplative religious asks them to pray for the successful use of the media by the Church. Preparation to better preach the gospel to all people forms a chief motivation for training priests in using modern means of communication. Such a goal not only motivates their studies but also serves as one of the apostolates for priests (*Guide to the Training of Future Priests*). *Aetatis Novae* sets the "development and promotion of the Church's own media of social communications" as one of the priorities for the Catholic Church and argues that "media work is not simply one more program alongside all the rest of the Church's activities: social communications have a role to play in every aspect of the Church's mission" (*AN*, par. 17). The very same thinking appears with regard to the Internet (*Church and the Internet*, par. 5).

The pope's return to the theme many times. In addition to encouraging Church use of communication in his annual Communication Day addresses in 1967, 1973, and 1974, Paul VI wrote quite forcefully about using the media for evangelization in his apostolic exhortation *Evangelii Nuntiandi* ("Announcing the Gospel"):

> When they are put at the service of the Gospel, [mass media] are capable of increasing almost indefinitely the area in which the Word of God

is heard; they enable the Good News to reach millions of people. The Church would feel guilty before the Lord if she did not utilize these powerful means that human skill is daily rendering more perfect. It is through them that she proclaims "from the housetops" [Matthew 10:27] the message of which she is the depositary. In them she finds a modern and effective version of the pulpit. Thanks to them she succeeds in speaking to the multitudes. (par. 45)

John Paul II included the topic in his encyclical *Redemptoris Missio* ("The Mission of the Redeemer," par. 37) as well as in the World Communication Day messages in 1984, 1989, 1992, 1997, 2000, and 2001.

CONCLUSION

Almost all Vatican comment and thinking about contemporary communication goes through the Pontifical Council for Social Communications, the agency set up in the 1960s for that purpose. In the eleven documents or statements that group has issued since 1971, six general themes or areas of concern emerge: the unity or solidarity of peoples as a goal for communication; a consciousness of the effects of the media on individuals and societies; an attempt to respond to specific problem areas or issues stemming from those media effects; the promotion of media education; the encouragement of individual and group responses, including the Church's pastoral care for communication professionals; and the Church's obligation and opportunity to make use of contemporary communication media to preach the gospel.

These areas of concern grow out of the Catholic theological worldview that stresses (or perhaps presumes) communion, sacramentality, and mediation as the three foci of the Catholic tradition. From these flow the more applied theological concepts such as the importance of conscience and its relationship to authority, the importance of the physical world and human invention, the understanding of hierarchy, and the dual motivation of human progress and love of God. More applied still are applications such as mentoring, education, and cooperative work.

As we have seen, Vatican opinion about modern communication does not so much apply the theological worldview in a set pattern but grows from it in an organic way. "The unity and advancement of people living in society: these are the chief aims of social communication and of all the means it uses," begins *Communio et Progressio* (par. 1). These goals and all things leading to them flow from God's creation and the model of God's love. Vatican opinion about modern communication calls people everywhere to live up to the example and gift of that love of God.

11: View from the News Desk

Mocha and Meditation Mats

David Crumm

After nearly two decades of reporting on the impact of religion on American life, I get occasional invitations to appear as a guest on religious radio stations. So in the summer of 2003, I sat on one end of a telephone line and talked on the air with an evangelical radio host who was trying to pose provocative questions.

"So, what's the biggest threat Christians face now? Is it gay-rights activists? Radical feminists? Politicians who'll say anything? The removal of God from the schools?" he asked.

At first, I was stumped. I didn't share his particular laundry list of prejudices, and didn't want to signal agreement on those issues to his listeners. But, beyond that dilemma, I was disappointed by his shortsighted view of American culture. If he really cared about the orthodoxy of his brand of faith, I was surprised that he wasn't looking elsewhere, far closer to home.

"The biggest threat to orthodoxy?" I repeated into the telephone. "Well, I'd say it's the central aisle in a Target store."

247

BUYING INTO A SPIRITUAL MARKETPLACE

When I talk face to face with groups of readers, someone usually stands up during the question-and-answer period to tell me that they think "Media"—and the tone of voice usually suggests an ominous capital "M" entity—is opposed to organized religion. In response, I try not to sound too defensive, then I fall back on describing some of the top-notch religion writers I have known at major newspapers across the United States. As journalists, we're not out to destroy anyone's faith, I tell readers. That's true, as far as the answer goes, but there also is a deeper truth here. The real answer to the Media question is that the cutting edge of postmodern media has, indeed, evolved into a potent force that competes directly with organized religion. Image, word, sound, and even carefully designed scents and tastes now are used to create attractive spiritual landscapes that are luring millions of customers coast to coast. These products, services, and entire environments are alternatives to the worship services and support programs that organized religion has tried to actively market ever since religious leaders realized in the 1970s that millions of Americans were wandering away from mainline pews and were "church shopping."

The efforts to ever-more-vigorously market mainline churches fueled the problem. Since everyone from bishops to parishioners bought into the model of religion as a consumer choice, Americans felt justified in wholeheartedly welcoming a spiritual reformation. The change in terminology from "religion" to "spirituality" was a marker of a major cultural shift. Traditional definitions of religion usually emphasize core concepts of revelation, submission, acceptance, and discipline—coupled in the best cases with a compassion for the external world. Spirituality is more than a lilting synonym for religion and has come to signify quest, assertion, choice, and experimentation—usually focused on an interior search for solace. As a journalist who has talked with thousands of Americans while working on hundreds of stories about religion in recent years, I've come to believe that all of this spiritual questing boils down to this larger pattern: Spirituality in America is the postmodern deconstruction of religion. A key element in postmodernism is that symbols no longer retain their authoritative meaning, but they become elements that users can rearrange to try to communicate their own messages. That's exactly what's happening in the spiritual marketplace.

Analyzing the many social forces that brought Americans to this change of heart and mind has filled entire volumes, but the basic idea I am outlining here fits with my own reporting on powerful shifts in American life over the past decade and a half. The end of the Cold War transformed many Americans' views of the world from a dualist system of Communist and "free," implying bad and good, into a complex landscape of emerging groups asserting many values. At the same time, the baby boomer generation that was weaned on the Cold War worldview continues to age and now confronts mortality both in their parents' generation and in the onset of their own chronic health concerns. That phase of life inevitably triggers reflections on ultimate questions. On top of all that, the stresses associated with employment, from the pace of work to the likelihood that people will face unexpected changes in their jobs, also are unsettling. And the instant interconnectivity of media brings the potentially reassuring resources of all of the world's faiths—twenty-four hours a day, on demand—into every home with an Internet connection.

The three most pressing spiritual questions of our era have become: Why should I get out of bed in the morning? How can I make it through another stressful day? And, at the end of the day, Did anything I do today really matter? These are consumer-driven revisions of the classic religious queries: Why are we here? How shall we live? And, is there eternal value in the good we achieve?

Marketing executives, some with altruistic intentions and some merely pursuing profits, began to catch on that there is nothing essentially sacred left in this emerging spiritual marketplace. Instead, there are products that work and products that don't. Following this mantra, corporations were able to wheel out far more sophisticated marketing campaigns than cash-strapped mainline denominations, mired in traditional ways of defining these issues, could hope to match.

So, in the autumn of 2003, trying to approach these issues in a fresh way as a journalist, I assembled a pilgrimage team of twelve volunteers to spend three evenings exploring a sampling of emerging spiritual landscapes. The group admittedly was skewed, because all of the pilgrims were connected with a United Methodist church in Ann Arbor, Michigan, where we met before setting out each night and again at the end of each evening, to debrief on our individual experiences of the pilgrimage trail. But the group was diverse in other ways. The youngest of these pilgrims was my 14-year-old son. There were three other high-school students, a university student, some middle-aged adults, and (the oldest) a United Methodist pastor and his wife in their 60s. Ten of the twelve were lay people. Half were male; half were female. Not a perfect scientific sample, but the crew was suitable for a journalist simply trying to draw on the viewpoints of what amounted to a focus group.

STARTING AT THE HEART OF THE REFORMATION

Like most small American cities, Ann Arbor offers all of the commercial amenities needed for such a pilgrimage. We started at what arguably was the birthplace of this cultural shift, a bookstore. As a sample of today's larger bookstores, we chose to visit the Borders store that once was the flagship of the chain. Through the centuries, most reformations started with some reformulation of the Word; this postmodern reformation started with a fresh approach to words. Trying to identify a flagship in what has amounted to an explosion in spiritual publishing, I gathered our pilgrims at the start of our evening and retold the tale of the ubiquitous *Chicken Soup for the Soul* series. The story of Jack Canfield and Mark Victor Hansen searching unsuccessfully for a publisher in the early 1990s, then finally managing to launch their hugely popular series with a smaller publishing house, Health Communications, Inc., is now almost mythic in its proportions. As the tale is told on the "Chicken Soup" Web site, this series now has racked up sales of more than 80 million copies of more than 60 individual "Chicken Soup" titles, tailored for everyone from teenagers and senior citizens to golfers, nurses, and pet owners.

Given the current prominence of religion in publishing, it was no surprise for our pilgrims to walk into Borders that night and notice the huge "RELIGION" department sign hanging from the ceiling. What amazed them was the realization of how widely spiritual messages have moved into nearly every department of the store, from music CDs with soothing inspirational themes to slick comic books, now called graphic novels, that relate apocalyptic tales of good vs. evil, often with dialogue straight out of old revivalist sermons. In the children's department, picture books like *What You Will See Inside a Mosque* (Skylight Paths) now are common.

One of our pilgrims found a prime example of cross-over, consumer-driven spirituality. In the African-American Studies department of Borders, a prominent display offered colorful boxes of "Empowerment Cards" (Smiley Books), produced by nationally known African-American radio commentator Tavis Smiley. The cover illustration showed an abstract image of a solitary human figure cupping its ears much like a Muslim at prayer. The back cover of the box described the messages on the inspirational deck of cards inside as "testimonies" and "words of wisdom," phrases borrowed directly from religious tradition. But the box's overall message was a twist on the idea of external religious authority. A blurb on the box cover told shoppers: "The answer to every question in any situation lies within you. The intelligence inside you has all the answers. Consult your inner wisdom. Don't question, analyze, or doubt the first answer it gives you. Listen and obey and you won't go wrong."

Oh, and while you're listening to that inner voice: Psst! Please buy this box.

Even hard-edged corners of the store had adapted to the soft curves of spiritual allure. Among the racks of news magazines, we found an issue of *Time* magazine with a "Science of Meditation" cover story, a headline telling readers that this business of meditation was no longer "New Age mumbo jumbo." Millions of Americans now meditate, *Time* editors told their readers. It probably didn't hurt sales of the issue that sexy actress Heather Graham was shown on the cover, sitting in a near lotus-position, wearing a low-cut dress. This photo wasn't mere pandering, *Time* assured readers. The cover caption read: "Actress Heather Graham has been practicing Transcendental Meditation since 1991."

This wasn't far from another rack, boasting an array of specifically spiritual magazines. An issue of *Body and Soul Magazine* boasted a cover story on "MIND BODY MAKE OVER: Breakthrough plan GETS YOU FIT from the INSIDE OUT" along with layouts on "3 MANTRAS for your worst workday" and "TAKE A PERSONAL DAY to retreat and recharge."

And what lay in the store's core RELIGION section, where people expect to find inspirational volumes? Even traditional-looking inspirational books we examined had titles like *The Saints' Guide to Happiness: Everyday Wisdom from the Lives of the Saints* by Robert Ellsberg (North Point Press), and *Breakthrough Prayer: The Secret of Receiving What You Need from God*, by Jim Cymbala (Zondervan).

In the spiritual marketplace, our pilgrims already had sensed this mantra: There are products that work and products that don't. To that original mantra, after the night at Borders, we added this footnote: What "works" spiritually these days is tested in an arena not much wider than one's own daily needs.

THROUGH A NEO-CLASSICAL CATHEDRAL

Some entrepreneurs, especially those who jumped into the spiritual realm a decade or more ago, designed holistic responses to the spiritual needs they perceived and wound up creating entire commercial environments. So I invited our pilgrims to spend an evening observing the fastest-growing denomination of urban temples in America: Starbucks. When Howard Schultz took a 1970s Seattle coffee shop and reinvented it in the 1980s to resemble European coffee bars, the firm was well on its way toward blossoming in the 1990s as an international chain that sold solace as much as java. Certainly, some minimalist Starbucks stands in busy cities are little more than retail counters, but the full-scale shops in cities like Ann Arbor attempt to shelter customers from the cares of the world with environments painstakingly designed from the furniture and wall coverings to the Starbucks-blend of music pumped from the sound system. They are basically mini-cathedrals.

The architecture of the Starbucks we visited even suggested a liturgical space, with the front doors opening onto a broad center aisle, flanked by seating areas, leading toward the high altar where the Starbucks staff awaited the proper words of institution from pilgrims—then chanted the cryptic lines from one initiate to another.

One pilgrim offered his petition in a soft voice: "Venti nonfat latte?"

The aproned woman at the cash register nodded her approval. She was signaling that this pilgrim clearly knew the liturgy by heart. Next, the aproned woman picked up the petition and chanted it reverently: "Venti non-fat latte!"

An aproned man to her right, springing into action, echoed the chant: "Venti nonfat latte."

The pilgrim made an offering of several dollars, charitably dropping the coins that came back in change into a bin for later distribution to the staff.

Another chant already was commencing from the next person in the procession: "Decaf white chocolate mocha?"

"Decaf white chocolate mocha!"

"Decaf white chocolate mocha!"

And soon, atop an elevated oval platform, the made-to-order chalices appeared.

The clergyman in his 60s who was part of our pilgrimage said later that, once he began to envision the Starbucks experience in this way, the parallels were stunning.

"Did you all see the poster on the wall, when we walked in the door? It showed a tall cup of coffee and a pastry? That's the host: the bread and wine served Starbucks style," he said. "They're offering us communion."

"But did you notice what they've managed to achieve in there?" said another pilgrim. "Some people want to go to church for community—to be in relation with other people—but others don't want that. They just want to be alone, and sometimes they don't feel comfortable in our churches, where we're trying to push people together. At Starbucks, you can do both very comfortably. You've got circles of people, and you've got very solitary people who want to be all alone, but they can sit in the middle of this really very comforting community."

Another pilgrim chimed in: "All the elements of a church are there. They've even got confessionals! I moved around and listened to little groups of people. I overheard a conversation among three girls—and it was a confessional. It really was. The one girl had been out the night before and drank way too much. The others were advising her that she wasn't alone and didn't need to feel guilty."

"We could learn from this," the pastor added. "Look at this."

He pulled out several Starbucks brochures—one recruiting new employees, another asking for customer feedback, and a third offering a Visa card—all of them couched in altruistic phrases. "You could change the text on these brochures and sell your church this way," he said.

To lure job candidates, a flier said, "Create Community," and "Make a difference in someone's day." Even the credit-card leaflet pointed out that, when one's application is accepted, Starbucks would make a charitable donation to "literacy, diversity and environmental initiatives." The flier promised: "It's a card that gives back. Some to you. Some to others."

The experience inspired a bemused respect: Starbucks has designed an environment where millions of people gladly pay for what churches are trying to give away for free.

PILGRIMAGE TO A POSTMODERN TEMPLE

For our third evening, we adopted the perfect postmodern mascot: the helpful hero of preschool television, Bob the Builder. As we gathered to set out for the final point in our pilgrimage, I brought out a 6-inch-tall figurine of the smiling fellow in his trademark yellow hardhat, known to millions of children for his cheery, can-do attitude about community life. For French audiences, the TV show and playsets are labeled, "Bob Le Bricoleur." It's no coincidence that he has been embraced so instinctively into American culture. Bricolage is one of the most common responses to the fragmentation of postmodernism. Despite the term's exotic sound, it describes perfectly the American ethos in such a situation.

The authoritative meaning of our religious revelation is crumbling? Our symbols are falling apart? Well, then, let's pull on our toolbelts, survey the rubble, and get to work. We'll rebuild something to fill the void.

On the afternoon before our final journey together, I had stopped by the Target store we would visit as a group and found rows of Bob figurines lining one aisle in the toy section—like the rows of plastic saints at a Vatican gift shop. I purchased a Bob and placed him that night in the center of our circle as we gathered to make this last trip. I told the group: "Like Bob, Americans have learned to shoulder their spiritual challenges, usually by picking up what materials are readily available and seem most helpful in patching up a better day. According to a Gallup Poll, about 4 of 10 Americans continue to claim that they attend weekly worship services, although actual church attendance statistics call into question the accuracy of their claims. Nevertheless, about 40 percent of Americans are saying that they continue to meet their religious needs each week in houses of worship. That's a sizeable minority of the population. But consider: Nearly everyone shops."

I asked each pilgrim to move through the Target store that evening and jot down a list of products they could buy to bring spiritual inspiration or solace to their morning, their midday break at school or work, and their evening as a typical day drew to a close.

We might have chosen another nationwide retailer, since most of the products at a typical Target are available elsewhere. But one of Target's signatures is its attention to design, from its trendy, corporate brands of housewares and small appliances to its ever-changing promotional posters and banners.

As we walked into the store, a huge banner greeted us in the women's clothing section, promoting "Yoga" garb with a color photo of an attractive young woman in a yoga stance with both palms pressed together in a meditative mood.

"I'll start right here," one woman said as other pilgrims fanned out into side aisles.

The challenge I had posed proved easy to fulfill.

For the morning, pilgrims chose CDs of music and ambient sounds mixed to help achieve "Tranquility" and "Inner Peace." Tea bags and fruity beverages in bottles promised a cosmic range of soothing or energizing therapies. A line of soaps offered "a calm oasis." One younger pilgrim wandered into the camping section and decided that a "Personal Navigator," complete with global-positioning-satellite technology, was the technological guru he wanted to consult at the start of a new day.

Even the cosmetics aisles bore slogans with a wry nod to transcendent values. As a woman starts her day, one makeup brand told customers, she knows that "real beauty comes from within. The rest is for you to make up."

There were lots of useful products, especially beverages and more music CDs, for a midday revival. "They even had a Sound Spa for only $12.99," one pilgrim said. "You plug it in and get the sounds of rain or the ocean. For the whole ocean, that's a pretty good price. I'd find that spiritually refreshing during a midday break."

A companion disagreed. "No, I want the fiber-optic bonsai for my office. That was remarkable. I could buy that little tree and watch it as I meditate."

For the end of the day, a host of companies vied for the chance to meet customers' spiritual needs.

Many picture frames to display family photos at home now come laser-etched with sage advice about the enduring values of family connections. On the cover of a blank journal for reflecting on one's day are the words, "I get up. I walk. I fall down. But I keep dancing." And, of course, there were countless books, magazines, and calendars with spiritual themes.

"Did you check out the pillows?" one pilgrim said. "For $6.99, I could get something called Perfect Sanctuary Pillow Spray. I want to try that! Sounds like the perfect way to end a day."

Finally, most pilgrims chose at least one end-of-the-day product from the aisle jammed with exotic-sounding candles, including one complete set of candles apparently guaranteed to provide the proper "Feng Shui" of light in your home.

Our group had agreed not to actually buy anything to keep our pilgrimage on a purely spiritual plane, but one woman simply couldn't resist a 2-foot-tall, amber, wax lantern.

"I had to buy it," she apologized. "It's perfect to light in the middle for our final talk."

She lit it in a room at the Methodist church as we gathered to debrief one last time at the end of our pilgrimage trail. And she was right. Its subtle glow was the perfect touch. I added my little Bob the Builder figurine to make it a tableau. Even after we finished sharing our notes—the three-night task now complete—we found ourselves lingering in the circle of chairs, watching the flame and eyeing little Bob's confident smile. For the modest price of a lantern and a toy, Target had provided a new ritual to this mainline church: meditation by lantern light and Bob.

"It was funny," said one pilgrim at length. "Even knowing how all of this is working on us doesn't change its appeal. This stuff 'works,' you know? You want it. Like tonight at Target, even though I knew what all of these marketing campaigns were trying to do to me, I still wanted to just buy, buy, buy."

CONCLUSIONS AND THE ROAD AHEAD

Please, *do* try this at home.

Journalists often employ focus groups and reader panels to evaluate new ideas, as I did with our dozen pilgrims who helped me to spot and interpret the many spiritual markers I have reported here. But educators could easily replicate this experiment with classes in religion, sociology, anthropology, and even urban planning. Lots of resources exist to light the way. Many guidebooks helped to refocus my vision in recent years so that I could see these common pieces of the urban mosaic as emerging spiritual landscapes—and could understand the all-encompassing, consumers'-eye-view of the world. Among the guides I found helpful were Juliet Schor's *The Overspent American: Why We Want What We Don't Need* (Perennial), Don Lattin's *Following Our Bliss: How the Spiritual Ideals of the Sixties Shape Our Lives Today* (HarperSanFrancisco), and, for a good anthropological portrait of the role of an American *bricoleur*, Douglas Harper's *Working Knowledge: Skill and Community in a Small Shop* (University of California Press).

As I conclude this essay, signs indicate that even traditional religious groups are acknowledging that the real competition for followers lies in the media marketplace. Family Christian Stores, a nationwide chain of more than 300 shops headquartered in Grand Rapids, Michigan, announced this autumn that it has surrendered its longstanding commitment to closing on the Sabbath. Even evangelical Christian consumers now expect shopping to be a part of their Sunday schedule, store executives told reporters as they announced the change in policy. And the mainline United Methodist Church was successful, after a brief controversy, in convincing Reuters to carry its new television ads on the 7,000-square-foot electronic billboard of Reuters in Times Square. Meanwhile, in November, the United States Conference of Catholic bishops spent hours in their plenary sessions in Washington, D.C., approving the publication of five, user-friendly pamphlets on subjects ranging from the rosary, which the bishops favor, to artificial birth control, which the bishops do not. This is the same body of men who only a decade ago put most of their collective efforts into publishing dense, book-length instructions to their faithful. Now they acknowledge that nobody read those books—and some better marketing and savvy design may help them to sell church teachings.

But all of these efforts seem like rather desperate attempts to catch up with the rest of American commerce.

As more research and reflection turns to these issues, I also wonder whether we can identify antecedents to this cultural shift. Perhaps past religious groups with utopian dreams are a close parallel to today's religious expectations, expressions, and experiences. In the eighth century, Caliph Al-Mansur ordered the construction of the famous Round City of Baghdad with all major roads in the circular design leading toward a central mosque and palace. This certainly was a dramatic spiritual landscape, blending secular and religious in the medium of architecture, as the city sprang up along the Tigris River. Later, the Crusades arguably were an effectively marketed reshaping of entire communities in Europe and the Middle East as the pilgrimages of thousands of men, women, and children turned into mass migrations eastward. Centuries later across the Atlantic, American utopian groups specialized in blending spiritual values with the production of trademark products. Shaker villages, for example, specialized in seed packets for home gardens, flat brooms, and sturdy chairs, some of their original creations now considered works of art. In the middle of the twentieth century, painter Warner Sallman's "Head of Christ" became closely associated with America's Cold War paranoia and was reproduced in so many formats that his mournful, Nordic-looking Jesus was placed even in civic centers and public schools. Much smaller formats of the painting, mass-produced on card stock, were carried in thousands of U.S. servicemen's pockets along with family photos. And, of course, for more than a century Christmas has been the granddaddy of all mixed-message, multimedia, marketing schemes, now virtually defining the shape of the fiscal year for many retailers in the United States.

Wherever the origins may lie for the present shift at the dawn of this new millennium, our pilgrims ended their journey convinced that something does seem different now. Our conclusion is that the fuel powering this dramatic change of gears is, indeed, media itself. While it is true that religious media stretch back to the ancient world, media today are flexing muscles with a computer-powered and networked sophistication that none of the efforts in past centuries could match. Never before have a suburban mother, a rural dairy farmer, and a big-city executive all been able to wake up from a fitful sleep at 2 a.m., grab a tissue from a bedside dispenser box preprinted with images of hovering angels, brew a soothing cup of tea that promises Asian forms of relaxation, punch up a Celtic CD of ancient spiritual melodies, and then fire up an Internet connection to hear the streaming chants of Buddhist monks direct from Thailand.

Walls are crumbling and are being rebuilt in new patterns in this postmodern bricolage. And the good news, perhaps, is that for most ordinary

Americans these new religious constructions they are assembling with the stuff they find at hand do not seem dangerously warlike. They're not associated, for the most part, with confronting enemies. Rather than conquering external worlds, the patterns of spiritual building blocks in these emerging landscapes seem designed to help us retreat from a confusing world.

Excuse us, we are saying. Can we have a moment's solace? After all, we really need some help in soothing our inner demons—and we're happy to pay for it.

Conclusion

A Relationship of Overlapping Conversations

Gustav Niebuhr

During my years as a newspaper reporter, I occasionally answered my ringing desk phone to listen to a request that managed to be at once flattering and annoying. The caller—usually someone working for a television or radio interview program—would typically begin by praising a story of mine that had just appeared, then ask my help in contacting one of my sources, usually an academic expert with a specialty relevant to the day's news. I rarely cooperated, in part because I suspected the caller was making good enough money to do his own spadework. But I also resisted the idea of having a story plucked apart—one that I may have spent considerable time researching, finding people who could speak credibly about the issue at hand. I did not want to think about someone else coming along and scissoring out a core element.

I cite these incidents because, although I thought little about them at the time, they now seem to hold a certain symbolic value. Regardless of how distinctive I might have considered my work, it existed within the very broad context of the ways in which religion and the media interact with one another. There were times in which a story may have appeared to others as but a link in a long chain.

As a journalist, I have always regarded covering religion as a craft demanding a special level of care and commitment. To put it another way, it is a privilege to have it as one's job to describe so fundamental a part of our culture as religion. The religious life of Americans touches an almost endless variety of major subjects, including politics, sports, business, the arts, and more.

I have told younger reporters and journalism students interested in the subject that religion should be approached without preconceptions. There are no templates on which one can rely to create good, informative stories about religion. Indeed, the dynamics that exist within a single religious group or the way a particular issue unfolds often require a fresh and open-minded approach each time one attempts a story on that group or issue. To report well about religion, a journalist must be prepared to be surprised.

Avoiding preconceptions means, in part, that he or she ought to cast a wide net in reaching those who can speak about the issue at hand. The more sources, usually, the better, by which I mean participants as well as scholarly experts. Good reporting on religion demands an ability to ask questions, listen carefully, ask again, and listen at length. What matters is that the journalist cultivates a spirit of attentiveness such that people feel free to speak about their concerns with a depth and detail that conveys how religious ideas are vitally present in their lives. Similarly, the task demands that a journalist select judiciously from among outside experts those whose insights show them to be truly engaged with the subject. I have felt dismay when reading or seeing stories whose authors have taken on complicated subjects but have relied on only a couple of quickly quoted sources, so that the reporter's commentary dominated the piece. Accuracy can be lost along with the nuance.

That said, a writer must realize that what control he or she exercises over the way a story is told exists only within the specific limits of that story. What happens next is unpredictable, although it may well illuminate how religion and media can meet. If you are quoted in a story—specifically a story primarily involving religion—you become a public figure, at least for that day, and a media property as well. Once that caller I mentioned above tracks you down, you may wind up as a guest on a drive-time radio program, or your special project may become the butt of a comedian's joke on late-night television, or you may even receive an invitation to the White House. It's a big media universe out there; the journalist occupies but a part of it.

The philosopher William James once declared that he would not attempt a single definition of religion. To do so, he said, risked sounding absolutist or dogmatic. Delivering the prestigious Gifford Lectures at the University of Edinburgh, he asked his audience to consider the word *government*, which, he said, one person might define as a legislative assembly, while another would say it was a system of laws, and a third might describe as authority itself. So too with religion, James said, "we may find no one essence, but many characters which may alternately be equally important to religion."[1]

James's observation can be applied as well to the media, for it too has many characters. When the person sitting in the seat next to mine on an airplane turns to me with a remark about "the media," I silently prepare myself for a conversation that may go in any number of directions. We may discuss newspapers and network news programs. Or our subject may be talk radio, or perhaps Hollywood. Or will my seatmate raise something very specific, like last night's roundtable of high-decibel talking heads on cable television? In the public mind, the media is this and much more.

Because of their inherent diversity, religion and media meet each other as decentralized forces at many points within the contexts of news, opinion, and entertainment. Yet the complexity of this encounter can be obscured by a popular tendency to reduce these meetings to a single, limited narrative of conflict. That story might insist that religion and the media embody opposing values, such that they can interact only with antipathy. To state the case as a series of slogans—the level on which such discussion too often proceeds—it is a contest of the foundational against the effervescent; enduring values against fashion; truth against whim.

No journalist covering religion can avoid the shibboleth that the news media are hostile to the spiritual, particularly in its organized forms. That idea coexists with an equally harsh portrayal of the entertainment media as fostering a sort of antimorality. In a survey conducted in 2002 on behalf of Public Broadcasting's *Religion & Ethics Newsweekly* and the magazine *U.S. News & World Report*, nearly half of the 2,002 adults interviewed answered yes to the question of whether movies, television, and popular music threaten religious faith.[2]

What such sweeping criticisms ignore is how broad religious ideas, embedded as American cultural assumptions, are often present in news coverage and turn up in popular entertainment as well.[3] In addition, television as a medium can provide a stage for the display of overtly religious acts and expressions, especially during the broadcasts of sporting events and news reports of catastrophes. Professional athletes often signal an attention to the divine by making the sign of the cross or praying on the field. People who survive various calamities typically tell reporters that they owe their wellbeing to God. Such short testimonies are often given without any critical challenge or comment by those doing the interviews.

The encounter between religion and the media cannot be likened to a simple back-and-forth exchange. It takes place, not on a two-way street, but rather on a three-dimensional chessboard with multiple points of contact.

Consider a news event related to one of the essays included in this book, Virgilio Elizondo on Our Lady of Guadalupe as the transforming figure in Mexican identity. In July 2002, Pope John Paul II traveled to Mexico on a pastoral visit during which he canonized Juan Diego, the sixteenth- century Aztec Indian to whom the Virgin Mary is said by tradition to have appeared. The trip and its focal point, the canonization, were heavily covered by the news media, as the Vatican undoubtedly expected. Papal trips are news stories; in this case, radio, television, and print media could be counted on to tell and retell this story of faith.

The case of the canonization also illustrates other important dimensions in the complex religion-media encounter. Among them is the element of extended time over which the religion-media relationship can play out. This particular event has a history going back four centuries, to the earliest days of Spain's conquest of Mexico. Another element is how a symbol outside a dominant religious institution came to be so embraced by that institution that its highest official would travel around the world to demonstrate its acceptance—an acceptance sealed by extensive news media coverage.

As Elizondo writes, the Guadalupe tradition has the Virgin, a figure of dark complexion clad in a blue mantle, miraculously appearing on Juan Diego's cloak, which he showed to Roman Catholic authorities in post-conquest Mexico. In this case, an article of clothing acts as a medium of authenticity, inspiring enough popular devotion eventually to overcome the resistance of church officials to recognizing the apparition's validity. Since then, the icon of the apparition has not simply endured but proliferated, as it has been reproduced countless times on the simplest of media—posters and wall paintings. By summer 2002, these images were being picked up by far more sophisticated media for broadcast worldwide.

There are many other instances in which religious use of media become a subject of attention by media outside religious control. Beginning with television's advent, independent operators have used that medium to disseminate overtly religious messages to mass audiences. Practitioners range from the Rev. Billy Graham, whose organization has repeatedly shown itself to be highly adept at using television to disseminate an event once restricted to those who entered a revival tent, to less successful operators like some televangelists whose operations either fell apart or were diminished in various scandals in the 1980s. The national reach of religious broadcasting made it a focus of interest to the news media and to scholars of religious studies: both devoted considerable time to describing its achievements and failures.

At times one can describe the religion and media encounter as occurring, if not exactly within a loop, then as a progressive series of encounters in which the forms of religion undergo change and different media become involved at different times. I will cite an example from my own experience.

The cartoon superhero Batman began life as a comic book action figure, went on to become a television series, and eventually emerged as a lavishly produced trilogy of Hollywood movies beginning in the late 1980s. One can certainly argue that superheroes, endowed with capacities beyond the mortal, represent an idea of the sacred. But the point here is that these particular movies became, in the style of Hollywood blockbusters, a national event, whose drawing power vividly illustrated the allure of the cinema, in contrast to that of the typical church.

One minister, stopping with a friend at the local shopping mall, chanced upon a long line of people waiting in the sun to get in to see the latest Batman installment. What could the church ever do to create something so exciting that people would wait for hours to get inside?

As a servant of the gospel, he had encountered a challenge from the media that he felt impelled to meet. He told me about this during an interview I did with him as part of a series of stories I wrote for the *New York Times* on the rise of suburban megachurches. The latter are big congregations whose sociologically savvy ministers are ever on the lookout for what the surrounding culture might teach them about ways to reach the nonpracticing or the marginally affiliated in the name of Jesus Christ.[4]

By the time we spoke, the pastor could point to an obvious measure of success: he had built up his congregation so that it numbered in the thousands. Church staff cultivated a friendly atmosphere; worship services emphasized different degrees of formality and tradition; there was a wide range of offerings in religious education and voluntary service. Among other features, the church had recently launched a Saturday night service in which a band played contemporary Christian music with a country beat. A survey of local radio showed country music to be popular. Why not communicate a Christian message through that medium, he asked? He must have known he had a sterling precedent for such an approach in Martin Luther, who had chosen to set his great hymn, "A Mighty Fortress," to a tune popular in his day.

The stories I wrote now strike me as illustrative of the complicated way in which religion and the media interact, a process that in this case involved one form of religious expression meeting a particular medium, being transformed, then encountering another as a result. I as a reporter had come to explore the ways in which the megachurches were adapting ideas from the culture to enhance their ministries. For the vehicle for their message, the ministers drew some of their inspiration from the media, broadly defined—the movies, theater, mass-circulation magazines, pop radio, and more. By the time I reached them, I found churches producing their own music, scripting dramas to be used in worship services, and advertising on billboards—all in the service of communicating the 2,000-year-old Christian story.

If one tried to diagram the encounters at work here, one would write the word media, followed by an arrow pointing to the word religion, followed by another arrow, pointing toward media. But that would hardly capture the process entirely. I suspect the encounter went further, after my stories were published in the *Times* and distributed on its newswire throughout the United States and beyond.

The relationship I'm describing is not a dialogue, which might be possible if either religion or media could be reduced to a single character. Instead, the way in which these two forces interact is better described as a series of overlapping conversations. Some will be short, others immensely long; some raucous, some convivial. At best, their overall effect is to enrich and diversify human experience.

Notes

Introduction

1   Benedict Anderson, *Imagined Communities* (London: Verso, 1983).

2   Diana L. Eck, *A New Religious America* (San Francisco: Harper, 2001).

3   Charles Haynes, ed. *Finding Common Ground: A First Amendment Guide to Religion and Public Education* (Nashville, Tenn.: Freedom Forum First Amendment Center at Vanderbilt University, 1994).

4   Donald W. Shriver Jr., *An Ethic for Enemies: Forgiveness in Politics* (New York: Oxford University Press, 1995).

5   Rosemary Radford Ruether and Herman J. Ruether, *The Wrath of Jonah: The Crisis of Religious Nationalism in the Israeli-Palestinian Conflict* (Minneapolis: Fortress Press, 2002).

6   Martin Marty and R. Scott Appleby, *Religion, Ethnicity and Self-Identity: Nations in Turmoil* (Hanover, N.H.: University Press of New England, 1997).

7   See Shriver, *An Ethic for Enemies*; Corwin Smidt, ed., *Religion as Social Capital: Producing the Common Good* (Waco, Tex.: Baylor University Press, 2003).

8   Robert Wuthnow, *Loose Connections: Joining Together in America's Fragmented Communities* (Cambridge, Mass.: Harvard University Press, 1998).

9   John Dart and Jimmy Allen, "Bridging the Gap" (Nashville: Freedom Forum First Amendment Center at Vanderbilt University, 1993).

10   Bart Pattyn, ed., *Media Ethics: Opening Social Dialogue* (Leuven, Belgium: Peeters, 2000).

11   Mark Silk, *Religion in the News*; vols. 1–6 (Hartford, Conn.: Leonard Greenberg Center for the Study of Religion in Public Life, Trinity College, 2002–4).

12   Stewart Hoover and Knut Lundby, eds. *Rethinking Media, Religion and Culture* (Thousand Oaks, Calif.: Sage, 1997), 3–14, 298–310; Claire Badaracco, "A Utopian on Main Street," in *Rethinking Media, Religion and Culture*, 263–82; William Dean, *The American Spiritual Culture and the Invention of Jazz, Football and the Movies* (New York: Continuum, 2003).

13   Sherry Ortner, *The Fate of "Culture": Geertz and Beyond* (Berkeley: University of California Press, 1999).

14   Stewart Hoover and Lynn Clarke, *Mediating Religion and Identity* (New York: Columbia University Press, 2002); Ronald Grimes, *Deeply into the Bone: Reinventing Rites of Passage* (Berkeley: University of California Press, 2000).

15   Carolyn Marvin, *Blood Sacrifice and the Nation* (New Haven: Yale University Press, 2001).

16   Meike Bal, *Quoting Caravaggio* (Chicago: University of Chicago Press, 1999).

17   John of the Cross, *Living Flame of Life*, trans. Jane Ackermann (Binghamton: Medieval and Renaissance Texts and Studies, 1995).

Chapter 1

1   See Gaye Tuchman, "Objectivity as Strategic Ritual," *American Sociological Review* 77, no. 1 (1972): 660–79; Michael Schudson, *Discovering the News: A Social History of the American Newspaper* (New York: Basic Books, 1978); Herbert Gans, *Deciding What's News* (New York: Random House, 1979).

2   For a morally engaged vision of the journalistic profession, see Jay Rosen, *What Are Journalists For?* (New Haven: Yale University Press, 2001).

3   Hayden White, *The Content of the Form* (Baltimore: Johns Hopkins University Press, 1987), xi.

4   Michael Schudson, *The Power of News* (Cambridge, Mass.: Harvard University Press, 1995), 55.

5   James Ettema and Theodore Glasser, "Narrative Form and Moral Force: The Realization of Innocence and Guilt Through Investigative Journalism," *Journal of Communications* 383 (1998): 11.

6   Gans, *Deciding What's News*, 205.

7   My larger study, *People of Faith: Religious Conviction in American Journalism and Higher Education* (Ithaca: Cornell University Press, 2003), examines the place of religion in the careers of forty Catholics and evangelicals who work in the national news media and the social sciences (in the disciplines of sociology, history, and political science). Those interviewed for the project include journalists Cokie Roberts, Fred Barnes, E. J. Dionne, Kenneth Woodward, and Peter Steinfels, along with scholars Andrew Greeley, George Marsden, Mark Noll, Elizabeth Fox-Genovese, Jay Dolan, and John DiIulio.

8   On cultural resources, see Rhys Williams, "Visions of the Good Society and the Religious Roots of American Political Culture," *Sociology of Religion* 60, no. 1 (1999): 1. On narrative, see Robert Wuthnow, *Christianity in the Twenty-First Century: Reflections on the Challenges Ahead* (New York: Oxford University Press, 1995); Robert Bellah, *The Broken Covenant: American Civil Religion in a Time of Trial* (Chicago: University of Chicago Press, 1992); Andrew Greeley, *The Catholic Myth* (New York: Simon & Schuster, 1997);

Stanley Hauerwas and L. Gregory Jones, eds., *Why Narrative? Readings in Narrative Theology* (Grand Rapids: Eerdmans, 1989).

9   On "culture as toolkit," see Ann Swidler, "Culture in Action: Symbols and Strategies," *American Sociological Review* 51, no. 2 (1986): 273–87; For use of the cultural "building blocks" concept, see Stephen Hart, *What Does the Lord Require? How American Christians Think About Economic Justice* (New Brunswick: Rutgers University Press, 1996).

10   Greeley, *Catholic Myth*, 46, 44.

11   Robert Bellah, "Religion and the Shape of National Culture," *America*, 31 July 1999, 10.

12   See Paul Giles, *American Catholic Arts and Fictions* (London: Cambridge University Press, 1992); Lee Lourdeaux, *Italian and Irish Filmmakers in America: Ford, Capra, Coppola, and Scorsese* (Philadelphia: Temple University Press, 1990); Richard Blake, *Afterimage: The Indelible Catholic Imagination of Six American Filmmakers* (Chicago: Loyola Press, 2000).

13   Andrew Greeley, *The Catholic Imagination* (Berkeley: University of California Press, 2000), 1.

14   Peter Thuesen, "The Leather-Bound Shrine in Every Home," *Books and Culture* (March–April 2000), 20.

15   For an account of evangelicalism's high view of the authority of Scripture, see James D. Hunter, *American Evangelicalism: Conservative Protestantism and the Quandary of Modernity* (New Brunswick: Rutgers University Press, 1983).

16   Colleen McDannell convincingly argues that Protestants value material culture (religious pictures, objects, and so on) as much as do Roman Catholics. At the same time, McDannell points out that much of Protestant material culture consists of words (usually biblical quotations or words) made into things (*Material Christianity* [New Haven: Yale University Press, 1995]).

17   David Tracy, *The Analogical Imagination: Christian Theology and the Culture of Pluralism* (New York: Crossroad, 1981).

18   A phrase from Gerard Manley Hopkins's poem "God's Grandeur."

19   Tracy, *Analogical Imagination*, 408, 415.

20   See also Andrew Greeley's summary of Tracy in *Catholic Myth*, 289–309.

21   On the evangelical penchant for boundaries, see Christian Smith, *American Evangelicalism: Embattled and Thriving* (Chicago: University of Chicago Press, 1998).

22   Greeley, *Catholic Imagination*, 111.

23   Bellah, "Religion."

24   Smith, *American Evangelism*, 189. On evangelical individualism, see Dennis Hollinger, *Individualism and Social Ethics: An Evangelical Syncretism* (Lanham, Md.: University Press of America, 1983); James L. Guth et al., *The Bully Pulpit: The Politics of Protestant Clergy* (Kansas City: University Press of Kansas, 1997); Harold Bloom, *The American Religion* (New York: Simon and Schuster, 1992). On the communalism of the Catholic social ethic, see Greeley, *Catholic Myth*, 289–309.

25   See William Dinges et al., "A Faith Loosely Held: The Institutional Allegiance of Young Catholics," *Commonweal*, 17 July 1998, 13–19; William J. Byron argues that social justice is an integral component of Catholic social thought in "Ten Building Blocks of Catholic Social Teaching," *America*, 31 October 1998, 10–11.

26   Guth et al., *Bully Pulpit*, 14.

27   Christian Smith, *Christian America? What Evangelicals Really Want* (Berkeley: University of California Press, 2000), 13, 7.

28   David J. O'Brien, *Public Catholicism* (Maryknoll, N.Y.: Orbis, 1996), 7.

29   Twenty journalists were interviewed for the project. Catholic journalists: E. J. Dionne, Colman McCarthy, Mary McGrory, Dan Balz (*Washington Post*); Peter Steinfels, Robin Toner (*New York Times*); Kenneth Woodward (*Newsweek*); Brian Healy (*Eye to Eye with Connie Chung*); Donald Wycliff (*Chicago Tribune*, formerly *New York Times*); Cokie Roberts (*ABC News/ National Public Radio*). Evangelical journalists: David Aikman, Richard Ostling (*Time*); Fred Barnes (*New Republic*); Marianne Kyriakos (*Washington Post*); Don Holt (*Fortune*); Wesley Pippert (formerly United Press International); Jeff Sheler (*U.S. News and World Report*); Cal Thomas (*Los Angeles Times Syndicate*); Russ Pulliam (editor, *Indianapolis News*; formerly Associated Press, New York City). In some cases the journalists are no longer at the news organizations listed above. The sample was drawn through snowball sampling. One journalist has withdrawn from the study.

30   In the case of two broadcast journalists and some print journalists, I was not able to look at fifty LexisNexis stories. In a few cases, more than fifty stories were examined in the initial analysis.

31   Peter Steinfels, "Constraints of the Religion Reporter," *Nieman Reports* 473, no. 5 (1993): 5.

32   Mark Silk, *Unsecular Media: Making News of Religion in America* (Chicago: University of Chicago Press, 1995).

33   See Schmalzbauer, *People of Faith*, for a treatment of these five storylines (including the "testing the scriptures," "communitarian," and the "peace and justice" storylines).

34   Tracy, *Analogical Imagination*, 415.

35   Gaye Tuchman, *Making News: A Study in the Construction of Reality* (New York: Free Press, 1978), 23.

36   For a discussion of evangelicals as bricoleurs in the secular world, see Paul A. Bramadat, *The Church on the World's Turf: An Evangelical Christian Group at a Secular University* (New York: Oxford University Press, 2000), 147.

37   Smith, *American Evangelicalism*, 124.

38   James D. Hunter, *Culture Wars: The Struggle to Define America* (New York: Basic Books, 1992).

39   David Astor, "Cal Thomas in Select 500 Club for Columnists," *Editor and Publisher* 8 (May 1999): 44.

40   Dean Ridings, Review of *Occupied Territory*, in *Fundamentalist Journal* 7 (April 1988): 58.

41   On one side are "conservatives" ("W." B7), "social and religious conservatives" ("Lost Virtue" B7), "Christians" ("Christians" B5), the "Christian Right" ("Religious Right" B7), and the "champions of traditional morality" ("Confronting" B7). On the other side are the "liberal secularists" ("Guns" B7; "Making Sense" B7), the "pagan left" ("Religious Right" B7), the "'heroes' and 'heroines' of the '60s" ("Final Insult" B7), the "'60s flower children" ("Fair" B7), "feminists" ("GOP" B5), "television journalists," the "big media" ("Newt" B7), the "entertainment industry" ("Apathy" B7), the "tenured radicals" ("Surveying" B5), the "bigots" (against Christian conservatives), and the "protected classes" ("Religious Right" B7).

42   Hunter, *Culture Wars*, 144.

43   On the use of public opinion data in the culture wars, see Hunter, *Culture Wars*.

44   Michael Lienesch, *Redeeming America: Piety and Politics in the New Christian Right* (Chapel Hill: University of North Carolina Press, 1993), 193.

45   James D. Hunter, "Before the Shooting Begins," *Columbia Journalism Review* (July–August 1993): 29–33.

46   Gans, *Deciding What's News*, 56–60.

47   Guth et al., *Bully Pulpit*, 14.

48   Gans, *Deciding What's News*, 20, 62–68. See also Tuchman, *Making News*, for the recurring phrase "news net."

49   Ridings, Review of *Occupied Territory*, 58.

50   Gans, *Deciding What's News*, 56–60.

51   Cal Thomas and Ed Dobson, *Blinded by Might: Can the Religious Right Save America?* (Grand Rapids: Zondervan, 1999), 97.

52   Ibid., 36, 88, 143.

53   For "consensus" see E. J. Dionne, "A Shift Looms; The President Sees Consensus, While Religious Leaders Disagree About the Church-State Divide," *Washington Post*, 3 October 1999, B1; see also Peter Steinfels, "Beliefs," *New York Times*, 25 June 1994, A12. For "agreement" see Peter Steinfels, "Beliefs," *New York Times*, 31 December 1993, A8; see also E. J. Dionne, "A Political Classic," *Washington Post*, 1 August 1997, A21. For "dialogue" see Peter Steinfels, "Beliefs," *New York Times*, 30 October 1999, A13; see also E. J. Dionne, "The Minnesota Compact," *Washington Post*, 11 July 1995, A17. For "complicated" see Peter Steinfels, "Beliefs," *New York Times*, 6 June 1992, section 1, 10; see also E. J. Dionne, "Radical Realist," *Washington Post*, 19 January 1997, W8.

54   Steinfels, "Constraints," 5.

55   E. J. Dionne, *Why Americans Hate Politics* (New York: Simon & Schuster, 1992), 32–33.

56   Tracy, *Analogical Imagination*, 408.

57   Greeley, *Catholic Imagination,* 6.

58   Philip Gleason, "The New Americanism in Catholic Historiography," *U.S. Catholic Historian* 113 (1993): 16.

59   Steinfels, "Constraints," 5.

60   Peter Steinfels, "Prophet and Politician," in *Generation of the Third Eye*, ed. Daniel Callahan (New York: Sheed & Ward, 1965), 220.

61   On Cogley and the Catholic Worker movement, see Mel Piehl, *Breaking Bread: The Catholic Worker and the Origin of Catholic Radicalism in America* (Philadelphia: Temple University Press, 1982).

62   On the relationship between Catholicism and liberalism, see Philip Gleason, *Keeping the Faith: American Catholicism Past and Present* (Notre Dame, Ind.: University of Notre Dame Press, 1987); John McGreevy, *Catholicism and American Freedom* (New York: Norton, 2003).

63   In *Why Americans Hate Politics* (New York: Simon & Schuster, 1991), Dionne favorably cites both Bell's *The End of Ideology* (New York: Free Press, 1962) and Schlesinger's *The Vital Center: The Politics of Freedom* (Boston: Houghton Mifflin, 1962). In the interview, he noted the impact of Niebuhr's *Children of Light and the Children of Darkness* (New York: Scribner, 1972) on his personal intellectual development.

64   Godfrey Hodgson, *America in Our Time: From World War II to Nixon* (New York: Random House, 1976), 93. On the affinities between ideological traditions and tropes, see Hayden White, *Metahistory: The Historical Imagination in Nineteenth-Century Europe* (Baltimore: Johns Hopkins University Press, 1975); Robert Nisbet, *Social Change and History: Aspects of the Western Theory of Development* (New York: Oxford University Press, 1969).

65   See Gans, *Deciding What's News*, 51; Tuchman, "Objectivity as Strategic Ritual."
66   See John McGreevy, "Thinking On One's Own: Catholicism in the American Intellectual Imagination, 1928–1960," *Journal of American History* 84, no. 1 (1997): 97–132; Gleason, *Keeping the Faith*.
67   See Gleason, *Keeping the Faith,* on the response of liberal Catholics to the charge of Catholic authoritarianism.
68   An example of the emphasis of *Commonweal* on the "neutral grays" can be found in John Kane, "Catholic Separatism," in *Catholicism in America,* ed. William Clancy (New York: Harcourt, Brace, and Company, 1954), 47–57.
69   E. J. Dionne, "Response," in *Disciples and Democracy*, ed. Michael Cromartie (Grand Rapids: Eerdmans, 1994), 19.
70   George M. Marsden, *The Outrageous Idea of Christian Scholarship* (New York: Oxford University Press, 1995), 59.
71   Bellah, "Religion," 10.
72   I am indebted to Blake's *AfterImage* for the term "theological footprints."
73   Blake, *AfterImage*; Giles, *American Catholic Arts and Fictions*; Lourdeaux, *Italian and Irish Filmmakers in America*.

Chapter 1: View from the News Desk

1   The views expressed in this essay are the author's own and do not necessarily reflect those of the Voice of America.
2   For more on VOA Tibetan, see John B. Buescher, "The Buddha's Conventional and Ultimate Tooth," in *Changing Minds: Contributions to the Study of Buddhism and Tibet in Honor of Jeffrey Hopkins*, ed. Guy Newland (Ithaca: Snow Lion Press, 2001), 19–48; and Alan L. Heil Jr., "To the Roof of the World: The Tibetan Service Miracle," in *Voice of America: A History* (New York: Columbia University Press, 2003), 302–10. For a view of international broadcasting in general as a propaganda instrument, see Michael Nelson, *War of the Black Heavens: The Battles of Western Broadcasting in the Cold War* (Syracuse: Syracuse University Press, 1997). For more on the complex modern exchange of information between Tibet and the rest of the world, see Donald S. Lopez Jr., *Prisoners of Shangri-La: Tibetan Buddhism and the West* (Chicago: University of Chicago Press, 1998); Orville Schell, *Virtual Tibet: Searching for Shangri-La from the Himalayas to Hollywood* (New York: Metropolitan Books, 200); and Thierry Dodin and Heinz Rather, eds., *Imagining Tibet: Perceptions, Projections and Fantasies* (Boston: Wisdom Publications, 2001). A memoir of travel to the region that touches some of the issues of cross-cultural exchange through the mirror of the media is Pico Iyer, *Video Night in Kathmandu and Other Reports from the Not-So-Far East* (New York: Knopf, 1988). For information regarding the first radio service for Tibet, a small network set up by the Tibetan government in Lhasa shortly before the Chinese People's Liberation Army invaded Tibet in 1949, see Robert Ford, *Captured in Tibet* (London: Harrap, 1957).

Chapter 2

1   Richard T. Cooper, "General Casts War in Religious Terms," *New York Times*, 16 October 2003.
2   This comment, made during a "Celebrate America" event in Good Shepherd Church, Sandy, Oregon, 21 June 2003, was broadcast on *NBC News*.

3   Osama bin Laden, "World Islamic Front Statement: Jihad Against the Jews and Crusaders," *Al Quds al'Arabi*, 23 February 1998. His statements dividing the world into believers and infidels were repeated in recorded comments that were broadcast on Al-Jazeera television on 7 October 2001.

4   Stephen Mansfield, *The Faith of George W. Bush* (New York: J. P. Tarcher, 2003), 108–9.

5   On February 8, 2003, registrants in the 2003 annual meeting of the association of National Religious Broadcasters passed a resolution (*Resolution 2003–03*) that stated in its conclusion: "We recognize . . . that God has appointed President George W. Bush to leadership at this critical period in our nation's history, and give Him thanks."

6   Alan Cooperman, "Bush's Remark About God Assailed," *Washington Post*, 22 November 2003, A6.

7   "Remarks by the President on the Loss of Space Shuttle," 1 February 2003, www.whitehouse.gov/news/releases/2003/02/2003020-2html.

8   For more information on this subject, see Deborah Caldwell, "George Bush's Theology: Does the President Believe He Has a Divine Mandate?" *National Catholic Reporter*, 21 February 2003.

9   "President or Preacher? Elaine Pagels and Rev. Dr. C. Welton Gaddy on the President's Irresponsible Use of Religious Language," Audio News Conference, Douglas Gould & Company, 11 February 2003.

10   Ibid.

11   "Presidential Remarks," 10 February 2003, www.whitehouse.gov/news/releases/2003/02/20030210-2.html. Accessed 4 April 2004.

12   "Address to Joint Session of Congress and the American People," 20 September 2001, www.whitehouse.gov/news/releases/2001/09/20010920-8.html. Accessed 4 April 2004.

13   Quoted in Forrest Church, *The American Creed: A Biography of the Declaration of Independence* (New York: St. Martin's Griffin, 2002).

14   Interfaith Alliance, *Election-Year Guide for Political Candidates*, 2000, 11.

15   William Pryor, "Commencement Address," Northeast Louisiana University, 15 May 1999.

16   Quoted in Church, *American Creed*, 85.

17   Quoted in Church, *American Creed*, 116.

18   Church, *American Creed*, ix.

19   Ibid, 139.

20   Quoted in Church, *American Creed*, 116.

21   See Robert S. Alley, *So Help Me God: Religion and the Presidency from Wilson to Nixon* (Richmond: John Knox Press, 1972), 94.

22   See Eck, *A New Religious America*.

23   See Pew Research Center for the People and Press and the Pew Forum on Religion and Public Life, "Religion and Politics: Contention and Consensus," July 24, 2003.

24   Informed by his study of politics, religion, and the presidency, Bob Alley observed, "Politics needs humanization, not deification" (*So Help Me God*, 147).

25   Pagels, "President or Preacher?" See also comments on the Christian Identity Movement in Jessica Stern, *Terror in the Name of God* (New York: Ecco, 2003).

26   A 1998 national survey conducted by the *Washington Post*, the Henry J. Kaiser Family Foundation, and Harvard University showed that the American electorate is deeply religious and prizes spirituality. Pollsters concluded

that religion contributed significantly to people's decisions about voting. See also: Hanna Rosin, "The Politics of Religion: Issues of Faith Shape Debates," *Washington Post*, 29 October 1998. Late in 2003 nearly two-thirds of the American electorate indicated that religious beliefs would be a major factor in their decisions about which candidates they would vote for in the 2004 elections.

27   See Geneive Abdo, "Religious Voting Blocs Shift Allegiances," *Chicago Tribune*, 17 December 2004. Abdo wrote, "Some Jewish and Muslim voters appear to be abandoning their past party affiliations and fewer evangelical Christians may go to the polls, adding to the volatility of the race."

28   After his rather exhaustive study of religion and the presidency, Bob Alley concluded that the rise, character, and form of any civil religion in the nation are always directly related to the words and actions of the president (*So Help Me God*, 24).

Chapter 2: View from the News Desk

1   H. Y. Amin, "Freedom as a Value in Arab Media: Perceptions and Attitudes Among Journalists," *Political Communication* 19 (2002): 128.

2   See W. Rugh, *The Arab Press: News Media and Political Processes in the Arab World*, 2nd ed. (Syracuse: Syracuse University Press, 1979).

3   See Abdel Rahman, A. Abdel, L. Mageed, and N. Kamel, *Communicator in the Egyptian Press* (Cairo: School of Mass Communication Press, 1992).

4   *Study of Media Laws and Policies for the Middle East and Maghreb* (London: Stanhope Center for Communications Policy Research, 2003).

5   See Amin, "Freedom as a Value in Arab Media," 125–35.

6   See: N. Sakr, *Satellite Realms: Transnational Television, Globalization and the Middle East* (London: I. B. Tauris, 2001).

7   See *Study of Media Laws.*

8   "Attacks on the Press in 2001," *Committee to Protect Journalists*, http://www.cpj.org. Retrieved 3 January 2004.

9   *Study of Media Laws.*

10   See H. Y. Amin, "Arab World Audio-Visual Media," in *Censorship: A World Encyclopedia*, ed. D. Jones (London: Fitzroy Dearborn Publishers, 1998).

11   See *Study of Media Laws.*

12   M. F. Azet, *News Agencies in the Arab World* (Jeddah: The Sun Rise for Publication, Distribution and Print, 1992).

13   See O. A. Najjar, "The Middle East and North Africa," in *Global Journalism: Topical Issues and Media Systems*, ed. A. De Beer and J. Merrill (New York: Pearson Education, Inc., 2004).

14   Ibid.

15   See *Study of Media Laws.*

16   Amin, "Arab World Audio-Visual Media," 130.

17   See S. El Calamawy, "The Impact of Tradition on the Development of Modern Arabic Literature," in *Arab and American Cultures*, ed. G. H. Atieh (Washington, D.C.: American Enterprise Institute for Public Policy Research, 1977), 47–50.

18   "Attacks on the Press."

19   *Study of Media Laws.*

20   J. Alterman, *New Media, New Politics? From Satellite Television to the Internet in the Arab World* (Washington, D.C.: Washington Institute for Near East Policy, 1998).

21   See *Study of Media Laws.*

22   See M. el-Nawawy and A. Iskandar, *Al-Jazeera: The Story of the Network That Is Rattling Governments and Redefining Modern Journalism* (Boulder: Westview, 2003).

23   See *Study of Media Laws.*

24   See Sakr, *Satellite Realms.*

Chapter 3

1   For more information on the ethnic press in New York City, check the Web site of the Independent Press Association, www.indypress.org.

2   "Strike Hard on Falun Gong," *China Press*, 11 May 2002, A16. Plaintiffs' exhibit in *Friends of Falun Gong v. Pacific Culture Enterprises*; translation by plaintiffs (2003).

3   *Friends of Falun Gong v. Pacific Culture Enterprise, Inc.* 02-CV-4482 (CBA), U.S. District Court for the Eastern District of New York.

4   See Paul Moses and Mae Cheng, "Silencing the Movement," *Newsday*, 6 September 2001, B06.

5   Eckholm, Erik, "A Quiet Roar: China's Leadership Feels Threatened by a Sect Seeking Peace," *New York Times*, 4 November 1999, A10.

6   Moses and Cheng, "Silencing the Movement," B06.

7   Liu Xiaoming. "China-U.S. Partnership in the New Century Address by Hon. Liu Xiaoming, Charge d'Affaires of the Chinese Embassy at the Reception to Mark the Tenth Anniversary of the China Press, New York, January 4, 2000." http://www.china-embassy.org/eng/sgxx/sggg/sggyth/t34 773.htm. Retrieved 23 February 2004.

8   Zhu Qizhen, "China-U.S. Partnership in the New Century," 1 January 2000. "Remarks by Ambassador Zhu Qizhen at Seminar on Combating Falun Gong in New York," http://www.chinaembassy.bg/eng/8296.html. Retrieved 23 February 2004.

9   "The China Press Is a Global News Leader and Gateway to Mainstreet U.S.A. and Mainland China," www.chinaPusa.com/images/intro2.htm. Retrieved 23 February 2004.

10   Lu Zidai, "What Does Evil Cult Harassing the China Press Tell Us?" *China Press*, 22 December 2001. Plaintiffs' exhibit in *Friends of Falun Gong v. Pacific Culture Enterprises*; translation by plaintiffs.

11   *Friends of Falun Gong, v. Pacific Culture Enterprise, Inc.* 02-CV-4482 CBA, U.S. District Court for the Eastern District of New York.

12   Moses, "Misprints? Falun Gong and the First Amendment," *Commonweal*, 6 June 2003, 11.

13   "Falun Gong Swaggers to *China Press*," *China Press*, 23 May 2002. Plaintiffs' exhibit in *Friends of Falun Gong v. Pacific Culture Enterprises*; translation by plaintiffs.

14   *Newsday*, 5 April 1989, 8.

15   For further resources on the Internet, visit the following sites: http://www.faluninfo.net/ [Falun Dafa Information Center, for Falun Gong's news about itself]; http://www.nyconsulate.prchina.org/eng/index.html [Consulate-general of the People's Republic of China in New York; site can be searched for releases concerning Falun Gong]; http://www.chinapres-susa.com/images/intro2.htm [*China Press*]; http://www.state.gov/g/drl/rls/ irf/ [The U.S. State Department's Annual Report on International Religious

Freedom]; http://www.oyez.org/oyez/resource/case/65/ [Abstract and link to text of *Cantwell v. Connecticut*]; http://www.oyez.org/oyez/resource/ case/ 136/resources [Abstract and link to text of *Gertz v. Welch*]; http://www. indypress.org [Web site of the Independent Press Association, offers translations of articles in ethnic press]; http://www.gothamgazette.com [offers translations of articles from ethnic press in New York City].

Chapter 4

1   George M. Marsden, *Fundamentalism and American Culture: The Shaping of Twentieth-Century Evangelicalism, 1870–1925* (New York: Oxford University Press, 1980), 4.

2   Karen Armstrong, *The Battle for God* (New York: Ballantine Books, 2000), xiii.

3   Martin E. Marty and R. Scott Appleby, "Conclusion: An Interim Report on a Hypothetical Family," in *Fundamentalisms Observed*, ed. Marty and Appleby (Chicago: University of Chicago Press, 1991), 835.

4   Jerrold M. Post, Ehud Sprinzak, and Laurita M. Denny, "The Terrorists in Their Own Words: Interviews with 35 Incarcerated Middle Eastern Terrorists," *Terrorism and Political Violence* 15, no. 1 (2003): 175.

5   Armstrong, *Battle*, xii.

6   J. Gordon Melton, "Al-Qaeda as a New Religion," paper presented to New Religious Movements Section, American Academy of Religion, Toronto, Canada, 2002, p. 5.

7   Charles Selengut, *Sacred Fury: Understanding Religious Violence* (Walnut Creek, Calif.: Altamira Press, 2003), 164–65.

8   Melton, "Al-Qaeda," 5.

9   Paul Heelas, "Introduction: On Differentiation and Dedifferentiation," in *Religion, Modernity and Postmodernity*, ed. Paul Heelas, David Martin and Paul Morris (Oxford: Blackwell, 1998).

10   The Institute for Creation Research's Web site is http://www.icr.org.

11   Armstrong, *Battle*, 140.

12   Razelle Frankl, "Transformation of Televangelism: Repackaging Christian Family Values," in *Media, Culture, and the Religious Right*, ed. Linda Kintz and Julia Lesage (Minneapolis: University of Minnesota Press, 1998), 177.

13   Sean Elder, "The Family Guy," *Salon* 2000, 3 July 2003, http://archive. salon.com/media/col/Elde/2000/01/08/paxson/.

Chapter 5

1   See Paul Boyer, *When Time Shall Be No More: Prophecy Belief in Modern American Culture* (Cambridge, Mass.: Harvard University Press, 1992), 1–18, esp. 3–4.

2   For a summary of Darby's system of prophetic interpretation and its diffusion in the United States, see Boyer, *When Time Shall Be No More*, 87–112.

3   Dispensationalists cite numerous scriptures foretelling the return of the Jews to the Promised Land, as well as Jesus' parable of the leafing of the fig tree as summer approaches (Mark 13:28), which is seen as a prophecy of the restoration of the Jews.

4   A key scripture for rapture believers is 1 Thessalonians 4:16-17: "For the Lord himself shall descend from heaven with a shout . . . and the dead in Christ shall rise first: Then we which are alive and remain shall be caught up together with them in the clouds, to meet the Lord in the air."

5   "And it shall come to pass, that in all the land, saith the Lord, two parts therein shall be cut off and die; but the third shall be left therein" (Zech 13:8). In the dispensationalist scenario, Antichrist's forces will also persecute and kill "Tribulation Saints"—Gentiles who missed the rapture but who realize their error, reject Antichrist's claims, and turn to Christ. The adventures of a group of Tribulation Saints form the basic plot of the popular "Left Behind" novels.

6   For a full discussion of this topic, with numerous citations of specific works by dispensationalists, see Boyer, *When Time Shall Be No More*, ch. 6, "The Final Chastisement of the Chosen," 181–224.

7   Yaacov Ariel, *Philosemites or Antisemites? Evangelical Christian Attitudes Toward Jews, Judaism, and the State of Israel* (Jerusalem: Hebrew University of Jerusalem, 2002), 1.

8   Darby based this portion of his end-time scenario on Revelation 16-22, especially 16:16; 17:11-14; 19:11-21, 20:1-15, and 21:1-6.

9   Daisy Maryles, "Armageddon Has Arrived," *Publishers Weekly*, 21 April 2003.

10   E.g., 2 Peter 3:10: "The heavens shall pass away with a great noise, and the elements shall melt with fervent heat, the earth also and the works that are therein shall be burned up."

11   Boyer, *When Time Shall Be No More*, ch. 4, "The Atomic Bomb and Nuclear War"; ch. 5, "Ezekiel as the First Cold Warrior"; and ch. 8, "Antichrist, 666, and the Mark of the Beast," 115–81, 254–90.

12   http://www.endtimeprophecy.net/~tttbbs/EPN1/GroupPages/grupend1. html. For a graphic description of the harlot of Babylon, who drinks the blood of the saints and is "full of abominations and filthiness of her fornication," see Revelation 17:3-6.

13   Boyer, *When Time Shall Be No More*, 331–38.

14   For a more extensive discussion, see Boyer, *When Time Shall Be No More*, 326–31; "The Middle East in Modern American Popular Prophetic Belief," in *Abbas Amanat and Magnus T. Bernhardsson, Imagining the End: Visions of the Apocalypse from the Ancient Middle East to Modern America* (London: I. B. Tauris, 2002), 312–35; and "John Darby Meets Saddam Hussein: Foreign Policy and Bible Prophecy," *Chronicle of Higher Education*, 14 February 2003, B10–11.

15   *Jerusalem Post*, 22 October 2000, cited in Ariel, *Philosemites or Antisemites?*, 43. n. 1.

16   See Jews for Jesus advertisements in *New York Times*, 18 March 1991, A9; and in *Boston Globe*, 28 March 1991, 22.

17   See Neil MacFarquhar, "Hussein's Babylon: A Beloved Atrocity," *New York Times*, 19 August 2003.

18   Jerry Falwell, "Muhammad, 'A Demon-Possessed Pedophile'?" *WorldNet-Daily*, 15 June 2002.

19   Benjamin Beit-Hallahmi, "Rebirth and Death: The Violent Potential of Apocalyptic Dreams," manuscript essay, ca. 2001, p. 173. This essay appears in somewhat different form in *The Psychology of Terrorism*, vol. 3, ed. Chris E. Stout (Westport, Conn.: Praeger, 2002), 163–89.

20   Ruth H. Bloch, *Visionary Republic: Millennial Themes in American Thought, 1756–1800* (New York: Cambridge University Press, 1985); James W. Davidson, *The Logic of Millennial Thought: Eighteenth-Century New England* (New Haven: Yale University Press, 1977), 237.

21   Ernest Lee Tuveson, *Redeemer Nation: The Idea of America's Millennial Role* (Chicago: University of Chicago Press, 1968).

22   Quoted in Gary Wills, "With God on His Side," *New York Times Magazine*, 30 March 2003, 26.

23   Arthur M. Schlesinger Jr., "Eyeless in Gaza," *New York Review of Books*, 23 October, 2003, 26.

24   Mark Thompson, "A Long Career of Marching with the Cross," *Time*, 3 November 2003, 30.

25   "Bush Repudiates General in Remarks Flap," *Guardian Unlimited* U.K., 22 October 2003, http://www.guardian.co.uk.

26   Ibid.

27   Wills, "With God on His Side," 26.

28   Henry Munson, "'Fundamentalism,' Ancient and Modern," *Dædalus* 132, no. 3 (2003): 40.

29   See Samuel P. Huntington, *The Clash of Civilizations and the Remaking of World Order* (New York: Touchstone, 1997).

30   See, for example, Herman Kahn and Anthony J. Wiener, *The Year 2000: A Framework for Speculation on the Next Thirty-Three Years* (New York: Macmillan, 1967).

31   Martin E. Marty, "Our Religio-Secular World," *Dædalus* 132, no. 3 (2003): 42.

32   Jean Bethke Elshtain, "Against Liberal Monism," *Dædalus* 132, no. 3 (2003): 79.

Chapter 5: View from the News Desk

1   Ziauddin Sardar, "The Forgotten Inheritance," *New Statesman*, 7 April 2003.

2   Karen Armstrong, "The True, Peaceful Face Of Islam. The War on Terror/Why the Hate?" MN - Minitex Statewide Database Access Program Expanded Academic ASAP, 1 October 2001, 158.5: 48; 10 November 2002.

3   Huntington, *Clash of Civilizations*, 14.

4   For further reading on this subject, see: Paul Findley, *Silent No More: Confronting America's False Images of Islam* (Beltsville, Md.: Amana Publications, 2001); Charles Haynes, "Watch Out: War on Terrorism Should Not Mean War on Islam," *Inside the First Amendment*, 23 September 2002, http://www.freedomdforum.org; Samuel Huntingon, "Why International Primacy Matters," *International Security*, Spring 1993; id., *The Clash of Civilizations and the Remaking of World Order* (New York: Touchstone, 1997); "Islam—A Religion of Terror?" *Invitation to Islam* 5, 5 October 1998; Muqtedar Khan, "A Memo to American Muslims," 29 September 2002, http://www.ijtihad.com; Abdul-Hakim Murad, "Recapturing Islam from Terrorists," 14 September 2001, 4 November 2002, http://www.themodernreligion.com; Greg Noakes, "Muslims and the American Press," in *Muslims on the Americanization Path*, ed. Yvonne Yazbeck Haddad and John L. Esposito (New York: Oxford University Press, 2000); Tariq Ramadan, "To be a European Muslim," The Islamic Foundation, 1999; Ann Rodgers-Melnick, "'Jihad' Misused, Misunderstood, Scholar Says," *Pittsburgh Post Gazette*, 23 September 2001; Munir Shafiq, "Secularism and the Arab-Muslim Condition" in *Islam and Secularism in the Middle East,* ed. Azzam Tamimi and John L. Esposito (London: Hurst, 2000); James Turner Johnson, "Jihad and Just War." *First Things: A Monthly Journal of Religion and Public Life* (June–July 2002): 12–15.

Chapter 6

1   W. Porter, "Some Sociological Notes on a Century of Change in the Funeral Business," *Sociological Symposium* 1 (1968): 36–46.
2   R. Fulton and G. Owen, "Death and Society in Twentieth Century America," *Omega* 18 (1987–88): 379–95.
3   "In Memoriam: Mrs. Cinderella E. Laughridge," Louisville, KY *Courier-Journal*, 14 January 1874.
4   A. Whitman, *The Obituary Book* (New York: Stein & Day, 1971), 7–8.
5   B. Storm, "A Different Type of Obit Page," *Editor & Publisher*, 6 June 1987, 100, 149.
6   B. Griffin, "Reconsider Policy," *Courier-Journal*, 21 September 1995, A8.
7   G. Cranberg, M. Brindley, and K. Putnam, "More Newspapers are Charging Readers for Life and Death News," *ASNE Bulletin* (May–June 1992): 16–18.
8   C. Heredia, "Memorials—Road Hazard or Reminder?" *San Francisco Chronicle*, 19 January 1998, A13.
9   B. Buote, "Roadside Memorials Pay Tribute to Lost Lives," *Boston Globe*, 4 August 2002, 1.
10 J. Ripley, "The Crosses They Bear," *North Pinellas Times*, 22 July 2000, 8.
11 C. Leimer, "Roadside Memorials: Marking Journeys Never Completed," n.d., http://www.tombstonetravel.com/spont.html.
12 L. Stroklund, "Montana American Legion White Cross Highway Fatality Marker Program," n.d., http://www.mtlegion.org/White%20Cross/White%20Cross.html.
13 P. Lloyd, "'X' marks the spot," *MADDvocate,* Summer 1998.
14 Heredia, "Memorials."
15 C. Burbach, "Memorials Say: We Won't Forget," *Omaha World Herald,* 25 May 2002, A1.
16 M. Hunter, "Slowing Motorists Cause 3-Car Pileup at Crash Site," *Times-Picayune*, 19 January 2002, 1.
17 K. Merk, "Roadside Memorials Convey Message of Comfort, Caution," *Courier-Journal*, 9 September 1996, A1, A10.
18 B. Radford, "Religion on the Roadside," *Free Inquiry* 22 (2001–02): 59.
19 Merk, "Roadside," A1, A10.
20 P. Maller, "I-43 Memorials Restored Again," *Milwaukee Journal Sentinel*, 24 April 2003, B4.
21 Ripley, "Crosses," 8.
22 Merk, "Roadside," A10.
23 Burbach, "Memorials," A1.
24 S. Miller, "Conspiracy Theories: Public Arguments as Coded Social Critiques—a Rhetorical Analysis of the TWA Flight 800 Conspiracy Theories," *Argumentation and Advocacy* 39 (2002): 40-56.
25 "The Web Sites of Flight 800," *U.S. News & World Report*, 5 August 1996, 8.
26 "Families of TWA flight 800."
27 A. Harmon, "Real Solace in a Virtual World," *New York Times*, 11 September 2002, G39.
28 "Cantor Families Memorial," 14 January 2004, http://www.cantorfamilies.com/cantor/jsp/index.jsp.
29 "Arrive Alive: Don't Drink & Drive," 14 January 2004, http://www.arrivealive.com.
30 "Noah Allen Gray." n.d., http://www.noahsmommy20.freeservers.com.
31 D. Hayes, "CompuTech of Kansas City, Mo., Offers Online Memorial Site," *Knight Ridder Tribune Business News*, 25 May 2002, 1.

32   B. Zelizer, "Reading the Past Against the Grain: The Shape of Memory Stud-ies," *Critical Studies in Mass Communication* 12 (1995): 214.

Chapter 6: View from the News Desk

33   Andrew Greeley, *God in Popular Culture* (Chicago: Thomas Moore, 1988), 124–29.
34   Hal Boedeker, "Death on the Airwaves," *Orlando Sentinel*, 9 May 2002.
35   Ibid.
36   Ibid.
37   Alessandra Stanley, "TV Watch: No Simple Rules for Dealing With Death," *New York Times*, 5 November 2003.

Chapter 7

1   In January of 2000, Aum changed its name to Aleph. Most in Japan, how-ever, continue to refer to the group as Aum. For the sake of simplicity, I have referred to the group as Aum throughout. "Aum Affair" is a translation of the Japanese *oumu jiken*. The term has come to be used frequently in Eng-lish language discussions of Aum and has the advantage, in its broadest meaning, of providing a way of conveniently referring to all the events related to Aum and the crimes committed by some of its members.
2   The "war period" refers to most of the 1930s up through 1945. From a Japanese or Asian perspective, the term World War II is misleading since Japan was, to one degree or another, at war throughout much of the 1930s.
3   These terms were used extensively throughout 1995 both in discussions of Aum and of the war.
4   Despite frequent criticisms of Japan for failing to reflect on the war years, it might well be argued that Japan has devoted more energy to reflection on the tragic dimensions of its past than the nations of many of its critics.
5   Murakami Shigeyoshi, *Japanese Religion in the Modern Period* (Tokyo: Uni-versity of Tokyo Press, 1980); and Helen Hardacre, *Shintō and the State, 1868–1988* (Princeton: Princeton University Press, 1989), provide histories of the relations of state and religion throughout the period. Fujitani Takashi, *Splendid Monarchy: Power and Pageantry in Modern Japan* (Berkeley: University of California Press, 1996), an analysis of how pageantry and other means were used to define and orchestrate the authority of the state and emperor, also contains valuable discussions of the role of the media. As far as possible, I will limit myself to citing key English language sources. Most of the works cited, particularly those relating to Aum, contain exten-sive references to sources in Japanese.
6   On the mass media in this period, see Katō Shūichi, "The Mass Media," in *Political Modernization in Japan and Turkey*, ed. Robert E. Ward and Dankwart A. Rustow (Princeton: Princeton University Press, 1994), 263–54; Gregory Kasza, *The State and the Mass Media, 1918–45* (Berkeley: University of Cali-fornia Press, 1988); and James Huffman, *Creating a Public: People and the Press in Meiji Japan* (Honolulu: University of Hawaii Press, 1997).
7   Katō, "Mass Media," 242. Japanese names are given throughout in the Japanese order, family name first and given name second.
8   On censorship, see Richard Mitchell, *Censorship in Imperial Japan* (Prince-ton: Princeton University Press, 1983), and Jay Rubin, *Injurious to Public Morals: Writers and the Meiji State* (Seattle: University of Washington Press,

1984). The importance of the topic of censorship, as well as the degree of attention the Japanese give it, is suggested by an examination of the articles related to media to be found in the Kodansha Encyclopedia of Japan. The article on censorship by Tamai Kensuke is given nearly as much space, three and a half pages, as the articles on mass communication, broadcasting, and newspapers combined (five pages, with considerable overlap in content).

9   Murakami, *Japanese Religion in the Modern Period*, 70–81, 95–109.

10   John Dower, *War Without Mercy: Race and Power in the Pacific War* (New York: Pantheon Books, 1986).

11   See the accounts of the experiences of Japanese during the war period collected in Haruko Taya Cook and Theodore F. Cook, *Japan at War: An Oral History* (New York: New Press, 1992).

12   Ian Buruma, *The Wages of Guilt: Memories of War in Germany and Japan* (New York: Farrar, Straus, Giroux, 1994), provides a very engaging account of reflection on the war in Japan as well as in Germany. Laura Hein and Mark Selden, eds., *Censoring History: Citizenship and Memory in Japan, Germany, and the United States* (Armonk, N.Y.: M. E. Sharpe, 2000) also contains relevant discussions.

13   For discussion of these issues, particularly in regard to American scholarship on Japan, see William LaFleur, "A Half-Dressed Emperor: Societal Self-Deception and Recent 'Japanokritik' in America," in *Self and Deception: A Cross-Cultural Philosophical Inquiry*, ed. Roger T. Ames and Wimal Dissanayake (West Futton: State University of New York Press, 1996), 263–86.

14   The essays collected in Tamaru Noriyoshi and David Reid, eds., *Religion in Japanese Culture: Where Living Traditions Meet a Changing World* (Tokyo: Kodansha International, 1996), discuss most of the points covered in this paragraph.

15   For an excellent overview of the conflicting evaluations of the mass media in Japan, see Susan Pharr, "Media and Politics in Japan: Historical and Contemporary Perspectives," in *Media and Politics in Japan*, ed. Susan J. Pharr and Ellis S. Krauss (Honolulu: University of Hawaii Press, 1996), 3–17.

16   Pharr, "Media and Politics," 13.

17   Ofer Feldman, *Politics and the News Media in Japan* (Ann Arbor: University of Michigan Press, 1993), 199.

18   For an analysis of media coverage of Sôka Gakkai in Japan, see Watanabe Takesato, "The Movement and the Japanese Media," in *Global Citizens: The Soka Gakkai Buddhist Movement in the World*, ed. David Machacek and Bryan Wilson (Oxford: Oxford University Press, 2000), 205–32.

19   See Ian Reader, "Consensus Shattered: Japanese Paradigm Shift and Moral Panic in the Post-Aum Era," *Nova Religio* 4 (2001): 225–34; and Watanabe Manabu, "Opposition to Aum and the Rise of the 'Anti-Cult' Movement," in *Religion and Social Crisis in Japan: Understanding Japanese Society through the Aum Affair*, ed. Robert J. Kisala and Mark Mullins (New York: Palgrave, 2001), 87–106.

20   For an excellent analysis of how the funeral of Emperor Shôwa reflected concerns relating to national and cultural identity, see Fujitani Takashi, "Electronic Pageantry and Japan's 'Symbolic Emperor,'" *Journal of Asian Studies* 51 (1992): 824–50.

21   A compelling account of how issues relating to the war were still alive at the time of the emperor's death can be found in Norma Field, *In the Realm of a Dying Emperor* (New York: Pantheon Books, 1991).

22   For an overview, see Mark Mullins, "The Legal and Political Fallout of the 'Aum Affair,'" in *Religion and Social Crisis in Japan*, ed. Kisala and Mullins, 71–86.

23   Ian Reader, *Religious Violence in Contemporary Japan: The Case of Aum Shinrikyō* (Richmond, UK: Curzon Press, 2000), provides an excellent study of Aum, and excellent studies of various responses to the Aum Affair in Japan may be found in *Religion and Social Crisis in Japan*, ed. Kisala and Mullins. Both works cite extensive Japanese sources.

24   I draw here and in the next two paragraphs on one of the more succinct and helpful accounts of Aum's early confrontations with society, Watanabe, "Opposition to Aum," as well as my own essay, "Aum and the Media: Lost in the Cosmos and the Need to Know," in *Religion and Social Crisis in Japan*, ed. Kisala and Mullins, 133–63, which is a slightly revised version of "Lost in the Cosmos and the Need to Know," *Monumenta Nipponica* 54 (1999): 217–46.

25   Parents were particularly concerned about being unable to contact their children who had renounced the world and entered into full-time residence at Aum facilities. Also at issue were Aum's demand that members renouncing the world donate all of their worldly possessions to the group.

26   For a discussion of Japanese laws regarding religious groups, including changes in the laws following the Aum Affair, see Mullins, "The Legal and Political Fallout of the Aum Affair," in *Religion and Social Crisis in Japan* (New York: Palgrave, 2001).

27   For a more detailed account of these events as well as an analysis of the symbolic role Sakamoto and his family would come to play later in the Aum Affair, see Gardner, "Aum and the Media," 136, 154–56.

28   Suggestions have been made that the police were reluctant to aggressively investigate Aum because of its status as a religious organization. The police, in other words, were reluctant to be viewed as persecuting religion as they had done in the war years (Reader, *Religious Violence,* 224). Their reluctance might also be linked to animosity toward Sakamoto, who had participated in several successful lawsuits against the police (Gardner, "Aum and the Media" 154–56).

29   Watanabe, "Opposition to Aum," 99–101.

30   An overview of the development of Aum's apocalyptic views as well as its conspiracy theories may be found in Reader, *Religious Violence,* 126–61.

31   The February 1995 issue of one of Aum's journals, *Vajrayāna Sacca*, was devoted to explaining how the mass media mind-controls the Japanese people. Questions can be raised, however, about whether Aum members or even the authors actually really believed what was published in the magazine. When I bought a copy of the magazine at an Aum bookstore in the spring of 1995, the two Aum clerks dismissed much of the claims made in the articles as silliness.

32   On the role of the mass media in creating new religious interests if not new religions themselves, see Shimazono Susumu, "Aspects of the Rebirth of Religion," *Religion in Japanese Culture: Where Living Traditions Meet a Changing World*, ed. Noriyoshi Tamaru and David Reid (Tokyo: Kodansha International, 1996), 181–82.

33   Gardner, "Aum and the Media," 138, includes a brief discussion of and reference to the relevant Japanese sources.

34   It is possible to argue here that the wartime legacy also had a role in TBS's actions. Though threatened with a lawsuit, TBS's decision not to broadcast the program concerning Aum may well have involved a desire not to be perceived as persecuting a religious group.

35   Helen Hardacre, "Aum Shinrikyō and the Japanese Media: The Pied Piper Meets the Lamb of God," *Institute Reports*, November 1995, provides an extensive analysis of the television coverage of Aum in Japan; see also Kisala and Mullins, *Religion and Social Crisis in Japan*, 8–9, and Ishii Kenji, "Aum Shinrikyō," in *Religion in Japanese Culture,* ed. Tamaru and Reid, 213–14. I draw here in particular on my essay "Aum and the Media," 133–41.

36   Though it gave extensive coverage of Aum, NHK's coverage was considerably less sensationalized than that of the private networks. Being state-funded, NHK is relatively free of the pressures generated by the competition for viewer ratings.

37   Aum members seem to have been drawing here on Ikeda Akira's defense of Aum in 1990.

38   Gardner, "Aum and the Media," 139. It should also be noted here that TBS thus confirmed Aum's claims that the mass media were attempting to mind-control people through the use of subliminal messages.

39   For a discussion of the influence of the American anticult movement on anticult activists in Japan, see Watanabe, "Opposition to Aum."

40   Gardner, "Aum and the Media," 138.

41   For more on this issue and how it related to the trials of Aum members, see Watanabe, "Opposition to Aum."

42   Gardner, "Aum and the Media," 139.

43   Richard Gardner, "'The Blessing of Living in a Country Where There Are Senryū!': Humor in the Response to Aum Shinrikyō," *Asian Folklore Studies* 50 (2002): 35–75.

44   *Asahi shinbun*, April 11. A critique of the wide shows' coverage of Aum.

45   *Yomiuri shinbun*, April 15. Criticism of the television stations for paying Aum members to appear.

46   *Yomiuri shinbun*, April 29. Aum "scientists" had developed electronic headgear meant to attune the wearer's brain waves to those of Asahara. Such headgear were, of course, often taken as evidence of the group's mind-control techniques. Here it is television mind-controlling the Japanese populace.

47   *Yomiuri shinbun*, May 15. Former Aum members were in great demand because their appearance in programs was thought to boost ratings.

48   See Gardner, "Lost in the Cosmos," and "Aum and the Media," which include extensive bibliographies of Japanese language discussions of the films as well as of reactions to Aum in Japan.

49   Gardner, "Aum and the Media," 42.

50   Shortly before this it had finally been revealed that TBS had previewed to Aum members a documentary about Aum and then decided not to air it after Aum threatened legal action. In the program, the lawyer Sakamoto voiced criticism of Aum. Though Sakamoto's disappearance occurred shortly after this, TBS did not report Aum's viewing of the program to police. The spring of 1996 was, in short, a time when television networks were very sensitive about coverage of Aum.

51   Mori shot more than one hundred and fifty hours of film over the course of a year or so.

52   Mori's insistence on not taking any steps to hide the identity of Aum members led to delays in getting the cooperation of Aum members in making the film. In its coverage, the film is thus limited to members who were not concerned that their identities be known.

53   I summarize here a longer analysis appearing in my "A Revisited," *Monumenta Nipponica* 57 (2002): 339–48.

54   Both films were finally released in DVD format in July of 2003. The films come, however, with a warning: the distributor is not to be held responsible for any adverse influence the films may have on the viewer.

55   Though the film is not named, the rumor that A was produced by Aum is reported as fact in Daniel Métraux, *Aum Shinrikyo and Japanese Youth* (New York: University Press of America, 1999). Relying on Metraux, two non-Japanese journalists (who knew little if any Japanese) told me they thought the movie was produced by Aum and was simply Aum propaganda. This illustrates the dangers of forming judgments about Japan by relying on works making scant use of Japanese sources, though in this case coverage of the film even in the English language newspapers in Japan should have set the matter straight.

56   A fuller argument may be found in my "Lost in the Cosmos."

57   For a discussion of the Japanese sources here, see Gardner, "Aum and the Media," 138.

58   Discussions of the criticism directed at scholars of religion can be found in Watanabe, "Opposition to Aum" as well as in Ian Reader, "Scholarship, Aum Shinrikyō, and Integrity," *Nova Religio* 3 (2000): 368–82, and "Consensus Shattered: Japanese Paradigm Shift and Moral Panic in the Post-Aum Era," *Nova Religio* 4 (2001): 225–34. Ian Reader, "Identity, Nihonjinron, and Academic Dishonesty," *Monumenta Nipponica* 58 (2003): 103–16, offers a broader discussion of academic integrity in Japan that relates to issues raised concerning Aum and scholars of religion.

59   Gardner, "Aum and the Media," 138.

60   For a discussion of Kaji and related views, see Matsudo Yukio, "Back to Invented Tradition: A Nativist Response to a National Crisis," in *Religion and Social Crisis in Japan*, ed. Kisala and Mullins, 163–78.

61   Gardner, "Aum and the Media," 138.

62   Richard A. Gardner, Review of *A Poisonous Cocktail?*, by Ian Reader, *Monumenta Nipponica* 51 (1996): 402–5.

63   Richard A. Gardner, Review of *Destroying the World to Save It*, by Robert J. Lifton, *Monumenta Nipponica* 56 (2001): 125–28.

Chapter 8

1   For detailed descriptions of this chant/song preaching style, see Howard Dorgan, *Giving Glory to God in Appalachia* (Knoxville: University of Tennessee Press, 1987), 55–85. See also Bruce A. Rosenberg, *The Art of the American Folk Preacher* (New York: Oxford University Press, 1970).

2   For a discussion of some of the preaching of the "First Great Awakening," see John Sparks, *The Roots of Appalachian Christianity* (Lexington: University Press of Kentucky, 2001), 15–33. For additional detail concerning the "Great Western Revival," see Deborah McCauley, *Appalachian Mountain Religion, a History* (Urbana: University of Illinois Press, 1995), 190–95.

3   The title of Jack Weller's demeaning study of the West Virginia natives he worked among while trying to build a Presbyterian mission among Pente-

costal Holiness and "Old-Time" Baptists. See Jack Weller, *Yesterday's People: Life in Contemporary Appalachia* (Lexington: University of Kentucky Press, 1965).

4   McCauley, *Appalachian Mountain Religion*, 476–77.

5   Discussion with the author, September 2, 2001, at the annual association meeting of the Elkhorn Primitive Baptist Association, Pilgrim's Rest Church, Jewell Ridge, Virginia. Elder Davis is moderator of Elkhorn Association, one of the four Primitive Baptist Universalist clusters in Central Appalachia. His assistance was very helpful during my research for and writing of *In the Hands of a Happy God: The "No-Hellers" of Central Appalachia* (Knoxville: University of Tennessee Press, 1997).

6   See David L. Kimbrough, *Taking Up Serpents* (Chapel Hill: University of North Carolina Press, 1995), 29.

7   Thomas Burton, *Serpent Handling Believers* (Knoxville: University of Tennessee Press, 1991; Kimbrough, *Taking up Serpents*; Fred Brown and Jeanne McDonald, *The Serpent Handlers: Three Families and Their Faith* (Winston-Salem, N.C.: John E. Blair, Publisher, 2000).

8   See my account of this debate in my work, *The Old Regular Baptists of Central Appalachia: Brothers and Sisters in Hope* (Knoxville: University of Tennessee Press, 1989), 147–50.

9   Burton, *Serpent Handling*, 32–60.

10   See Howard Dorgan, "Old Time Baptists of Central Appalachia," in *Christianity in Appalachia: Profiles in Regional Pluralism*, ed. Bill J. Leonard (Knoxville: University of Tennessee Press, 1999), 117–37.

11   For a more complete discussion of Old Regular Baptist family memorials and a detailed examination of the Smith family memorial, see Howard Dorgan, *Old Regular Baptists*, 88–102.

Chapter 9

1   For an excellent exposition of this point in relation to the popular religion of Mexico, see Jean Meyer, *La Cristiada* (Mexico: Siglo Veintiuno Editores, 1974), 316–23.

2   "Culture" is used here as all those solutions that a group finds in order to survive its natural and social situation. It is the complete world vision—norms, values, and rituals—of a group. Spain and Mexico had very highly developed cultures at the time of the clash.

3   Tepeyac is the hill north of Mexico City where the sanctuary of Tonantzin (which means our Mother)—the female aspect of the deity—was located. It was one of the most sacred pilgrimage sites of the Americas. Bernardino de Sahagún, *Historia general de las cosas de Nueva España* (Mexico, written in mid-1500s), 3:352.

4   Mestizo is the Spanish word for a person born from parents of different races. In contemporary Latin America it is acquiring a positive meaning, and the arrival of Columbus is celebrated as the day of la raza (the race), meaning the new race formed of Europe and Native America. There is no English translation of this concept, since the English term "half-breed" (a social rather than a biological term) is very derogatory and would have a completely different meaning.

5   For the first twelve missionaries who came to Mexico, "New World" was a theological term indicating the place where the new Christianity was now to emerge. It would not be simply a continuation of the Christianity of

Europe, but a new, evangelical Christianity. Silvio Arturo Zavala, *Recuerdo de Vasco de Quiroga* (Mexico: Editorial Porrua, 1965); Jacques Lafaye, *Quetzalcoatl et Guadalupe* (Paris: Gallimard, 1974), 52–67.

6   Some of the Native American cultures were very well-developed and in many ways superior to those of the Europe of the sixteenth century. For a good description of this, see Miguel León-Portilla, *Aztec Thought and Culture* (Norman: University of Oklahoma Press, 1963), esp. 134–76.

7   Octavio Paz, *The Labyrinth of Solitude* (New York: Penguin, 1961), 93–96.

8   León-Portilla, *Aztec Thought*, 74–79.

9   See Jacques Soustelle, *La vie quotidienne des Aztèques à la veille de la conquête espagnole* (Paris: Hachette 1955).

10   For a good description of the development of the Guadalupe tradition, see Lafaye, *Quetzalcoatl et Guadalupe*, 281–396.

11   León-Portilla, *Aztec Thought*, 102.

12   For a good example of a scholar who has been able to penetrate the historical consciousness alive in the folklore of the people, see Nathan Wachtel, *La vision des vainçus* (Paris: Gallimard, 1971); see also, Rodolfo Acuña, *Occupied America* (New York: Harper & Row, 1981).

13   See Pope Paul VI, *Evangelii Nuntiandi* (8 December 1975), sections 48 (on popular piety) and 63 (on adaptation and fidelity in expression). See also Meyer, *La Cristiada*, 307, which brings out the false way that North American and European missionaries have judged Mexican Catholicism.

14   See Meyer, *La Cristiada*, 275–323.

Chapter 10

1   John Rivera, "Gazing into the Spiritual Future: Expectations in an Age of Information and Technology," *Sun Baltimore*, 12 March 2000, 2A.

2   G. Bishop, "The Religious Worldview and American Beliefs About Human Origins," *Public Perspective* 9 (1998): 39–44.

3   DYG Inc., "Poll: Public Wants Evolution, Not Creationism, in Science Class," *U.S. Newswire*, 10 March 2000.

4   S. Benen, "Science Test," *Church & State* 53 (2000): 8–12, 14.

5   Rivera, "Gazing," 2A.

6   Mark E. Cohen, *The Canonical Lamentations of Ancient Mesopotamia* (Potomac, Md.: Capital Decisions Limited, 1988).

7   Thomas Aquinas, *Summa contra Gentiles* 3.66–67.

8   Nomanul Haq, "Moments in the Islamic Recasting of the Greek Legacy: Exploring the Question of Science and Theism," in *God, Life, and the Cosmos: Christian and Islamic Perspectives*, ed. T. Peters, M. Iqbal, and S. N. Haq (Burlington, Vt.: Ashgate Publishing, 2002), 153–71; Seyyed H. Nasr, "Islamic Cosmology: Basic Tenets and Implications, Yesterday and Today," *Science and Religion in Search of Cosmic Purpose*, ed. J. F. Haught (Washington, D.C.: Georgetown University Press, 2000), 42–57.

9   David C. Lindberg, *The Beginnings of Western Science: The European Scientific Tradition in Philosophical, Religious, and Institutional Context, 600 B.C. to A.D. 1450* (Chicago: University of Chicago Press, 1992), 242.

10   See D. C. Goodman, ed. *Science and Religion: From Conflict to Conversation* (New York: Paulist Press, 1995), 12–49, 131–36.

11   Ian Barbour, *Religion and Science: Historical and Contemporary Issues* (San Francisco: HarperSanFrancisco, 1997), 45–47.

12   "Four Letters from Sir Isaac Newton to Doctor Bentley," in *Science and Religious Belief: 1600–1900*, ed. D. C. Goodman (Bristol: John Wright & Sons, 1973), 131–36.

13   See Frank Manuel, *The Religion of Isaac Newton* (Oxford: Clarendon Press, 1974); Barbour, *Religion and Science*, 23.

14   J. J. O'Connor and E. F. Robertson, *Robert Boyle*, January 2000, http:// www-groups.dcs.st-and.ac.uk/~history/Mathematicians/Boyle.html and http:// www-gap.dcs.st-and.ac.uk/~history/Mathematicians/Boyle.html.

15   Michael J. Buckley, "The Newtonian Settlement and the Origins of Atheism," in *Physics, Philosophy, and Theology: A Common Quest for Understanding*, ed. R. J. Russell, W. R. Stoeger, and G. V. Coyne (Vatican City: Vatican Observatory, 1988), 81–102.

16   Barbour, *Religion and Science*, 184–87.

17   Louis Jacobs, *The Book of Jewish Belief* (Springfield, N.J.: Behrman House, 1984).

18   Ibid., 110. Also see the detailed explanation of Midrash and extensive Midrash bibliography provided by the hebrew Union College, Jewish Institute of Religion at http://www.huc.edu/midrash/intro.html.

19   Barbour, *Religion and Science,* 113, 158–59.

20   Ibid., 306–7.

21   Sayyed Nasr, "What is the Koran?" 14 November 2003, http://www.islamamerica.org/articles.cfm?article_id=32.

22   Nomanul Haq, "Islam and Ecology: Toward Retrieval and Reconstruction,"*Dædalus* 130, no. 4 (2001): 141–78.

23   Nasr, "What is the Koran?"

24   Jacobs, *Book of Jewish Belief,* 53.

25   Barbour, *Religion and Science*, 157.

26   John F. Haught, *Science & Religion: From Conflict to Conversation* (New York: Paulist Press, 1995), 22.

27   Richard H. Bube, *Putting it All Together: Seven Patterns for Relating Science and Christian Faith* (Lanham.: University Press of America, 1995).

28   Barbour, *Religion and Science*, 107–10.

29   See Ian Barbour, "Ways of Relating Science and Theology," in *Physics, Philosophy, and Theology: A Common Quest for Understanding*, ed. R. J. Russell, W. R. Stoeger, S.J., and G. V. Coyne, S.J. (Vatican City: Vatican Observatory, 1988), 21–48; Barbour, *Religion and Science*; Haught, *Science and Religion*; Bube, *Putting it All Together*; Ted Peters, "Theology and Natural Science," in *The Modern Theologians*, 2nd ed. ed. D. Ford (Oxford: Blackwell, 1997), 649–68.

30   Haught, *Science and Religion*, 9–12.

31   William A. Dembski, "The Intelligent Design Movement," in *An Evolving Dialogue: Theological and Scientific Perspectives on Evolution*, ed. J. B. Miller (Harrisburg: Trinity Press International, 2001), 439–44.

32   Barbour, *Religion and Science*, 78–79.

33   Henry M. Morris, ed., *Scientific Creationism* (Green Forest, Ark.: Master Books, 1985).

34   Philip Kitcher, *Abusing Science: The Case Against Creationism* (Cambridge: MIT Press, 1982).

35   Langdon Gilkey, "Theories in Science and Religion," in *Religion and the Natural Sciences: The Range of Engagement*, ed. J. Huchingson (Fort Worth: Harcourt Brace Jovanovich College Publishers, 1993), 61–65.

36   Haught, *Science and Religion*, 15.

37   John Paul II, "Message," in *Physics, Philosophy, and Theology: A Common Quest for Understanding*, ed. R. J. Russell, W. R. Stoeger, and G. V. Coyne (Vatican City: Vatican Observatory, 1988), 1–15.

38   Barbour, *Religion and Science*, 18–105.

39   See Norma J. Emerton, "Arguments for the Existence of God From Nature and Science," in *Science and Theology: Questions at the Interface*, ed. M. Rae, H. Regan, and J. Stenhouse (Grand Rapids: Eerdmans, 1994), 72–86.

40   In *Science and Relgious Belief: 1600–1900*, ed. D. C. Goodman (Bristol: John Wright & Sons, 1973), 12–17.

41   Ibid, 17–27.

42   Nasr, "Islamic Cosmology," 53.

43   Professors at local colleges and universities may provide the most immediate views on issues that intersect religion and science. Public affairs and media outreach offices are usually able to identify the scholars who have agreed to speak to reporters on this topic.

      Experts at the various religion-science centers on the North American continent are well prepared to respond to media requests. Among these is the Center for Theology and the Natural Sciences (CTNS) in Berkeley, California (http://www.ctns.org/), which has been "building bridges" between religion and science for more than twenty years through an expanding program that includes religion-science courses at the graduate and seminary level, public lectures, symposia, course development programs, and conferences around the world. CTNS can provide information about the series of biennial conferences cosponsored with the Vatican Observatory during which theologians, natural scientists, and philosophers shared their research on specific topics and explored possible ways in which God's action in the world can be plausibly articulated.

      Other excellent sources of information on religion-science issues include the Metanexus Institute (http://www.metanexus.net/index.asp) located in Philadelphia, Pennsylvania, which advances the constructive engagement of religion and science through an on-line forum, lectures, funding of local initiatives, and conferences. The Center for Islam and Science (http://www.cis-ca.org/), based in Sherwood Park, Alberta, Canada, provides an on-line forum, publishes biannually the scholarly journal *Islam & Science*, and sponsors conferences with the conviction that there is underlying unity of all knowledge based on the concept *Tawhid*, the unity of God. The Columbia University Center for the Study of Science and Religion (http://www.columbia.edu/cu/cssr/) in New York City has sponsored lectures, conferences, and courses that bring religionists and scientists together to share their perspective on issues of mutual concern. For several years, the Zygon Center for Religion and Science (http://zygoncenter.org/), formerly the Chicago Center for Religion and Science, has been sponsoring lectures, conferences, and an "Epic of Creation" course open to seminarians, university students, and the public.

      The John Templeton Foundation (http://www.templeton.org/), based in Radnor, Pennsylvania, also welcomes media interest in constructive efforts to relate religion and science. The Foundation has aided religion-science course development at colleges and universities around the world, sponsored international conferences, and funded a variety of initiatives aimed at pursuing new spiritual and theological insights on issues from cosmology to health care.

For more in-depth understanding of issues, at least four scholarly journals can be helpful to reporters. They are *Islam & Science*, published biannually by the Center for Islam and Science; *Perspectives on Science and Christian Faith*, published quarterly on behalf of the American Scientific Affiliation; *Theology & Science*, published biannually by the Center for Theology and the Natural Sciences; and *Zygon: Journal of Religion & Science*, published quarterly on behalf of the Institute for Religion in an Age of Science and the Center for Advanced Study in Religion and Science.

Library shelves are burgeoning with monographs that cover the gamut from general to detailed examinations of religion and science in relation to one another. For an introduction to the religion-science relationship, see John F. Haught's readable *Science and Religion: From Conflict to Conversation* (New York: Paulist Press, 1995) and Ian Barbour's more in-depth *Religion and Science: Historical and Contemporary Issues* (London: SMC Press, 1998).

Chapter 10: View from the News Desk

1   "Catholics Gaze Toward Heavens; Mars Brings Into Focus Church's Longstanding Battle to Reverse Galileo Error," *Associated Press*, 25 August 2003.
2   Edith M. Lederer, "United Nations Delays Treaty on Human Cloning, a Setback for U.S. Effort to Ban it," *Associated Press*, 6 November 2003.
3   See Scott Gold, "Religion, Science May Turn a Page Over Textbook in Texas," *Los Angeles Times*, 6 November 2003, 11.
4   Gold, "Religion."

Chapter 11

1   See Lloyd Baugh, *Imaging the Divine: Jesus and Christ-Figures in Film* (Kansas City, Mo.: Sheed & Ward, 1997).
2   For further information on the World Council of Churches, see D. Gill, ed., *Gathered for Life: Official report, VI Assembly, World Council of Churches, Vancouver, Canada, 1983* (Geneva: WCC, 1983).
3   For a readily available, edited summary of all relevant statements from 1935 to 1971, see Appendix I of the *Guide to the Training of Future Priests Concerning the Instruments of Social Communication* (Pontifical Council, 1986).
4   R. F. Trisco, "Vatican Council II," in *New Catholic Encyclopedia* (New York: McGraw-Hill, 1967), 565.
5   Richard P. McBrien, *Catholicism*, 2 vols. (Minneapolis: Winston Press, 1980), 1180–81; italics in original.
6   Ibid., 1183–84; italics in original.
7   Blake, *Afterimage*, 15–21.
8   Paul A. Soukup, "Church Documents and the Media." *Concilium: revue internationale de theologie* (December 1993): 77.

Conclusion

1   Henry James, *Varieties of Religious Experience* (Lakewood, Colo.: Collier, 1961), 39.
2   Poll by Mitofsky International and Edison Media Research, conducted for *Religion & Ethics Newsweekly* and *U.S. News & World Report,* cited in "Exploring Religious America," booklet accompanying videotape published by Public Broadcasting Corp. Channel 13, WNET, New York, 2002, p. 12.

3   Mark Silk, *Unsecular Media: Making News of Religion in America* (Chicago: University of Illinois Press, 1995).
4   Gustav Niebuhr, "Megachurches: The Gospels of Management; The Minister as Marketer: Learning from Business," *New York Times*, 18 April 1995, 1.

Bibliography

Abdel Rahman, A., L. Abdel Mageed, and N. Kamel. *Communicator in the Egyptian Press*. Cairo: School of Mass Communication Press, 1992.

Abdo, Geneive. "Religious Voting Blocs Shift Allegiances." *Chicago Tribune*, 17 December 2004.

Acuña, Rodolfo. *Occupied America*. New York: Harper & Row, 1981.

Alexander, Jeffrey. "Citizen and Enemy as Symbolic Classification: On the Polarizing Discourse of Civil Society." *Cultivating Differences: Symbolic Boundaries and the Making of Inequality*. Ed. Michele Lamont and Marcel Fournier, 289–308. Chicago: University of Chicago Press, 1992.

Alley, Robert S. *So Help Me God: Religion and the Presidency, Wilson to Nixon*. Richmond: John Knox Press, 1972.

Alterman, J. *New Media, New Politics? From Satellite Television to the Internet in the Arab World*. Washington, D.C.: Washington Institute for Near East Policy, 1998.

Amanat, Abbas, and Magnus T. Bernhardsson. "The Middle East in Modern American Popular Prophetic Belief." *Imagining the End: Visions of the Apocalypse from the Ancient Middle East to Modern America*. London: I. B. Tauris Publishers, 2002.

Amin, H. Y. "Freedom as a Value in Arab Media: Perceptions and Attitudes Among Journalists." *Political Communication* 19 (2002): 125–35.

Anderson, Benedict. *Imagined Communities*. London: Verso, 1983.

Antoun, Richard T. *Understanding Fundamentalism: Christian, Islamic and Jewish Movements*. Walnut Creek, Calif.: Altamira Press, 2001.

Aquinas, Thomas. *Summa Contra Gentiles*. Ed. R. Busa. Opera Omnia #005. CD-ROM. Milano: Editoria Elettronica Editel, 1992.

Ariel, Yaacov. *Philosemites or Antisemites? Evangelical Christian Attitudes Toward Jews, Judaism, and the State of Israel.* Jerusalem: Hebrew University of Jerusalem, 2002.

Ariès, Philippe. *Western Attitudes Toward Death from the Middle Ages to the Present.* Trans. Patricia M. Ranum. Baltimore: Johns Hopkins University Press, 1974.

Armstrong, Karen. *The Battle for God.* New York: Ballantine Books, 2000.

Astor, David. "Cal Thomas in Select 500 Club for Columnists." *Editor and Publisher* 8 (May 1999): 44.

"Attacks on the Press in 2001." *Committee to Protect Journalists.* 3 January 2004. http://www.cpj.org/attacks0/mideast01.html.

Azet, M. F. *News Agencies in the Arab World.* Jeddah: The Sun Rise for Publication, Distribution and Print, 1992.

Bacon, Francis. *The Advancement of Learning.* Ed. M. Kiernan. New York: Oxford University Press, 2000.

Badaracco, Claire. "A Utopian on Main Street." *Rethinking Media, Religion and Culture.* Ed. Stewart Hoover and Knut Lundby, 263–82. Thousand Oaks, Calif.: Sage, 1997.

Bal, Meike. *The Practice of Cultural Analysis: Exposing Interdisciplinary Interpretation.* Palo Alto: Stanford University Press, 1999.

———. *Quoting Caravaggio.* Chicago: University of Chicago Press, 1999.

Barbour, Ian. *Religion and Science: Historical and Contemporary Issues.* San Francisco: HarperSanFrancisco, 1997.

———. "Ways of Relating Science and Theology." *Physics, Philosophy, and Theology: A Common Quest for Understanding.* Ed. R. J. Russell, W. R. Stoeger, S.J., and G. V. Coyne, S.J., 21–48. Vatican City State: Vatican Observatory: 1988.

Baugh, Lloyd. *Imaging the Divine: Jesus and Christ-Figures in Film.* Kansas City, Mo.: Sheed & Ward, 1997.

Beit-Hallahmi, Benjamin. "Rebirth and Death: The Violent Potential of Apocalyptic Dreams." *The Psychology of Terrorism*, vol. 3. Ed. Chris E. Stout, 163–89. Westport, Conn.: Praeger, 2002.

Bellah, Robert. *The Broken Covenant: American Civil Religion in a Time of Trial.* Chicago: University of Chicago Press, 1992.

———. "Religion and the Shape of National Culture." *America*, 31 July 1999, 10.

Belluck, P. "Science Expands, Religion Contracts." *New York Times*, 13 August 1999, 4.1.

Benen, S. "Science Test." *Church & State* 53 (2000): 8–12, 14.

Bishop, G. "The Religious Worldview and American Beliefs About Human Origins." *Public Perspective* 9 (1998): 39–44.

Blake, Richard A. *Afterimage: The Indelible Catholic Imagination of Six American Filmmakers.* Chicago: Loyola University Press, 2000.

Blanshard, Paul. *American Freedom and Catholic Power.* Boston: Beacon Press, 1949.

Bloch, Ruth H. *Visionary Republic: Millennial Themes in American Thought, 1756–1800.* New York: Cambridge University Press, 1985.

Bloom, Harold. *The American Religion.* New York: Simon & Schuster, 1992.

Bloomfield, Arthur. *Before the Last Battle: Armageddon.* Minneapolis: Bethany House Publishers, 1971.

Boyer, Paul. "John Darby Meets Saddam Hussein: Foreign Policy Meets Bible Prophecy." *Chronicle of Higher Education*, 14 February 2003, B10–11.

———. "The Middle East in Modern American Popular Belief." *Imagining the End: Visions of the Apocalypse from the Ancient Middle East to Modern America.* Ed. Abbas Amanat and Magnus T. Bernhardsson, 312–35. London: I. B. Tauris, 2002.

————. *When Time Shall Be No More: Prophecy Belief in Modern American Culture.* Cambridge, Mass.: Harvard University Press, 1992.

Brackett, D. W. *Holy Terror: Armageddon in Tokyo.* New York and Tokyo: Weatherhill, 1996.

Bramadat, Paul A. *The Church on the World's Turf: An Evangelical Christian Group at a Secular University.* New York: Oxford University Press, 2000.

Brown, Fred, and Jeanne McDonald. *The Serpent Handlers: Three Families and Their Faith.* Winston-Salem: John E. Blair, Publisher, 2000.

Bruce, Steve. *Fundamentalism.* Cambridge, UK: Polity, 2000.

Bube, Richard H. *Putting It All Together: Seven Patterns for Relating Science and Christian Faith.* Lanham, Md.: University Press of America, 1995.

Buckley, Michael J. "The Newtonian Settlement and the Origins of Atheism." *Physics, Philosophy, and Theology: A Common Quest for Understanding.* Ed. R. J. Russell, W. R. Stoeger, and G. V. Coyne, 81–102. Vatican City: Vatican Observatory, 1988.

Buckna, David. "The Pop Gospel." *Calgary Herald,* 19 July 2003.

Buescher, John B. "The Buddha's Conventional and Ultimate Tooth." *Changing Minds: Contributions to the Study of Buddhism and Tibet in Honor of Jeffrey Hopkins.* Ed. Guy Newland, 19–48. Ithaca: Snow Lion Press: 2001.

Buote, B. "Roadside Memorials Pay Tribute to Lost Lives." *Boston Globe,* 4 August 2002, 1.

Burbach, C. "Memorials Say: We Won't Forget." *Omaha World Herald,* 25 May 2002, A1.

Burton, Thomas. *Serpent-Handling Believers.* Knoxville: University of Tennessee Press, 1991.

Buruma, Ian. *The Wages of Guilt: Memories of War in Germany and Japan.* New York: Farrar, Straus, Giroux, 1994.

Byron, William J. "Ten Building Blocks of Catholic Social Teaching." *America,* 31 October 1998, 10–11.

Caldwell, Deborah. "George Bush's Theology: Does the President Believe He Has a Divine Mandate?" *National Catholic Reporter,* 21 February 2003.

Callahan, Daniel, ed. *Generation of the Third Eye.* New York: Sheed & Ward, 1965.

Carter, Stephen L. *The Culture of Disbelief: How American Law and Politics Trivialize Religious Devotion.* New York: Basic Books, 1993.

"Catholics Gaze Toward Heavens; Mars Brings into Focus Church's Longstanding Battle to Reverse Galileo Error." Associated Press, 25 August 2003.

Chu, Pauline. "Media Distorts Meaning of Islamic Faith." 18 September 2002. http://www.dailytexanonline.

Church, Forrest. *The American Creed: A Biography of the Declaration of Independence.* New York: St. Martin's Griffin, 2002.

Cohen, Mark E. *The Canonical Lamentations of Ancient Mesopotamia.* Potomac, Md: Capital Decisions Limited, 1988.

Coleman, Louis. Personal Interview with Peter Smith. 1 May 2003.

Cook, Haruko Taya, and Theodore F. Cook. *Japan at War: An Oral History.* New York: New Press, 1992.

Cooper, Richard T. "General Casts War in Religious Terms." *New York Times,* 16 October 2003.

Cooperman, Alan. "Bush's Remark About God Assailed." *Washington Post,* 22 November 2003, A06.

Cranberg, G., M. Brindley, and K. Putnam. "More Newspapers are Charging Readers for Life and Death News." *ASNE Bulletin* (May–June 1992): 16–18.

Dart, John. *Deities and Deadlines*, First Amendment Center, 1995, 1998.

Davidson, James W. *The Logic of Millennial Thought: Eighteenth-Century New England.* New Haven: Yale University Press, 1977.

Dean, William. *The American Spiritual Culture and the Invention of Jazz, Football and the Movies.* New York: Continuum Press, 2003.

De Beer, A., and J. Merrill, eds. *Global Journalism: Topical Issues and Media Systems.* New York: Pearson Education, Inc., 2004.

Dembski, William. A. "The Intelligent Design Movement." *An Evolving Dialogue: Theological and Scientific Perspectives on Evolution.* Ed. J. B. Miller, 439–44. Harrisburg: Trinity Press International, 2001.

Demereth, N. J. *Crossing the Gods: World Religions and Worldly Politics.* New Brunswick: Rutgers University Press, 2001.

Dionne, E. J. *Why Americans Hate Politics.* New York: Simon & Schuster, 1992.

Dobson, Ed, Ed Hindson, and Jerry Falwell. *The Fundamentalist Phenomenon: The Resurgence of Conservative Christianity,* 2nd ed. Grand Rapids: Baker Book House, 1986.

Dodin, Thierry, and Heinz Rather, eds. *Imagining Tibet: Perceptions, Projections and Fantasies.* Boston: Wisdom Publications, 2001.

Dorgan, Howard. *The Airwaves of Zion.* Knoxville: University of Tennessee Press, 1993.

———. *Giving Glory to God in Appalachia.* Knoxville: University of Tennessee Press, 1987.

———. *In the Hands of a Happy God: The "No-Hellers" of Central Appalachia.* Knoxville: University of Tennessee Press, 1997.

———. *The Old Regular Baptists of Central Appalachia: Brothers and Sisters in Hope.* Knoxville: University of Tennessee Press, 1989.

———. "Old Time Baptists of Central Appalachia." *Christianity in Appalachia: Profiles in Regional Pluralism.* Ed. Bill J. Leonard, 117–37. Knoxville: University of Tennessee Press, 1999.

Dower, John W. *War Without Mercy: Race and Power in the Pacific War.* New York: Pantheon Books, 1986.

Draper, John W. *History of the Conflict Between Religion and Science.* New York: D. Appleton & Company, 1874.

Duty, Guy. *Escape from the Coming Tribulation.* Minneapolis: Bethany Fellowship, 1975.

Dyer, Charles. and Angela Elwell Hunt. *The Rise of Babylon: Sign of the End Times.* Wheaton: Tyndale House Publishers, 1991.

DYG Inc. "Poll: Public Wants Evolution, Not Creationism, in Science Class." *U.S. Newswire,* 10 March 2000.

Eck, Diana L. *A New Religious America.* San Francisco: Harper, 2001.

Eckholm, Erik. "A Quiet Roar: China's Leadership Feels Threatened by a Sect Seeking Peace." *New York Times,* 4 November 1999, A10.

El Calamawy, S. "The Impact of Tradition on the Development of Modern Arabic Literature." *Arab and American Cultures.* Ed. G. H. Atieh, 47–50. Washington, D.C.: American Enterprise Institute for Public Policy Research, 1977.

Eliade, Mircea. *The Encyclopedia of Religion.* New York: Macmillan, 1987.

el-Nawawy, M., and A. Iskandar. *Al-Jazeera: The Story of the Network That Is Rattling Governments and Redefining Modern Journalism.* Boulder: Westview, 2003.

Elshtain, Jean Bethke. "Against Liberal Monism." *Dædalus: Journal of the American Academy of Arts & Sciences* 132, no. 3 (2003): 78–79.

Emerton, Norma. "Arguments for the Existence of God From Nature and Science." *Science and Theology: Questions at the Interface.* Ed. M. Rae, H. Regan, and J. Stenhouse, 72–86. Grand Rapids: Eerdmans, 1994.

Ettema, James S., and Theodore L. Glasser. "Narrative Form and Moral Force: The Realization of Innocence and Guilt Through Investigative Journalism." *Journal of Communications* 383 (1998): 11.

Evans, Michael D. *Beyond Iraq: The Next Move—Ancient Prophecy and Modern Day Conspiracy Collide.* Lakeland, Fla.: White Stone Press, 2003.

Feldman, Ofer. *Politics and the News Media in Japan.* Ann Arbor: University of Michigan Press, 1993.

Field, Norma. *In the Realm of a Dying Emperor.* New York: Pantheon Books, 1991.

Findley, Paul. *Silent No More: Confronting America's False Images of Islam.* Beltsville, Md.: Amana Publications, 2001.

Finney, Joseph C. *Culture Change, Mental Health, and Poverty.* Lexington: University of Kentucky Press, 1969.

Ford, Robert. *Captured in Tibet.* London: Harrap, 1957.

Frankl, Razelle. "Transformation of Televangelism: Repackaging Christian Family Values." *Media, Culture, and the Religious Right.* Ed. Linda Kintz and Julia Lesage, 163–89. Minneapolis: University of Minnesota Press, 1998.

Friends of Falun Gong v. Pacific Culture Enterprise, Inc., 02-CV-4482 CBA. U.S. District Ct. for the Eastern District of New York, 2003.

Froese, Arno. "The Comforter." *Midnight Call,* February 2004.

Fujitani, Takashi. "Electronic Pageantry and Japan's 'Symbolic Emperor.'" *Journal of Asian Studies* 51 (1992): 824–50.

———. *Splendid Monarchy: Power and Pageantry in Modern Japan.* Berkeley: University of California Press, 1996.

Fulton, R., and G. Owen. "Death and Society in Twentieth Century America." *Omega* 18 (1987–88): 379–95.

Gaines, Jane M., and Michael Renov, eds. *Collecting Visible Evidence.* Minneapolis: University of Minnesota Press, 1999.

Galilei, Galileo. "To the Most Serene Grand Duchess Mother." *Science and Religious Belief: 1600–1900.* Ed. D. C. Goodman, 29–49. Bristol: John Wright & Sons, 1973.

Gans, Herbert. *Deciding What's News.* New York: Random House, 1979.

Gardner, Richard A. "Aum and the Media: Lost in the Cosmos and the Need to Know." *Religion and Social Crisis in Japan: Understanding Japanese Society through the Aum Affair.* Ed. Robert J. Kisala and Mark R. Mullins, 133–63. New York: Palgrave, 2001.

———. "'The Blessing of Living in a Country Where There Are Senryû!': Humor in the Response to Aum Shinrikyô." *Asian Folklore Studies* 50 (2002): 35–75.

———. "Lost in the Cosmos and the Need to Know." *Monumenta Nipponica* 54 (1999): 217–46.

———. "Revistited," *Monumenta Nipponica* 57 (2002): 339–48.

———. Review of *A Poisonous Cocktail?* by Ian Reader. *Monumenta Nipponica* 51(1996): 402–5.

———. Review of *Destroying the World to Save It* by Robert J. Lifon. *Monumenta Nipponica* 56 (2001): 125–28.

Geertz, Clifford. *After the Fact: Two Countries, Four Decades, One Anthropologist.* Cambridge, Mass: Harvard University Press, 1995.

Giles, Paul. *American Catholic Arts and Fictions.* London: Cambridge University Press, 1992.

Gilkey, Langdon. "Theories in Science and Religion." *Religion and the Natural Sciences: The Range of Engagement.* Ed. J. Huchingson, 61–65. Fort Worth: Harcourt Brace Jovanovich College Publishers, 1993.

———. *Creationism on Trial.* Minneapolis: Winston Press, 1985.

Gill, D., ed. *Gathered for Life: Official Report, VI Assembly, World Council of Churches, Vancouver, Canada, 1983.* Geneva: WCC, 1983.

Gleason, Philip. *Keeping the Faith: American Catholicism Past and Present.* Notre Dame: University of Notre Dame Press, 1987.

———. "The New Americanism in Catholic Historiography." *U.S. Catholic Historian* 113 (1993): 16.

"A Globalization That Will Benefit You." *Awake!* 83, no. 10 (2002): 11–13.

Gold, Scott. "Religion, Science May Turn a Page Over Textbook in Texas." *Los Angeles Times,* 6 November 2003, 11.

———. "Vote in Texas Is One for the Science Books; State Board, in What Is Seen as a Rebuke to Religious Conservatives, Adopts High School Biology Texts That Teach the Theory of Evolution." *Los Angeles Times,* 7 November 2003, 18.

Golshani, Mehdi. "Islam and the Sciences of Nature: Some Fundamental Questions." *Islamic Studies* 39 (2000): 597–611.

Greeley, Andrew. *The Catholic Imagination.* Berkeley: University of California Press, 2000.

———. *The Catholic Myth.* New York: Simon & Schuster, 1997.

———. *God in Popular Culture.* Chicago: Thomas Moore, 1988.

Grimes, Ronald. *Deeply into the Bone: Reinventing Rites of Passage.* Berkeley: University of California Press, 2000.

Guth, James L., et al. *The Bully Pulpit: The Politics of Protestant Clergy.* Kansas City: University Press of Kansas, 1997.

Haddad, Yvonne, and John Esposito, eds. *Muslims on the Americanization Path.* Oxford: Oxford University Press, 2000.

Hagee, James. *Final Dawn Over Jerusalem.* Nashville: Thomas Nelson Publishers, 1998.

Hall, David A., ed. *Lived Religion in America: Toward a History of Practice.* Princeton: Princeton University Press, 1997.

Hammond, Phil, ed. *Cultural Difference, Media Memories: Anglo-American Images of Japan.* London: Cassell, 1997.

Haq, Nomanul. "Islam and Ecology: Toward Retrieval and Reconstruction." *Islam and Ecology: A Bestowed Trust.* Ed. R. C. Foltz, F. M. Denny, and A. Bahuraddin, 121–54. Cambridge, Mass.: Harvard University Press, 2003.

———. "Islam and Ecology: Toward Retrieval and Reconstruction." *Dædalus* 130, no. 4 (2001): 141–78.

———. "Moments in the Islamic Recasting of the Greek Legacy: Exploring the Question of Science and Theism." *God, Life, and the Cosmos: Christian and Islamic Perspectives.* Ed. T. Peters, M. Iqbal, and S. N. Haq, 153–72. Burlington, Vt.: Ashgate Publishing, 2002.

Hardacre, Helen. "Aum Shinrikyō and the Japanese Media: The Pied Piper Meets the Lamb of God." *Institute Reports* of the East Asian Institute, Columbia University (November 1995).

———. *Shintō and the State, 1868–1988.* Princeton: Princeton University Press, 1989.

Hart, Stephen. *What Does the Lord Require? How American Christians Think About Economic Justice.* New Brunswick: Rutgers University Press, 1996.

Hauerwas, Stanley, and L. Gregory Jones, eds. *Why Narrative? Readings in Narrative Theology.* Grand Rapids: Eerdmans, 1989.

Haught, John F. *Science and Religion: From Conflict to Conversation*. New York: Paulist Press, 1995.

Hayden White. *Metahistory: The Historical Imagination in Nineteenth-Century Europe*. Baltimore: Johns Hopkins University Press, 1975.

Hayes, D. "CompuTech of Kansas City, Mo., Offers Online Memorial Site." *Knight Ridder Tribune Business News*, 25 May 2002, 1.

Haynes, Charles, ed. *Finding Common Ground: A First Amendment Guide to Religion and Public Education*. Nashville, Tenn.: Freedom Forum First Amendment Center at Vanderbilt University, 1994.

Heelas, Paul. "Introduction: On Differentiation and Dedifferentiation." *Religion, Modernity and Postmodernity*. Ed. Paul Heelas, David Martin and Paul Morris, 1–18. Oxford, UK: Blackwell, 1998.

Heil, Alan L., Jr. "To the Roof of the World: The Tibetan Service Miracle." *Voice of America: A History*, 302–10. New York: Columbia University Press, 2003.

Hein, Laura, and Mark Selden, eds. *Censoring History: Citizenship and Memory in Japan, Germany, and the United States*. Armonk, NY: M. E. Sharpe, 2000.

Herman, Edward S., and Noam Chomsky. *Manufacturing Consent: The Political Economy of the Mass Media*. New York: Pantheon Books, 2002.

Hodgson, Godfrey. *America in Our Time: From World War II to Nixon*. New York: Random House, 1976.

Hollinger, Dennis. *Individualism and Social Ethics: An Evangelical Syncretism*. Lanham, Md.: University Press of America, 1983.

Hooker, John. *Working Across Cultures*. Palo Alto: Stanford University Press, 2003.

Hoover, Stewart, and Lynn Shoefield Clark, eds. *Practising Religion in the Age of Media: Explorations in Media, Religion and Culture*. New York: Columbia University Press, 2002.

Hopkins, Gerard Manley. *The Later Poetic Manuscripts of Gerard Hopkins in Facsimile*. Ed. Norman H. MacKenzie. New York and London: Garland Publishing, 1991.

Huffman, James L. *Creating a Public: People and the Press in Meiji Japan*. Honolulu: University of Hawaii Press, 1997.

Hunter, James D. *American Evangelicalism: Conservative Protestantism and the Quandary of Modernity*. New Brunswick: Rutgers University Press, 1983.

———. "Before the Shooting Begins." *Columbia Journalism Review* (July–August 1993): 29–33.

———. *Culture Wars: The Struggle to Define America*. New York: Basic Books, 1992.

Hunter, M. "Slowing Motorists Cause 3-Car Pileup at Crash Site." *Times-Picayune* 19 January 2002, 1.

Huntington, Samuel P. *The Clash of Civilizations and the Remaking of World Order*. New York: Touchstone, 1997.

———. "Why International Primacy Matters." *International Security* 17, no. 4 (1993): 69–83.

Intermedia Department, National Council of Churches of Christ. *Global Communication for Justice*. New York: NCCC, 1992.

Ishii, Kenji. "Aum Shinrikyō." *Religion in Japanese Culture: Where Living Traditions Meet a Changing World*. Ed. Noriyoshi Tamaru and David Reid, 209–16. Tokyo: Kodansha International, 1996.

Iyer, Pico. *Video Night in Kathmandu and Other Reports from the Not-So-Far East*. New York: Knopf, 1988.

Jacobs, Louis. *The Book of Jewish Belief*. Springfield, N.J.: Behrman House, 1984.

James, William. *The Varieties of Religious Experience*. Lakewood, Calif.: Collier, 1961.

Jeffrey, David Lyle. *Houses of the Interpreter: Reading Scripture, Reading Culture*. Waco, Tex.: Baylor University Press, 2003.

———. *People of the Book: Christian Identity and Literary Culture*. Grand Rapids: Eerdmanns, 1996.

John of the Cross. *Living Flame of Life*. Trans. Jane Ackermann. Binghamton: Medieval and Renaissance Texts and Studies, 1995.

Johnson, James Turner. "Jihad and Just War." *First Things: A Monthly Journal of Religion and Public Life* (June–July 2002): 12–15.

Jones, Loyal. "Mountain Religion: The Outsider's View." *Mountain Review* 2, no. 3 (1976): 43–46.

Kahn, Herman, and Anthony J. Wiener. *The Year 2000: A Framework for Speculation on the Next Thirty-Three Years*. New York: Macmillan, 1967.

Kane, John. "Catholic Separatism." *Catholicism in America*. Ed. William Clancy, 47–57. New York: Harcourt, Brace, & Company, 1954.

Kaplan, David E., and Andrew Marshall. *The Cult at the End of the World: The Incredible Story of Aum*. London: Arrow Books, 1996.

Kasza, Gregory J. *The State and the Mass Media, 1918–45*. Berkeley: University of California Press, 1988.

Katô, Shûichi. "The Mass Media." *Political Modernization in Japan and Turkey*. Ed. Robert E. Ward and Dankwart A. Rustow, 263–54. Princeton: Princeton University Press, 1994.

Kepler, Johannes. "Mysterium Cosmographicum." *Science and Religious Belief: 1600–1900*. Ed. D. C. Goodman, 12–17. Bristol: John Wright & Sons, 1973.

Kimbrough, David L. *Taking Up Serpents: Snake Handlers of Eastern Kentucky*. Chapel Hill: University of North Carolina Press, 1995.

Kisala, Robert J., and Mark Mullins, eds. *Religion and Social Crisis in Japan: Understanding Japanese Society through the Aum Affair*. New York: Palgrave, 2001.

Kitcher, Philip. *Abusing Science: The Case Against Creationism*. Cambridge, Mass.: MIT Press, 1982.

Kobayashi, Yoshinori. *Sensôron*. Tokyo: Gentôsha, 1998.

Lafaye, Jacques. *Quetzalcoatl et Guadalupe*. Paris: Gallimard, 1974.

LaFleur, William R. "A Half-Dressed Emperor: Societal Self-Deception and Recent 'Japanokritik' in America." *Self and Deception: A Cross-cultural Philosophical Inquiry*. Ed. Roger T. Ames and Wimal Dissanayake, 263–86. West Futton: State University of New York Press, 1996.

Lederer, Edith M. "United Nations Delays Treaty on Human Cloning, a Setback for U.S. Effort to Ban It." *Associated Press*, 6 November 2003.

Leimer, C. "Roadside Memorials: Marking Journeys Never Completed." n.d. 14 January 2004. http://www.tombstonetravel.com/spont.html.

León-Portilla, Miguel. *Aztec Thought and Culture*. Norman: University of Oklahoma Press, 1963.

Lienesch, Michael. *Redeeming America: Piety and Politics in the New Christian Right*. Chapel Hill: University of North Carolina Press, 1993.

Lifton, Robert J. *Destroying the World to Save It: Aum Shinrikyô, Apocalyptic Violence, and the New Global Terrorism*. New York: Henry Holt & Company, 1999.

Lindberg, David C. *The Beginnings of Western Science: The European Scientific Tradition in Philosophical, Religious, and Institutional Context, 600 B.C. to A.D. 1450*. Chicago: University of Chicago Press, 1992.

Lindberg, David C., and Ronald L. Numbers. "Beyond War and Peace: A Reappraisal of the Encounter Between Christianity and Science." *Church History* 55 (1986): 338–54.

Lindsey, Hal. *Blood Moon*. Palos Verdes, Calif.: Western Front Publishing, 1996.

———. *The Late Great Planet Earth*. Grand Rapids: Zondervan, 1970.

Loizeaux, Elizabeth Bergmann, and Neil Fraistat. *Reimaging Textuality: Textual Studies in the Late Age of Print*. Madison: University of Wisconsin Press, 2002.

Lonergan, Bernard. *Method in Theology*. Minneapolis: Seabury Press, 1972.

Long, Douglas. *Fundamentalists and Extremists*. New York: Facts on File, 2002.

Lopez, Donald S., Jr. *Prisoners of Shangri-La: Tibetan Buddhism and the West*. Chicago: University of Chicago Press, 1998.

Lourdeaux, Lee. *Italian and Irish Filmmakers in America: Ford, Capra, Coppola, and Scorsese*. Philadelphia: Temple University Press, 1990.

Lu, Zidai. "What Does Evil Cult Harassing The *China Press* Tell Us?" *China Press*, 22 December 2001. Plaintiffs' exhibit in *Friends of Falun Gong v. Pacific Culture Enterprises*; translation by plaintiffs.

MacFarquhar, Neil. "Hussein's Babylon: A Beloved Atrocity." *New York Times*, 19 August 2003.

Mansfield, Stephen. *The Faith of George W. Bush*. New York: J. P. Tarcher, 2003.

Manuel, Frank. *The Religion of Isaac Newton*. Oxford: Clarendon Press, 1974.

Marsden, George M. *Fundamentalism and American Culture: The Shaping of Twentieth-Century Evangelicalism, 1870–1925*. New York: Oxford University Press, 1980.

————. *The Outrageous Idea of Christian Scholarship*. New York: Oxford University Press, 1997.

Marty, Martin E. "Our Religio-Secular World." *Dædalus: Journal of the American Academy of Arts & Sciences* 132, no. 3 (2003): 42–49.

Marty, Martin E., and R. Scott Appleby. "Conclusion: An Interim Report on a Hypothetical Family." *Fundamentalisms Observed*. Ed. Martin E. Marty and R. Scott Appleby, 814–42. Chicago: University of Chicago Press, 1991.

————. *Religion, Ethnicity and Self-Identity: Nations in Turmoil*. Hanover: University Press of New England, 1997.

Marvin, Carolyn. *Blood Sacrifice and the Nation: Totem Rituals and the American Flag*. Cambridge: Cambridge University Press, 1999.

Maryles, Daisy. "Armageddon Has Arrived." *Publishers Weekly*, 21 April 2003.

Matsudo, Yukio. "Back to Invented Tradition: A Nativist Response to a National Crisis." *Religion and Social Crisis in Japan: Understanding Japanese Society through the Aum Affair*. Ed. Robert J. Kisala and Mark Mullins, 163–78. New York: Palgrave, 2001.

McBrien, Richard P. *Catholicism*, 2 vols. Minneapolis: Winston Press, 1980.

McCauley, Deborah. *Appalachian Mountain Religion, A History*. Urbana: University of Illinois Press, 1995.

McDannell, Colleen. *Material Christianity*. New Haven: Yale University Press, 1995.

McGreevy, John. *Catholicism and American Freedom*. New York: Norton, 2003.

————. "Thinking On One's Own: Catholicism in the American Intellectual Imagination, 1928–1960." *Journal of American History* 841 (1997): 97–132.

McLuhan, Marshall. *Media Studies*. New York: New York University Press, 2000.

McMullin, Ernan. "Natural Science and Belief in a Creator: Historical Notes." *Physics, Philosophy, and Theology: A Common Quest for Understanding*. Ed. R. J. Russell, W. R. Stoeger, and G. V. Coyne, 49–79. Vatican City: Vatican Observatory, 1988.

Métraux, Daniel A. *Aum Shinrikyo and Japanese Youth*. New York: University Press of America, 1999.

Meyer, Jean. *La Cristiada*. Mexico: Siglo Veintiuno Editores, 1974.

Miller, S. "Conspiracy Theories: Public Arguments as Coded Social Critiques—A Rhetorical Analysis of the TWA Flight 800 Conspiracy Theories." *Argumentation and Advocacy* 39 (2002): 40–56.

Millman, Joyce. "Praise the Lord and Pass the Remote: Christian Values Collide with Big Money on Fox Family Channel and Pax TV." *Salon*, October 1998.

Mitchell, Richard H. *Censorship in Imperial Japan*. Princeton: Princeton University Press, 1983.

Morris, Henry M., ed. *Scientific Creationism*. Green Forest, Ark.: Master Books, 1985.

Moses, Paul. "Misprints? Falun Gong & the First Amendment." *Commonweal*, 6 June 2003, 11.

Moses, Paul, and Mae Cheng. "Silencing the Movement." *Newsday*, 6 September 2001, B06.

Mullins, Mark R. "The Legal and Political Fallout of the 'Aum Affair.'" *Religion and Social Crisis in Japan: Understanding Japanese Society through the Aum Affair*. Ed. Robert J. Kisala and Mark Mullins, 71–86. New York: Palgrave, 2001.

Munson, Henry. "'Fundamentalism' Ancient and Modern." *Dædalus: Journal of the American Academy of Arts & Sciences* 132, no. 3 (2003): 31–42.

Murad, Abdul-Hakim. "Recapturing Islam from Terrorists." 14 September 2001. http://www.themodernreligion.com.

Murakami, Shigeyoshi. *Japanese Religion in the Modern Period*. Tokyo: University of Tokyo Press, 1980.

Nasr, Seyyed H. "Islamic Cosmology: Basic Tenets and Implications, Yesterday and Today." *Science and Religion in Search of Cosmic Purpose*. Ed. J. F. Haught, 42–57. Washington, D.C.: Georgetown University Press, 2000.

———. *Science and Civilization in Islam*. Cambridge, Mass.: Cambridge University Press, 1987.

Nasr, Seyyed H., and Oliver Leaman, eds. *History of Islamic Philosophy*. New York: Routledge, 2001.

Nelson, Michael. *War of the Black Heavens: The Battles of Western Broadcasting in the Cold War*. Syracuse: Syracuse University Press, 1997.

Newton, Isaac. "Four Letters from Sir Isaac Newton to Doctor Bentley." *Science and Religious Belief: 1600–1900*. Ed. D. C. Goodman, 131–36. Bristol: John Wright & Sons, 1973.

Niebuhr, Gustav. "Megachurches: The Gospels of Management; The Minister as Marketer: Learning from Business." *New York Times*, 18 April 1995, 1.

Nisbet, Robert. *Social Change and History: Aspects of the Western Theory of Development*. New York: Oxford University Press, 1969.

O'Brien, David J. *Public Catholicism*. Maryknoll: Orbis, 1996.

Ortner, Sherry. *The Fate of "Culture": Geertz and Beyond*. Berkeley: University of California Press, 1999.

Pagels, Elaine, and C. Welton Gaddy. "President or Preacher? Elaine Pagels and Rev. Dr. C. Welton Gaddy on the President's Irresponsible Use of Religious Language." Audio news conference. Douglas Gould & Company, 11 February 2003.

Pattyn, Bart, ed. *Media Ethics: Opening Social Dialogue*. Leuven, Belgium: Peeters, 2000.

Paz, Octavio. *The Labyrinth of Solitude*. New York: Penguin, 1961.

Peters, Ted. "Theology and Natural Science." *The Modern Theologians*, 2nd ed. Ed. D. Ford, 649–68. Oxford: Blackwell Publishing, 1997.

Pew Research Center for the People and Press and the Pew Forum on Religion and Public Life. *Religion and Politics: Contention and Consensus*. July 24, 2003.

Pharr, Susan J. "Media and Politics in Japan: Historical and Contemporary Perspectives." *Media and Politics in Japan*. Ed. Susan J. Pharr and Ellis S. Krauss, 3–17. Honolulu: University of Hawaii Press, 1996.

Pharr, Susan J., and Ellis S. Krauss, eds. *Media and Politics in Japan*. Honolulu: University of Hawaii Press, 1996.

Piehl, Mel. *Breaking Bread: The Catholic Worker and the Origin of Catholic Radicalism in America*. Philadelphia: Temple University Press, 1982.

"Poll by Mitofsky International and Edison Media Research conducted for *Religion & Ethics Newsweekly* and *U.S. News & World Report*." *Exploring Religious America*. PBS, WNET, New York, 2002, 12.

Pontifical Council for Social Communications. *100 Years of Cinema*. 1995–1996. 18 October 2003. http://www.vatican.va/roman.

———. *Aetatis Novae: On Social Communications on the Twentieth Anniversary of Communio et Progressio*. 1992. 18 October 2003.

———. *An Appeal to all Contemplative Religious*. 1973. 18 October 2003.

———. *The Church and Internet*. 2002. 18 October 2003.

———. *Communio et Progressio: On the Means of Social Communication Written by Order of the Second Vatican Council*. 1971. 18 October 2003.

———. *Criteria for Ecumenical and Inter-religious Cooperation in Communications*. 1989. 18 October 2003.

———. *Ethics and Internet*. 2002. 18 October 2003.

———. *Ethics in Advertising*. 1997. 18 October 2003.

———. *Ethics in Communications*. 2000. 18 October 2003.

———. *Guide to the Training of Future Priests Concerning the Instruments of Social Communications*. 1986. 18 October 2003.

———. *Pornography and Violence in the Communications Media: A Pastoral Response*. 1989. 18 October 2003.

Porter, W. "Some Sociological Notes on a Century of Change in the Funeral Business." *Sociological Symposium* I (1968): 36–46.

Post, Jerrold M., Ehud Sprinzak, and Laurita M. Denny. "The Terrorists in Their Own Words: Interviews with 35 Incarcerated Middle Eastern Terrorists." *Terrorism and Political Violence* 15, no. 1 (2003): 171–84.

Powell, Michael. "The Chinatown Clampdown." *Newsday*, 5 April 1989, 8.

Powers, William. "The Roman Legion." *National Journal*, 15 August 1980.

Radford, B. "Religion on the Roadside." *Free Inquiry* 22 (2001–2): 59.

Ramadan, Tariq. *Western Muslims and the Future of Islam*. Oxford: Oxford University Press, 2004.

Ray, John. "The Wisdom of God Manifested in the Works of Creation." *Science and Religious Belief: 1600–1900*. Ed. D. C. Goodman, 17–27. Bristol: John Wright & Sons, 1973.

Reader, Ian. "Consensus Shattered: Japanese Paradigm Shift and Moral Panic in the Post-Aum Era." *Nova Religio* 4 (2001): 225–34.

———. "Identity, Nihonjinron, and Academic (Dis)honesty." *Monumenta Nipponica* 58 (2003): 103–16.

———. *A Poisonous Cocktail? Aum Shinrikyō's Path to Violence*. Copenhagen: Nordic Institute of Asian Studies Publications, 1996.

———. *Religious Violence in Contemporary Japan: The Case of Aum Shinrikyō*. Richmond, UK: Curzon Press, 2000.

———. "Scholarship, Aum Shinrikyō, and Integrity." *Nova Religio* 3 (2000): 368–82.

Richardson, James T., and Bryan Edleman. "Falun Gong and the Law: Development of Legal Social Control in China." *Nova Religio: The Journal of Alternative and Emergent Religions* (forthcoming).

Riddell, Frank S., ed. *Appalachia: Its People, Heritage and Problems*. Dubuque: Kendall Hunt Publishing Company, 1974.

Ridings, Dean. Review of *Occupied Territory* by Cal Thomas. *Fundamentalist Journal,* 7 April 1988, 58.

Rivera, John. "Gazing into the Spiritual Future: Expectations in an Age of Information and Technology." *Sun Baltimore,* 12 March 2000, 2A.

Robertson, Pat. *The New World Order.* Dallas: Word Publishing, 1991.

Roof, Wade Clark, ed. *Contemporary American Religion.* New York: MacMillan, 2000.

Rosen, Jay. *What Are Journalists For?* New Haven: Yale University Press, 2001.

Rosenberg, Bruce A. *The Art of the American Folk Preacher.* New York: Oxford University Press, 1970.

Rosin, Hanna. "The Politics of Religion: Issues of Faith Shape Debates." *Washington Post,* 29 October 1998.

Rubin, Jay. *Injurious to Public Morals: Writers and the Meiji State.* Seattle: University of Washington Press, 1984.

Ruether, Rosemary Radford and Herman J. Ruether. *The Wrath of Jonah: The Crisis of Religious Nationalism in the Israeli-Palestinian Conflict.* Minneapolis: Fortress Press, 2002.

Rugh, W. *The Arab Press: News Media and Political Processes in the Arab World,* 2nd ed. Syracuse, N.Y.: Syracuse University Press, 1979.

Said, Edward. *Orientalism.* New York: Pantheon, 1978.

Sakr, N. *Satellite Realms: Transnational Television, Globalization & the Middle East.* London: I. B. Tauris Publishers, 2001.

Sardar, Ziauddin. "The Forgotten Inheritance." *New Statesman,* 7 April 2003.

Schechter, Danny. *Falun Gong's Challenge to China: Spiritual Practices or "Evil Cult"?* New York: Akashic Books, 2001.

Schell, Orville. *Virtual Tibet: Searching for Shangri-La from the Himalayas to Hollywood.* New York: Metropolitan Books, 2000.

Schlesinger, Arthur M., Jr. "Eyeless in Gaza." *New York Review of Books,* 23 October 2003.

Schmalzbauer, John. *People of Faith: Religious Conviction in American Journalism and Higher Education.* Ithaca: Cornell University Press, 2003.

Schudson, Michael. *Discovering the News: A Social History of the American Newspaper.* New York: Basic Books, 1978.

———. *The Power of News.* Cambridge, Mass: Harvard University Press, 1995.

Selengut, Charles. *Sacred Fury: Understanding Religious Violence.* Walnut Creek, Calif.: Altamira Press, 2003.

Shimazono, Susumu. "Aspects of the Rebirth of Religion." *Religion in Japanese Culture: Where Living Traditions Meet a Changing World.* Ed. Noriyoshi Tamaru and David Reid, 171–83. Tokyo: Kodansha International, 1996.

———. "The Evolution of Aum Shinrikyō as a Religious Movement." *Religion and Social Crisis in Japan: Understanding Japanese Society through the Aum Affair.* Ed. Robert J. Kisala and Mark Mullins, 19–52. New York: Palgrave, 2001.

Shriver, Donald W., Jr. *An Ethic for Enemies: Forgiveness in Politics.* New York: Oxford University Press, 1995.

Silk, Mark. *Religion in the News,* vols. 1–6, Hartford, Conn.: Leonard Greenberg Center for the Study of Religion in Public Life, Trinity College, 2002–4.

———. *Unsecular Media: Making News of Religion in America.* Chicago: University of Illinois Press, 1995.

Smidt, Corwin, ed. *Religion as Social Capital: Producing the Common Good.* Waco, Tex.: Baylor University Press, 2003.

Smith, Christian. *American Evangelicalism: Embattled and Thriving.* Chicago: University of Chicago Press, 1998.

————. *Christian America? What Evangelicals Really Want.* Berkeley: University of California Press, 2000.

Soukup, Paul A. "Church Documents and the Media." *Concilium: revue internationale de theologie* (December 1993): 71–79.

Soustelle, Jacques. *La vie quotidienne des Aztèques à la veille de la conquête espagnole.* Paris: Hachette, 1955.

Sparks, John. *The Roots of Appalachian Christianity.* Lexington: University Press of Kentucky, 2001.

Steinberg, Leo. *Leonardo's Incessant Last Supper.* New York: Zone Books, 2001.

Steinfels, Peter. "Constraints of the Religion Reporter." *Nieman Reports* 473, no. 5 (1993).

Stern, Jessica. *Terror in the Name of God.* New York: Ecco, 2003.

Stock, Brian. *Listening for the Text: On the Uses of the Past.* Philadelphia: University of Pennsylvania Press, 1990.

Study of Media Laws and Policies for the Middle East and Maghreb. London: The Stanhope Center for Communications Policy Research, 2003.

Swidler, Ann. "Culture in Action: Symbols and Strategies." *American Sociological Review* 512 (1986): 273–87.

Sylvan, Robin. *Traces of the Spirit: The Religious Dimensions of Popular Music.* New York: New York University Press, 2002.

Tamaru, Noriyoshi, and David Reid, eds. *Religion in Japanese Culture: Where Living Traditions Meet a Changing World.* Tokyo: Kodansha International, 1996.

Tamini, Azzam, and John L. Esposito, eds. *Islam and Secularism in the Middle East.* New York: New York University Press, 2000.

Thomas, Cal, and Ed Dobson. *Blinded by Might: Can the Religious Right Save America?* Grand Rapids: Zondervan, 1999.

Thompson, Mark. "A Long Career of Marching with the Cross." *Time,* 3 November 2003.

Tracy, David. *The Analogical Imagination: Christian Theology and the Culture of Pluralism.* New York: Crossroad, 1981.

Trisco, R. F. "Vatican Council II." *New Catholic Encyclopedia.* New York: McGraw-Hill Book Co., 1967.

Tuchman, Gaye. *Making News: A Study in the Construction of Reality.* New York: Free Press, 1978.

————. "Objectivity as Strategic Ritual." *American Sociological Review* 77, no. 1 (1972): 660–79.

Tuveson, Ernest Lee. *Redeemer Nation: The Idea of America's Millennial Role.* Chicago: University of Chicago Press, 1968.

United Nations Development Program. *Arab Human Development Report.* New York: UN, 200 October 2003.

Wachtel, Nathan. *La vision des vainçus.* Paris: Gallimard, 1971.

Wallace, William A., O.P. "A History of Science and Faith." *Readings in Faith and Science.* Ed. R. Brungs, S.J., 7–31. St. Louis, MO: ITEST Faith/Science Press, 1997.

Watanabe, Manabu. "Opposition to Aum and the Rise of the 'Anti-Cult' Movement." *Religion and Social Crisis in Japan: Understanding Japanese Society through the Aum Affair.* Ed. Robert J. Kisala and Mark Mullins, 87–106. New York: Palgrave, 2001.

Watanabe, Takesato. "The Movement and the Japanese Media." *Global Citizens: The Soka Gakkai Buddhist Movement in the World.* Ed. David Machacek and Bryan Wilson, 205–43. Oxford: Oxford University Press, 2000.

"The Web Sites of Flight 800." *U.S. News & World Report,* 5 August 1996, 8.

Weller, Jack. *Yesterday's People: Life in Contemporary Appalachia.* Lexington: University of Kentucky Press, 1965.

Westfall, Richard S. "The Rise of Science and the Decline of Orthodox Christianity: A Study of Kepler, Descartes, and Newton." *God and Nature: Historical Essays on the Encounter Between Christianity and Science.* Ed. D. C. Lindberg & R. L. Numbers, 218–37. Berkeley: University of California Press, 1986.

Westfall, Richard S. *Never at Rest: A Biography of Isaac Newton.* Cambridge, Mass.: Cambridge University Press, 1984.

White, Andrew D. *A History of the Warfare of Science with Theology in Christendom,* 2 vols. New York: D. Appleton & Company, 1929.

White, Hayden. *The Content of the Form.* Baltimore: Johns Hopkins University Press, 1987.

White, Robert. "New Approaches to Media Ethics: Moral Dialogue, Creating Normative Paradigms, and Public Cultural Truth." *Media Ethics.* Ed. by Bart Pattyn, 59–80. Leuven, Belgium: Peeters, 2000.

Whitman, A. *The Obituary Book.* New York: Stein & Day, 1971.

Wills, Garry. "With God on His Side." *New York Times Magazine,* 30 March 2003.

Woodward, Bob. *Bush at War.* New York: Simon & Schuster, 2002.

World Council of Churches. *The Church and the Media of Mass Communication.* Geneva: World Council of Churches, 1968.

Wuthnow, Robert. *Christianity in the Twenty-First Century: Reflections on the Challenges Ahead.* New York: Oxford University Press, 1995.

———. *Loose Connections: Joining Together in America's Fragmented Communities.* Cambridge, Mass.: Harvard University Press, 1998.

"Your Enemies Are My Enemies." *Temple Mount and Eretz Yisrael Faithful Movement.* 2001. http://www.templemountfaithful.org/enemies/htm.

Zavala, Silvio Arturo. *Recuerdo de Vasco de Quiroga.* Mexico: Editorial Porrua, 1965.

Zbigniew, Brzezinski. *The Grand Chessboard: American Primacy and Its Geostrategic Imperatives.* New York: Basic Books, 1997.

Zelizer, B. "Reading the Past Against the Grain: The Shape of Memory Studies." *Critical Studies in Mass Communication* 12 (1995): 214–39.

About the Contributors

ASLAM ABDALLAH edits the monthly *Minaret* (Los Angeles), the weekly *Observer* (Detroit), and hosts a radio talk show on Islamic Broadcasting Network (IBN.net). Proficient in English, Urdu, Hindi, Arabic, and Persian, he has published eleven books, and more than four hundred papers on topics pertaining to Muslims and Islam in the West. His articles are translated and published worldwide. Vice chairman of the Muslim Public Affairs Council, he is a naturalized U.S. citizen, born in India.

CLAIRE BADARACCO is professor of communication at Marquette University. A graduate of the University of California, Berkeley, and Rutgers University, she has published widely in academic journals, including *Merton Annuals*; contributed book chapters and written several books, including *Trading Words* (1995) and *American Culture and the Marketplace* (1993); edited *The Cuba Journal of Sophia Peabody Hawthorne* (1982); and served as associate editor of the *Journal of Communication*, vols. 50–52.

PAUL BOYER, the Merle Curti Professor of History Emeritus at the University of Wisconsin-Madison, is the author of *When Time Shall Be No More: Prophecy Belief in Modern American Culture* (1992). Among his other works are *Salem Possessed: The Social Origins of Witchcraft* (with Stephen Nissenbaum, 1974); *Urban Masses and Moral Order in America, 1820–1920* (1978); *By the Bomb's Early Light: American Thought and Culture at the Dawn of the Atomic Age* (1985); and *Purity in Print: Book Censorship in America* (2nd ed., 2002). He is also editor-in-chief of *The Oxford Companion to United States History* (2001).

JOHN B. BUESCHER received his Ph.D. in religious studies from the University of Virginia, has taught at the University of North Carolina at Wilmington, and has worked at the National Endowment for the Humanities. In 1991 he joined the Voice of America as chief of the Tibetan Broadcast Service, where he directs Tibetan reporters and stringers in producing four hours of daily shortwave radio programming in Tibetan to Tibet and the Tibetan-speaking regions of Asia.

DAVID CRUMM has written about the impact of religion on American life for the *Detroit Free Press*, the statewide morning newspaper in Michigan, since 1986. While his work as the religion writer of the *Free Press* focuses mainly on Michigan, he has reported from across the United States, Europe, and the Middle East. His journalistic work spans three decades, including posts as an investigative reporter, news editor, media critic, and Sunday magazine editor.

JOHN DART, news editor of the *Christian Century*, was a religion reporter for the *Los Angeles Times* for thirty-one years. He coauthored *Bridging the Gap: Religion and the News Media* (1993), a benchmark study of their tensions, and wrote *Deities and Deadlines* (1995, 1998), a primer for new religion writers. His latest book is *Decoding Mark* (2003).

HOWARD DORGAN, emeritus professor of sociology, Appalachian State University, has devoted thirty-two years to his study of Appalachian religious practices and to the respective theologies of a highly diverse set of "Old-Time Baptist" subdenominations and a correspondingly wide range of Pentecostal/Holiness groups, the two religious movements that most typify the spiritual culture of the region. In 1997–98 his colleagues in the Appalachian Studies Association elected him their president, and in 2000 they granted him the highest ASA honor, the Cratis Williams/James Brown Award for Service to the Association and the Region.

VIRGILIO ELIZONDO is professor of religion at University of Notre Dame, author of ten books, and recipient of five honorary doctorates. His most recent book, *San Fernando Cathedral: Soul of the City* (1998), breaks ground in secular and religious studies. He is often interviewed by media to interpret Latino religious issues. *Time* magazine named him one of the "leading spiritual innovators" for the year 2000 for his work on mestizo theology.

MOHAMMED EL-NAWAWY, Egyptian-born and raised, has worked as a journalist in the Middle East and the United States. An expert on Arab media, he is the author and coauthor of two books: *The Israeli-Egyptian Peace Process in the Reporting of Western Journalists* (2002), and *Al-Jazeera: The Story of a Network That is Rattling Governments and Redefining Modern Journalism* (2003). He is assistant professor of international communication and journalism at Georgia State University.

JOHN P. FERRÉ is professor of communication at the University of Louisville, where he investigates ethical, religious, and historical dimensions of mass media in the United States. In addition to numerous articles and reviews, he has written several books, including *Good News: Social Ethics and the Press with Clifford G. Christians and P. Mark Fackler* (1993).

COREY FLINTOFF has been a newscaster and reporter at National Public Radio since 1990. Prior to that, he worked for the Alaska Public Radio Network and at public radio stations in Alaska after his graduation from the University of California, Berkeley. He was in Mongolia on a Knight International Press Fellowship, a "journalistic Peace Corps" dedicated to fostering independent, public-service journalism in developing democracies. He has also conducted journalism and radio-production training in Finland and Kosovo.

WELTON GADDY has written more than twenty books about religion and politics. He leads the national nonpartisan grassroots and educational organizations, The Interfaith Alliance and The Interfaith Alliance Foundation and serves as the pastor for preaching and worship at Northminster (Baptist) Church in Monroe, Louisiana. He also provides regular commentary to the national media on issues relating to religion and politics. Some of his appearances include CNN's *The World Today* with Wolf Blitzer, PBS's *The Newshour* with Jim Lehrer, *NBC Dateline*, *NBC Evening News* with Tom Brokaw, and ABC's *World News Tonight*.

RICHARD GARDNER is professor of religion in the faculty of comparative culture, Sophia University, Tokyo, Japan and director of Sophia's Summer Session of Asian Studies. In addition to articles on the response to Aum in Japan, he has written on the relation of theater and religion in medieval Japan as well as on the relation of religion and humor.

REBECCA MOORE is professor of religious studies at San Diego State University, specializing in new religious movements. She has written and published several books and articles on the subject. She is currently working on a coauthored volume on Jewish and Christian historical origins.

PAUL MOSES is an associate professor of English at Brooklyn College of the City University of New York, where he teaches journalism. He is a former city editor at *Newsday* and holds an M.F.A. in English from the University of Massachusetts at Amherst. He twice covered the religion beat at *Newsday* and was the lead writer in a team that won the 1992 Pulitzer Prize for Spot News Reporting at *New York Newsday*.

GUSTAV NIEBUHR, formerly a reporter with the *New York Times, Wall Street Journal*, and *Washington Post*, currently teaches religious studies and communication at Syracuse University.

ADAM PHILLIPS is a features reporter for the Voice of America, based in New York City, honored as Religion Reporter of the Year (radio) by the Religion Newswriters Association (2001). At Voice of America, he specializes in religion, urban and immigrant life, and the arts.

MARK PINSKY, a former staff writer for the *Los Angeles Times*, covers religion for the *Orlando Sentinel*. He is the author of *The Gospel According to The Simpsons: The Spiritual Life of the World's Most Animated Family* (2001) and *The Gospel According to Disney: Faith, Trust and Pixie Dust* (2004).

RICHARD RODRIGUEZ, a 1993 recipient of the National Humanities Medal, is a well-known essayist. He worked for twenty years as a journalist for the Pacific News Service and has been a contributing editor for *Harper's Magazine* and the Sunday Opinion section of the *Los Angeles Times*, and wrote *Days of Obligation: An Argument with My Mexican Father* (1993).

JAME SCHAEFER is an assistant professor of theology at Marquette University, where she specializes in the relationship between religion and science and directs the Interdisciplinary Program in Environmental Ethics. She is a recipient of awards from the Center for Theology and the Natural Sciences and the John Templeton Foundation.

JOHN SCHMALZBAUER is the author of *People of Faith: Religious Conviction in American Journalism and Higher Education* (2003). From 1996 to 1998 he was a postdoctoral research associate at the Center for the Study of Religion and American Culture in Indianapolis. He is currently completing a study on the resurgence of religion in American higher education with historian Kathleen Mahoney and psychologist James Youniss, and is on the faculty of Holy Cross College.

PETER SMITH is the religion writer for the *Courier-Journal* of Louisville, Kentucky. With nearly twenty years of experience as a journalist, he has worked as a correspondent for Religion News Service in Europe and North America and has written for the *Boston Globe*, *MSNBC*, *Self Magazine*, *Modern Maturity*, the *Lutheran*, the *Boston Phoenix*, the *Prague Post*, and other publications. He was the recipient of the American Academy of Religion's award for Best In-Depth News Reporting on Religion in 2002.

PAUL A. SOUKUP, S.J., has explored the connections between communication and theology since 1982. His publications include *Communication and Theology* (1983); *Christian Communication: A Bibliographical Survey* (1989), *Media, Culture, and Catholicism* (1996), *Mass Media and the Moral Imagination with Philip J. Rossi* (1994), and *Fidelity and Translation: Communicating the Bible in New Media with Robert Hodgson* (1999). This latter publication grows out of his work on the American Bible Society's *New Media Bible*. In addition, he and Thomas J. Farrell have edited four volumes of the collected works of Walter J. Ong, S.J., *Faith and Contexts* (1992–99). Soukup teaches in the communication department at Santa Clara University.

TERESA WATANABE is a religion reporter for the *Los Angeles Times*. She has extensive experience as a religion reporter in Asia, and served as the bureau chief in Tokyo for the *Los Angeles Times*.

JOE WILLIAMS covers the education beat for the *New York Daily News* and was a reporter for the *Milwaukee Journal Sentinel* after graduating from Marquette University's journalism program.

Index